Walter Benjamin's Philosophy

Why read Walter Benjamin today? The simplicity of the question is disarming. There are as many answers as there are Walter Benjamins: Benjamin the Critic, Benjamin the Modernist, Benjamin the Marxist, Benjamin the Jew. Yet it is Benjamin the Philosopher who, in one way or another, stands behind all of these. This collection explores what Adorno described as his 'philosophy directed against philosophy'.

The essays cover all aspects of Benjamin's writings, from his early work in the philosophy of art and language, through his cultural criticism, to his final reflections on the concept of history. The experience of time and the destruction of tradition are identified as the key themes in Benjamin's understanding of history.

The contributors are Howard Caygill, Alexander Garcia Düttman, Peter Osborne, Werner Hamacher, John Kraniauskas, Irving Wohlfarth, Rodolphe Gasché, Gertrud Koch, Andrew Benjamin, Rebecca Comay.

Andrew Benjamin is Senior Lecturer in Philosophy at the University of Warwick. His publications include *Art, Mimesis and the Avant-Garde* (1991) and *The Plural Event* (1993), both published by Routledge.

Peter Osborne is Senior Lecturer in Philosophy at Middlesex University. He is the editor of *Socialism and the Limits of Liberalism* (Verso, 1991) and co-editor of *Thinking Art: Beyond Traditional Aesthetics* (ICA, 1991) and *Socialism, Feminism and Philosophy: A Radical Philosophy Reader* (1990), also published by Routledge.

Warwick Studies in European Philosophy
Edited by Andrew Benjamin
Senior Lecturer in Philosophy, University of Warwick

This series presents the best and most original work being done within the European philosophical tradition. The books included in the series seek not merely to reflect what is taking place within European philosophy, rather they will contribute to the growth and development of that plural tradition. Work written in the English language as well as translations into English are to be included, engaging the tradition at all levels – whether by introductions that show the contemporary philosophical force of certain work, or in collections that explore an important thinker or topic, as well as in significant contributions that call for their own critical evaluation.

Walter Benjamin's Philosophy

Destruction and Experience

Edited by Andrew Benjamin and
Peter Osborne

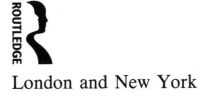

London and New York

First published 1994
by Routledge
11 New Fetter Lane, London EC4P 4EE

Simultaneously published in the USA and Canada
by Routledge
29 West 35th Street, New York, NY 10001

Phototypeset in 10 on 12 point Times by Intype
Printed in Great Britain by T.J. Press (Padstow) Ltd, Padstow, Cornwall
Printed on acid free paper

British Library Cataloguing in Publication Data
Walter Benjamin's Philosophy: Destruction and Experience
  I. Benjamin, Andrew   II. Osborne, Peter
  913

Library of Congress Cataloging in Publication Data
Walter Benjamin's Philosophy: Destruction and Experience / edited by
  Andrew Benjamin and Peter Osborne.
      p.   cm. – (Warwick studies in European philosophy)
  Includes bibliographical references and index.
  1. Benjamin, Walter, 1892–1940.   I. Benjamin, Andrew E.
  II. Osborne, Peter   III. Series.
B3209.B584W35 1993
193–dc20   93–16566

ISBN 0–415–08368–0 (hbk)   ISBN 0–415–08369–9 (pbk)

Contents

Notes on Contributors

Howard Caygill teaches at the University of East Anglia and is author of *Art of Judgement* (Blackwells, 1989).

Alexander García Düttmann is a Mellon Fellow in the Department of Philosophy at Stanford University. His publications include *La parole donnée* (Galilée, 1990).

Peter Osborne is Senior Lecturer in Philosophy at Middlesex University. He is the editor of *Socialism and the Limits of Liberalism* (Verso, 1991) and co-editor of *Socialism, Feminism and Philosophy: A Radical Philosophy Reader* (Routledge, 1990) and *Thinking Art: Beyond Traditional Aesthetics* (Institute of Contemporary Arts, 1991). He is an editor of the journal *Radical Philosophy*.

Werner Hamacher is Professor of German at Johns Hopkins University. He has published widely in the area of modern German studies.

John Kraniauskas is Lecturer in Latin American Cultural History at Birkbeck College, University of London. He is an editor of the journal *Traversia*.

Irving Wohlfarth is Professor of German at the University of Reims. He has edited special editions of the *New German Critique* on Benjamin and has two forthcoming studies of Benjamin.

Rodolphe Gasché is Professor of Comparative Literature at the State University of New York at Buffalo. His many publications include *The Tain of the Mirror* (Harvard University Press, 1989). He has a forthcoming book on Derrida and Paul de Man.

Gertrud Koch teaches at the University of Bochum. She is the author of *'Was ich erbeute sind Bilder': Zum Diskurs der Geschlechter im Film* (Frankfurt, 1989). She is an editor of the journal *Babylon*.

Andrew Benjamin teaches philosophy at the University of Warwick. His publications include *Art, Mimesis and the Avant-Garde* (Routledge, 1991) and *The Plural Event* (Routledge, 1993).

Rebecca Comay is Associate Professor of Philosophy and Literary Studies at the University of Toronto. She has published widely on nineteenth- and twentieth-century European philosophy. Her most recent publication is *On The Line: Reflections on the Bad Infinite* (New York, 1993).

Acknowledgements

The assistance of the publishers of the journals *Qui Parle*, *Cardoza Law Review*, *Diacritics* and *Modern Language Notes* for allowing articles by Gertrud Koch, Werner Hamacher, Irving Wohlfarth and Alexander García Düttmann to be reprinted is gratefully acknowledged. Thanks must also be given to Peter Pollner for his translation of the letter by Eric Auerbach.

Introduction

Destruction and Experience

Andrew Benjamin and Peter Osborne

> *'Construction' presupposes 'Destruction'*
> (Walter Benjamin, *Passagen-Werk* N 7, 6)

Why read Benjamin today? The simplicity of the question is disarming. There are as many answers as there are Benjamins: Benjamin the Critic, Benjamin the Marxist, Benjamin the Modernist, Benjamin the Jew. . . . Behind each of them, however, in one way or another, stands Benjamin the philosopher. Following a period in which the reception of Benjamin's writings in the English-speaking world was dominated by Arendt's portrayal of him as an alchemist-critic,[1] the fundamentally philosophical character of Benjamin's thought has come increasingly into view.[2]

Yet to speak of Benjamin 'the philosopher' should not be mistaken for a disciplinary claim. If Adorno is misleading when he maintains that Benjamin 'chose to remain completely outside the manifest tradition of philosophy',[3] he is nonetheless right to emphasize the distance of his thought from philosophy in its institutionalized, academic form. In this sense, Benjamin's is indeed 'a philosophy directed against philosophy'.[4] However, with the important exception of Heidegger, such 'anti-philosophical' philosophy could be said to make up the mainstream of the post-Hegelian tradition. Benjamin's work is located beyond the parameters of an institutionalized 'philosophy', but it is not thereby to be sought at its margins. Rather, it occupies another space altogether: that distinctively modern space where historical and philosophical reflection combines with the thoughts of the day: criticism. For the most part, Benjamin wrote criticism, but what he wrote was nonetheless 'philosophical' for that.

Benjamin aimed, notoriously, to make philosophy embrace the totality of experience.[5] He sought, thereby, to render experience philosophical: the experience of truth. It was in the breadth of this ambition that he parted company with the predominantly neo-Kantian philosophy of his day and came to ally his work to literature. In a context in which institutionalized philosophy had given up the claim to totality of its tradition, Benjamin remained true to that tradition by rejecting its institutional form and philosophizing 'directly' out of the objects of cultural experience. 'The object of philosophical criticism', he wrote in 1925, 'is to show that the function of artistic forms is . . . to make historical content . . . into a philosophical truth.'[6] Rather than being opposed to his philosophical concerns, Benjamin's interest in literature (and later, an increasingly wide variety of other cultural forms) was the means for their pursuit.

Initially, it was in works of art that Benjamin found the self-contained form of totality he thought necessary for experience to participate in truth. Later, it was history as a redemptive whole which he took as the totality in relation to which the lived (*das Erlebnis*) might be experienced as truth. Central to both periods was the idea of destruction (*Destruktion*) as a condition of the possibility of experience (*Erfahrung*) in the strong, philosophical sense of an experience of truth.

For Benjamin, 'destruction' always meant the destruction of some false or deceptive form of experience as the productive condition of the construction of a new relation to the object. Thus, in *The Origin of German Tragic Drama*, allegory is seen to destroy the deceptive totality of the symbol, wrenching it out of context and placing it in new, transparently constructed, configurations of meaning.[7] The portrayal of politics as a part of nature (the will of the intriguer) destroys the 'historical ethos'.[8] Similarly, photography is seen to destroy the aura of the object, opening up the possibility of a radically new knowledge (the optical unconscious).[9] In Benjamin's own work, montage destroys the continuity of narrative as the condition for a new construction of history;[10] while now-time destroys the experience of history as progress, replacing it with the apocalyptic doublet of catastrophe and redemption.[11] It is the destructive element that 'guarantees the authenticity of dialectical thought'.[12] The destructive character is 'the consciousness of historical man'.[13]

Crucial to each of these instances of destruction is Benjamin's understanding of the temporality of the present as the moment of destruction. It is through his interest in time that Benjamin's theory of experience is connected up to his philosophy of history. Above all, this interest is an interest in the present as the site of historical experience. In this respect, albeit in a novel way, Benjamin's work is first and foremost a version of what Habermas has called the 'philosophical discourse of modernity'.[14] It is a philosophical discourse on and of modernity, in the form not of a 'philosophy of history', but a philosophy of historical time. The fundamental question that it addresses is the question of the character of the present.

In opposition to that historicism for which the present is either a moment in the unfolding of progress, like any other, or a part of a backward and forward succession of facts, or is subsumed in some other way under a conception of history as a completing or completed whole, for Benjamin the present is both the moment and site of the actuality of the past. The past is contingent upon the action of the present: 'every image of the past that is not recognised by the present as one of its own threatens to disappear irretrievably'.[15] Such a present holds itself apart from chronology. It cannot be defined as a mere point in time. It is not the *nunc stans*. Rather, it is the result of a complex act of temporalization which is always contested: 'In every era the attempt must be made anew to wrest tradition away from a conformism that is about to overpower it.'[16] It is through such wresting that both tradition and the present are constituted. The present is constructed in the destruction and reconstitution of tradition. As the temporality of history is rethought under the pressure of such a conception of the present, so this rethinking comes to define the present (this present, now), philosophically.

This link between action and the present (the present as temporal construction) establishes both the proximity and distance of Benjamin's thought to Heidegger's – the theme of a number of the chapters in this volume. Heidegger, like Benjamin, is concerned to differentiate the present from the time set by clocks. There are affinities between what Heidegger calls 'resoluteness' (*entschlossenheit*) and the politics of Benjamin's time of the 'now' (*Jetztzeit*). The repetition of the given as the same was as problematic for Heidegger as it was for Benjamin. Yet an absolute differentiation must be made on the question of Being. The comfort granted to Heidegger's thought by the determination of the present as the presence of Being is contrary to Benjamin's whole concept of history. Now-time eschews all ontological reduction by thinking the past in terms of the monadic structure of remembrance.

Nonetheless, for all their differences, Benjamin's relations to Heidegger underline his place within 'the manifest tradition of philosophy' which Adorno claimed he forsook, but of which he was always a part, however deviant. The essays collected together in this volume insist on this connection. To do so, however, is as much to insist on the necessity for a reinterpretation of that tradition as it is to maintain the need for a 'philosophical' reading of Benjamin. To adapt the terms of Benjamin's own work on translation: philosophy must expand and deepen its conception of itself if it is to recognize itself in Benjamin's writings.[17] These essays undertake this task at a time at which the phenomenon known as post-structuralism may have made Benjamin's work 'easier to read' in the literary sphere of the US academy,[18] but it has not necessarily made it any more easily understood.

Benjamin's writings continue to provoke, and resist, reception from a variety of standpoints. It is through this resistance – what Arendt referred to as their *sui generis* character – that they continue to live. And it is through this after-life, as much if not more than in the time of their writing, that they contribute to the philosophical tradition, by transforming it. It is hoped that these essays will help extend that after-life.

NOTES

1 Hannah Arendt, 'Walter Benjamin: 1892–1940' (1968), published as the Introduction to Walter Benjamin, *Illuminations* (London: Fontana, 1973).

2 See in particular the introductory essay to Gary Smith (ed.) *Benjamin: Philosophy, Aesthetics, History* (Chicago, IL: Chicago University Press, 1989), pp. vii–xlii.

3 'A Portrait of Walter Benjamin', in Theodor W. Adorno, *Prisms*, translated by Samuel and Shierry Weber (London: Neville Spearman, 1967), pp. 239–40.

4 Ibid., p. 235.

5 Walter Benjamin, 'On the Program of the Coming Philosophy' (1917–8), translated by Mark Ritter, in Smith, *Benjamin*, pp. 1–12.

6 Walter Benjamin, *The Origin of German Tragic Drama* (1925), translated by John Osborne (London: New Left Books, 1977), p. 182.

7 Ibid., pp. 177–9.

8 Ibid., pp. 88–91.

9 'A Short History of Photography' (1931), in Walter Benjamin, *One-Way Street and Other Writings*, translated by Edmund Jephcott and Kingsley Short (London: New Left Books, 1979), pp. 240–57. Certain photographs of Atget's of the 'unremarked, forgotten, cast adrift' fragments of cities, Benjamin writes, 'pump the aura out of reality like water from a sinking ship' (p. 250).

10 Walter Benjamin, 'N [Re the Theory of Knowledge, Theory of Progress]', translated by Leigh Hafrey and Richard Sieburth, in Smith, *Benjamin*, pp. 43–83; (N 1, 10) and (N 1a, 8) in particular.

11 'Theses on the Philosophy of History' (1940), *Illuminations*, pp. 255–66.
12 'Eduard Fuch, Collector and Historian' (1937), *One-Way Street*, p. 360.
13 'The Destructive Character' (1931), *One-Way Street*, p. 158.
14 Jurgen Habermas, *The Philosophical Discourse of Modernity*, translated by Frederick Lawrence (Cambridge: Polity Press, 1987). See also Jurgen Habermas, 'Taking Aim at the Heart of the Present: On Foucault's Lecture on Kant's *What is Enlightenment?*', in J. Habermas, *The New Conservatism: Cultural Criticism and the Historians' Debate*, translated by Shierry Weber Nicholson (Cambridge: Polity Press, 1987), ch. 7.
15 'Theses on the Philosophy of History', *Illuminations*, p. 257 (Thesis V).
16 Ibid. (Thesis VI).
17 Cf. Walter Benjamin, 'The Task of the Translator' (1923), *Illuminations*, p. 81.
18 Rainer Nagele, 'Reading Benjamin', in Rainer Nagele (ed.) *Benjamin's Ground: New Readings of Walter Benjamin* (Detroit, IL: Wayne State University Press, 1988), p. 8.

1 Benjamin, Heidegger and the Destruction of Tradition

Howard Caygill

It is there that I shall find Heidegger on my path, and I expect
some sparks to fly from the clash [*l'entre-choc*] of our two very
different ways of viewing history.
>   (Benjamin, letter to Scholem, 20 January 1930)

The imagined meeting of Benjamin and Heidegger would be an apt
subject for a modern allegorical painting, perhaps by Kitaj with the
title *l'entre-choc*. Two iconic figures meet in a rancid *Heimat* landscape punctuated by distant 'factory' chimneys and traversed by a
gleaming Autobahn. Surrounded by a cluster of emblems drawn
from Judaism, Catholicism, and the 'contemporary mass movements' of Communism and Fascism, they contemplate a bullet-
scarred bust of Hölderlin. And between them flash the sparks from
the collision of their 'two very different ways of viewing history'.

Such an image would illustrate the extent to which the differences
between Heidegger and Benjamin are traversed by broader political
and religious oppositions, with the one figuring the unrepentant
beneficiary of the National Socialist regime and the other its exiled
and terrorized victim. Yet there is a danger of this image becoming
a sentimental idyll, a 'left melancholic' alibi for not examining the
possible complicity between their two views of history. Nor is the
danger of a Manichean separation of Benjamin and Heidegger aver-
ted by simply harmonizing their opposition, whether through the
liberal equanimity of intellectual history or the neo-Marxist resolution of a dialectical opposition. Such approaches to the staging of
the opposition prescribe in advance the terms on which Benjamin
and Heidegger will or will not meet, and in so doing forgo the
sparks thrown up by their *l'entre-choc*. They also sacrifice the light
which these sparks might cast upon prevailing assumptions about
the relationship between history, politics and art under modernity.

The clash between Heidegger and Benjamin's thought cannot be described in terms of a 'debate' – there was no institutional space in which Benjamin and Heidegger could engage in a liberal 'exchange of views'. Benjamin's comments on Heidegger's work were uniformly hostile, and never directly addressed the author: he planned in 1930 to establish a reading group with Brecht which would 'demolish Heidegger' (*Briefe*, 514) and a year later claimed to prefer the 'preposterous and uncouth analyses of Franz Mehring' to the 'profound description of the realm of ideas undertaken by the Heideggerian school' (p. 524). Nor is there any evidence of Heidegger's critical engagement with Benjamin's work. And yet in spite of this absence of 'debate' the encounter of Benjamin and Heidegger's thought is of crucial importance not only for understanding the development of Benjamin's thought but also for understanding the directions taken by German philosophical and political radicalism during the 1920s and 1930s.

The thematic parallels between Heidegger and Benjamin's thought are striking. Both were critical to the point of hostility of prevailing neo-Kantian and Hegelian liberal progressive philosophies of history, and both engaged with a constellation of themes which included 'tradition', 'origin', 'technology' and 'art'. Both explored these themes within the context of an analysis of the grain of everyday experience in modernity: Heidegger in the analyses of Division 1 of *Being and Time* and Benjamin in the 'Arcades Project'. Finally, both sought to comprehend the changes in the modern political occasioned by what Benjamin described as the 'tremendous shattering of tradition' and its 'intimate connection with the contemporary mass movements' (Benjamin 1935: 223). Their accounts of these changes stressed the role played by technology in the emergence of a political realm riven by the opposition between the mass movements of the left and the right.

The thematic similarities are complemented by a chronological parallel between their writings and publications. These began in 1916 with Benjamin's critique of Heidegger's *Der Zeitbegriff in der Geschichtswissenschaft* (*The Concept of Time in the Science of History*) (1916) and to a lesser extent *Die Kategorien- und Bedeutungslehre des Duns Scotus* (*Scotus's Doctrine of the Categories and Signification*) (1916). Heidegger's development of the themes of tradition and temporality announced in these early works and their systematic critique by Benjamin set the stage for the composition and publication of their contemporaneous masterpieces *Being and Time* (1927) and *The Origin of German Tragic Drama* (*Ursprung des deutschen Trauerspiels*) (1928). The same set of themes was to resurface almost a decade later in the two classic meditations on art, politics and technology written in 1935 – Heidegger's 'The Origin of the Work of Art' and Benjamin's 'The Work of Art in the Age of Mechanical Reproduction'.

These thematic and chronological parallels are not coincidental but issue directly from Benjamin's initial critique of Heidegger's philosophy of history in 1916. Central to this critique is a severe difference with Heidegger over the nature of tradition. Benjamin's insistence upon the destructive character of tradition and its relation to history and subjectivity established the terrain not only for his critique of Heidegger but also for the development of his thought as a whole. This first *entre-choc* in 1916 thus formed the matrix for the subsequent differences which were to emerge between the two thinkers.

TRADITION AND HISTORICAL TIME

The dedication to *The Origin of German Tragic Drama* reads

Entworfen 1916   Verfasst 1925
Damals wie Heute meiner Frau gewidnet

and translates as 'Sketched 1916   Composed 1925   Dedicated then as now to my wife'. The 'sketch' of 1916 has survived in the six fragments mentioned in a letter to Herbert Belmore late in 1916. They were written over the summer of that year, beginning with 'The Happiness of Classical Humanity' and 'Socrates' written in June. These were followed by the three fragments written over the summer months, 'On the Middle Ages', 'The Mourning-Play and Tragedy' and 'The Significance of Speech in the Mourning-Play and Tragedy' (I follow Gillian Rose's felicitous translation of *Trauerspiel* as mourning-play). The series of fragments was concluded in mid-November with the consummate commentary on Genesis 2–3: 'On Language in General and on Human Language'. The significance of these fragments for understanding Benjamin's thought cannot be overstated. Together they form the matrix not only of the *Trauerspiel* book and the associated essays on language and translation prior to 1925, but also of the 'Arcades Project' and its paralipomena from the 1930s.

The fragments of 1916 are also significant with respect to the *entre-choc* between Benjamin and Heidegger. In a letter to Gershom Scholem dated 11 November 1916, Benjamin refers Scholem to the

Heidegger essay 'The Concept of Time in the Science of History' which was first given as a *venia legendi* lecture in Freiburg on 27 July 1915 and was published in the first half of 1916 in the *Zeitschrift für Philosophie und philosophische Kritik*, vol. 161. Benjamin seems to have read this essay during the summer, and the last four fragments show clear signs of a critical engagement with it. The programmatic sketch for his *Trauerspiel* book, and indeed for his authorship as a whole, thus emerged from a critique of Heidegger.

Benjamin's comments on Heidegger's essay are far from complimentary: he told Scholem 'it shows precisely how not to deal with the matter. A terrible piece of work, which you should perhaps look at, if only to confirm my suspicion, that most of what the author says about historical time is nonsense (which I am in a position to judge) but also, to confirm that what he says about mechanical time is wrong too!' (*Briefe*, 130–1). Yet this categorical rejection of Heidegger's early work on time conceals the extent of Benjamin's critical engagement, and indeed the several points of agreement between them.

Superficially, Heidegger's text appears as an academic exercise in neo-Kantianism, but one with several novel twists which point forward to the subsequent development of his thought. Heidegger begins with the received neo-Kantian distinction of the natural and cultural sciences, proposing to compare the concepts of time which are used in each of them. Still in a neo-Kantian vein, he examines the 'function' of the concept of time which is proper to the goals of the two sciences.

The first part of the essay examines the function of time in modern natural science. Heidegger describes the 'goal' of modern science as the expression of the 'unity of the physical image of the world [*Weltbild*], the tracing-back of all appearances to the mathematically established laws of general dynamics, back to the laws of motion of a still undetermined mass' (Heidegger 1916: 363; 5, translation amended). In physical science, the concept of time functions as a mathematical measure, as the fourth-dimensional variable t added to the three-dimensional system of Cartesian co-ordinates x, y, z. This requires that the 'sensible-intuitive qualities of a defined phenomenon are eliminated and transformed into mathematical ones' (Heidegger 1916: 365; 6) and that 'time then become an homogeneous ordered series of points, a scale, a parameter' (pp. 366; 6). With these arguments Heidegger anticipates his later analysis of the mathematization of modern science in *What is a Thing?*, but the emphasis in the 1916 text is on developing a concept of historical time by means of a comparison with the concept of time used in physical science.

In his discussion of the function of time in history, Heidegger establishes many of the tropes which will inform his later discussions of history, tradition and origin. He admits that there is little consensus among historians over the goal of history, but draws out those 'moments' of the science of history which elucidate the function performed in it by the concept of time. Two of these moments are substantive. They concern the historical *object* and the *relation* of past and present. The next two moments are methodological. In them Heidegger reflects upon the concept of time implied in the testing of historical sources and the construction of historical narratives. The fifth and final moment brings out the understanding of time presupposed by historical chronology. From all this Heidegger concludes that the historical concept of time is qualitative, but on the way to this unremarkable conclusion he makes several important and suggestive points which were later developed more fully.

Heidegger claims that the object of history is humanity 'not as a biological entity, rather to the extent that its spiritual-physical accomplishments embody the ideal of culture' (pp. 368; 7). The idea of culture is realized through *Kulturschaffen* (creation of culture), which appears on occasions to be itself the agent of history. Yet at the moment when Heidegger is describing it in terms of an 'objectification of spirit in the medium of time' a dissonance enters into his account:

> This *Kulturschaffen* in its fullness and variety proceeds in time, it passes through a development, underlies the most varied forms of recasting and retrieval, and gathers what is past in order to work it through further, or to combat it.
>
> (pp. 368; 8, translation amended)

In the first part of the sentence Heidegger prosecutes a logic of objectification; in the second he intimates a differential view of time and history. In the remainder of the essay, the second view increasingly prevails.

When Heidegger describes the object of history as the temporal objectification of spirit, he reduces time to a neutral medium of objectification. However, when he broadens his analysis to include the relation between past and present he gains some fresh insights into the phenomenon of historical time. He does not then succumb to a pseudo-Hegelian synthesis of past and present in the continuous present of the 'objectification of spirit' as in the first half of the sentence cited above, but instead pursues the paradox of historical time intimated in its second half. The claim that the present must gather what is past in order to work it through further or combat it intimates a new, differential notion of historical time. The historical object is always separated from the present by an interval of time, but it is precisely this interval that allows it to be retrieved and worked through or resisted again. It is time that makes the past into what Heidegger will later call an 'endowment', but this is time not as a medium for unifying past and present but as a difference that divides them.

Time separates the present from the past as well as bringing the past into the present. The present of the past was 'other' to our present, and yet it is not 'incomparably other'. There is a 'temporal rift between the historian and the object' and for history to be possible this rift must be both overcome and preserved. This movement is identified by Heidegger as the main 'goal' of history, and he intimates that it is only possible through the paradoxical function of time, which brings the past into the present while ineluctably consigning it to the 'past'. Time, in the later language, both presences and withdraws the past; it performs the work of carrying over the past to the present while also making it something other than the present.

Various perplexities follow from the simultaneous presencing and withdrawing of the past through time, and these are explored by Heidegger in his reflections on historical methodology. These reflections are beset by the anxiety of the 'labyrinth of errors' opened by viewing time as both presencing and absencing the past. Heidegger is particularly intrigued by the problem of the authenticity of historical sources provoked by this movement. If the past exists only for the present but not entirely in it, what then *is* the past, is there an authentic past, or is it but the forged coin of the present? This problem is explored in an excursus on historical source criticism, the guaranteeing of the 'authenticity' of received sources. Time once again plays an equivocal role: it raises the possibility of forgery, while supplying the touchstone for a genuine source; it is the condition both for the authenticity and inauthenticity of a source.

Heidegger maintains that sources – documentary and other – are 'stamped' by their time, especially by the legal and cultural forms which for him comprise their 'time'. Such past structurings of time are visible to the present, and the authenticity of a source may be established by comparing it with the structuring of time characteristic of the epoch in which it is supposed to have arisen. Here

Heidegger retrieves his earlier argument for *Kulturschaffen* as the source of the structuring of time. If a source is incongruent with what has become known as 'its time', then it is suspect. He cites the pseudo-Isadorean decretals as an example of an exposed forgery, concluding that a source's 'value as evidence depends on how far removed it is in time from the historical fact to which it is to testify' (pp. 372; 9). The trope informing Heidegger's analysis is becoming clearer – time enables historical truth to be established while simultaneously distancing and undoing its claims.

Time also obeys this structure in the methodological discussion of historical narrative. Presenting the past as a historical object allows once present events to become elements of a narrative, while at the same time removing them from any possibility of narrative by locating them in their proper epoch. The narrative is of the present, but claims to present the past. Time is both the condition of a true narrative and the prime threat to its authenticity. A similar trope obtains with Heidegger's analysis of historical chronology, the calibration of time in terms of days, weeks, years. This he says is a condition for historical understanding, yet also an obstacle, since historical events obey a qualitative temporality which cannot be contained by chronology. The latter calibrates the presencing and withdrawing of time from the standpoint of an eternal present in which every moment is identical, but cannot capture differences in the qualitative experience of time.

Although couched in the numbing idiom of academic neo-Kantianism, Heidegger's analysis of historical time is already far beyond it. It points to a radical understanding of time as *tradition*, that is, as a passing on of the past to the present which is also the present's constitution of its past. It regards historical time or tradition as deeply equivocal. It is both the 'passing on' and 'carrying over' of a historical object or heritage, and that which opens the dangerous intervals of time across which the heritage must be carried. Furthermore, while it is the guarantee of a genuine 'heritage' – a past owned by a present – it also undermines the truth and validity of the past in the act of passing it on to the present. The heritage is different for each present, but this unsettles its claim to be 'true' and threatens to expose it as a forgery. Historical time, or tradition, is no less than the condition of history which makes history impossible; it allows the present to constitute a past which was never present to itself, never true. Time, which promised to be a condition for the present's gathering the past to itself, now appears to have become the means by which the past and the present ruin and scatter each other.

Even at this early stage of his career Heidegger's analysis is characteristically ambiguous. He complicates the thought of historical time (tradition) by showing how it both enables and undermines history. Yet when faced with the prospect of dissemblance and inauthenticity opened by this perspective, he attempts to re-establish truth and authenticity. Thus in one sentence he can regard objectification in time as the substance which underlies the continuous 'recasting and retrieval' of history as well as the differential power which breaks continuity and allows for the past to be 'taken up' and 'worked through or combatted'. Historical time or tradition is both the medium or vehicle of truth and its greatest threat.

Heidegger remains with the thought that the 'substance' of historical time is continually beset by a differential time; he does not attempt in a dialectical fashion to reconcile them in a higher unity. He could have done so by resting everything on the eternal present of the *Kulturschaffen* underlying past and present, and thus remained a sound neo-Kantian in the tradition of the 'southwestern school'. That he did not do so is largely the outcome of his recognizing the temporal heterogeneity of past and present: the past can never be present to itself, but is always parasitic upon another present somewhere in its future. However, there is a distinct sense that in this text Heidegger is searching for the basis of authentic experience in time. This he subsequently discovered not in the continuous present of the *Kulturschaffen* but in the ecstatic temporality of a subject open to the future. In *Being and Time* he draws out and thematizes the dimension of futurity, and uses it to establish the desired authentic relation of past and present.

In his critique of Heidegger's account of historical time, Benjamin arrives at very different conclusions. He accepts Heidegger's account of historical time as the condition of the simultaneous possibility and impossibility of history, but does not share his preoccupation with establishing authenticity. Benjamin's work, as we shall see, represents a radical development of Heidegger's insights, presaging the work of the post-*Kehre* Heidegger and avoiding the language of restoration and authenticity which haunted Heidegger's work in the 1920s and early 1930s to such unhappy effect.

The germs of Benjamin's later thinking are evident above all in the two fragments from 1916 on 'Tragedy and *Trauerspiel*' and 'On the Significance of Speech in Tragedy and *Trauerspiel*'. It is in the former fragment that Benjamin engages most directly with Heidegger's account of historical time. The piece is structured around a neo-Kantian trump of Heidegger's neo-Kantian hand. Instead of restricting the analysis of historical time to the contrast of natural and historical science, Benjamin introduces the function of time in aesthetics, specifically in the distinction between the dramatic forms of tragedy and *Trauerspiel*. However, he remains close to Heidegger in trying to specify the paradoxical character of historical time or tradition.

In this extremely allusive fragment Benjamin uses tragedy and *Trauerspiel* to exemplify two forms of historical time. Tragic time is authentic, and marks a present which is redeemed and completed by gathering its past to itself, while time for *Trauerspiel* is inauthentic, the past ruining the present and making it entirely in vain. While the two art forms correspond to the distinction of authentic and inauthentic time, and are explored as such throughout the fragment, they are never called to serve as the opposed moments of a dialectic. The fragmentary and elliptical form of the essay resists the temptation present in Heidegger's treatise to restore authenticity by any move towards a dialectical resolution. The fragment begins with some reflections on tragedy as a schema of historical time, and then breaks into a disquisition on historical time addressed to Heidegger but without mentioning his name or identifying citations. This is followed by some reflections on the representations of death in tragedy and *Trauerspiel*, followed by a meditation upon the experience of time proper to the two dramatic genres.

Benjamin adopts Heidegger's distinction between quantitative and qualitative time, agreeing with him that time is 'not simply a measure by which the duration of a mechanical alteration may be measured' (Benjamin 1916: 134). On the nature of historical time, however, Benjamin and Heidegger differ in several respects. First of all, Benjamin defines the time of history as 'infinite in every direction and unfulfilled in every moment' (p. 134), that is, he defines it as resisting any bid for authenticity or fulfilment in the present moment. He makes a further distinction between historical time and the historical events that take place 'within' it: 'the determining force of the historical form of time cannot be understood in terms of empirical events nor can it be entirely contained by any' (p. 134). Benjamin here appears to claim, in fairly orthodox Kantian fashion, that historical time is transcendental – the condition of the possibility of historical events. This appears to be common ground with Heidegger; but on closer examination their positions fall far apart.

In some respects Heidegger can be read in 1916 as developing a transcendental account of historical time, laying out the conditions for the possibility of historical events whether as the 'substance of continuity' underlying them or as the interruption in continuity which allowed past and present events to be distinguished from each other. Benjamin too stresses the transcendental discontinuity of historical time, but unlike Heidegger he does not do so on the basis of a contrast between a continuous, substantial time and discontinuous time founded upon interruption. Instead he introduces another factor into the equation: redeemed time for him is not a continuous substance underlying past, present and future, but the Messianic interruption of the temporal order itself.

Heidegger keeps open the possibility that historical time may be a suitable vehicle for authenticity, an option which Benjamin utterly refuses to entertain. For him, an authentic, redeemed historical time is only possible at the end of history with the advent of the Messiah – 'This idea of a fulfilled time is called in the Bible, where it is the dominant historical idea, Messianic time' (p. 134). He continues:

> the idea of a fulfilled historical time cannot be thought in the same way as the idea of an individual time. This determination, which naturally completely changes the meaning of redemption, is what distinguishes tragic from Messianic time. Tragic time is to the latter, as individually fulfilled is to divinely fulfilled time.
>
> (p. 134)

It is the distinction between fulfilment *in* historical time and the fulfilment *of* historical time which marks the difference between Heidegger and Benjamin. Benjamin identifies Heidegger's understanding of historical time as tragic, one in which past, present and future can be gathered in time, whereas for him fulfilled time is Messianic, a gathering *of* time which is not *in* time.

Heidegger keeps open the possibility of redemption in historical time, with the implication that present guilt may be redeemed in time by 'working through' and 'combating' the past. For Benjamin there can be no redemption *in* historical time, only the redemption *of* it. There can be no 'working through' or 'combat', no gathering of a heritage in the present. As if anticipating Heidegger's development of ecstatic time as the horizon for gathering together past, present and future in *Being and Time*, Benjamin insists on the complete exteriority of Messianic time, one whose advent brings with it the 'cessation of happening'. In the absence of the Messianic fulfilment of time there can be none in time: all events in time are not only inauthentic, but they can never attain authenticity.

Benjamin stages the distinction between authentic and inauthentic historical time by contrasting tragedy and *Trauerspiel*. He focuses on their treatments of the moment of death, distinguishing the authenticity of the tragic death from the inauthentic death of *Trauerspiel*. Tragic death marks a moment of fulfilment; all the events of a life gather significance from the anticipation of this moment. This is of course an ironic and a paradoxical moment; time is fulfilled at the moment in which it ceases. Death in *Trauerspiel* does not fulfil a life; here the moment of death is but one of a series of insignificant moments. Each moment is a fraud, a repetition of a repetition – 'all play until death ends the game, only to continue in an enlarged repetition of the same game in another world' (p. 136). The events of such a life are 'parabolic schemas, sensible mirror images of another game'. The events of historical time are inauthentic, repeats and copies of earlier repetitions. There is no possibility of an authentic 'source'; historical time drains its events of any significance. There is no moment or place where the 'passing over' of tradition can be gathered; its sole issue is ruination and dispersal.

Benjamin further explores the difference between his and Heidegger's views of historical time in the fragment 'On the Significance of Speech in *Trauerspiel* and Tragedy'. The tragic word conveys a meaning; it had a meaning when it was spoken, and this meaning is preserved in being passed on: 'The word as the bearer of its significance is the pure word.' In its tradition the word gathers to it fresh significance; it is given life by being passed on. With *Trauerspiel*, however, the word has no authentic or intrinsic meaning, no word is pure. Its meaning changes according to the circumstances of its transmission and reception: 'The word in the process of transformation is the linguistic principle of *Trauerspiel*' (p. 138). Once again, there is no genuine or authentic meaning which can be conveyed by the word; its meaning and its conveyance interrupt and undermine each other and 'The counterpoint between sound and meaning remains spectral in *Trauerspiel*' (p. 139). It does not gather significance to itself around an original meaning which is augmented and given life by being passed over, but only repeats an original absence of meaning.

Benjamin emphasizes the destructive work of historical time or tradition over Heidegger's attempts to secure authenticity through it. He sees any attempt to derive authenticity or significance from the handing-over of tradition as obeying the mythic laws of the tragic genre in which a historical subject may be redeemed in time, gather the past and future into a present. For Benjamin this was only possible in the apocatastasis at the Messianic end of history in which all time and events will be gathered, and not just those befalling a subject in time. In the absence of this fulfilment of time he saw no possibility of the existence of an authentic historical subject. This difference with Heidegger was taken further in *The Origin of German Tragic Drama*; meanwhile Heidegger too had developed the ambiguities of his early position in the discourse on historical authenticity which forms the second division of *Being and Time*.

AUTHENTICITY AND BETRAYAL

Both Heidegger and Benjamin opposed the progressive view of history which regarded the present as the untroubled heir of the past. This view was shared by both the Enlightenment liberal and counter-Enlightenment conservative understandings of the relation between past and present. It assumed tradition to be a neutral medium, whether for the unfolding of reason in history or for the bestowal of the accumulated wisdom of the past upon the present. For Heidegger and Benjamin, however, tradition was not the smooth and uninterrupted transmission of the past to the present but a handing over of tradition fraught with danger and risk.

In questioning the understanding of tradition shared by both Enlightenment and counter-Enlightenment, Heidegger and Benjamin retrieved a forgotten aspect of the notion of tradition. Originating in Roman law, *traditio* was a legal term denoting 'delivery', 'conveyance' or 'surrender'. Its use was extended to religion by Tertullian in the second century CE as part of his wholesale translation of Christian religious experience into the language of Roman law. At this stage tradition was an extremely equivocal term, with the familiar sense of the 'handing down' of an oral doctrine coexisting with the less familiar one of 'surrender' and 'betrayal'. Theologians, for example, described Christ's betrayal by Judas as the 'tradition' which initiated the events of his 'passion'. 'Tradition' was further defined as the ecclesiastical crime of surrendering sacred texts in a time of persecution – delivering them over to destruction by unbelievers. One guilty of the crime of 'tradition' was a 'traditor' or, in later usage, a 'traitor'.

While the Enlightenment and counter-Enlightenment adopted the sense of tradition as a 'handing down', Heidegger and Benjamin retrieved its treacherous and dangerous sense of a potentially destructive surrender. The act of 'handing over' destroys the object it surrenders; it is in no sense a 'medium', let alone a *neutral* medium for the transmission of the past to the present. As both agreed in 1916, tradition is not only that which is handed over within a given time, but also the giving of that time itself in the distinction of past and present. Tradition paradoxically establishes the distance between past and present while overcoming it by delivering them to each other; it both founds and presupposes the time within which it takes place. As Heidegger and Benjamin pointed out in 1916, tradition is a paradoxical, even destructive, phenomenon characterized by a delivery which both exceeds and is contained by what is delivered.

Both Heidegger and Benjamin analyse the paradoxical operation of tradition in terms of the concept of 'origin' which names the 'simultaneous' immanence and transcendence of the act of delivery over what is delivered. But in *Being and Time* and *The Origin of German Tragic Drama* they draw extremely different conclusions from their analyses of origin. For Heidegger, origin and tradition are equivocal; they can be either authentic or inauthentic, fulfilling or destructive. For Benjamin there is no such equivocation: origin and tradition are unequivocally destructive. The difference hinges around the possibility of an authentic site where tradition can be gathered. This site has to be granted a privileged status with respect to tradition; in modernity this status is described topologically in terms of 'the subject' or 'that which lies under'. Heidegger in 1916 and later in *Being and Time* grants the possibility of gathering tradition on the ground of the subject, while Benjamin refuses it. The reasons for these distinct stances may be clarified by a comparative analysis of origin and tradition as developed in the two main texts of the 1920s.

In the second division of *Being and Time* on 'Dasein and Temporality' Heidegger translates many of the thoughts of the 1916 essay on historical time into the language of the analytic of Dasein. The exposition of authentic and inauthentic tradition is immeasurably clarified by the introduction of ecstatic temporality, the futurity of Dasein. Tradition retains its ambiguity and risk – it may surrender Dasein to inauthenticity – but it also gives it the opportunity to become 'authentic' in a moment of resolute decision. The moment of resolution marks the site where past, present and future are gathered together; but occupying this site brings with it the danger of irresoluteness and indecision.

The ambiguity of the site becomes evident in the two senses of 'origin' which inform the exposition of authenticity: it is both the retrospective moment of ruination and decay *and* the ecstatic moment of vision (*Augenblick*). The first sense appears in the following reference to the 'ontological source' from 'Temporality and Everydayness':

> The ontological source of *Dasein's* Being is not 'inferior' to what springs from it, but towers above it in power from the outset; in the field of ontology, any 'springing from' is degeneration.
>
> (1927: 334)

With reference to origin, the action of 'springing from' puts everything ontic into question, denudes it of any intrinsic significance. The 'ontological source' disrupts any attempt on the part of Dasein to gather itself; it ruins any attempt to describe a place or a moment from which to draw together past, present and future. Here the excessive moment of tradition betrays any attempt to establish a site from which to receive from the past and pass on to the future.

At this moment of betrayal and ruination the power of origin also provides an opportunity for a re-inauguration of tradition. Viewed from the perspective of a present 'now' described in terms of the borders between what it receives (the past) and what it passes on (the future), origin degrades the 'now' into an indifferent moment of transition. But if origin itself – the act of receiving and passing on – is made the present, then the moment of transition may be transformed into a 'moment of vision':

> The moment of vision is a phenomenon which *in principle* can *not* be clarified in terms of the *now* [dem *Jetzt*]. The 'now' is a temporal phenomenon which belongs to time as within-time-ness: the 'now' 'in which' something arises, passes away, or is present-at-hand. 'In the moment of vision' nothing can occur; but as an authentic Present or waiting-towards, the moment of vision permits us *to encounter for the first time* what can be 'in a time' as ready-to-hand or present-at-hand.
>
> (p. 338)

The thought of origin cannot be restricted to moments in time or things present or ready to hand, since they are parasitic upon the act of 'handing over' which is a condition of time and things present in time. The origin is thought both as a disempowering destruction of whatever is handed down and as a potentially empowering authentic encounter, a repetition made for the first time.

The equivocal sense of origin as degeneration and as authentic present is unfolded in the analysis of 'Temporality and Historicality' in Section V of *Being and Time*. Here Heidegger develops the thought of the 1916 essay that the past is constituted as wholly other by the present, while yet also, indeed only, existing for and in the present. Tradition gives the past to the present, but at the price of its simultaneous proximity and remoteness. The past is at once of no significance – it is not even present to itself as 'past' – yet also replete with significance, being always 'encountered for the first time' in the present. Heidegger writes:

> Thus 'the past' has a remarkable double meaning; the past belongs irretrievably to an earlier time; it belonged to the events of that time; and in spite of that, it can still be present-at-hand 'now' – for instance, the remains of a Greek temple. With the temple, a 'bit of the past' is still 'in the present'.
>
> (p. 478)

The past 'belongs irretrievably' to another time, and yet it has been 'handed over' to the present, and is as past only by grace of the present. But such gathering of the past to the present cannot be accomplished by a present which situates itself between what has been and what will be.

The equivocality of the past, or its 'enigma', has a considerable impact on Heidegger's analytic of Dasein. If the past only exists for the present and never existed for itself (as past), why is it yet determinative of Dasein in the present? In Heidegger's words:

> when one designates a time as 'the past', the meaning of this is not unequivocal; but the past is manifestly distinct from *one's having been*, with which we have become acquainted as something constitutive for the ecstatic unity of Dasein's temporality. This, however, only makes the enigma ultimately more acute; why is it that the historical is determined *predominantly* by the 'past', or, to speak more appropriately, by the character of having-been, when that character is one that temporalizes itself equiprimordially with the Present and the future.
>
> (p. 381)

Heidegger dispels the enigma through the distinction between an authentic and inauthentic relation between past, present and future. The past is always a repetition, but one which may be thought 'degeneratively' as stripping the present of its significance – as being irretrievably other as 'past' – or it can be thought resolutely in a 'moment of vision'. The 'moment of vision' is 'a *disavowal* of that which in the "today", is working itself out as the "past". Repetition does not abandon itself to the past, nor does it aim at progress'

(p. 386). An inauthentic stance toward tradition allows features of the present to give themselves the alibi of being past; a resolute stance accepts that the past is a temporalization of the present and future: 'the phenomena of handing down and repeating . . . are rooted in the future' (p. 386). Here it becomes clear that the moment of vision is ecstatic and not Messianic, for by attending to the future it allows for an authentic relation to the past and present. The Messianic moment, on the contrary, collapses past, present and future into the cessation of events.

Heidegger's account of an authentic relation between past and present founded in the future allows him to describe a site or a 'now' where they may be gathered. However, he very quickly and tendentiously transforms this site first into 'the Subject' as something underlying past, present and future, and then into discrete 'subjects'. The 'handing over' of the past is taken to constitute or be the work of a historical subject. The subject may be inauthentic, *das Mann*, whose present is drained of meaning by the burden of the past. This is the subject Heidegger speaks of when he says: 'When, however, one's existence is inauthentically historical, it is loaded down with the legacy of a "past" which has become unrecognisable, and it seeks the modern' (p. 391). Or the subject can be authentic, possessing that 'authentic resoluteness . . . in which *Dasein hands* itself *down* to itself, free for death, in a possibility which it has inherited and yet has chosen' (p. 384). Here tradition is acknowledged to be the work of the present and future subject; it hands itself down to itself through 'the past' which is recognized as but a way of acknowledging its present and future. The past is the freely chosen inheritance, the other which Dasein has chosen to give itself. In both cases it is assumed that the site of tradition is properly described in the topologically specific terms of 'a subject'.

The authentic historical subject is the one capable of resolutely choosing its past. This choice is no less than the active repetition of tradition:

> The resoluteness in which Dasein comes back to itself, discloses current factical possibilities of authentic existing, and discloses them *in terms of the heritage* which that resoluteness, as thrown, *takes over*. In one's coming back resolutely to one's thrownness, there is hidden a *handing down* to oneself of the possibilities that have come down to one, but not necessarily *as* having thus come down.
>
> (p. 383)

Such a stance toward tradition, which assumes responsibility for it, is proper to an authentic subject – *'Repeating is handing down explicitly'* – but why is this handing down reserved to a subject, and who is this subject? Heidegger's second sentence in the above passage insinuates a reflexive structure of subjectivity in order to transform the site of tradition into the place of a subject. It would be possible to read it without this structure, as 'In . . . coming back resolutely to . . . thrownness, there is hidden a *handing down* . . . of the possibilities that have come down . . . but not necessarily *as* having thus come down.' Here the ellipses bring out the questions regarding time, tradition and the present which are raised by the thought, and shows how they are narrowed and even smothered by superficial addition of the reflexive structures of 'subjectivity'. What is worse, the imposition of a logic of the subject upon the site of tradition makes it possible to insert familiar and at hand subjects into its place. As a result the site of tradition is surrendered to the subject of tradition, be it the hero, the poet, the leader or the people.

Heidegger has nevertheless shown that the site of tradition is always endangered, even when it seems at its most authentic. But by introducing the dialectical logic of subjectivity – which risks its present in order to regain in the future what it has lost in the past – he transforms the paradox of tradition into the agonal and tragic struggle of the subject. The resolute subject struggles with tradition in the guise of fate and destiny, and in the struggle finds freedom:

> Our fates have already been guided in advance, in our Being with one another in the same world and in our resoluteness for definite possibilities. Only in communicating and in struggling does the power of destiny become free.
>
> (p. 384)

The struggle clears the space for a moment of decision, one in which the past and future may be gathered and granted significance in the present. In the anticipation of death, the 'connected life' is envisaged ecstatically, and this shows the past to be but a part of this life, not exterior to it. The place where tradition is gathered is the subject, but its 'connected life' is always endangered by what is more than the subject, and that is not just the past and the future but tradition's very gathering of past, present and future.

In bringing together tradition and the analytic of Dasein, Heidegger has developed and deepened his earlier account of historical time. The handing over of tradition is ambiguous – it may disem-

power or empower Dasein – it may strip past and present of significance, or it may fulfil the moment by resolutely binding together
past, present and future. However, he very rapidly translated the
handing over of tradition into the agonal, or dialectical, logic of
subjectivity. It was the second stage of this analysis which Benjamin
had anticipated, and already found unacceptable, in 1916. The broad
outline of his critique of Heidegger's earlier text formed the 'draft'
of *The Origin of German Tragic Drama* in which he insisted upon
the destruction of tradition. His reading of tradition and the work
of origin maintains that tradition betrays whatever it hands over.
For him there is no possibility of an authentic relation to tradition
within tradition; there is only the Messianic completion of tradition
itself, which is its destruction. With this argument Benjamin retained
the radical insight into the destruction of tradition which he shared
with Heidegger, but avoided any temptation to transform the site
of tradition into the place of the subject.

In the 'Epistemo-Critical Prologue' to *The Origin of German
Tragic Drama* Benjamin is close to Heidegger in insisting that origin
cannot be described in terms of the objects and events to which it
gives rise. The act of handing over that forms tradition is in excess
of such objects and events. It gives rise to history and historical
time, but its content is not exhausted by them:

> Origin [*Ursprung*], although an entirely historical category, has,
> nevertheless, nothing to do with genesis [*Entstehung*]. The term
> origin is not intended to describe the process by which the exist-
> ent came into being, but rather to describe that which emerges
> from the process of becoming and disappearance.
>
> (1928: 45)

Two things emerge from the process of 'becoming and disappearance': one is the object or event which comes and goes, and the
other is the coming and going of objects and events, their tradition.
For Benjamin the price of becoming an object of tradition is inauthenticity and imperfection; such an object can never be authentically
there, integral in itself, since it only is there by grace of being
handed over by tradition. Its emergence is always already its disappearance – the site of tradition is not a place where past, present
and future are gathered together for resolute action, but one where
the present is haunted not only by its past but also by its future of
becoming past. It is a place of *mourning*. Here origin and its objects
can never attain authenticity, but are always indebted to something
which does not disclose itself:

That which is original is never revealed in the naked and manifest existence of the factual; its rhythm is apparent only to a dual insight. On the one hand it needs to be recognised as a process of restoration and re-establishment, but, on the other hand, and precisely because of this, as something imperfect and incomplete.

(p. 45)

In order for the past to be handed over to the present, it has to be destroyed, made into a different kind of object, one which is past. Origin then is destructive, with no place for authenticity or fulfilment – it is, in Benjamin's words, 'a whirlpool in the flow of becoming whose rhythm consumes the materials of becoming' – tradition is catastrophic, taking when it would seem to give, a perpetual state of emergency.

For Benjamin, tradition is a play of sadness, a ruination. It offers no possibility of authenticity, no moment of decision, no meaning to a life. It is not the place for a subject to play out its tragedy of loss and gain. This is in stark contrast to Heidegger's tragic schema in which Dasein gathers tradition to itself in the struggle between past, present and future and can thus gain authenticity even in the moment of death. For Benjamin, death leaves everything incomplete, the subject becomes a haunting presence to be mourned:

Whereas the tragic hero, in his 'immortality', does not save his life, but only his name, in death the characters of *Trauerspiel* lose only the name bearing individuality, and not the vitality of their role. This survives undiminished in the spirit world.

(p. 136)

The death of *Trauerspiel* is not final, nor does its anticipation permit an authentic stance toward the present; it offers no opportunity to make a resolute decision. Benjamin exemplifies this point by a discussion of the death of Hamlet, which he claims was not a tragic death:

He wants to die by some accident, and as the fateful stage properties gather around him, as around their lord and master, the drama of fate flares up in the conclusion of this *Trauerspiel* as something that is contained, but of course overcome, in it. Whereas tragedy ends with a decision – however uncertain this may be – there resides in the essence of *Trauerspiel*, and especially in the death scene, an appeal of the kind which martyrs utter.

(p. 137)

This death did not complete a life, give it meaning, but cut it off and left it in question. There is no final decision which would give meaning to the events which preceded it, simply indecision and accident in the face of catastrophe.

For Benjamin, the work of tradition cannot be captured by the schema of tragedy. It has no room for the establishment of an authentic subject making resolute decisions; for it, authenticity is always *haunted* by its opposite just as 'restoration is haunted by the idea of catastrophe' (p. 66). Benjamin insists that *Trauerspiel* knows no completion, it knows no possibility of achieving fulfilment in time:

> it possesses no mechanism by which all earthly things are gathered in together and exalted before being consigned to their end.
>
> (p. 61)

For *Trauerspiel* the world was empty, a place of 'never-ending repetition' with no possibility of ever becoming genuine or authentic: 'For those who looked deeper saw the scene of their existence as a rubbish heap of partial, inauthentic actions' (p. 139). The world handed down to us by tradition is uncanny, undecipherable, always other. History becomes an allegory, withholding its meaning just as it seems to offer it.

Benjamin's reading of tradition stays with its destructive aspect: instead of authenticity within tradition, in a tragic fulfilment within time, tradition itself is inauthentic. Benjamin considered that the excessive moment of tradition, the moment of origin which ruined the integrity of the originated, could be employed against tradition. Tradition as the scene of handing over might itself be made an object of contemplation, as in the description of 'melancholy immersion' at the end of *The Origin of German Tragic Drama* when

> its ultimate objects, in which it believes it can most fully secure for itself that which is vile, turn into allegories, and that these allegories fill out and deny the void in which they are represented, just as, ultimately, the intention does not faithfully rest in the contemplation of bones, but faithlessly leaps forward to the idea of resurrection.
>
> (p. 233)

The sense of futility and uncanniness which tradition bestows on what it hands over is now extended to the act of handing over itself, in the clear hope of freeing objects from its thrall. There is a clear analogy here with the baroque death, which can only have any meaning if death itself dies.

For both Heidegger and Benjamin tradition is the event of 'handing over' and not just the handing over of events. Both agree that the action of 'handing over' is immanent and excessive, but against this shared background crucial differences emerge. In Benjamin the encounter of immanence and excess in the moment of origin is catastrophic – immanence or meaning in history is repeatedly shattered by excess – the act of handing over *ruins* what it hands over. The site where tradition gathers itself cannot be located in a present with its past and future; it is deferred to a future which is not ecstatic, not the future of *this* present; in Kafka's words, 'there is infinite hope, but not for us'. For Heidegger, such ruination is potentially, but not necessarily, the issue of tradition, since for him the excessive moment of origin not only destroys but can also *gather*, it can allow things and events to be revealed.

This difference leads on to the question of the subject in the two accounts of tradition. For Benjamin, the moment of origin or 'handing over' is characterized by confusion and indecision – in the act of 'handing over' there is no community or subject to give or receive, the subject is indeed ruined by tradition. For Heidegger, the moment of origin is potentially a moment of clarity and resolute decision, one which enables a subject, be it a 'hero' or a 'people', to decide, in the words of the first version of 'The Origin of the Work of Art', 'who they are and who they are not'. This moment of origin is one of historical decision, enabling Dasein to choose as a subject its own destiny. For Benjamin such a choice of destiny is characteristic of tragedy which 'ends with a decision', while *Trauerspiel* ends with indecision and uncathartic catastrophe. Heidegger's moment of origin can be a moment of decision, resoluteness unto death, while Benjamin's origin provokes sadness and mourning for the death it brings about.

The differences over origin and tradition extend repeatedly into the two theories of art. In Benjamin tradition is ruination – barbarism – it destroys what it hands over; yet without this destruction nothing would be handed over. The work of art is a ruin, a site of mourning where the destruction of tradition can be acknowledged. For Heidegger tradition may gather what it would hand over, deliver it into the light, and for him the work of art is a temple which presents this gathering. Heidegger celebrates tragedy as a place of witness to this handing over, while Benjamin discounts tragedy in favour of *Trauerspiel* as a communal lament for ruination. The aesthetic and political differences between the two thinkers which are becoming evident in their opposed understandings of the destruction of tradition emerge most clearly in their reflections on art, technology and the political from the mid-1930s.

ART, TECHNOLOGY AND TRADITION

In the two essays written in 1935 – 'The Origin of the Work of Art' and 'The Work of Art in the Age of Mechanical Reproduction' – Heidegger and Benjamin explore the impact of technology on tradition, art and politics. The focus on technology is not new, but goes back to their work of the 1920s. It featured for Heidegger in the guise of equipmentality in the First Division of *Being and Time*, and was prominent in Benjamin's 'One-Way Street'. However, by 1935 it plays a central role in both Heidegger and Benjamin's accounts of tradition, art and politics. For Heidegger, planetary technology marks the erasure of the 'rift design' or configuration of world and earth, and poses a threat to the site of tradition, a threat which can no longer convincingly be met by a resort to the subject. For Benjamin technology also possesses the potential fundamentally to reconfigure the site of tradition, perhaps even bringing about its destruction, and opening new scenes and possibilities for gathering past, present and future.

Heidegger's text, which underwent considerable change between its first and second versions, shows signs of a new engagement with the question of the *site* of tradition. There is considerable evidence for a turn from the precipitate identification of this site with the reflexive structures of the subject. He focuses now upon the configuration of this site itself – the 'rift design' – which is inscribed in the artwork. The 'rift design' of earth and world marks a new questioning of the site for the handing over of tradition. Heidegger no longer assumes, as he did in *Being and Time*, that this configuration can be aligned with the autonomous subject gathering past, present and future in a moment of resolute decision. Yet he is more cautious than Benjamin with regard to technology's potential to offer new configurations for gathering past, present and future; he sees in it rather the triumph of a particular kind of gathering, one which is the apogee of subjectivity.

Benjamin saw the object of tradition as ineluctably inauthentic; what is 'handed over' is never complete, never entirely there. The site of tradition is always one of ruination, a place of mourning. Those who gathered there did *not* do so in order to decide who they were and what they would become, but in order to mourn. This view of the gathering at the site of tradition changed considerably in 'The Work of Art in the Age of Mechanical Reproduction'. The place where past, present and future are gathered in tradition is no longer one of mourning, but one of politics. Although the details of this change are sketchy, it is clear that Benjamin does not mean here the politics of a subject who gathers past, present and future to itself in the manner of Heidegger's tragic hero or *Volk*. What is at stake is a new political configuration of the site of tradition, one which does correspond to the topology of the subject and which is not preoccupied with the tragic dialectic of authenticity and inauthenticity.

For Benjamin authenticity, or continuous presence through time, rested on the unwarranted assumption that tradition was continuous. This held especially for works of art. In the tradition of a work of art, the work itself is both present and absent, a phenomenon described as the uncanny experience of 'aura'. The aura of an artwork is an effect of its tradition: this presents the artwork as present and absent, unique to the here and now, and yet distant, and elsewhere. Benjamin observes that 'An ancient statue of Venus, for example, stood in a different traditional context with the Greeks, who made it an object of veneration, than with the clerics of the Middle Ages, who viewed it as an ominous idol' (1935: 225). Both eras regarded the statue as possessing an aura, being present yet distant, its meaning unexhausted by its being here. For this reason, such works of art were 'in the service of a ritual – first the magical, then the religious kind' (p. 225); they transported their viewers by their combination of immanence and transcendence.

However, in the epoch of technological reproducibility, the simultaneous distance and proximity of the object handed over by tradition is abolished. The configuration of the site of tradition is no longer determined by the play of presence and absence, nor consequently can the work of art be viewed any longer in terms of aura, for 'Even the most perfect reproduction of a work of art is lacking in one element: its presence in space and time, its unique existence at the place where it happened to be' (p. 222). The missing presence is a 'lack' only from the standpoint of a tradition which gathered past, present and future under the sign of a continuous present. With technical reproducibility, the play of presence and absence loses its significance, and the ritual basis of art is succeeded by 'another practice – politics' (p. 226). The site of tradition is no longer configured in terms of a ritual performance of presence and absence, but by politics.

Benjamin's understanding of the replacement of ritual by politics may be clarified by contrasting his view of aura with Heidegger's analysis of the artwork. In 'The Origin of the Work of Art' Heidegger no longer configures the site of tradition in terms of the reflexive tropes of the subject – the past is no longer appropriated by a tragic subject risking its present for the sake of its future. Yet his retreat from this position returns tradition to what Benjamin described as 'ritual'. This is evident in the analysis of the work of art in terms of the 'worlding of the world'.

Heidegger translates his earlier language of 'origin' and 'tradition' into that of 'worlding' and the 'world'. The worlding of the world is the work of origin: 'Wherever those decisions of our history that relate to our very being are made, are taken up and abandoned by us, go unrecognized and rediscovered by new inquiry, there the world worlds' (1935: 44–5). The things which are handed over in and by this world are both present and absent, coming and going: 'By the opening up of a world, all things gain their lingering and hastening, their remoteness and nearness, their scope and limits' (p. 45). The world does not hand things over as they are, but draws back from them even as it hands them over. The experience of this phenomenon in art, what Benjamin called its aura, is for Heidegger its voice, a voice which transports its listener. Van Gogh's painting of the boots, for example, 'spoke' and in doing so magically transported the viewer: 'In the vicinity of the work we were suddenly somewhere else than we tend to be' (p. 35). This ability to distance its viewer marks the authenticity of the work of art, and is what Benjamin described *critically* as its 'cult value'.

It is the ritual confirmation of tradition that Benjamin claims has been succeeded by politics, a change manifest above all in the status of the work of art. Yet with this claim Benjamin does not move to configure the site of tradition in terms of a historico-political subject, but sees the breakdown of ritual as opening possibilities for new ways of configuring past, present and future. While previously he saw tradition as destructive of whatever it handed over, now he suggests that it may itself be destroyed by technology.

Tradition worked by distancing its objects as past in order to bring them to presence in the present; technology, however, destroys this distance. Benjamin sees this phenomenon as based in two social circumstances, both of which are related to the increasing significance of the masses in contemporary life. Namely, the desire of contemporary masses to bring things 'closer' spatially and humanly, which is just as ardent as their bent towards overcoming the uniqueness of every reality by accepting its reproduction.

(Benjamin 1935: 225)

The reproduction of the object as neither distant nor unique does not for Benjamin entail its devaluation. It was tradition which destroyed the integrity of its object in the act of 'handing over'; it was tradition which distanced the object from itself and its recipient. But with its destruction by technology the object is freed from tradition, for 'in permitting the reproduction to meet the beholder or listener in his own particular situation it reactivates the object reproduced' (p. 223). The object is reactivated when the qualities of distance and uniqueness are removed from it; it becomes something different, something which need no longer be experienced in terms of presence and absence.

Benjamin describes this phenomenon as a 'tremendous shattering of tradition', and sees in it the characteristic ambiguities of a moment of origin: this means that its positive features are 'inconceivable without its destructive, cathartic aspect, that is, the liquidation of the traditional value of the cultural heritage' (p. 223). He explores the 'origin' that inaugurates the epoch of technology on several occasions in the essay; what is common to them is the feature of reality becoming thoroughly permeated by technology. Technology succeeds tradition as the means by which objects are 'handed over', and this, Benjamin argues, means that technology now determines our experience of space and time. Technology breaks down the distance established by tradition, and by doing so poses a moment of crisis or decision – 'renewal of mankind' or its destruction – which can be met either 'ritually' in the 'aestheticization of politics', or politically in the 'politicization of art'.

Heidegger's essay also echoes the theme of the replacement of tradition by technology, and he like Benjamin sees technology as both revealing and concealing. 'Earth' in the technological world withdraws the more it is forced by technology to reveal itself:

Earth thus shatters every attempt to penetrate into it. It causes every merely calculating importunity upon it to turn into a destruction. This destruction may herald itself under the appearance of mastery and progress in the form of the technical-scientific objectivation of nature, but this mastery nevertheless remains an impotence of will.

(Heidegger 1935: 47)

Technology is a 'world' and thus has some of the properties of tradition – 'even this doom of the god remaining absent is a way in which world worlds' – and it might be expected that it would possess the potential for resolute decision. But it seems as if the potential for resoluteness is less marked in the world of technology than in the world of tradition. The bid for technological mastery of the earth fails because the necessity of the struggle with the earth is forgotten. The world of technology seeks total transparency and control, but cannot produce works which 'fight the battle between world and earth'. The world, says Heidegger, 'cannot soar out of the earth's sight if, as the governing breadth and path of all essential destiny, it is to ground itself on a resolute foundation' (p. 49). For Benjamin, it is precisely this property of technology to demolish all traditional foundations that raises the possibility of no longer having to fight battles between world and earth.

In these passages Heidegger seems once again to be seeking a means by which resolution and authenticity may be attained with respect to tradition. The same search in 1916 led him to configure the site of tradition in terms of the tragic subject seeking authenticity. Now, although the configuration of tradition in terms of the subject is abandoned, there is still a tendency to search for a foundation for resolution, something that 'lies under' and remains present through time as a crypto-subject. But this is only a tendency, and one that is opposed in the same text by another direction of thought which addresses the question of configuration through the discussion of the 'rift design'. Alongside his discussion of the ruination of tradition by technology, with its subtext on the failure of the National Socialist movement properly to engage with 'planetary technology' mentioned in the contemporary *Introduction to Metaphysics*, there emerges an attempt to rethink the forms of gathering and configuration. The place for this new inquiry is the work of art.

The turn to the work of art is made in the full knowledge that, in the epoch of technology, art is, in Hegel's terms, no longer a formative experience. Nevertheless, it remains for Heidegger a privileged site for 'the becoming and happening of truth' (p. 71) with truth defined earlier as the 'conflict between lighting and concealing in the opposition of world and earth' (p. 63). This conflict is not an opposition, but a 'source of unity by virtue of their common ground. It is a basic design, an outline sketch, that draws the basic features of the rise of the lighting of beings' (p. 63). The rift design as a work of art must respect both the openness of the world and the withdrawing of the earth, and this respect Heidegger expresses in terms of the materiality of the artwork: 'The rift must set itself back into the heavy weight of stone, the dumb hardness of wood, the dark glow of colours' (p. 63). The rift design offers a configuration of openness and withdrawing, lighting and concealing, that forms the origin of the work of art.

The configuration of the rift design does not only gather together world and earth, but also configures tradition and politics. The origin of the work of art is 'the origin of both the creators and the preservers, which is to say of a people's historical existence' (p. 78). The rift design now configures creation and preservation, the relationship between past endowment, present condition and future possibility that constitutes historical existence. In a technological world, which drives for complete openness and the vanquishment of the earth, there is no place for the 'rift design' – no source of configuration between world and earth. But in the face of this, Heidegger's text fluctuates between seeing in the erasure of the rift design the possibility of new, unprecedented configurations, and the resort to superimposing a subject – the people – upon the rift design as if in this way to protect it from technology.

Benjamin by contrast emphasizes the potential for reconfiguration presented by technology. He does so by exploring the technological medium of film, trying to establish whether it falls back into the condition of auratic art – the play of presence and absence – or whether it presents possibilities for new configurations. For Benjamin, what is viewed in the film is the 'handing over' of an object not by tradition, but by technology; in it the subject matter cannot be distinguished from the way it is presented. What is delivered by technology is above all its mode of delivery. The film 'comprises certain factors of movement which are in reality those of the camera, not to mention special camera angles, close ups, etc.' (1935: 230). The audience are not potential participants in a religious rite, contemplating the play of presence and absence, but are 'able to take the position of a critic':

> The audience's identification with the actor is really an identification with the camera. Consequently the audience takes the position of the camera; its approach is that of testing. This is not the approach to which cult values may be exposed.
>
> (1935: 230–1)

Film then is a potentially unauratic art, although Benjamin is also aware that it can be used for auratic ends.

The abolition of distance and uniqueness through technology requires the perpetual redrawing of boundaries between human beings and the world, and with each other. For this reason technology for Benjamin raises the necessity of politics: limits and boundaries have to be drawn on the basis of deliberation, not simply given through tradition. The film is potentially a thoroughly politicized art; the picture of the cameraman 'consists of multiple fragments which are assembled under a new law' (p. 236). In the era of technology, it is possible for the 'mass' to reconfigure not only the law but the site where it is received, the way in which it is given, and themselves. They need not necessarily be thought of as subjects who reflexively legislate for themselves as legislators and legislated, since all aspects of this giving of law are open to reconfiguration.

Benjamin further explores the potential offered through technology for the reconfiguration of politics in the 'Arcades Project', but he is by no means naively optimistic. He is convinced that the technological reconfiguration of the site of tradition is ineluctable, and may lead either to the 'renewal' or 'destruction' of humanity. Through the power of technology it is possible to create giant auratic works of art – cities and entire peoples – who are simultaneously present and absent to themselves. The configuration of this presence and absence may be managed ritually or politically. In the former the people are staged as present and absent: they participate avidly in their own history while spectating it as someone else's history; they participate in political action and view it from a distance; they participate in their own destruction and enjoy the spectacle:

> Mankind, which in Homer's time was an object of contemplation for the Olympian Gods, now is one for itself. Its self alienation has reached such a degree that it can experience its own destruction as an aesthetic pleasure of the first order. This is the situation of politics which Fascism is rendering aesthetic. Communism responds by politicising art.

> (p. 244)

In the politicization of art, the management of presence and absence is itself deliberative, the configuration of the site is itself at issue; it is no longer simply given as the stage upon which the play of presence and absence may be performed.

THE CONDITION OF POLITICS

Benjamin refers to a condition of politics that Fascism is rendering aesthetic but which may be rendered political. It is the fate of this 'condition' that is the object of decision for him. The condition itself is marked by the 'proletarianisation of modern man and the increasing formation of masses' (p. 243), a process in which all previous understandings of property – of what it means to possess – are up for renegotiation. Politics is no longer necessarily the work of self-possessed subjects who unite their past and their future in a moment of resolute decision, for this scenario itself has come into question. The site of tradition where past, present and future are gathered together need no longer be thought in terms of what is proper to a subject – be it hero or *Volk* – what does and does not, what should and should not belong to it.

When the question is asked what the new configurations of tradition might be, what shape the new gathering of past, present and future might take, Benjamin is almost silent. He does make some comments about the emergence of a new mode of perception emphasizing tactile as opposed to visual experience, but these remain sketchy. On the whole he remains true to his earlier anarchist political programme of the 'Critique of Violence' which maintained that the shape of the new law was unimaginable. For this reason he was able to say far more about the 'aestheticization of politics' – indeed, to dedicate a decade to uncovering its genealogy in the 'Arcades Project' – than about the 'politicization of art'. He saw the reconfiguration of tradition through technology as a momentous revolution, one fraught with danger, but also with the potential for establishing new terrains of politics and subjectivity. Yet these remained unexplored.

Although Heidegger resorts on occasions in 'The Origin of the Work of Art' to a subject who would gather together their endowment and their destiny in the moment of resolution, he too introduced arguments which pointed in different directions. He was as aware as Benjamin of the destructive side of tradition, and was responding to the same problem of the management of simultaneous presence and absence which it entailed. And on occasions his text goes much further than Benjamin's in surveying the terrain of possible new sites of tradition. In these Heidegger begins to consider possible shapes of the political which might follow the destruction of tradition.

An important and suggestive occasion is the discussion of 'double concealment' – of the refusal of Being to reveal itself in beings and the dissemblance of one being by another. This implies a radical rethinking of the scene of the political, one which is far removed from the spectacular dramaturgy of Fascist aestheticized politics: 'the open place in the midst of beings, the clearing, is never a rigid stage with a permanently raised curtain on which the play of beings runs its course. Rather, the clearing happens only as this double concealment' (1935: 54). In the 'double concealment' the condition of politics is not the neutral space where the past, present and future are gathered, but one in which the gathering dissembles itself, never seeking or attaining authenticity. It is one in which the opposition of authentic presence and inauthentic absence is suspended, one in which the scene itself, or 'clearing', is not 'a rigid stage' but is itself negotiable and continually in play.

With Benjamin's 'politicized art' and Heidegger's doubly concealed clearing, the site of tradition is given the potential to assume a new shape. The gathering of past, present and future which takes place on or in it need not obey the total ruination and loss of *Trauerspiel* nor the reflexive movements of a subject's loss and gain characteristic of tragedy. From their early insights into the destructive character of tradition, and through their different views of what it meant, both thinkers arrived at insights into the revolutionary transformations undergone by the political realm under modernity. Neither of them underestimated the gravity of these transformations, many of which are still under way. They showed that they involved negotiations not only of the political present but also of its past and future. By bringing together the questions of the site of tradition and the condition of modern politics they were able to point to reconfigurations of the political which would be appropriate to the fundamental changes in subjectivity produced by modernity. For this reason it is important not to drive a wedge between these two thinkers, but to read them together, each against the other's grain.

BIBLIOGRAPHY

Benjamin, Walter (1916) *Gesammelte Schriften*, vol. II.1, ed. Rolf Tiedemann and Hermann Schweppenhauser, Frankfurt am Main: Suhrkamp, 1977.
—— (1928) *The Origin of German Tragic Drama*, translated by John Osborne, London: New Left Books, 1977.
—— (1935) 'The Work of Art in the Age of Mechanical Reproduction', in *Illuminations*, translated by Harry Zohn, London: Fontana, 1977.

—— *Briefe*, ed. Gershom Scholem and Theodor Adorno, Frankfurt am Main: Suhrkamp, 1978.

Heidegger, Martin (1916) 'Der Zeitbegriff in der Geschichtswissenschaft', in his *Frühe Schriften*, Frankfurt am Main: Klostermann, 1972; translated by Harry S. Taylor and Hans W. Uffelmann as 'The Concept of Time in the Science of History', *Journal of the British Society for Phenomenology* 9 (1) (January 1978).

—— (1927) *Being and Time*, translated by John Macquarrie and Edward Robinson, Oxford: Basil Blackwell, 1978.

—— (1935) 'The Origin of the Work of Art', in *Poetry, Language, Thought*, translated by Albert Hofstadter, San Francisco, CA: Harper & Row, 1971.

2 Tradition and Destruction

Walter Benjamin's Politics of Language

Alexander García Düttmann
Translated by Debbie Keates

What is Fascism? How does Communist revolution resist Fascism? These prove to be the implicit questions in a text by Benjamin whose first version dates from 1935.[1] It is called 'The Work of Art in the Age of Mechanical Reproduction'. But doesn't posing the question of Fascism and of Communist revolution in terms which imply an aesthetic treatise or a cultural critique already preclude the range of the response? and run the risk of falling into ideology? It is perhaps in order to confront this type of objection that Benjamin's text begins with a series of methodological remarks. They demonstrate that it is possible to pose the question of Fascism and of Communist revolution in terms of an analysis of the transformations which inaugurate what Benjamin will call the age of mechanical reproduction of the work of art. These transformations consist in the destruction of the unity and authenticity attributed to traditional art; they affect any relation to tradition in so far as, according to Benjamin, the concept of tradition is itself essentially linked to the idea of the work of art, to the values which attach themselves to it, and which, without that idea, would never have been able to take on a stable and recognizable form.

The methodological remarks contained in the preface leave no room for doubt: to describe what has happened to the work of art, and what is at the origin of Fascism and of Communist revolution (no Fascism or Communist revolution without mechanical reproducibility), Benjamin makes use of the distinction superstructure/ infrastructure, and nevertheless refuses the dissymmetry that Marx establishes between them. This dissymmetry cannot be dissociated from historical development, nor from the doubled speed which is proper to it: it both prescribes the speed of history and is already inscribed in history's temporality.

When Marx undertook his critique of the capitalistic mode of production, this mode was in its infancy. Marx directed his efforts in such a way as to give them prognostic value. He went back to the basic conditions underlying capitalistic production and through his presentation showed what could be expected of capitalism in the future. The result was that one could expect it not only to exploit the proletariat with increasing intensity, but ultimately to create conditions which would make it possible to abolish capitalism itself. The transformation of the superstructure, which takes place far more slowly than that of the infrastructure, has taken more than half a century to manifest in all areas of culture the change in the conditions of production. Only today can it be indicated what form this has taken. Certain prognostic requirements should be met by these statements. However, theses about the art of the proletariat after its assumption of power or about the art of a classless society would have less bearing on these demands than theses about the developmental tendencies of art under present conditions of production. Their dialectic is no less noticeable in the superstructure than in the economy. It would therefore be wrong to underestimate the value of such theses as a weapon.[2]

In order to understand Benjamin's particular manner of posing the question of Fascism and of Communist revolution, it is crucial to understand the displacement that he implements in his methodological remarks. In the age of mechanical reproduction, the superstructure no longer lags behind the infrastructure. From this fact, Benjamin deduces that the dialectic of the conditions of production (*Produktionsbedingungen*) is discovered as easily in art as in the economy. Admittedly art is considered the expression of this dialectic; but in so far as art and culture no longer submit to a determination which assigns them an ideological function (we know that the dissymmetrical relation between culture and the economy entailed such a determination as its major effect), the distinction between infrastructure and superstructure, inseparable from this determining dissymmetry, becomes problematic.[3]

When the question of Fascism is posed, the question of an artistic production which goes beyond the limits of ideology cannot not be posed. Fascism, for Benjamin, is a renewal of ideology; it checks the destructive process to which it owes its existence. In other words, it reintroduces a dissymmetry while presupposing, as its condition of possibility, a development which results in the abolition of the dissymmetrical relation between infrastructure and super-structure. This development allows the problem of the work of art in the age of mechanical reproduction to be raised as a problem of Fascism. Benjamin rejects 'a number of outmoded concepts, such as creativity and genius, eternal value and mystery [the first version of the text adds style, form, content, but does not mention mystery], concepts whose uncontrolled (and at present almost uncontrollable) application would lead to a processing of data in the Fascist sense'.[4,5] It would be wrong to believe that it is here a question of avoiding particular traditional and outmoded concepts which could no longer be used because they already and inevitably fall into a usage which escapes control. There are no good and no bad traditional concepts: it is the tradition as such that is at stake.

It can now be seen why Benjamin's discourse cannot be a simple critique of ideology. But this is in no way to suggest that it remains a purely descriptive discourse, as Jürgen Habermas would seem to imply.[6] At the end of the preface, Benjamin evokes the authority of an inventive and innovative character (is it possible to conceive of an innovation which would not entail an inventive dimension?); because of this invocation, his discourse exceeds, or allows us to think about that which exceeds, the limitations of a description which would be restricted to retracing the lines of a historical move-ment or development. Everything is argued as though ideology critique and theoretical description were deemed inadequate respon-dents to the questions of Fascism and of Communist revolution as they appear in the domain of art and of the reproduction of the work of art. Let us note that it is never in the name of parliamentary democracy that Benjamin intends to oppose himself to Fascism. In the age of mechanical reproduction, the age in which cinemato-graphic reproduction programmes a 'new selection' in which only 'the star' and 'the dictator'[7] remain, parliamentary democracy and the theatre derive from the same anachronism: neither can escape the crisis of – traditional – *representation*. Even if Communist revolu-tion remains bound to a particular representation of work, and even if Benjamin does not maintain, as Alain Badiou does at the moment of the collapse of state Marxism, that 'democracy and totalitarianism are the two epochal versions of the fulfilment of the political in the doubled category of social bond and representation',[8] the require-ment of an invention or of an innovation is indicative of a crisis in representation as a model of tradition. Benjamin aims therefore at a radical innovation: 'The concepts which are introduced into the theory of art in what follows differ from the more familiar terms in that they are completely unusable [*volekommen unbrauchbar*] for the purposes of Fascism.'⁹ An analysis of Fascism which begins with a conceptual invention, one required to provoke a mutation or an irreversible change in the realm of theory and in the politics of art, is necessarily limited if it is not also an analysis of economic constraints and contradictions. This necessary limitation does not, however, affect the truth of the analysis once it is understood that a parallelism relates the superstructure to the infrastructure. The redoubling of these structures no longer inverts and veils the truth. Not that the question of ideology disappears. On the contrary, ideology is capable of affirming itself with a force and a violence which are revealed to be uncontrollable in so far as they are the force and violence of destruction itself and are constantly regenerated by the destructive process. Fascism is all the more dangerous because it does not simply pit itself against destruction.

If, as Benjamin claims, politics – and this is as true for Fascism as it is for Communism – depend on the exposure and the control of the body that cinematographic and photographic reproduction make possible (film and photography being the most representative, as well as the most efficacious, of the reproductive techniques that Benjamin analyses), then it is possible to consider the politics of art or the politics of the mechanical reproduction of the image as exemplary of all politics. Two recent examples: since Tienanmen Square and Bucharest we no longer underestimate television's role in the rise of revolts and revolutions. The introduction of concepts 'completely unusable for the ends of Fascism' is in and of itself a political gesture. If it is indeed the case that Fascism only re-establishes links with tradition and its concepts, then, to be precise, its form of destruction lacks radicality: Fascist destruction has catastrophic effects because it is never sufficiently radical. The claim of an inventiveness which would not be limited by a tradition, and would thus be irrecuperable, brings to light a difference whose trace is erased by the haste with which Benjamin's text is identified as a theoretical description. As was the case with an ideology critique based on the dissymmetrical relation of superstructure to infrastructure, theoretical description remains too traditional. It requires, as its minimal condition of possibility, a detachment which devotes the conscious subject to spiritual contemplation. It is true that Benjamin would not have been able to write his text if he had not been in a position to detach himself, however slightly, from the destructive process. But it is also true that, in this text, he states the impossibility of remaining within a contemplative attitude, an attitude of reflection which presupposes the unity of its object.

Invention is a political gesture. But not a gesture which can be reduced to voluntarism, as though invention were evidence only of a will to opposition. It is destruction which demands invention.[10] Fascism responds to this demand by instituting a restricted economy of destruction whose characteristic traits are the maintenance of traditional categories and the attempted conservation of capitalist conditions of ownership. To answer the question 'what is Fascism?' without also answering to the demand of destruction is to risk subscribing to Fascism and to the answer it gives to this demand.

How then to invent concepts 'completely unusable for the purposes of Fascism'?[11] In other words, what is an invention which fulfils destruction? Benjamin points to the introduction of a series of concepts which the other will not be able to use, or will only be able to use if it in turn becomes other. The concept which the other cannot use takes away its breath, and makes it speak otherwise. Let us assume that a concept could be 'entirely unusable': are we not obliged to admit that this single concept affects the entirety of language and that we cannot continue to use a language in which a concept remains unusable? To seek out an unusable concept is to be carried toward the *unusable of language*, towards an unusable language. Indeed, what does 'use a language' mean? Maybe it is impossible to use a language which is not exposed to the other, to a usage which diverts meaning and divides intention. Usage involves alterity and alteration. An unusable language is always a language without an other: it remains absolutely singular and absorbs all alterity even before the other can show itself.[12] If the other cannot use it, this is because it withdraws from usage and is unusable for those who speak it, not only for the other who has never spoken it and never will. It is not the language of communication, for as soon as a language is used it is submitted to the discipline of *communication*, to the transmission of some content. But the unusable language, whose usage is by definition impossible, is the language of the *communicability* which precedes any usage or utility.[13] From this perspective, Communist revolution does not replace the purposes of Fascism with its own. It would be another mistake to confine the opposition between 'the politicization of art' and the '(Fascist) aestheticization of politics', which Benjamin sets up at the end of the text, to a mere homogeneous, binary opposition.

In his 1916 text 'On Language in General and the Language of Man in Particular',[14] Benjamin conceives a genealogical order of language proceeding from an irruptive event whose particularity is attached to a rupture which introduces discontinuity into language itself. The loss of originary language – of the language of names, which has no acquaintance with exteriority and where name and thing coincide almost absolutely[15] – is equal, in Benjamin's eyes, to a multiplication of languages. Language is dispersed and transformed into a system of arbitrary signs. 'To name' now signifies 'to add a name to a thing'. Consequently, there is only one single language which can assert that it is 'entirely unusable', and that is the language of names. Before a name can be used, the language of names will have anticipated any use. From the moment that language is stamped by convention, and at which denomination also names something other than the thing, from the moment at which 'overdenomination' breaches the name, language becomes useful. The language of names is not an instrument used to express a content. But once languages are multiplied, once multiplicity has marked language and language is exposed to the other (language), one is caught irredeemably in the world of tools, and under the sway of utility. One is constrained to make use of language, even if it leads to certain difficulties. As insurmountable as they may appear, these difficulties are finally accidental and provisional, not because they are situated at a different level from those which result from the use of an unusable language, but because the other which is implicated in any use only arrives after, or at the instant of, the loss of the language of names. The other is other because it is in keeping with a language whose use is more or less difficult without thereby being impossible. How do we overcome the difficulties we encounter as soon as we use a language? Let us beware of confounding this question – which has a technical or economical valence – with a question of principle.

Benjamin calls upon a 'series of concepts completely unusable for the purposes of Fascism'. But he does not name the language of names at any moment of his meditation on the technical reproducibility of art. This is not so surprising: the idea of a language of names seems to conform to the traditional idea of the work of art. Within the tradition, the work of art is presented as an authentic, singular existence, as the *hic et nunc* of an irreducible and irreplaceable event, as the apparition of that which remains shielded from general reproducibility. The traditional work of art entails an effect of sacralization which refers back to a ritual function; in some sense it is a *name*. Let us retain one point from this excursus through the language of names, through the metaphysico-theological conception of language: one cannot use a language which the other will not also be able to use. Each time it is used, the other has already used it.

Why does Benjamin not explain what he understands by a 'series of completely unusable concepts'?[16] The invention of this series is indispensable in the light of the *mise en série* of the work of art, and no doubt inscribes itself in the cause of the destruction of tradition. It accomplishes this destruction, since there would otherwise be no difference between Fascist and Communist strategies, nor between the 'aestheticization of politics' and the 'politicization of art'. If Benjamin is silent on the subject of language use, and about the language of his own discourse, it is due to – or so it would appear – his greater interest in the image, in visual imagination, and in the collective imaginary determined by cinematographic reproductions. He is more interested in the image produced by technical reproduction than in any literary language or painterly image:

In the case of films, mechanical reproduction is not, as with literature and painting, an external condition for mass distribution. Mechanical reproduction is inherent in the very technique of film production. This technique not only permits in the most direct way but virtually causes mass distribution. It enforces distribution because the production of a film is so expensive that an individual who, for instance, might afford to buy a painting no longer can afford to buy a film. In 1927 it was calculated that a major film, in order to pay its way, had to reach an audience of nine million. With the sound film, to be sure, a setback in international distribution occurred at first: audiences became limited by language barriers. This coincided with the Fascist emphasis on national interests. It is more important to focus on this connection with Fascism than on this setback, which was soon minimized by synchronization. The simultaneity of both phenomena is attributable to the depression. The same disturbances which, on a larger scale, led to an attempt to maintain the existing property structure by sheer force [*mit offener Gewalt*; the first version is more explicit: *also in faschistischer Form*] led the endangered film capital to speed up the development of the sound film. The introduction of the sound film brought about a temporary relief, not only because it again brought the masses into the theaters but also because it merged new capital from the electrical industry with that of the film industry. Thus, viewed from the outside, the sound film promoted national interests, but seen from the inside it helped to internationalize film production even more than previously.[17]

This long note, incorporated into the body of the text in the first version, teaches us something about Benjamin's reasons for leaving aside the problems of language, particularly those which concern the inscription of his discourse in the destructive process. But it is significant in several other ways as well: Benjamin here makes evident the complexity of the relation between economic constraints and the technical progress which modifies the essence of the work of art. A summary must take account of three motifs.

1 The destruction of destruction   The possibility that the destruction of tradition will turn against itself can never be excluded. In such a case, the destruction of the destruction arrives from the interior of destruction – even if Benjamin speaks of an 'exterior' perspective. It is a contradiction, an impasse that prohibits the representation of destruction as a linear and continual process. To the extent that destruction carries within itself the ability to stop its own movement, to shield itself from its force and violence by using force and violence – by using *its own* force and *its own* violence – to that extent it can awaken and revive ideology. Fascism, whose goal is to conserve tradition in the midst of the very destruction which protects and threatens it, profits from this ability: it exploits the consequences and so institutes a tradition of destruction. In the interval which separates the invention of the talkie and the (commercial) use of post-synchronization, the language is better suited to Fascism than to Communist revolution. The invention of the talkie is not simply the coupling of image and language in the space opened up by technical reproducibility (and it is in this space that Benjamin situates the unconscious), but also, and primarily, it is the invention of a language more accessible to Fascist than to Communist discourse. The inventive dimension is implicated in the fact that a national language, which does not allow for reproduction without a supplementary mediation, that is, a translation, and the image, which is *a priori* and immediately reproducible, align themselves and constitute what could be called a *national talkie*. This is the paradoxical structure of nationalism in general, and hence of the national and nationalist interests of Fascism: because it privileges *one* language and suppresses all others, nationalism tends to conserve the multiplicity of tongues and their national imprints. *At the same time* that it erects linguistic barriers, it abolishes them. Here the language of names inevitably comes to mind: like all nationalisms, Fascist nationalism pretends to found a language of names which, as we have suggested, is without other and thus unusable and tautological. But even as it so pretends, it is conserving the multiplicity of tongues, and so the very principle of multiplicity. Fascism does not carry destruction to term (but what is involved in such a term?); it does not allow itself to be entirely carried away by destruction, even if it is only in and through destruction that it finds its condition of possibility.

2 The new dissymmetry Benjamin traces the invention of the talkie back to an economic constraint. The crisis in capitalism provoked so violent a reaction from those who were deferring destruction in order to safeguard their own existence that it made the violence and injustice at the origin of the appropriation and distribution of goods in capitalist societies even more apparent. What is the *offene Gewalt*, that violence which is considered Fascist in the first version of the text, and which openly intends to conserve capitalism, if not the manifestation of the violence which confers consistency to capitalist societies at their constitutive and consolidating moment? The crisis forced the film industry to develop a new technique which would attract the masses. As a result, and this is not unrelated to the fact that the electronics industry also benefited from these efforts, the technical innovation contributed to the stabilization of the film industry. The invention of the talkie is thus an ideological supplement; to the extent that such a supplement can act on the economy, it guarantees a certain efficacy and a certain profitability. It matters little whether this presentation of the socioeconomic and historical data corresponds to the reconstitution of the facts which could be undertaken today. It is far more instructive to follow the turns and deviations of Benjamin's discourse, especially as the analysis found in the passage cited above seems to contradict the methodological remarks in the preface. If the invention of the talkie is an ideological supplement, then the dissymmetry which produces ideology also determines the age of the mechanical reproduction of the work of art. Indeed, this dissymmetry determines the age *before* any ideological recuperation of the technique, and *before* any transmission of the contents of traditional ideology. The dialectics of the conditions of production is, contrary to what the preface would have us believe, less perceptible in the superstructure than in the economy. But it is no longer anachronism which engenders ideology. Consequently, it is not a question of the *same* dissymmetry. The symmetry which establishes an equilibrium between infrastructure and superstructure becomes itself the ground where ideological effects gather; the symmetry establishes a *precarious* equilibrium because it is the meeting ground of ideology. It will be noticed, therefore, that ideology is intrinsic to the mechanical reproduction of art, to destruction, and not only to the tradition or to what remains of it. In the age of mechanical reproduction of the work of art, ideology is never simply that which remains of a tradition which is being progressively destroyed, nor does it simply exhaust itself in the reanimation of a tradition in the midst of destruction. Ideology is also that destruction itself, but as that which remains, as pure innovation, even as pure repetition without content. Benjamin shows that mechanical reproduction reproduces ideology in the innovations it makes possible. The same diagnosis can be found in the chapter of the *Dialektik der Aufklärung* in which Adorno and Horkheimer attack the 'culture industry':

> The culture industry consists of repetition. That its characteristic innovations are never anything more than the improvements of mass reproduction is not external to the system. It is with good reason that the interest of innumerable consumers is directed to the technique, and not to the contents – which are stubbornly repeated, outworn, and by now half-discredited. The social power which the spectators worship shows itself more effectively in the omnipresence of the stereotype imposed by technical skill than in the stale ideologies for which the ephemeral contents stand in.[18]

3 The paradoxical import of destruction   This third motif may be the most troubling. All of the difficulty of Benjamin's discourse comes back, in effect, to a decision about the import of destruction. In the passage which distinguishes works of literature and painting from works of film (*Filmwerke*), the same destructive process reinforces ideology (it does so by national limitation and transgressive internationalism) and leaves it only one, last resort: destruction itself. Whence the *paradox of destruction*: the more tradition is destroyed, the greater the risk of destruction itself becoming a tradition through repetition, repetition here understood as perhaps the most impoverished but least used 'form' of tradition. Does not invention, the introduction of a series of 'unusable' concepts, ultimately aim at a destruction which is not reconstituted as tradition? Such an invention is perhaps not an invention in the ordinary sense of the term; in a referential language, an 'unusable' concept is already an unpronounceable name, and thus necessarily situated beyond or behind tradition. That which remains 'unusable' remains always, and so does not remain (to be a remainder, that which remains must always be threatened with disappearance). And so, the technical reproducibility of the work of art, or, more precisely, the destruction which becomes manifest in technical reproduction, allows us finally to think the *absolutely reproducible irreproducible*. It allows us to think that which undoes the opposition between reproducibility and the irreproducible, between destruction and the transmission of an essentially unreproducible object (which is nevertheless delivered to reproduction).

In following the main thread of an interpretation which recognizes tradition as the ideological dimension of history (let us not forget that, for Benjamin, the application of traditional concepts leads to the 'processing of factual data in a Fascist sense'), we see the paradox of destruction take on the form of a paradox of ideology and be enunciated in inverted terms: the *more* powerful ideology is shown to be (it is never as powerful as when it results neither from a determinate content nor from a lag in the superstructure), the *more* it is exposed to its own destruction. This translation of the paradox of destruction opens up the possibility that it can always be recuperated by a schema which reattaches it to social contradictions, to a contradictory historical reality, or to an interpretation of history as contradiction and ideology. But the generality of the paradox goes beyond the limits of any proposed interpretation. Why? Because it is part of tradition's essence (of tradition as ideology as well as of non-ideological tradition), as long as it is figured as a transmission of a content or a form which is opposed to the violence of the destructive process, to abandon itself to destruction. It is only in repeating and in conserving destruction that tradition escapes it. Tradition is affirmed for the last time, and thus for the first time, when all that remains is the empty repetition of destruction.

How is the insistent return of the paradox of destruction in this century to be interpreted? and in thoughts which could not be more diverse and incompatible? Two proper names could be called upon here to serve as examples: Heidegger and Adorno. What Heidegger says about *Ge-stell* in the seminar on *Time and Being* can be transcribed without too destructive a violence into the terms of a paradoxical 'hyperbologic'. The *Ge-stell* is the place, the between-two where everything plays itself out and decides itself, where everything has occurred and not yet come to pass, where everything remains outside the event (*Ereignis*) so as already to prefigure it. This suggests that it is the *trace* which is in question in the paradox of destruction, the *trace* as that which defers presence and refers to a deferred presence, to a fulfilment or an apocalypse that disappoints.

> Between the epochal formations of Being [epoch is the fundamental trait of the sending] and the transformation of Being into the event stands *Ge-stell*. *Ge-stell* is an in-between stage, so to speak. It offers a double aspect, one might say, a Janus head. It can be understood as a kind of continuation of the will to will, thus as an extreme formation of Being. At the same time, however, it is a first form of the event itself.[19]

Several years earlier, in 1954, Adorno discerned the double possibility of catastrophe and salvation in destruction. Destruction erases the difference between ideology and reality; ideology therefore resists any revelatory disclosure:

> Ideology is no longer a veil, but only the threatening aspect of the world. It is not only by virtue of its entanglement with propaganda, but on account of its own character, that ideology turns into terror. Because ideology and reality thus move toward one another, because reality in the absence of any other convincing ideology itself becomes that ideology, only a slight mental effort would be necessary to shed an illusion which is at once omnipotent and empty.[20]

The paradox of destruction makes language turn. But the whirlpool swallows neither the language of names nor the language composed entirely of citations.

Mechanical reproduction destroys the authenticity (*Echtheit*) of the traditional work of art. If the introduction of a series of concepts which the other will not be able to use comes back to the fulfilment of destruction, then one will look for these concepts (which are not concepts) in the destruction of authenticity, that is, in the process which submits language to the principle of technical reproduction. Benjamin states in his essay on Karl Kraus that the Austrian writer's purpose was to unmask the unauthentic (*das Unechte*); to this end, Kraus attacked the press, journalistic language, stock phrases as so many 'monstrous creatures of technique (*Ausgeburt der Technik*)'. Writing and speaking in stock phrases: this is the form that language takes in the age of mechanical reproduction. When we 'make phrases' we use, each and every time, expressions which are so worn out that they finally assert that the language created by the press, by the institution of mechanical reproducibility, is a language of *citations without references*. A language which would be composed only of citations would always be a *language of the other*, a language without an other of the other. Like the language of names, the language of citations designates a language which is no longer involved in communication.

Tradition and destruction, name and citation, these are *effects of* difference as a trace of communicability within communication. The language of communicability is scarcely a language; it is the thing itself of language, or language as the thing itself. Language is 'unusable' for the purposes of the other (and the other of the other) because difference inscribes communicability in the place of communication. But language allows itself to be used by the other (and by the other of the other) because communicability is only a trace of language, it is language as a trace, and not at all another language in which we could install ourselves. Is this to say that language will continue to be used? Having announced, and promised, the introduction of a series of concepts 'unusable for the purposes of Fascism', Benjamin adds: 'They are, on the other hand, usable [*brauchbar*] for the formulation of revolutionary demands in the politics of art.'[21] Must one negotiate with Fascism to destroy restricted destruction? How can enough be destroyed? In what does the experience of communicability consist?

We read a text or a commentary, an analysis or an interpretation; but instead of beginning by imprisoning ourselves in knowledge, in an apprenticeship to and a reproduction of dogmas and contents, of instituted forms and acquired rules, we suffer a shock which throws us forward and backward, which paralyses us and devotes us to thinking and writing. This experience of excess, this excessive experience, is only the experience of communicability. Accordingly, tradition in the guise of a gift, a gift which gives nothing and yet only gives, exceeds communication (but excess never exceeds any other thing). If the determination of communication rests on the double possibility of enchaining and refusing enchainment, and if the refusal to enchain makes up part of communication, as Niklas Luhman stresses in his book on speech and silence,[22] then a communication which does not let itself be determined by this alternative overwhelms its proper determination and is turned back into communicability. Such is what occurs when one is simultaneously paralysed by and devoted to thought and writing.

There would be no tradition in general, tradition would be

unthinkable and inaccessible, if it was not essentially a *tradition of communicability*. The law of tradition, which we here introduce, requires that a work or a thought have access to it – to tradition – only by breaking with traditional standards. These same standards decide what may and may not have value within the domain of tradition. A tradition which would have already set its standards once for all time would be one which delivered itself to oblivion. It would sink into indifference, and would fill in the temporal gap only by annulling itself and thus becoming a sterile preservation. In an American interview, Jacques Derrida implicitly enunciates this law of tradition. What Derrida attempts to produce in his thought and his writing, and what the latter themselves produce, follows tradition, at least if we understand it according to its law, to the contradiction that here makes law:

> In a work such as *Glas*, or other recent ones like it, I am trying to produce new forms of catachresis, another kind of writing, a violent writing which stakes out the faults (*failles*) and deviations of language; so that the text produces a language of its own, in itself, which while continuing to work through tradition emerges at a given moment as a *monster*, a monstrous mutation without tradition or normative precedent.[23]

It happens that tradition is inscribed in one of the columns of *Glas* as a motif of the speculative dialectic presented in the Jena Philosophy:

> One desires, one consum(mat)es, one labors, it passes (away) and dies. As empiric individuals. So tradition (that is Hegel's word) is what resists this loss and constitutes the maintained ideality; not the finite and elaborated object, but the labour tool that can yet be of service, because of its generality structure. The tool is endowed with an ideal, reproducible, perfectible identity, gives rise to accumulation, and so on. So one cannot desire without desiring to produce tools, that is, production tools.[24]

A law which results from a contradiction, and is a law only in as much as it states the irreducibility of this contradiction, is never simply a law. (Note that this law does not precede the contradiction, for if it did, it would have already surpassed it in rising to the level of a generality or a non-contradictory totality.) No generality or ideality could procure a sufficient stability for this law. The law of tradition is invented each time thought or writing break with tradition. Structure and history are here no longer opposed to one

another. Such a necessity to invent and reinvent the law permits us
to say that there is no tradition and yet there is always some.
Singular and irreproducible, Derrida's thought is perhaps unique in
its invention of the law which does not neglect the writing to which
it must be devoted: it re-emerges in his thought as the condition of
all tradition.[25] Meanwhile, to be recognizable as monsters, as monstrous creatures which erupt, which emerge from the tradition only
to destroy it, these forms of thought and writing also and irremedi-
ably maintain themselves in a residual and minimal ideality or generality which make reproduction and citation possible. The desire to
produce monsters translates into the desire to start a family. A
discourse which does not allow itself to be worked over by this
double desire (it is both antagonistic and complementary) lacks
force, is not innovative enough, and is no longer able to integrate
past discourses into a tradition whose origin it would be. Different
discourses come back and come towards us from the singular event
(*événement*) of every discourse. This event is the only point of
reference; tradition is not, as those who recuperate destruction
would have it, an archive of points of reference to which one could
easily refer for orientation in a time of crisis or distress. Tradition
is not shielded from crisis because it is nothing other than crisis
prior to any periodization. Each discourse is the survivor of its own
catastrophe, or, in other words, of its own event. It destroys past
and future discourses because it is a monster, and because it cannot
risk being recognized by those same discourses who would accordingly destroy it. It destroys itself because it guards, and must guard,
a certain aspect of monstrosity which it cannot guard without
renouncing it, which it can guard only under conditions in which it
lets itself be recognized and calls upon another tradition. Survival
and tradition are confounded here; if 'tradition is always threatened
with only being a survival', as Jean-François Lyotard teaches us, it
is because of this originary confusion which is the confusion of the
origin.

We are now perhaps in a position to propose a sort of *axiom* of
philosophy and the appearance of philosophical discourse. Let us
not be too quick to identify philosophy with a conceptual generality.
The philosopher remains subject to the law of tradition because he
or she always *continues* to think. Philosophical discourse must
appear in a monstrous aspect at the very heart of a tradition which
is never present to itself, which exists and does not exist, which
only exists *après-coup*, that is, which will only exist after the new
discourse will have given way to one tradition and will already call

for another invention or an invention of an other. In Benjamin's language, we could say that the thing whose character must be certified as evenemential and non-reproducible is susceptible to reproduction at the very moment of its production. We will see that, in a certain sense, Benjamin says just that. In pleading for the introduction of a series of 'unusable' concepts, he is not taking tradition lightly, nor is he sacrificing it to a facile radicalism which is easily recuperable. He is more likely to be embedding himself in tradition. No tradition would be constituted without the attempt to invent concepts, terms, words and expressions which are more or less 'unusable'. Fascism, as Benjamin seems to understand it, marks the *forgetting* of tradition, while revolution is tradition's *memory*.

The law of tradition prescribes the engenderment of diverse forms and styles of writing which do not immediately disappear in their reproduction or citation. It prescribes the generation of concepts which, from the very fact of their singularity and their evenemential character, are concepts without being. But then again, this law also prescribes the foundation of a family which, even while remaining under the injunction of heteronomy and exteriority (a monster can only present itself, but it must never be able to present itself as such), lets itself be recognized and gives writing, singularity and event a recognizable form. Derrida proposes to distinguish 'normal monstrosities' from 'monstrous monstrosities which never present themselves as such'.[26] But this distinction must be made within the interiority of the monster, which has no interiority, and so has no assured limits at its disposal. Simultaneously with name and citation, the event is the *époché* of knowledge and communication. It is the undialectical moment in which we have an experience of communicability.[27]

Benjamin's theses permit two different discourses to be held. If 'in principle a work of art has always been reproducible'[28] (the first thesis begins with this question of principle, a principle which logically implies that all which is not reproducible does not belong – in principle – to the space of art), and if it is thus necessary to be able to reproduce the work of art in order to identify it as such, then traditional reproduction and tradition as reproductive transmission have not affected the authentic character of their object. Reproduction is not contrary to authenticity. Tradition and traditional reproduction authenticate the work of art by (temporal) distance and (spatial) propagation. But it would be oversimplifying Benjamin's discourse to want to reduce it to a principle of general reproducibility which contained within it a scission that would destroy the unity of technique and destruction, and would come to separate out two techniques (manual and mechanical) or two ways of reproduction (traditional and non-traditional). The second thesis of 'The Work of Art' seems not to reproduce the argument of the first: Benjamin now claims that reproduction (manual or mechanical, traditional or non-traditional) misses the work of art (which always allows itself to be reproduced and which never lacks for reproductions). Reproduction misses the work of art, the work of art always lacks for reproductions, because in reproductions the *experience of place* is always missing. 'Even the most perfect reproduction of a work of art is lacking in one element: its presence in time and space, its unique existence at the place where it happens to be.'[29] The singularity of the work of art is attached to the singularity of place, and it is this singular unity of the place and the thing (neither of which is singular except in the *hic et nunc* which they together constitute) that reproduction, even perfect reproduction – that which excels in being undistinguishable from its model – never reproduces. Reproduction reproduces an object, but it does not have the capacity to reproduce the unity which makes up the uniqueness of the object. As a consequence, as soon as the work of art is no longer found in a spot where it was originally placed (this emplacement is its origin itself) it becomes a reproduction. To reproduce a work of art, it is sufficient to destroy the unity of the place and the thing. There is therefore a reproduction prior to (mechanical or manual) reproduction.

Does tradition, which conserves the work and invests it with historical testimony, protect the unity of any given unreproducible, sensible certainty?

> This unique existence of the work of art determined the history to which it was subject throughout the time of its existence. This includes the changes which it may have suffered in physical condition over the years as well as the various changes in its ownership. The traces of the first can be revealed only by chemical or physical analyses which it is impossible to perform on a reproduction; changes of ownership are subject to a tradition which must be traced from the situation of the original.[30]

A note lets slip the fact that reproduction also has historical value, and that tradition should be dissociated from history, at least if tradition *per se* does not already necessarily dissociate the place and the thing: 'Of course the history of art encompasses more than this [changes in physical condition and in ownership]. The history of the

"Mona Lisa", for instance, encompasses the kind and number of its copies made in the 17th, 18th, and 19th centuries.'[31] The history of the work of art does not recover its tradition. The latter is certainly a 'very vital reality', but it does not touch the uniqueness of the work. It rather constitutes it: 'the uniqueness of the work of art is inseparable from its being imbedded in the fabric of tradition.'[32] Tradition transmits the object 'as being the same and self-identical', *als ein Selbes und Identisches* (which is the formula Benjamin employs in the first version of the text[33]). At the same time, art could not be thought of as a *historical* phenomenon if the work was only its own reproduction, if it was not also an exception to its own principle, if it did not have the property of being in principle, inside its principle without principle. History depends on the unity in which place and thing are crossed and remain, in the last instance, indiscernible: they come to pass only in their crossing. It will be deduced from this fact that the destruction of tradition, as well as of all that inaugurates tradition, is also a destruction of history and of the historical value attributed to a certain type of reproduction (manual reproduction).

The gesture which discloses the fundamental trait of the work of art by bringing back out its originary unity with the place draws together this text on technical reproducibility and the lectures that Heidegger devoted to the origin of the work of art. In 1935, Heidegger characterized the 'essential traits of the being-work of the work [*Werksein des Werkes*]': a building, a Greek temple, portrays nothing. It simply stands there

in the middle of a rock-cleft valley. The building encloses the figure of the god, and in this concealment lets it stand out into the holy precinct through the open portico. By means of the temple, the god is present in the temple. The presence of the god is in itself the extension and delimitation of the precinct as a holy precinct. The temple and its precinct, however, do not fade away into the indefinite. It is the temple-work that first fits together and at the same time gathers around itself the unity of those paths and relations in which birth and death, disaster and blessing, victory and disgrace, endurance and decline acquire the shape of destiny for human being. The all-governing expanse of this open relational context is the world of this historical people. Only from and in this expanse does the nation first return to itself for the fulfilment of its vocation. Standing there, the building rests on the rocky ground. This resting of the work draws up out of the rock the mystery of that rock's clumsy yet spontaneous support. Standing there, the building holds its ground against the storm raging above it and so makes the storm itself manifest its violence. The lustre and the gleam of the stone, though itself apparently glowing only by grace of the sun, yet first brings to light the light of day, the breadth of the sky, the darkness of night. The steadfastness of the work contrasts with the surge of the surf, and its own repose brings out the raging of the sea. Tree and grass, eagle and bull, snake and cricket first enter into their distinctive shapes and thus come to appear as what they are. The Greeks early called this emerging and rising in itself and in all things *physis*. It clears and illuminates, also, that on which man bases his dwelling. We call this ground *earth*. What this world names is not to be associated with the idea of a mass of matter deposited somewhere, or with the merely astronomical idea of a planet.[34]

How shall we not remark upon, in this place, the affinity between Heidegger and Benjamin's discourses, which date from the same year and yet differ in so many ways? It is not only the determination of the work of art as the unity of the place and the thing (nothing takes place, not even place itself, without this unity) which allows us to pass from one text to the other; both Benjamin and Heidegger let the religious foundation of the work of art appear. They found the unity of the work of art, its being-work, on the unity of the rite and the sacred precinct.

For Benjamin, the sacred is the origin of art, of tradition and of traditional (manual) reproduction. This is to say that art carries with it a sacred memory and a promise; it transmits and reproduces the sacred as a memory and a promise. Technical reproduction perverts the origin – its memory and its promise – to such an extent that it seems difficult to reconcile art with its principle: namely, the general reproducibility of the work. What we know of the sacred we know through the art that technical reproduction destroys in destroying its foundation – the sacred and its unity. In the first version of 'The Work of Art' Benjamin notes that 'the unique value of the "authentic" work of art' (*einzigartiger Wert des 'echten' Kunstwerks*: quotation marks here encircle authenticity) is always based on theology (*ist immer theologisch fundiert*). The phrase undergoes a modification in the later versions of the text. But the modification does not concern the foundation of the work of art: 'the unique value of the "authentic" work of art has its basis in ritual, the location of its original use value.'[35] If Maurice de Gandillac, the French translator, renders *einzigartiger Wert* by 'value of unicity' instead of 'unique value', he is not altogether wrong. The work of art is unique in virtue of its unity; its value of unicity is therefore a unique value, as it is scarcely a value which could be attributed to just anything. The thing which is distinguished by a unity which brings to the fore that which it unites is always in some relation to the work of art, even if that relation is not recognized.

To radicalize Benjamin's argument, it could be said that the work of art, the work and art, the unity of the work and art, are an *effect* of the unity which unites place and thing in their apparition. As soon as something remains because its foundation is unique and guarantees its unicity (Benjamin describes tradition as (the transmission of) what remains, (of) what remains by reason of the unity and unicity of what was founded), there is *sacralization* and *aestheticization*. The aestheticization is reactive, in the sense that Nietzsche understood this term, that is, in the sense of a limitation and a recuperation of destruction:

> The ritualistic basis, however remote, is still recognizable as secularized ritual even in the most profane forms of the cult of beauty. The secular cult of beauty, developed during the Renaissance and prevailing for three centuries, clearly showed that ritualistic basis in its decline and the first deep crisis which befell it. With the advent of the first truly revolutionary means of reproduction, photography, simultaneously with the rise of socialism, art sensed the approaching crisis which has become evident a century later. At that time, art reacted with the doctrine of *l'art pour l'art*, that is, with a theology of art.[36]

Originating in theology and the sacred, art ends by sacralizing itself: aestheticization is an *auto-sacralization*. But the aestheticization also affects politics: the 'aestheticization of politics', which the Fascist project typifies, also inscribes itself in the tradition founded on the unity of the sacred which is at the origin of the work of art. As long as tradition is affirmed for a last and a first time in the empty repetition of the destructive gesture, as long as destruction remains paradoxical, as long as language comes up against the paradox of destruction, this destruction will never be able to avoid the risk of an aestheticization, an aestheticization of the destructive gesture, at least not if the fact of remaining refers back to the possibility of a fundamental unity which assures the unity of that which remains.

A double affinity, then, links the discourse on mechanical reproducibility to that on the origin of art. It is not a question of assimilating two discourses which inhabit their arguments and styles in very different ways. Nonetheless, looked at more closely, it is hard not to remark upon the passages which communicate with each other. Benjamin and Heidegger both conceive of the – traditional – work of art as the singular unity of place and thing; and both discover in that unity the unity of the sacred. If for Benjamin technical reproduction destroys the *hic et nunc* of the original, which constitutes its unity and is the origin of tradition in its role as transmission of all that the authentic 'contains of the originarily transmissible', Heidegger interprets the origin of the work of art as the function of a presence which is never supplementary.

> Both men and animals, plants and things, are never present and familiar as unchangeable objects, only to represent incidentally also a fitting environment for the temple, which one fine day is added to what is already there. We shall get closer to what *is*, rather, if we think of all this in a reverse order:. . . . The temple, in its standing there, first gives to things their look and to men their outlook on themselves. This view remains open as long as the work is a work, as long as the god has not fled from it.[37]

The affinity between these two discourses goes perhaps even deeper: if one allows oneself to be seduced by the fascination which the name and the language of names has for Benjamin (at least a certain Benjamin), and if one dares to breach the apparently unbreachable distance separating the 1916 text (on the unicity and singularity of the name) from the 1935 text (on the unicity and singularity of the – traditional – work of art), then one will no longer be able to read Heidegger's sentence in which 'world' translates the Greek word *physis* without hearing Benjamin. This sentence is also a warning: 'What this word names is not to be associated with . . . .' The word names, the word is a name which wants to name – the thing. The word is that which does not want not to name; but to understand it, the force of naming – the thing – must be left in the word. The experience of language is necessary and one must not be imprisoned in representations. To think the origin of the work of art is to trust oneself to the force of language's denomination and to distrust those representations which have come to veil the truth of the name, that is, of the truth named and uttered by the name. The origin of the work of art, its singular unity, occurs through the originary unity of language; it occurs through the name and names itself in its singularity.

Let us return to the question of principle. *One the one hand*, reproducibility is general: the work of art has always been reproducible and would not be capable of escaping reproduction, be it manual, mechanical or otherwise. There is no discrimination between techniques: nothing stops us from distinguishing mechanical from manual reproduction; on the contrary, everything forces us to this distinction, but it does not then permit us to distinguish the work of art from something which is not one. The inclusion of the work of art is part of the order of reproduction. Men can redo what they have done, but the work of art lends itself to reproduction and use in the same moment that it is created or produced. Since it is a question of principle, the following type of affirmation can be found trivial or tautological: the work of art reproduces itself. Benjamin will never stop insisting on the irreversible character of the destructive process, and will attempt to determine the destruction of the traditional work of art, which means the passage from manual to technical or mechanical reproducibility, as revolutionary opportunity. He will so generously give his blessing to destruction that Adorno will reproach him for having sacrificed dialectical reflection to barbarism. But, *on the other hand*, the – traditional – work of art does not, under any circumstances, fold under to general reproducibility, and must be excepted from reproduction, be it manual, mechanical, or otherwise. Its authenticity and its authority, its originality and its transmissibility, its material devotion and its capacity as historical testimony all depend on its exceptional status, on the unreproducible *hic et nunc* which also assures its identity. No doubt one of the massive effects of this unique status is the aggravation of the tension which marks the relation between manual and technical reproductions. How can access be had to a principle of general reproductibility if the – traditional – work of art is not essentially reproducible?[38] One can respond to this question: Certainly, the work of art is always reproducible, but this does not suggest, as might a reading which is too keen on dissociating and polarizing the elements of the text, that it does not present itself at the origin as a traditional unity which inserts it into tradition and founds its transmissibility. All the strings of the argument must be pulled. The cleavage between the two forms of reproduction is shown to be even more violent, and the destruction more ineluctable, when the destructive force does not achieve authenticity, authority and tradition. In a catastrophic reversal, tradition – in its Fascist form – succeeds in destroying destruction. It can reach this point only because the principle of destruction already has established a resistance to tradition. It would be wrong to think that the limitations of general reproducibility provide any sort of regulatory principle which could regulate the destruction by subjecting it to a horizon while interdicting its over-excessiveness which attacks the originary identity. Such an apology for equilibrium and symmetry, for a compensatory economy and the conservation of the destructive gesture, forgets that destruction is destined to failure as soon as it is obliged to turn back on itself and is recuperated by its own paradox.

There is no accurate measure for destruction. All destruction is by definition *excessive* and therefore fragile, vulnerable and disposed to destruction. This strange vulnerability at the very heart of destruction is perhaps nothing other than love, the love of destruction. Let us listen to how destruction sounds to Blanchot's ear. He accepts the word 'destruction', pronounced like the word of an oracle, from a book by Marguerite Duras: 'One must love to destroy, and she or he who could destroy with a pure movement of loving, would not injure, would not destroy, would only give, giving the empty immensity in which destroy becomes a non-private word, non-positive, the neutral speech which carries across neutral desire.'[39] In saying this, Blanchot also says that this word belongs to a book which gives it to us as though it were an unknown word, 'proposed by an entirely other language whose promise it would be, a language which has, perhaps, only this single word to say'. Is it too hazardous to suggest that the language of destruction is that unusable language whose possibility and necessity we are trying to determine? The language of destruction only says destruction, it has nothing to say, it communicates nothing. The speech of an oracle: if destruction is essentially excessive, then so is the language which speaks it. It exposes itself to misunderstanding, to confusion and to violent reappropriation. Destroy, she says in the voice of a priestess or a young adolescent, it is she who says it, the *other* who says it each time, if it is true that destruction proves to be excessive. We have been paraphrasing Blanchot's text: '*Destroy*. It is only a murmur. Not a unique term, glorified by its unity, but a word which multiplies itself in rarefied space, and such that she who pronounces it, pronounces anonymously, a young figure who comes from a place without horizon, youth without age, from a youth which makes one very old or too young to appear simply young. Thus the Greeks greeted in each adolescent girl the expectation of an oracle's word.'[40] We are paraphrasing this text, but in the same gesture we are bringing it into an encounter with another; in his notes on the destructive character (1931), Benjamin says that destruction rejuvenates (*denn Zerstören verjüngt*), and that the destructive character is exposed to misunderstanding. Just like the oracle (which Benjamin describes as a destruction established by the state), the destructive character calls forth misunderstanding and incomprehension (*fordert das Missverstandenwerden heraus*). There is no language of destruction and no discourse on destruction which does not incite polemics and equivocations and warnings, wars and destructions. Destruction, the language of destruction, and the discourse on destruction all arouse suspicion because of the extravagance and the excess which make destruction untenable. This excess confuses distinctions and oppositions; the distinction between good and bad reproduction and the distinction between good and bad destruction, distinctions which no metadiscourse can renounce, are premature and provisional, and yet they are not young enough. The most irresistible temptation would consist therefore in saying that good destruction is distinguished by excess and extravagance. But ceding to this temptation is again to be deceived: one would only try anew to give an identity to the *differance* (difference and deferral) of destruction, because it is precisely excess and extravagance, fragility and vulnerability (do we dare say love and the 'pure movement of loving'?) which permit destruction to be reinscribed in tradition. The excess is excessive in relation to any attribution; it even exceeds its representation in ruins.

NOTES

1 The pages which follow are not intended to be read as a commentary upon Benjamin's essay, a familiarity with which is here assumed. They rather intend to address a problem at work in this essay by asking what Benjamin can teach us about the relation between language, politics, destruction and tradition. The presentation of these problems is determined less by the rules of (philosophic) deduction than by the necessities of what Adorno calls 'constellation'. This may explain, in part, the occasionally apodictic, elliptical or contradictory character of certain passages. The use of individual concepts must be judged within the context of the text as a whole. All the analyses which seem to be guided by a vision which is at once over- and under-attentive (the strategic isolation of a single sentence would only be one example of such a vision) should not themselves be isolated in turn. It should also be noted that these pages are only an extract of a work in progress which is the subject of ongoing discussion. To those who have been willing to be a part of this discussion, I offer my thanks.

2 Walter Benjamin, 'Das Kunstwerk im Zeitalter seiner technischen Reproduzierbarkeit', in *Gesammelte Schriften*, vol. I.2 (Frankfurt am

Main: Suhrkamp, 1974), p. 473. Translated by Harry Zohn as 'The Work of Art in the Age of Mechanical Reproduction', in *Illuminations*, ed. Hannah Arendt (New York: Schocken Books, 1969), pp. 217–18.

3 The concept of ideology does not appear in the methodological remarks. It is not Benjamin who designates the delay of the superstructure by this concept. To justify its use it is enough, in this context, to cite Marx:

> At a certain stage of development, the material productive forces of society come into conflict with the existing relations of production or – this merely expresses the same thing in legal terms – with the property relations within the framework of which they have operated hitherto. From forms of development of the productive forces these relations turn into fetters. There begins an era of social revolution. *The changes in the economic foundation lead sooner or later to the transformation of the whole immense superstructure.* In studying such transformations it is always necessary to distinguish between the material transformation of the economic conditions of production, which can be determined with the precision of a natural science, and the legal, political, religious, artistic or philosophic – *in short, ideological forms* in which men become conscious of this conflict and fight it out.

> (Karl Marx, 'Zur Kritik der politischen Ökonomie', in Marx/Engels, *Werke*, vol. 13 (Berlin: Deitz Verlag, 1972), p. 9; translated by Rodney Livingstone and Gregor Benton as 'Preface to a *Contribution to a Critique of Political Economy*', in Karl Marx, *Early Writings*, ed. Lucio Colletti (New York: Vintage Books, 1975), pp. 425–6, my italics.)

4 Ibid.

5 The relation between control and revolution is not questioned in this essay. We have attempted elsewhere (and beginning from another text by Benjamin) to analyse (Communist) revolution as that which controls (uncontrollable) revolt. Cf. García Düttmann, *Das Gedächtnis des Denkens. Versuch über Heidegger und Adorno* (Frankfurt am Main: Suhrkamp, 1991).

6 Jürgen Habermas, *Philosophisch-politische Profile* (Frankfurt am Main: Suhrkamp, 1981), p. 343.

7 'Das Kunstwerk', p. 492; 'The Work of Art', p. 247.

8 Alain Badiou, *Peut-on penser la politique?* (Paris: Seuil, 1985), p. 17.

9 'Das Kunstwerk', p. 473; 'The Work of Art', modified, p. 218.

10 Here again it is necessary to insist that Benjamin does not make use of the concept of destruction to describe the effects of technical reproduction; in any case, no elaboration of this concept is proposed in the text which concerns us here. The reader will judge whether or not it is pertinent to speak of destruction.

11 We are suspending, for the moment, the question of concepts which would be useful for the purposes of Communist revolution.

12 Later in the essay (and *à propos* of what we will call the *destruction of destruction*) we will try to show why Fascism is a language without an other which erects itself upon an alterity or multiplicity of languages.

13 Rodolphe Gasché has examined the function of the concept of communicability (*Mitteilbarkeit*) in Benjamin, especially in his 'Saturnine Vision

and the Question of Difference: Reflections on Walter Benjamin's Theory of Language', in Rainer Nägele (ed.) *Benjamin's Ground* (Detroit, MI: Wayne State University Press, 1989).

14 In *Gesammelte Schriften*, vol. II.1 (Frankfurt am Main: Suhrkamp, 1977), pp. 140–57.

15 In *La parole donnée. Mémoire et promesse* (Paris: Galilée, 1989), p. 157, we show why Benjaminian logic implies that a 'departure of the name outside of itself is already prepared and effectuated at the moment in which the name is permitted to substitute for the verb and so closes the circle of divine sameness'.

16 Benjamin limits himself to asserting that the concept which is unusable for the purposes of Fascism is usable for the purposes of Communist revolution. Is this the sign of a relativism?

17 'Das Kunstwerk', pp. 481–2; 'The Work of Art', p. 244.

18 T. W. Adorno and M. Horkheimer, in *Gesammelte Schriften*, vol. 3 (Frankfurt am Main: Suhrkamp, 1981), p. 158; translated by John Cumming as *The Dialectic of Enlightenment* (New York: Continuum Press, 1982), p. 136.

19 Martin Heidegger, 'Zeit und Sein', in his *Zur Sache des Denkens* (Frankfurt am Main: Max Niemeyer, 1981), pp. 56–7; translated by Joan Stambaugh as *On Time and Being* (New York: Harper & Row, 1972), p. 53.

20 T. W. Adorno, 'Beitrag zur Ideologienlehre', in *Gesammelte Schriften*, vol. 8 (Frankfurt am Main: Suhrkamp, 1972), p. 477.

21 'Das Kunstwerk'; 'The Work of Art'.

22 Niklas Luhmann (with P. Fuchs), *Reden und Schweigen* (Frankfurt am Main: Suhrkamp, 1989).

23 'Deconstruction and the other', in R. Kearny (ed.) *Dialogues with Contemporary Continental Thinkers* (Manchester: Manchester University Press, 1984), p. 123.

24 Jacques Derrida, *Glas* (Paris: Galilée, 1974), p. 140; translated by John P. Leavey Jr. and Richard Rand (Lincoln, NE: University of Nebraska Press, 1986), pp. 121–2.

25 What happens when deconstruction receives its ('improper') name and marks itself off from tradition? We have examined this question in another context: cf. García Düttmann, 'Rien à voir. Radicalité d'une déconstruction', in *La part de l'oeil*, Art et phénoménologie, Brussels, 1991.

26 Jacques Derrida, 'Some Statements and Truisms . . .' in D. Carroll (ed.) *The States of Theory* (New York: Columbia University Press, 1990), p. 79.

27 'Communicability' designates that which makes possible and simultaneously interrupts communication. It is thus not opposed to a contrary concept, especially not to some sort of 'incommunicability'.

28 'Das Kunstwerk', p. 473; 'The Work of Art', p. 218.

29 Ibid., p. 475; p. 220.

30 Ibid., pp. 475–6; p. 220.

31 Ibid., p. 480; p. 243.

32 Ibid., p. 480; p. 223.

33 See 'Das Kunstwerk', p. 437.

34 Martin Heidegger, 'Vom Ursprung des Kunstwerks', quoted from the

French edition, ed. E. Martineau (Paris: Authentica, 1987) (a non-authorized translation), pp. 25–7; translated by Albert Hofstadter as 'The Origin of the Work of Art', in *Poetry, Language, Thought* (New York: Harper Colophon Books, Harper & Row, 1971), p. 41. The version of 'Vom Ursprung' translated by Martineau is earlier than and differs slightly from that referred to by Hofstadter and should be referred to by those interested.

35 'Das Kunstwerk', p. 480; 'The Work of Art', p. 224.

36 Ibid.

37 'Vom Ursprung', p. 27; 'The Origin of the Work', p. 43.

38 Recognizing that a work of art can in principle be reproduced, while simultaneously maintaining the contrary, namely, that a determinate here and now of the artwork in principle escapes reproducibility, Benjamin opens up the field of the political, which is not simply congruent with what the essay on the work of art calls politics. A thinking is political if, on the one hand, it is carried away by the incommensurable movement of destruction, and, on the other, if it respects the necessity of compromise and negotiation. It is under the name of 'politics' that we must think the way in which these two asymmetrical and irreconcilable tendencies relate to one another.

39 Maurice Blanchot, *L'amitié* (Paris: Gallimard, 1971), p. 132.

40 Ibid.

3 Small-scale Victories, Large-scale Defeats

Walter Benjamin's Politics of Time

Peter Osborne

The literary forms of expression my thought has forged for itself
over the last decades have been utterly conditioned by the
preventive measures and antidotes with which I have had to
counter the disintegration constantly threatening my thought as
a result of . . . contingencies. And though many – or a sizeable
number – of my works have been small-scale victories, they are
offset by large-scale defeats.

(Benjamin, letter to Scholem, July 1932[1])

The development of Benjamin's thought is marked by two founding
and two subsequent, transformative concerns. In the first place, we
find the desire for the philosophical articulation of an expanded or
'total' concept of experience (*Erfahrung*), a 'uniform and continuous
multiplicity of knowledge' which would exclude no domain, however
marginal, bizarre or esoteric, from its compass.[2] Alongside this
stands an emphatic concept of truth as a 'self-presenting realm of
ideas' (*sich darstellenden Ideenreiches*), an 'intentionless state of
being' (*intentionsloses Sein*), that pre-exists all constitutive activity
of the intellect.[3] The task of philosophy thus comes to be seen as
'the representation (*Darstellung*) of ideas by means of the empirical'
through the construction of configurations or constellations of 'concrete elements in the concept (*dinglicher Elemente im Begriff*)
which, through their mediating role, will rescue (*Rettung*) the
phenomena of experience for the experience of truth.[4]

In the early work, this project takes the twin form of an esoteric
philosophy of language and what Rabinbach has described as a
'programmatic anti-politics'.[5] A radically linguistic concept of truth
is opposed to the instrumentalism of 'all outwardly-directed communication'.[6] Thus, while much of Benjamin's earliest work may be
characterized as a form of modern Jewish Messianism, he rejected
political Zionism along with '*every* contemporary political

tendency'.[7] For Benjamin, immediately before and after the First World War, existing philosophy was charged with an academic impoverishment of the ideas of experience and truth; but Jewishness, 'Jewishness without Judaism' (Rabinbach), 'noble bearer and representative of the intellect', was to preserve them only in the form of the word and to renew them only through contemplation, to produce a promise of redemption incapable, in principle, of fulfilment in history.[8]

The key to this radical separation of thought and action, philosophically, is to be found in the atemporal stasis of Benjamin's quasi-Platonic 'ideas' and the monadic self-sufficiency it imposes upon them, in what is essentially an aesthetic model of philosophical representation, albeit one derived from a quite specific (Romantic) aesthetic. 'Ideas', Benjamin writes in *The Origin of German Tragic Drama*, 'are timeless constellations'. The extremes necessary to their comprehension are merely 'virtual' to the historical process. History is no more than 'the coloured borderline to their cystalline simultaneity'. Benjamin's ideas are monads, containing 'pre-stabilized' (*prästabiliert*) within them the representation of phenomena in their 'objective interpretation'. As such, each conceals within it 'the abbreviated and rarefied figure' or 'image' (*Bild*) of the rest of the world of ideas, recoverable through its philosophical representation.[9]

Yet, although ideas may be timeless, their philosophical representation is not. If the aim of philosophy is 'to establish the becoming of phenomena in their being', such representation will not be satisfied by a phenemonon until it has 'absorbed all of its history', since it is out of this history that it must construct its idea. Truth may be eternal, but its content is immanently historical: hence Benjamin's methodological excursus on the concept of origin in the 'Epistemo-Critical Prologue' to *The Origin of German Tragic Drama*, and the centrality to the book of the idea of natural history, whereby the dialectical identity of time and timelessness, history and eternity, 'outer' and 'inner', set out in the Prologue, is recapitulated *in concreto* in the interpretation of the allegories of Baroque drama. The metaphysical is to the historical as 'a stocking turned inside out'.[10]

If the impact of revolutionary politics, and the project for a pedagogic materialist historiography to which it ultimately gave rise, were to transform Benjamin's thought, they were to do so less through any simple rejection of these ideas than via a continual and unfinished process of 'recasting'.[11] The early, esoteric account of the structure of philosophical representation was slowly, sporadically, yet systematically transformed into the project for a theologically enriched historical and cultural materialism as Benjamin grappled with the problems of representation internal to his plan for a book on the history of the Paris arcades as an 'ur-phenomenon' of the nineteenth century. The template of this plan, through which the pressures of its great mass of historical material were to pass, was the elaboration of a new form of historiography: that 'Copernican revolution of remembering [*Eingedenken*]' to which Benjamin refers in his notes for the project, and which finds its most direct if still somewhat oblique presentation in his last surviving piece of writing, the theses 'On the Concept of History'.[12] Thus have we come to inherit what has long been the most disputed issue in Benjamin criticism – the relationship between the metaphysical and the materialist moments of the later work – associated with the two key questions of the theoretical coherence of its project (whether it could, in principle, ever have been successfully carried out) and the nature of its legacy.

At the centre of this debate lies the question of time and the temporal structure of what, generalizing from Benjamin's use of the phrase 'Surrealist experience', I shall call *avant-garde experience*, using the term to denote that experience of history towards which all of Benjamin's writings after 1927 are directed: the experience of history within the time of the 'now' in which, in the shock of the dialectical image, the continuum is exploded by a new experience of time.[13] Benjamin's conception of this experience as a *political temporalization of history*, alternative and preferable to that underlying prevailing forms of historiography (summed up by the term 'historicism'), was developed under the impact of a series of models of cultural experience (Proust, Kafka, Baudelaire, Brecht) of which Surrealism was the most strategically important. Yet it never received a direct philosophical presentation in which its multiple aspects appear together in the condensation of a fully elaborated idea. It has become a cliché to insist on the fragmented and incomplete nature of Benjamin's *oeuvre*, a cliché that turns all too quickly into an alibi for cavalier critiques and self-serving appropriations alike. Yet as Benjamin made clear in his discussion of the Romantics, a thinking can be 'systematically oriented' without being 'systematically developed'.[14] It is the aim of what follows to pursue the systematic orientation of Benjamin's thought through a variety of its manifestations to the point of a judgement on its politics of time.

The question underlying and motivating this reading is Benjamin's own: namely, what are the conceptual structure, terms and conditions of a 'political' experience of history adequate to the demands of a metaphysical concept of truth? For if in 1919 Benjamin was provoked by Bloch into an increasing engagement with politics which would soon take the form of an explicit identification with revolutionary Marxism (1924), he never followed him theoretically in his particular brand of Messianic Marxism, based on the Utopian identification of both Jewish and Christian concepts of redemption with the hopes of the revolution.[15] The question of the political as the historical realization of the metaphysical (the 'philosophical question of action'[16]) thus remained open for Benjamin in a way it never was for Bloch, open to both materialist and theological doubts about its possibility which, in their convergence on this point, laid the ground for their combination within Benjamin's work. It is the space of this opening that Benjamin's later thought explores. The route by which it arrived there was called Surrealism.

SURREALISM: THE SECRET CARGO

The porcelain stoppers from bottles of lemon soda and beer lined with little red circles for perfect air-tightness have as much value as all the water lilies in the world. A universe in pieces, abandoned, without hope, an image of the real. . . . Everything has taken on the miraculous tint of time.

(Louis Aragon, *Treatise on Style*, 1928[17])

Benjamin's essay on Surrealism is located at a crucial juncture in the development of his thought. Written during the period in which the *Passagen-Werk* was first conceived, as both is 'prolegomena' and 'screen',[18] it contains many of the tensions characteristic of his later work in condensed form. More specifically, it reveals Surrealism as the means by which Benjamin made the leap from his earlier ('idealist') theory of the artwork to his later ('materialist') account of the truth of history buried in the objectivity of outdated cultural commodities. Central to this mediating function was Benjamin's sense of the *ambiguity* of Surrealism as an artistic and political movement: Surrealism as the movement which both registered and went beyond that 'crisis in the arts' which was, for Benjamin, the index of a general crisis of experience; Surrealism as the movement which, oscillating between its loyalty to the revolution and its loyalty to itself (*La Révolution Surréaliste*), could never quite make up its mind about its relation to politics; Surrealism as the movement which, in transition from art to politics, came to stand for the moment of transition itself.[19] Benjamin's essay is a historico-philosophical interpretation of Surrealism as the seed-bed of a new and revolutionary form of historical consciousness. In the manner characteristic of his essays of the period – mapping the historical contours of their objects and judging them against the ideas of them thereby constructed – it was to become, in turn, the seed-bed of his own work.[20]

Whatever the 'deficiencies' of certain of its manifestations or the 'pernicious romantic prejudices' of particular interpreters, Benjamin is unequivocal about Surrealism's historical importance as a contribution to the expansion of the idea of political experience. It is the project of Surrealism, he argues, what we may call 'its most particular task', 'to win the energies of intoxication for the revolution'. We know that 'an ecstatic component lives in every revolutionary act', but for the Surrealists this is 'not enough'. It is their great inspiration to seek out the ecstatic in the everyday, the mysterious in the mundane, 'by virtue of a dialectical optic that perceives the everyday as impenetrable, the impenetrable as everyday'.[21] In this way, ecstasy is both *secularized* and *politicized*. As Adorno puts it in his essay on 'One-Way Street': 'The absurd is presented as though it were self-evident, in order to disempower what is self-evident.'[22] The self-evident becomes absurd.

More particularly, Breton is attributed with an 'extraordinary discovery' that will soon become the centre-piece of Benjamin's work: the perception of 'the revolutionary energies that appear in the "outmoded" '. In Surrealism, destitution, 'not only social but architectonic, the poverty of interiors, enslaved and enslaving objects', is transformed into 'revolutionary nihilism'. Breton and Nadja redeem (*einlosen*) everything we experience of the objects of the most recent past into 'revolutionary experience (*Erfahrung*)'.[23] But what, precisely, is 'revolutionary' about this experience? And how do the Surrealists bring it about? Benjamin's essay is rather less clear about these issues than it is in evoking and promoting Surrealism as a cultural movement which breaks the bounds of 'culture', opening up possibilities for politics that had yet to be fully envisaged, still less theorized. Nonetheless, there are sufficient hints which, taken in the context of Benjamin's earlier work, allow us to reconstruct something of the impact of Surrealism on Benjamin's thought.[24]

Four themes stand out: (1) the explosion of the bounds of the 'poetic' in the generalization of poetic experience to the objects of everyday life; (2) the secularization of the ecstatic and the conception of reality as a dreamwork; (3) the valorization of the image over the metaphor, its connection to the 'residual' metaphysical materialism of the body, and its identification with political action; (4) the opposition of 'political' to 'historical' views of the past. In each case, an element of Benjamin's earlier work is taken up, wrenched from its original context, and inserted into the crisis-ridden world of interwar Europe. In the process, a tension that was always implicit in Benjamin's thought comes decisively to the fore: a tension between the philosophical theory of experience and the history of experience. It is this tension, registered in the project for a *dialectical redemption of the destruction of tradition*, that forms the nerve-centre of Benjamin's later work, to which each of the impulses picked up by the individual studies ultimately returns.[25]

Surrealism celebrates and promotes the destruction of tradition in the two key areas of art and religion. It is in the imbrication of the two, and their joint replacement by a new sort of 'profane illumination', that Benjamin locates the source of Surrealism's charge; harnessing the energies of old cultural forms to destroy these forms themselves. In the process, both aestheticism and religiosity are revealed to have a historical meaning quite different from what might otherwise have been supposed. Art for art's sake 'was scarcely ever to be taken literally; it was almost always a flag under which sailed a cargo that could not be declared because it still lacked a name':[26] Surrealist experience as profane illumination. In sealing off the artwork from practical concerns, aestheticism made a religion out of art. It thereby provided the model of a secular religion which would inspire the Surrealists not only to attack all theisms, but also to shatter the institutional and conventional bounds of art, generalizing the aesthete's absolutization of the experience of the artwork into a secular aesthetic religion of everyday life, 'a materialistic, anthropological inspiration', that would break forever with 'a praxis that presents the public with the literary precipitate of a certain form of existence while withholding that existence itself'.[27]

Surrealism liberated the pent-up energy trapped in the autonomous work of art, setting free the consciousness of the 'aesthetic' as a domain for the experience of truth, free to roam over the entire world of cultural experience. Such was the 'secret cargo' of aestheticism. It is this, its avant-garde function of attacking the conceptual and institutional division between 'art' and other cultural practices, not by rejecting art but by universalizing it,[28] that established Surrealism as the basis for the transposition of Benjamin's theory of the artwork into the medium of a general theory of experience. Nor was the role of religion here restricted to its functioning as a metaphor: first, for the absolutization of art in aestheticism; and second, for its transformation into a generalized form of practical consciousness in Surrealism itself (a parallel which quickly earned Breton the nickname 'the Pope' from his critics). As Benjamin points out, it was in a 'bitter, passionate revolt against Catholicism' that Rimbaud, Lautréamont and Apollinaire brought Surrealism into the world.[29] The dialectical negation of religion is as important to Surrealism's impact on Benjamin as its corresponding negation of art. For it is this negation that establishes the connection to theology which, ironically, will allow Benjamin to reintroduce explicitly theological motifs into his 'materialist' work, as ciphers or figures for a philosophical consciousness of history that has no equivalent secular form. The Freudian concept of the unconscious may have provided Surrealism with a secular version of revelation and a model for the interpretation of reality as dreamwork – allowing 'its gaze to roam freely' over the ruins of the most recent past as the waking sleeper surveys the 'residues of dream-world' – but there was nothing in its formation to contribute to the comprehension of the *historical* dimension of this experience; nothing to help us understand these ruins as 'the ruins of the bourgeoisie'.[30] It is here that Benjamin's distinctive contribution lies: not as a historian of Surrealism, but as the theorist of Surrealist experience *as* historical experience.

If surrealist experience was the secret cargo of aestheticism, political experience (the political experience of history) was to be the secret cargo of Surrealism. The *Passagen-Werk*, Benjamin writes to Scholem in August 1935, 'represents both the philosophical application of surrealism – and thereby its sublation [*Aufhebung*] – as well as the attempt to retain the image of history in the most inconspicuous corners of existence – the detritus of history, as it were'.[31] The resonance of Breton's discovery of 'revolutionary energies in the outmoded' in the 'detritus of history' is clear. But Benjamin adds a distinctive element of his own, which links this philosophical application of Surrealism back, directly, to the epistemology of *The Origin of German Tragic Drama*: the image of history. Whereas Breton had classified these energies under the general heading of Surreality, Benjamin identifies them with history itself. It is in this move – the reintroduction of a Messianic idea of history as a redemptive whole into the context of Surrealist experience – that the originality of Benjamin's work as a theory of avant-garde experience is to be found. The thread connecting the two parts of the project (and hence the early to the later work) is the concept of the image.

We have already noted how, in *The Origin of German Tragic Drama*, each idea was held to conceal within itself the 'abbreviated and rarefied figure' or 'image' of the rest of that 'self-presenting realm of ideas' which was, for Benjamin, 'truth' – as opposed to the mere totality of objects of knowledge, the transcendental conditions of which had become the exclusive preoccupation of academic neo-Kantianism. Access to such images via the representation of ideas 'by means of the empirical' (constellations of 'concrete elements in the concept') was the task of philosophical representation. By the time of the essay on Surrealism, however, it is Surrealist experience, 'profane illumination', which has taken over this role. In the process, the concept of the image has undergone a correspondingly 'materialist' conversion. For whereas in the first case the image was only an 'abbreviated and rarefied figure' of a true reality (the realm of ideas) which was essentially linguistic in nature and required contemplation for its apprehension, in the latter case 'that image sphere to which profane illumination initiates us' is *itself* 'the world of universal and integral actualities', within which 'the *physis* that is being organized for . . . [the collective] in technology' is to be produced. So, not only has the sphere of images achieved a substantial actuality of its own, but, unlike the realm of ideas, it is both a bodily and a historical one, subject to and hence dependent upon action. And it is through action, the actions that generate profane illuminations, that its realm is to be entered: action that 'puts forth its own image and exists, absorbing and consuming it, where nearness looks with its own eyes'.[32]

Drawing, rather tenuously, on Aragon's *Treatise on Style*, Benjamin opposes the image to the metaphor, identifying the latter with both morality and an exclusively bourgeois form of intellectuality, while the former is associated with politics (specifically, the task of 'making contact with the proletarian masses') and justice. In the image sphere, 'political materialism and physical nature share the inner man, the psyche, the individual, or whatever else we wish to throw to them, with dialectical justice, so that no limb remains unrent.'[33] If the epistemology of *The Origin of German Tragic Drama* was nourished by reflection upon the beauty of truth, by the time of the essay on Surrealism it is its goodness with which Benjamin is primarily concerned. In fact, underlying the dense and contorted prose of the extraordinary final pages of the essay are a series of dichotomies, linked into a single almost Manichean opposition:

image	metaphor
action	contemplation
body	intellect
politics	morality
proletariat	bourgeoisie
justice	[oppression]

Noticeably absent from these lists – and from the apocalyptic resolution to their opposition projected in the final paragraph as the fulfilment of the demand of the *Communist Manifesto* for reality to 'outdo itself' (*sich ubertreffen*), 'when in technology body and image so interpenetrate that all revolutionary tension becomes bodily collective innervation, and all the bodily innervations of the collective become revolutionary discharge'[34] – are both truth and history, twin axes of Benjamin's thought. Yet it is the tension between them, nonetheless, which generates the dynamism of the picture. And if this tension is discharged in the conclusion, in mimetic identification with the ecstasy of Surrealist experience, essentially for reasons of *style*, Benjamin knows that the fulfilment of such exotic speculations depends on action of a wholly other kind; not least, because of the political critique of Surrealism's residual aestheticism articulated by Naville, which he explicitly endorsed.[35] The question thus arises of the politics of the essay, and more particularly, of the concept of the political at work within it, in its dual relations to 'truth' and 'history', respectively. We have already noted that it is the movement within Surrealism from 'art' to 'politics' that Benjamin picks up on as being of decisive historical significance, and unequivocally affirms in the face of more poetic interpretations. If the late nineteenth-century concept of art as an autonomous sphere of value was thereby exploded, it follows that the concept of the political will not have been left unaffected either. Precisely what this effect is, however, remains unclear.

The question of the political enters into Benjamin's essay in at least three ways. First and most directly, there is the question of Surrealism's orientation within the established field of politics – 'its highly exposed position between an anarchistic *fronde* and a revolutionary discipline'.[36] Second, there is the question of the effect of Surrealism as a practice upon the conception of the political. And finally, there is the question of the role of this new concept of the political in Benjamin's work; specifically, in the mediation of 'truth' (metaphysics) and 'history' (materialism). If the first and theoretically most straightforward of these questions is, ultimately, as unresolved within Benjamin's essay as it was historically within Surrealism itself, this is in part because of the way in which it is finessed by the shift in the concept of the political registered by the second. For if there is a redefinition of the political to be found in the essay, it is not in those passages where politics is explicitly thematized, but in the description of the allegedly 'revolutionary' character of Surrealist experience itself. And here, side-stepping the *aporias* of art and politics, experience and action, Benjamin redefines the political, neither as a particular kind nor a particular sphere of action, but rather as a particular *temporal mode of experience*: an action-generating, as opposed to a contemplative, orientation towards the past.

'The trick by which this world of things is mastered', Benjamin writes, summing up his reading of Breton's *Nadja*, and ' – it is more proper to speak of a trick than a method – consists in the substitution of a political for a historical view of the past.'[37] *The substitution of a political for a historical view of the past*: this is the phrase that links the 'Theological-Political Fragment' (1920–1) to the thesis 'On the Concept of History' (1940); the 'old' to the 'new'. This is the phrase which, in the context of the attempt simultaneously to read Surrealist experience as political experience and as a historically specific form of cultural experience, redefines political experience *as* historical experience, historical experience (*Erfahrung*) as 'political'. This is what is 'revolutionary' about Surrealist experience – revolutionary in the dual sense of constituting a radically ruptural sense of historical time, which would propel us into a quite different future, and hence of inaugurating a radically new conception of historical time (a 'Copernican revolution in the historical view'): the primary of politics over history.[38] Or to put it in another, albeit still preliminary way: what we are talking about here is the primacy of the present over the past in the perception of that (ever-present) past. 'History', Benjamin writes in Thesis XIV, 'is the subject of a structure whose site is not homogeneous, empty time, but time filled with the presence of the now [*Jetztzeit*]'.[39] It is the experience of this 'now', produced at the point of contact between a specific past and an equally specific present as a fleeting experience of the 'legibility' of history as a whole,[40] that Benjamin's later work seeks both to elucidate and to elicit. In it, truth (metaphysics) meets history (materialism) as 'political' experience. Before we examine the structure of this experience in more detail, however, we need to know more about both its conditions and its necessity; more about those other two forms of historical temporalization against which it is pitted and out of the refiguration of which it is to arise: our old friends, the siamese twins, modernity and tradition.

MODERNITY AND TRADITION (I): KAFKA'S FAILURE

To do justice to the figure of Kafka in its purity and peculiar beauty, one must never lose sight of one thing: it is the figure of a failure.

(Benjamin, letter to Scholem, June 1938[41])

If Surrealism furnished Benjamin with a prototype for a revolutionary experience of the presence of the past, Kafka provided him with the reverse: an archaic experience of the present. As such, Kafka's writings represent the pole of tradition: not tradition *per se*, tradition in its original form as the handing down of a heritage, wherein the continuity of history is assured by a doubling of the present as it simultaneously identifies itself with and distances itself from a specific past;[42] but tradition at grips with modernity, tradition in crisis – modernity under the *sign* of tradition (Kabbalah). In treating the present in this way, Kafka's writings place themselves at the crossroads of Benjamin's thought – the meeting place of Jewish mysticism and the sociology of modernity – holding 'the promise of a compass needle in uncharted territory'.[43] It is through these writings, and the interpretive disputes they occasioned, that Benjamin works out his conception of the relation of the present (his present, the present of interwar Europe) to the idea of tradition; and it is this relationship, in turn, that offers the key to the avant-garde element of his philosophy of history. For not only do Kafka's writings lay bare the experience of modernity in its primary, negative aspect as a destruction of tradition (a destruction of tradition's mode of destruction), but, Benjamin comes to argue, they reveal this destruction to be beyond recuperation by tradition, in however modern, negative or 'up-dated' a form. The indeterminacy of Kafka's mysticism, which was the central issue for all those involved in the Kafka debate of the 1930s, was for Benjamin ultimately the sign of 'tradition falling ill'.[44] Just as Surrealism is the nodal point for the dissolution of the concept of art in Benjamin's thought, so Kafka's work (not Marxism) is the privileged site for the investigation of its *critical* relation to the theological tradition.

Benjamin's interest in Kafka represents what one commentator has described as 'an undisguised return to the Messianic concerns that had dominated his early writings' (the concerns of the Jewish Messianic tradition).[45] Yet it is a fundamental error to suppose these concerns to be removed from Benjamin's interest in Marxism. The two interests make claims upon the same philosophical ground – the relationship of truth to history – from different historical and theoretical standpoints. This does not separate them from one another, it forces them together into the same interpretive space. Benjamin's reading of Kafka is one of a series of sites for the confrontation of their competing claims, but it is also the location of a decisive mutation in their relations: the place where we find, for the first time, a reflective theoretical recognition of something Benjamin had otherwise experienced only in the form of a practical demand: the necessity to transpose the theological structure of his thought, without remainder, into the terms of historical materialism.[46]

If the theological dimension to Benjamin's writing is increasingly, if inconsistently, attenuated, prior to its final appearance in the 1940s theses 'On the Concept of History', it was not because of a critique of its theoretical structure (it had always been maintained only in a secular form), but because of a growing concern about its capacity to communicate, as tradition. Such esotericism did not matter to the early Benjamin; in fact it was prized, as a sign of truth. Once he became interested in politics, however, it could no longer be justified. Conversely, Benjamin's interest in Marxism was foremost an interest in it as a collective intellectual form, through which a philosophical critique of the present could be actualized as politics (an interest, ironically, in Communism as a living *tradition* capable of expressing certain of Benjamin's formative experiences as a writer). Only secondarily was he interested in it as doctrine. The philosophical content of the Messianic tradition remained, for Benjamin, open to recovery in a 'materialist' form; not simply in order to preserve it (as doctrine), but as the medium for its actualization. As such, it would provide the standpoint from which to view its own destruction as tradition, and thereby, the condition for the reconstitution of the integrity of historical experience, in a new form.[47]

In Benjamin's work, 'historical materialism' is the name of a doctrine (*Lehre*) of which Communism is the tradition, but it does not denote any particular, fixed or authoritative interpretation of this doctrine. Rather, it names the site of interpretation. Benjamin deploys the hermeneutic and doctrinal resources of the Messianic tradition to reinterpret historical materialism, philosophically, as the historically appropriate medium for the theorization of what were, originally, theological insights. (Theology, 'as we know, is wizened and has to keep out of sight', but in the service of historical materialism it can still 'win all the time'.[48]) In the process, these insights must be translated into materialist terms. If such a translation is possible, however, it cannot be legitimate to describe its content, exclusively, as either 'theological' or 'materialist' in character, since according to Benjamin's theory of language it is truth that languages have in common as the condition of their translatability, and truth is beyond any particular language. Nor will the content be unaffected by its translation. It is the strategic significance of the attempt to translate the experience of modernity into the language of tradition – and its failure – that makes Kafka's work so central to Benjamin's thought.[49]

Benjamin's reading of Kafka develops between 1934 and 1938 in two distinct stages. Between them stands, on the one hand, 'The Work of Art in the Age of its Technical Reproducibility' (1935) and, on the other, 'The Storyteller' (1936).[50] In the former, the transition from tradition to modernity appears primarily from the standpoint of modernity, as possibility. In the latter, it appears from the standpoint of tradition, as loss. It is the increasing polarization of the categories of modernity and tradition, registered in these essays, that compelled Benjamin to rework his initial reading of Kafka. His interpretations are united by two themes: the inadequacy of the other prevailing interpretive approaches ('natural' and 'supernatural' or 'psychoanalytic' and 'theological' – as opposed to historical) and the judgement of Kafka's failure. However, whereas in the first version this failure, understood as a failure 'to convert poetry into doctrine', is more or less peripheral to the account of the literary success predicated upon it, it gradually comes to assume a far greater, symptomatic significance, undermining the historico-philosophical basis of the original interpretation and issuing in a far more incisive judgement. In the process, Kafka's work ceases to be a site for the exploration of productive combinations of Messianic and materialist motifs within Benjamin's thought (along the lines of the essay on Krauss) and comes instead to be seen as the terminus of the Jewish mystical tradition – a terminus that is symbolic of the sickness of tradition in general, as a form of historical temporalization, and cries out for a new form of historical experience. The final interpretation thus marks an emphatic reinforcement of the avant-garde element in Benjamin's philosophy of history. To comprehend it, it is necessary to place it in the context of, first, the initial reading out of which it grew, and second, the competing interpretations of Scholem and Brecht, in response to which Benjamin forged his view.[51]

If the form of Benjamin's 1934 essay on Kafka is problematic, its line of argument is nonetheless clear enough. Its starting point is an account of the prehistoric nature of Kafka's world derived from the place of law within it: 'In Kafka the written law is contained in books, but these are secret; by basing itself on them the prehistoric world [where 'laws and definite norms remain unwritten'] exerts its rule all the more ruthlessly.' The secrecy of the law's origin makes the plight of the accused hopeless. It is this hopelessness that 'brings out the beauty' in the accused. Kafka renders the despair of those suffering under an unknown law beautiful, through the depiction of their situation as hopelessness (whatever their individual hopes). It is this hopelessness that distances Kafka's work from the restoration of myth: 'Even the world of myth of which we think in this context is incomparably younger than Kafka's world, which has been promised redemption by myth. But if we can be sure of one thing, it is this: Kafka did not succumb to its temptation. A latter-day Ulysses, he let the Sirens go by "his gaze . . . fixed on the distance . . .".'[52] It is in the double reference here, to a world older than myth from a world that has surpassed it, that the complex historical logic of Benjamin's interpretation lies. Product of a world in which the lived reality of law as authoritative judgement is legitimated with reference to its written form, Kafka cannot but present the opacity of law to the individual in terms of the secrecy of some written origin. His world is thus at once 'prehistoric' (in its blind, incomprehensible, quasi-natural exteriority, without redemption, and hence prior to myth) and post-mythic (in its presentation of the rational *form* of law). It projects law into prehistory, prehistory into law.

The main consequence of this dual and contradictory historical projection is interpretive indeterminacy, at the level of both act and genre; an indeterminacy that is constitutive of the meaning of Kafka's work. (Kafka's world, one might say, is determinate only in its indeterminacy.) 'Kafka's entire work', Benjamin argues, 'constitutes a code of gestures which surely had no definite symbolic meaning for the author from the outset; rather the author tried to derive such a meaning from them in ever-changing contexts and experimental groupings' – just as his characters try, in vain, to derive an authoritative meaning from their circumstances. Kafka's stories demand yet refuse to be read as parables: 'they do not want to be taken at their face value; they lend themselves to quotation and can be told for purposes of clarification. But do we have the doctrine which Kafka's parables interpret and which K.'s postures and the gestures of the animals clarify? It does not exist; all we can say is that here and there we have an allusion to it. Kafka might have said that these are relics transmitting the doctrine, although we could regard them just as well as precursors. . . .' Either way: 'In the mirror which the prehistoric world held before him in the form of guilt . . . [Kafka] saw the future emerging in the form of a judgement.' But he 'did not say what it was like'. 'Kafka could understand things only in the form of a *gestus*', but he could not understand this *gestus* itself. In Kafka, narrative thus 'regains the significance it had in the mouth of Scheherazade: to postpone the future'.[53]

Yet it would be a mistake to seek, like Kafka's characters, hope in postponement. For it is infinite. The proceedings gradually take on the form of a judgement. Time *is* the trial. This is the measure of Kafka's despair. He 'did not consider the age in which he lived as an advance over the beginnings of time'. Benjamin quotes Kafka: ' "To believe in progress is not to believe that progress has already taken place. That would be no belief." '[54] Wherein, then, if anywhere, lies the basis of *Kafka's* hope? It is at this point that the question of his relation to the Jewish mystical tradition – posed most acutely by Scholem – comes to the fore. For it is the light thrown on Kafka's world by the perspective of the redemption that it is denied which, Benjamin agrees, introduces what hope there is. Yet, as Kafka says, this hope is 'not for us'. It is not for the living. Rather, it would seem, it is merely the metaphysical measure of our hopelessness. The question thus arises as to the status within Kafka's work of this nihilistic theology of hope. Is it, as Scholem insists, deepening the standard theological reading into a religious nihilism, a sign of the 'enormous' residual force of mystical impulses?[55] Or is it rather, as Benjamin increasingly came to think, the opposite: the death-mask of tradition? Or is it, as Brecht suggests, a secret Bolshevism?[56] The key lies in the way in which we understand the relationship between the temporalization of history and literary form in Kafka's work.

Benjamin's reflections on Kafka were part and parcel of his exchanges with Scholem on the Messianic philosophy of history from their very beginning: his reading of *The Trial* while in bed with jaundice in November 1927. Initially at least, Benjamin seems to have been interested in a reading of Kafka's work within the terms of Scholem's nihilistic interpretation of the Jewish Messianic tradition, which he had already drawn upon in *The Origin of German Tragic Drama*. This interpretation has three main parts: (1) the impossibility of redemption within historical time (as opposed to the fulfilment of history as a whole in Messianic time); (2) the constitutive status of the standpoint of redemption for the philosophy of history, as its primary category of totalization; (3) the consequent thesis of the 'nothingness of revelation' and the implied definition of historical time as infinite deferment (deferment of redemption).[57] Not surprisingly, Scholem encouraged Benjamin in this reading, arguing in the summer of 1931 that the possibility of divine judgement is 'the sole subject of Kafka's production'; that Kafka's work expresses a world in which 'redemption cannot be anticipated'; and most specifically of all, that it represents 'the moral reflection . . . of a halakhist who attempted a *linguistic* paraphrase of a divine judgement'. He concludes: 'the light of revelation never burned as unmercifully as it does here. This is the theological secret of perfect prose.' Scholem insists that Kafka has 'no position of any sort' in the continuum of German literature. It is to the history of Jewish literature that he belongs.[58]

Taking its cue from this reference to the Halakah (passages of law in the *Talmud*), Benjamin's 1934 essay nonetheless explicitly resists the exclusivity of Scholem's Judaic reading, acknowledging only that Kafka's prose pieces do not belong 'entirely in the tradition of Western prose forms'. Rather, he suggests, they have 'a similar relation to doctrine as the Haggadah [passages of lore, anecdote or parable in the *Talmud*] does to the Halakah'; although, as we have seen, crucially, in this case the doctrine does not exist. Kafka's reflections are thus not the reflections of a halakhist. Their indeterminacy does not derive from the unbridgeable gap between the divinity of law and its human interpretation. They are those of a haggadhist, seeking to fill the gap created by the loss of law (Halakah), seeking to *convert Haggadah into Halakah*. Kafka makes a 'grandiose attempt to convert poetry into doctrine, to turn it into a parable and restore to it that stability and unpretentiousness which, in the face of reason, seemed to him to be the only appropriate thing for it'. But he fails. Indeed, he was bound to fail, and he knew it. Failure was built into the structure of his project from the very beginning. For Benjamin, it was *this* that was the secret of the success of his prose.[59]

Whereas Scholem finds in Kafka's linguistic world an 'affinity to the language of the last judgement . . . the prosaic in its most canonical form',[60] Benjamin finds a matter-of-factness derived, not from theology, but from Kafka's peculiar projection of history. The 'prehistoric' force of Kafka's world presents everything, even the unknown, as always already known. As a result, ignorance takes on the form of forgetting. Benjamin quotes Willy Haas on *The Trial*: ' "The object of the trial . . . indeed, the real hero of this incredible book is forgetting, whose main characteristic is the forgetting of itself." ' He continues: 'What has been forgotten . . . is never something purely individual. Everything forgotten of the prehistoric world, forms countless, uncertain, changing compounds, yielding a constant flow of new, strange products. Oblivion is the container from which the inexhaustible intermediate world in Kafka's stories presses toward the light. . . . Forgetting always involves the best, for it involves the possibility of redemption.'[61]

Where Scholem finds judgement, Benjamin sees memory, a memory from which K. is forever estranged: 'Whenever figures in the novels have anything to say to K., no matter how important or surprising it may be, they do so casually and with the implication that he must really have known it all along. It is as though nothing new was being imparted, as though the hero was just being subtly invited to recall to mind something that he had forgotten.'[62] Yet to K., it remains unfathomable. Hence that peculiar combination of everydayness and metaphysical perplexity and anxiety that Kafka's linguistic world evokes: not the existentialist everyday, defence against an anxiety that nonetheless keeps breaking through, but perplexity and anxiety at the mundane way in which the incomprehensible presents itself *as* everyday, as something that is actually always already known. (Compare Benjamin's reading of Surrealism, outlined above.) Redemption is possible, but it is never present as a *concrete* possibility. Indeed, it is the very concreteness of Kafka's world that banishes it to the horizon. ('The absolutely concrete can never be fulfilled at all'.[63]) Hence the guilt and the shame: K.'s shame at having forgotten, indeed, at not even remembering what it is that he has forgotten, even after he has been reminded of it. This is not just a 'theological' but a profoundly *historical* experience. Or rather, it is a profound intimation of a crisis of historical experience that Benjamin aims to redeem *as* historical experience, through interpretation.

Benjamin rejects Scholem's appropriation of Kafka for the Jewish mystical tradition, but he does not thereby neglect the Jewish element in his work. Instead, he historicizes it. Scholem makes the connection through the doctrine of law, finding in Kafka an affirmation of his own nihilistic Messianism. His interpretation thus remains internal to doctrinal issues. Benjamin, on the other hand, sticking closer to the spirit of Scholem's work on the Kabbalah than Scholem himself, views Kafka from the standpoint of tradition (Kabbalah). His interpretation is historical – however theological the content of the tradition with which he is dealing. Faced with Scholem's polarization of literary history into the 'German' and the 'Jewish', Benjamin refuses the option, incorporating both as elements within a third form: 'In his depth Kafka touches the ground which neither "mythical divination" nor "existential theology" supplied him with. It is the core of folk tradition, the German as well as the Jewish.' His stories about legends are 'dialectical fairy tales'. They take the traditional form of tales about individuals' victories over the forces of myth and give each a new twist, reworking the legend in the light of a new experience of historical time.[64] 'A dialectical fairy scene [*Feen*]' was, of course, Benjamin's original (1927) subtitle for his essay on the arcades.[65] At this point, he would thus seem to be identifying with Kafka's historical projection, if not with his specific literary strategy (the story). Yet it was just this attempt to mediate the contradiction of Kafka's literary form (the idea of parables without doctrine) via the idea of the folk tradition (*Volkstums*) that was soon to lead him to view his own essay as an example of 'apologetics': the affirmation of a regressive aesthetic resolution to a crisis of historical representation.[66]

It is a distinctive feature of both Scholem's and Benjamin's Kafka interpretations that they offer no perspective on the future within historical time, except, in Benjamin's case, as a negation of a form of futurity now judged definitely past (tradition): 'The gate to justice is learning. And yet Kafka does not dare attach to this learning the promises which tradition has attached to the study of the Torah. His assistants are sextons who have lost their house of prayer, his students are pupils who have lost the Holy Writ. Now there is nothing to support them on their "untrammeled happy journey".'[67] The present is defined not just by its negation of the past, but by its negation of the past form of historical temporalization (tradition). However, since this negation is still registered within that form (Kafka as the modern master of the German-Jewish folk tradition), there is no future outside the mere extrapolation of this negative present; no new temporalization. Even Brecht, who characteristically stressed the 'visionary' side of Kafka's work, in conflict with its 'parabolic elements', dubbed his precision 'the precision of an imprecise man, a dreamer', who 'saw what was coming without seeing what *is*'. On this reading, Kafka offers us a future, but only as horror, and only in a prophetic manner; not in the concrete form of a new futurity. The Hence what Brecht saw as the political danger of his work: the opening it creates for an appeal to a leader to take responsibility for the ills of the world it depicts – not in the form of a heroic fascist 'solution', but as a need for someone to blame.[68] Yet if Benjamin's 1934 Kafka essay might be said to inhabit the world it depicts, by actively mimicking its form,[69] such mimetic identification was quickly transformed into the enabling condition of a more stringent critique. This process can be traced at two levels: first, in Benjamin's reflections on the fate of the story as a genre; and second, in his continuing correspondence with Scholem about Kafka.

Both 'The Storyteller' and 'The Work of Art' essays articulate their present (the present of interwar Europe), culturally, as 'a birth-time and a period of transition to a new era',[70] defined, on the one hand, by 'a tremendous shattering of tradition' and, on the other, by the prospect for a 'renewal of mankind'.[71] It was the perspective on this renewal opened up by his analysis of film that allowed Benjamin to take up once again the avant-garde stance of 'One-Way Street' and the Surrealism essay and to explore its consequences for literary form. His theme is the waning of 'communicable experience' and the 'new beauty' thereby imported to what is vanishing. (As in the Kafka essay, beauty is associated with the archaic.) However, rather than working within the simple sociological dualism of modernity and tradition, Benjamin offers a triadic schema within which the original unity of the epic is progressively broken up as its constituent elements appear separately in the story and the novel, respectively. Those elements associated with the story crystallize into a discrete form long before the emergence of the novel, but once it evolves the novel increasingly becomes the dominant form as the social basis of storytelling is first eroded and then collapses. Finally, however, the novel itself comes under threat as the intensification of the developmental tendencies that were the basis of its prior existence erode it in turn.

The art of the story belongs to an oral tradition grounded in the common experiences of specific communities of listeners, even when at a certain point in its development it begins to appear in written form. The novel on the other hand is essentially a written form, dependent on the private consumption of the book. The new forms of collective experience generated by the technologies of industrial work and modern warfare and 'the boundless maze of indirect relationships, complex mutual dependencies and compartmentations' of the city,[72] however, find their adequate expression only in film, and those literary forms carried along in its wake: journalism, advertisements, the pamphlet. (Film, one might say, is the secret truth of Brecht's epic theatre.) 'So long as the movie-makers' capital sets the fashion', however, film can only be 'revolutionary' in its 'criticism of traditional concepts of art'. Its potential for the expression of the possibilities inherent in the new forms of collective experience will remain untapped. It is this potential that Benjamin seeks to liberate as 'historical experience'.[73]

The implications of this analysis of the fate of the story for Benjamin's reading of Kafka are twofold. In the first place, the attempt to mediate the contradiction within Kafka's writings between their contemporary and their theological elements, via the idea of 'tradition without doctrine' (the Jewish and German folk traditions of the fairy tale and the story), breaks down. The story is as 'archaic', as lost to history, as the doctrine of the mystical tradition, the loss of which it is called upon to articulate. Kafka's story-form thus shifts from being seen as a novel aesthetic resolution to the representation of a historical contradiction, to a mystifying symptom of the contradiction itself.[74] It is not just Kafka's world that is archaic, but his writing as well: hence its novelty. Second and consequently, the historical aspect of Kafka's failure comes more clearly into view. Kafka 'surrendered' to tradition at a time when tradition had already 'fallen ill'. Wisdom, the epic side of truth, truth as a property of tradition, or as Benjamin calls it in his letter of 1938, 'truth in its aggadic consistency', has already been lost. However, and this is Kafka's originality, rather than renouncing the transmissibility of truth and holding onto its remaining, now esoteric core, Kafka 'sacrificed truth for the sake of clinging to transmissibility, to its aggadic element', to the *form* of tradition. His stories have the form of parables, but 'they *had* to become *more* than parables' (against Kafka's will), since there was no doctrine for them to convey. As a result, 'they do not modestly lie at the feet of doctrine, as aggadah lies at the feet of Halakah', as Benjamin's initial formulation might be taken to suggest. Rather, 'when they have crouched down, they unexpectedly raise a mighty paw against it'. They simultaneously mourn and *criticize* the law by hanging on, hopelessly, to the hope of its transmissibility. This is the positive, critical side of Kafka's failure to convert poetry into doctrine. The side from which it makes sense for Benjamin to say that, once Kafka was certain of eventual failure, 'everything worked out for him en route as in a dream'. It is in his failure that the deeper meaning of his work resides – as a demonstration of the hopelessness of the attempt to revive the form of tradition for the understanding of the modern world.[75]

Scholem's reassertion of his version of the theological reading, against Benjamin's essay, thus served as much to sharpen the difference between them as it did to enrich Benjamin's sense of Kafka's closeness to the Jewish tradition, just as his conversations with Brecht provided him with an alternative 'prophetic' reading against which to test his interpretation.[76] For it was precisely by deepening his appreciation of Kafka's closeness to the Jewish mystical tradition that Benjamin came to distance himself from his standpoint. This process reaches its apogee in early 1939, when Benjamin further radicalized his reading to encompass the humour in Kafka's writing, explicitly connecting up its clowning to its theological dimension. 'The key to Kafka's work', he now suggests, 'is likely to fall into the hands of the person who *is able to extract the comic aspects from Jewish theology*. Has there been such a man? Or,' he taunts Scholem, 'would you be man enough to be that man?' The comedy of Jewish theology, one cannot help but think, lies here in its utter inability to comprehend the modern world in a form through which it is possible to live (that is, to act) within it. 'What is actually and in a very precise sense *folly* in Kafka is that this, the most recent of experiential worlds, was conveyed to him precisely by the mystical tradition.' One is reminded of the final stanzas of Scholem's own didactic poem on *The Trial* (addressed to God), that was printed along with the sections of Benjamin's essay that appeared in the *Judische Rundschau* in late 1934, turned now by Benjamin's new interpretation of Kafka against their author:

Who is the accused here?
The creature or yourself?
If anyone should ask you
You would sink into silence.

Can such a question be raised?
Is the answer definite?
Oh, we must live all the same
Until your court examines us.

Benjamin's response at the time was that Kafka's work indicates 'a state of the world in which such questions no longer have a place, because their answers, far from being instructive, make the questions superfluous'. Now, he might have added that only clowns keep on asking them. The experience of the present in terms of its own, new and radically abstract form of historical time-consciousness ('modernity') poses questions enough of its own.[77]

Having seemingly left Scholem, along with Kafka, behind, it is to historiography rather than literary or cultural theory in any narrow sense that Benjamin turns to pursue his reflections on the present possibilities for a revolutionary experience of history. These grow directly out of his considerations on the history of literary forms in 'The Storyteller'. What gives this analysis its distinctiveness is the historiographic dimension it opens up by its treatment of narrative genres as embodiments of different kinds of memory. Historiography, Benjamin suggests, 'constitutes the creative indifference of the various epic forms'. 'Memory is the epic faculty *par excellence*. Only by virtue of a comprehensive memory can epic writing absorb the course of events on the one hand and, with the passing of these, make its peace with the power of death on the other.' 'Memory creates the chain of tradition.' The development of literary forms thus corresponds to a series of different historiographic forms, different forms of memory, different *temporalizations of history*. More particularly, Benjamin distinguishes between the unitary and 'perpetuating' remembrance (*Eingedenken*) of the novelist and the multiple 'short-lived' reminiscences (*Gedachtnis*) of the storyteller: forms of memory that were originally united in the epic.[78] Yet neither can provide the basis for a contemporary historiography.

The story is dying out. It had already begun to 'recede into the archaic' at the time of the appearance of the novel. It is no longer a 'present force', and if it persists, it nonetheless comes to us from another world, another time, in which we no longer live (hence, its beauty). To adopt it as a historiographic form would be pure nostalgia. At the same time, the novel is in crisis. It is being replaced by a new form of communication, 'information', the value of which derives from an economy of abbreviation and 'does not survive the moment in which it was new'.[79] In fact, Benjamin would soon argue, information is itself already being replaced by the experience of 'shock' ('the price for which the sensation of the modern age may be had: the disintegration of the aura in the experience of shock'). Consciousness shields the self from such shocks by registering them without retaining them, protecting the organism against over-stimulation by isolating them from memory. Their memory thus becomes unconscious. At the same time, in a potentially redemptive move, shock becomes the formal principle of perception in the film; the camera, the instrument of an 'unconscious optics'.[80]

The totalizing standpoint of the novel was always problematic, historiographically (as Lukács demonstrated in the thesis of its 'transcendental homelessness'[81]), since it is based on an individual, biographical model of closure. It soon begins to fracture once the lives of individuals become increasingly dependent on the mediations of impersonal social forms, the logics of which remain opaque. (This is the fundamental social experience underlying Kafka's work, for example.) Yet the reconstitution of the original unity of the epic (the reconstitution of history as the unity of the one and the many narratives) can be no more than a forlorn hope so long as no basis can be found for it within the new forms of social experience themselves. What is possible, though, is the remembrance (*Eingedenken*) of such a unity – the remembrance of the unity of remembrance and reminiscence (*Gedachtnis*) – as the standpoint from which to begin to think the possibility of such a history. The historiographic hope of the epic is thus preserved, renewed, by Benjamin in his own novelistic narrative of its evolving forms ('The Storyteller'). What it requires for its realization is a historiographic equivalent to the film.[82]

MODERNITY AND TRADITION (II): HISTORICISM'S SLEEP, BAUDELAIRE'S DREAM

The hero is the true subject of modernity. . . . it takes a heroic constitution to live the modern. . . . With [this] belief, Balzac and Baudelaire are in opposition to Romanticism.
(Benjamin, 'The Paris of the Second Empire in Baudelaire', 1938[83])

If 'memory creates the chain of tradition' and historiography is 'the record kept by memory', the shattering of the chain, the breakdown of memory, will set off a historiographic crisis. As Kafka saw, modernity is a form of forgetting. 'Historicism' responds to this crisis, to the amnestic temporality of modernity, with the twin ideas of historiography as a *science* and history as *progress*: historiography as the science of progress. In the process, it trades remembrance for the re-establishment of continuity between past and future, in a newly abstract, merely chronological form.[84] Elsewhere, however, in Baudelaire, we find a quite different response to this crisis: an explicit affirmation of the temporality of modernity – 'the ephemeral, the fugitive, the contingent' – in the desire 'to extract from fashion whatever element it may contain of poetry within history, to *distil the eternal from the transitory*'.[85] Modernism, as the affirmative cultural self-consciousness of the abstract temporality of modernity, starts here. Yet it concludes, in Baudelaire, only in the idea of a new classicism, as modern poetry seeks its place in the warehouse of cultural treasures, where 'the pathological aspect of the notion of "culture" ' is enthroned, in the alleged independence of its entities from the production process in which they survive.[86] In the form taken by its 'distillation' of the eternal, Baudelaire's modernism rejoins the indifferent, contemplative temporality of historicism as 'heritage'. What it leaves behind, however, apart from the shell of contingency, is an aspiration, a desire, to embrace modernity as a *living* form, and a set of motifs to guide its comprehension, the significance of which transcend the limitations of the idea of modernism within which they appear. It is these elements, reinterpreted from the standpoint of the present (the present of the 1930s) on the basis of a combination of Nietzschean and Marxist themes, that provided Benjamin with the foothold he needed within 'modernity' to relaunch historiography as remembrance (*Eingedenken*). In the process, his understanding of the temporal possibilities of modernity was transformed.[87]

Baudelaire's importance for Benjamin is bound up, inextricably, with both his historical location at the outset of the culture of modernity (modernism) and his choice of the lyric as his main literary medium. Together, they determine both the force of the shock of 'the new' upon his work and its intimate, almost incestuous, relation to the ancient or classical. It was the subsequent history of modernism (to which Art Nouveau is the key) that allowed Benjamin to read in Baudelaire its original form; and it was the very incompatibility between what Baudelaire lived through (*Erlebnis*) and the form in which he chose to express it (the lyric) that is seen to have made it possible for him to give it 'the weight of an experience (*Erfahrung*)'.[88] Just as it was the consistency with which Kafka was true to his historico-philosophical 'failure' that was taken to account for the peculiar success of his work, at the same time as it provided the vantage point for its critique, so with Baudelaire it is the single-mindedness and naivety with which he pursues a classical concept of the eternal, within the modern, that lays bare the dynamics of modernity in its 'original' state. Like Kafka's, Baudelaire's lesson was mainly negative. But unlike Kafka's, it contained the seeds of a different futurity. In rescuing Baudelaire's sense of the future from the limits of his conception, Benjamin prepares the ground for the elaboration of a distinctively 'modern' futurity of his own.

For Benjamin, unlike what has become the mainstream of the sociological tradition, 'modernity' is no mere name for a chunk of historical time and the social forms that happen to have occupied it. Rather, it designates a temporal structure of experience, a part of a phenomenology of historical consciousness, which finds its preliminary description in Baudelaire, but which is by no means adequately thought there.[89] It is thus, but only thus, and by implication, that it may be predicated of societies or social forms characterized by practices which give rise to such temporal experiences. Foremost among such practices for Benjamin were warfare in the age of technology, mechanized industrial labour, the jostling of the crowd in the great cities, gambling, run-away inflation, and film.[90] At the heart of his analysis of the temporality of these practices lies the fetish character of the commodity-form, planned centre-piece of the *Passagen-Werk*.[91] In the wake of the appearance for the first time in palpable form of the 'ever-always-the-same', the newness of the product acquires 'a hitherto unheard of significance', as a stimulus to demand. It is the pure temporal logic of this new social form (the commodity as fetish) that Benjamin detects in fashion (*mode*), and it is its projection as a form of historical consciousness that creates the 'homogeneous empty time' of historicism, in which historical events appear, indifferently, as 'mass-produced articles': each one new, yet, in terms of the character of the time it occupies and hence its relation to the present, 'ever-always-the-same'. In this process, the historiographic concept of 'the modern' is radically transformed. For whereas it used to be opposed to a conception of antiquity as a stable historical referent, now 'the centuries between the present moment and that which has just been lived . . . tirelessly constitute "antiquity" ' anew in the most recent past. 'Modernity' *antiquates* to a hitherto unheard of extent. The modern and the new become synonymous. Furthermore, as a result of this accelerating temporal rhythm, registered in Baudelaire's poetry, where it is actively constructed on the basis of his identification with the modern as the site of the eternal (modern*ism*), the new now appears *as* the ever-always-the-same, 'the ever-always-the-same within the new'. Hence the definition of fashion ('the eternal recurrence of the new' – a ritual, mythic repetition), its ultimate expression as death ('the only one radical novelty, and that is always the same'), and Benjamin's projected allegorical reading of modernity as Hell.[92]

What is of most interest in this network of ideas from the

standpoint of the philosophy of history is the equation it establishes between novelty and eternity. Baudelaire confronts this emergent identity with 'heroic effort', in the attempt to snatch the new away from the ever-same, in the name of the eternal; Nietzsche faces it with 'heroic composure', in the recognition that there never will be anything new; with Blanqui (in the late cosmological work that so fascinated Benjamin) 'resignation prevails'.[93] Yet Benjamin himself adopts none of these attitudes, since for him, this is not the temporal structure of history *per se*, but merely the 'hell' of a consciousness of time out of which he is seeking to escape, into a redeemed future. What he is looking for is a fissure in its temporal structure through which to break it open onto a new form of historical experience. He finds it in the instantaneous temporality of the 'now', which marks out the 'exact repetition' of the new as the ever-same.[94] For in the experience of the repetitive succession of identical instants, abstractly projected onto history as the blank chronologism of historicism's 'homogeneous empty time', we are returned, structurally, to the cosmological time of nature as an 'eternal and total passing away' – that very temporality the experience of which Benjamin had earlier declared 'Messianic' and identified with happiness.[95] The very *indifference* of the new as the ever-always-the-same that is the basis for the quantification of time in historicism becomes, for Benjamin, the ground for a quite different, *qualitative* experience of the 'now' as a historical present. Eternal recurrence, he notes, is 'an attempt to link the two antinomic principles of happiness with one another: namely that of eternity and that of the yet once again'. It 'conjures out of the wretchedness of time the speculative idea (or the phantasmagoria) of happiness'.[96] Benjamin aims to appropriate this twofold structure for a concrete experience of history. Elements of the time consciousness of modernism and historicism are to be refigured to produce a new quasi-Messianic experience of historical time.

The instantaneity of the 'now', experienced for the first time within modernity as a form of *historical* (rather than merely natural) temporality, is seen to contain within its monadic structure the possibility of an experience of eternity, a Messianic 'cessation of happening', combined with a 'recurrence', a 'yet once again', which can only be understood as a new form of remembrance (*Eingedenken*). In the time of this 'now', nature and history are one, as eternal. The past will be gathered up within the present, in the perspective of redemption, as an explosive historical 'experience' (*Erfahrung*). In opposition to the regressive, psychologically defensive, historicist experience of the temporal order of modernity, whereby an incident is assigned a precise point in time 'at the cost of the integrity of its contents', in order to transform it into 'a moment that has been lived (*Erlebnis*)'[97] – intellectually appropriating it as a merely quantitative relation, in compensation for the failure to establish any living relationship to it – we are offered a historico-metaphysical experience of the same temporal order: 'now-being' (*Jetztsein*).[98] But in what sense is this metaphysical experience 'historical' in its concrete content, rather than just its origin – as opposed to, for example, 'religious' or merely mystical? And what is its active, political dimension?

It is at this point that Benjamin's thought needs to differentiate itself most decisively from the Surrealist and Proustian models from which it draws so much inspiration. For both have an involuntary character that places them, subjectively, in the domain of *chance*. Their compelling force depends upon it. Yet as Benjamin shows in his discussion of gambling as the transformation of time into a 'narcotic', to embrace chance is to surrender to the temporality of modernity as *forgetting*: intellectual mastery through practical submission.[99] This is no basis for historiography as an enabling remembrance. But there is a problem here, since Benjamin acknowledges that experience (*Erfahrung*) is 'a matter of tradition, in collective as well as private life'. It is 'less the product of facts firmly anchored in [the individual] memory than of a convergence in memory of accumulated and *frequently unconscious* data'.[100] How are such data to be retrieved, if not through the experimental procedure of systematic chance? It was for allegedly failing to meet this challenge that Adorno famously accused Benjamin's work of being stranded at the 'crossroads of magic and positivism': a Surrealist philosophy whose dialectic lacks mediation, a 'blind processing of material', in which thought 'delivers itself over to luck and the risk of betting on experience and striking something essential'.[101]

JETZTZEIT: THE TIME OF HISTORY, THE TIME OF TRUTH

How long
Do works endure? As long
As they are not completed.
  (Bertolt Brecht, 'About the Way to Construct Enduring Works'[102])

Now-time receives a series of more or less apocalyptic descriptions in Benjamin's late work. It is 'the now of a specific recognizability [*bestimmten Erkenbarkeit*]' in which 'truth is loaded to the bursting-point with time'. It is 'a present which is not a transition, but in which time stands still and has come to a stop'; 'a Messianic cessation of happening' providing 'a revolutionary chance in the fight for the oppressed'. It is the 'moment of awakening' which 'rescues' history for the present, 'ignites the explosives that lie in the past', and 'blasts the epoch' out of the reified continuity of homogeneous time. It is a 'flash of lightning'. In it, the past is said to 'attain a higher degree of actuality than in the moment of its existence'. It 'coincides' with the birth of 'authentic historical time [*echten historischen Zeit*], the time of truth'. It is the site of the structure of which history is the subject.[103]

A flash of lightning, an awakening, a cessation of happening, a recognition. . . . The images cohere in the climax of a narrative, cut off, frozen, like the final frame of a film, on the threshold of a new beginning. But what of the conceptual structure of this process, this 'revolutionary' experience of stasis? What *kind of time* are we talking about here, exactly? Everything depends on how we understand the doubling of the 'now' as the point of intersection of two radically different forms of time, the Messianic and the immanently historical, as it opens up 'modernity' to the promise of fulfilment. Now-time is neither wholly inside nor wholly outside of history, but faces both ways at once. It is this combination of apparently contradictory temporal structures that gives Benjamin's conception both its force and its complexity. It is best approached by way of negation.[104]

In the first place, in terms of the form of its presence, now-time is neither the time of the blankly identical Aristotelian or cosmological instant, taken by historicism as the ontological ground of its chronologies (and interpreted by Heidegger as the basis of the 'ordinary conception of time'); nor, less still, is it the time of the extended, durational, phenomenological present described by Husserl, of which the idea of modernity is a historical form.[105] Rather, it aspires to condense into the punctual, one-dimensional space of the former, not just a longitudinal historical content, but the presence of history as a *whole*, refracted through the prism of the historical present. Neither instant nor present, Benjamin's now-time historicizes the structure of instantaneity, to produce it as interruption, simultaneously contracting the present into the stasis of its point-like source and expanding its historical content to infinity, in an 'enormous abridgement' of 'the entire history of humanity'.[106] Exploiting the dual, dialectical character of the present, as both durational extension and point-like source, it performs a twofold mediation: of nature (instant) with history (present), and of this historical present ('modernity') with history as a whole (eternity). Neither instant nor present, Benjamin's now-time is 'the present *as* now-time [*der Gegenwart* als *der "Jetztzeit"*]'. It is always a historically specific now.[107] But how can this work, if history is not yet over, if the future has yet to occur? How can history present itself as a whole, in the time of the 'now', outside the confines of the ultimately *time-denying* eternal present of Hegelianism?[108]

The trick lies in the monadic structure of the dialectical image, productive object of now-time. For rather than constructing a linear unidirectional series of successive instants (Aristotle's 'before/now *or* then/after'), or a three-dimensional temporal spectrum (Husserl's 'past/present/future'), Benjamin's dialectical images are constellations of the 'then' and the 'now', which, in the hermetic enclosure of their internal relations, mirror the structure of history as a whole, viewed from the standpoint of its end.[109] As such, they are not so much allegorical in their semantic structure as of the nature of theological symbols: 'the true conception of historical time is wholly based on the *image* of redemption'.[110] Each image, in its totalized if temporary self-sufficiency, reflects the structure of the yet-to-be-completed whole; each image thus carries within it the *perspective* of redemption.

Redemption itself, in the strict, absolute or Messianic sense, is not at stake. In this, Benjamin's later work remains steadfastly at one with his earlier writings, and with Scholem's nihilistic understanding of the Messianic idea. There is no redemption *within* historical time, only the redemption *of* history, as a whole.[111] The past may carry with it 'a temporal index by which it is *referred to* redemption', in the sense that 'only a redeemed mankind receives the fullness of its past'[112] – the very idea of the past as the 'totality' of what has been, projects a historical closure – but this does not make redemption itself a realizable *practical* goal. Indeed, quite the reverse, it retains it outside of history. Nor, it would seem, for Benjamin, is its truth a graspable cognitive goal, since 'an emphatic refusal of the concept of "timeless truth" ' is now in order.[113] This is the main difference between this network of ideas and the framework of *The Origin of German Tragic Drama*: ideas are no longer to be understood as 'timeless constellations'.[114] But nor is truth to be conceived as 'just a temporal function of knowledge' either. Rather, more difficultly, it is in some way 'bound to a time kernel [*Zeitkern*]' planted in history.[115] It is this 'time kernel' of truth that is exposed, momentarily, in now-time: at once complete within the structure of the now, yet radically incomplete in its immediate passing (its becoming past): ' "In relation to the history of organic life on earth . . . the history of civilized humanity would fill one-fifth of the last second of the last hour [of a twenty-four hour day]." Now-time . . . as a model of the Messianic . . . coincides exactly with the stature which the history of humanity has in the universe.'[116] It is this paradoxical structure of completeness/incompleteness that is the key to its political effect.

Cognitively, dialectical images work metonymically, with the part ('the now of a specific recognizability') imaging the whole (history as a redemptive whole). Politically, however, they work the other way around, generating their allegedly explosive practical charge from the contradiction between the transience or incompleteness of the historical present in terms of which they are constructed and the perspective of completion inherent in their metonymic structure. Adorno is correct to say that they lack mediation, if by this he means the kind of immanent *conceptual* mediation at stake in the structure of Hegelian logic. He is wrong, however, to suggest that they lack mediation altogether; wrong to reduce the concept of mediation to a narrowly Hegelian form. (After all, Hegel's logic is dependent upon precisely that 'eternal present' that would obliterate the past as past, and the future as the yet-to-be-determined.) There *is* mediation in the experience of the dialectical image: a mediation between the lived historical present of the 'now' and a specific past, via the perspective of history as a redemptive whole. But, as Buck-Morss has argued, it has more of the character of a switch between circuits (triggered, I would argue, by the metonymic structure of the image) than the production of a shared conceptual space.[117] The charge of arbitrariness in the choice of images is rebutted by their specific, *philosophically constructed*, historical contents. (Only the material in the *Passagen-Werk* can 'redeem' the philosophical argumentation which summarizes its methodological form. Unlike dialectical images themselves, the 'philosophy' here is not self-sufficient.) Buck-Morss is misleading, however, and undermines her own position, when she suggests that it is 'political action', rather than the experience of the image, that is the link between the two temporal registers. For political action (or at least, the *impulse* to such action) is the supposed effect, not the medium, of the experience. It derives from that very partiality of the Messianic presence that might otherwise seem to problematize the metaphysics of Benjamin's conception.

The political argument implicit in Benjamin's presentation of now-time is certainly an ambitious one (too ambitious, one might think), but it depends upon the *impossibility*, not the imminence, of a willed redemption. For only if the Messianic remains exterior to history can it provide the perspective of a completed whole (without the pre-determination of a teleological end) from which the present may appear in its essential transience, as radically incomplete. It is for this reason that Benjamin does not write of now-time as Messianic *per se*, but only as a 'model' (*Modell*) of the Messianic, 'shot through' with 'chips' (*Splitter*) of Messianic time, site of a *'weak'* (*schwache*) Messianic power. Redemption, the reception of the fullness of the past, does not come until Judgement Day: the end of time.[118] For all its suspension of immanent temporal succession, 'the present as now-time' is ultimately as transient, and hence as incomplete, as any other present. (Indeed, at one point, Benjamin even suggests that what is rescued there is already, in the next moment, 'irretrievably' lost.[119]) When he writes famously that 'every image of the past that is not recognized by the present as one of its own concerns threatens to disappear irretrievably',[120] Benjamin is not arguing for some kind of total recall. This is a myth of historicism: the recovery of the past 'the way it really was'. He is pointing to a politics of memory for which the character of the present, and hence the future, is determined by its relations to a series of specific pasts ('enslaved ancestors', for example, as opposed to triumphs of nation).[121] But this does not mean that the selection of pasts is a simple matter of 'choice'. It is governed by a strict *cognitive* criterion: the uncovering of what is 'truly new' in the present. It is for this reason that 'now-being' is to be understood as a form of avant-garde experience.

Benjamin's philosophy of history is a critique of the historicist concept of progress, but it is no historical nihilism. Its dialectical critique cannot but bring forth another, 'truer' notion of a progress that 'does not reside in the continuity of temporal succession, but rather in its moments of interference: where the truly new first makes itself felt, as sober as the dawn'.[122] When remembrance and futurity come together in the time of the now, 'the truly new makes itself felt'. It is because of the momentary character of this experience that it is an angel, not the Messiah, who watches over Benjamin's later work.[123]

OF ANGELS AND AVANT-GARDES: REMEMBERING THE FUTURE?

As strange as it may seem, the expression of the future does not appear to be situated on the same level of the human mind as the expression of the present and the past.

   (Jean-Richard Bloch, 'Language, Utilitarian and Poetic'[124])

Benjamin's angel of history (Klee's 'Angelus Novus') has been the object of intense biographical and philological scrutiny. I shall not add to it here. However, the image is central to Benjamin's politics of time, in so far as that politics is constructed at a point of tension between an avant-garde, action- and future-oriented impulse (a 'revolutionary' experience of the past that will 'blast open the continuum of history'), and an angelic, backward-looking, memorializing cognitivism of redemptive remembrance (*Eingedenken*). The intention is certainly, as Buck-Morss says, that 'theological illumination that redeems past history, and political education that condemns it' be 'one and the same endeavour'.[125] But do the two things really fit so neatly together? And what of the political not as a form of judgement but as 'the philosophical question of *action*'?[126] How does the figure of the angel fit into Benjamin's rethinking of the temporality of the avant-garde?

Two markers suggest themselves as guides: Schlegel's well-known aphorism to the effect that the historian is 'a prophet looking backwards',[127] and Benjamin's central metaphor for the experience of now-time as a form of historical consciousness, the metaphor of awakening. Condensed into the interplay of these images is the peculiar structure of what Habermas calls Benjamin's 'conservative-revolutionary understanding of criticism'.[128] The connection to Schlegel is a deep one, going back to Benjamin's 1919 dissertation on 'The Concept of Art Criticism in German Romanticism'.[129] In the *Passagen-Werk* the image of the historian-prophet crops up in another context, in a description of the dialectical image as a 'lightning flash', but the philosophical meaning is the same. Benjamin refers there to 'the metaphoric passage from the introduction to Jochmann on the prophet's gaze, which catches fire from the summits of the past'.[130] Is Benjamin's 'angel of history' such a backward-looking prophet?

Well, he is certainly 'turned towards the past', and he sees it differently from us: 'Where we perceive a chain of events, he sees one single catastrophe which keeps piling wreckage upon wreckage and hurls it in front of his feet.' But that is the end of the similarities. There is no futurity, no prophecy here, because there is no connection between the divine world from which the angel comes and the profane world of the living, prior to the appearance of the Messiah. The angel *would like* to be the Messiah, he 'would like to stay, awaken the dead, and make whole what has been smashed'. But the angel is not the Messiah. In the profane historical world over which he watches, the angel is impotent. The storm blowing from paradise 'has got caught in his wings with such violence that the angel can no longer close them'. He is propelled backwards, 'irresistibly', into a future from which history looks no different than before: 'the pile of debris before him grows skyward'.[131]

Commentators have often noted the unremitting gloom of this picture and connected it to events at the time of the composition of the piece; specifically, the effect on German communists of the Hitler-Stalin pact. Yet its pessimism is actually not historical at all, but Messianic. *All* of history appears as wreckage from the standpoint of redemption. This was, perhaps, a consoling thought at the time, but it derives from a quite different perspective from that of the historian (the backward-looking prophet) who is always a part of a specific historical present and relates through it only to specific pasts. The point of the passage is not to establish the standpoint of the angel as the standpoint of critique, but the reverse. It is a part of the critique of the concept of progress. 'This storm is what *we* call progress.' The homogeneous temporal continuum that underlies the idea of 'progress' mirrors, in a distorted form, the *indifference* to all historical specificity characteristic of the Messianic view. When placed in the context of the *Passagen-Werk*, the passage functions to distinguish the historian from the angel. For the angel, who at each moment sees history up to that point as a single whole, outside of any living relation to the present, it is 'one single catastrophe'. For the historian, on the other hand, who is always inside a specific present, and whose 'now' is thus always the now of a 'specific recognizability', history appears in the light of the idea of actualization, as possibility. Redemption offers a model of completion, and hence an impulse to action. The avant-garde is not that which is most historically advanced because it has the most history behind it (the angel), but that which, in the flash of the dialectical image, disrupts the continuity of 'progress', and is thus able (like the child) to 'discover the new anew'.[132] Benjamin's philosophy of history is a struggle to wrestle the idea of the 'new', essential to any concept of the avant-garde, away from the ideology of 'progress'.

At the centre of this struggle lies the image of awakening, waking up to the possibilities of the present: 'The now of recognizability is the moment of awakening.'[133] It is as awakening that remembrance is linked to both recognition and action: 'The new dialectical method of history writing presents itself as the art of experiencing the present as the waking world to which that dream that we call the past in truth relates'; 'awakening is the exemplary case of remembering'; 'awakening is the dialectical, Copernican revolution of remembrance'; 'utilization of dream elements upon awakening is the canon of dialectics'.[134] The difficulty here is that there would seem to be two rather different, conflicting temporalities at play within the idea of awakening. One, privileging the moment of waking, the borderline between sleep and consciousness, is 'a gradual process' (*ein stufenweiser Prozess*).[135] The other, associated with the physiological notion of shock, is a punctual event, hurling the subject from one world to another. Benjamin clearly wants to combine the two: 'the "Now of Recognizability" in which things put on their true – surrealistic – face', and the subsequent, more gradual process, 'the awakening of a knowledge not yet conscious of what has gone before', as the significance of the 'now' slowly dawns: the dissolution of the surrealist 'mythology' of the image into 'the space of history'.[136] Yet each subverts, as much as it depends upon, the other.

On the one hand, Benjamin needs to break down the threshold that separates the waking from the sleeping (dreaming) world, in order to make the contents of the latter accessible to the former's redemptive-Utopian critique. On the other hand, however, he needs to re-establish the distinction in order to distance the sober dawn of the new historical beginning from the mythological material from which it sets out. Or to put it another way, *Surrealism must be both constructed and denied.*[137] This tension manifests itself most sharply in relation to the question of action. The second, more reflective, hermeneutical moment would appear to dissipate the impulse to action, along with its dissolution of the mythological immediacy of the image. Yet it is a more politically meaningful, because more historical, form of knowledge. How, though, is it related to action? The complex cognitive structure of the dialectical redemption of myth produces an aporia about action that Benjamin hardly registers, let alone solves, leaving it instead to the stream of his imagery to secure the association (much like the end of the Surrealism essay). The act of interpretation is invested with 'all the insignia of praxis' (Habermas),[138] but praxis itself is nowhere to be seen. The 'gestalt of betweenness' (Manninghaus)[139] leaves us suspended between past and future, stuck on the threshold of a 'science of thresholds' that enacts as much as it theorizes its object. Revolutionary political action is evoked, but it is never actually thought.

The reason for this, according to Habermas, stems from the temporal structure of redemptive or 'rescuing' (as opposed to ideology) critique, since it projects a 'leap' into the future on the basis of a leap into the past.[140] At one level, as we have seen, this is misleading. The future is no more severed from the present than the past. The interruption of the continuity of history does not take us 'backwards', but outside of history altogether; outside, on the basis of a specific recognition from within. In a deeper sense, though, Habermas is right: the temporality of now-time and the temporality of praxis are incommensurable. However, this is not because now-time has no futurity, but rather, if anything, because it has too much. In 'blasting' us out of the extended durational present into the (ec)static time of the now, where the future is fixed, fulfilled, in the form of the image, we lose touch with the real concrete past as it lives in the present – that 'absolutely concrete' which 'can never be fulfilled at all'.

Yet this is perhaps less destructive for the prospects of Benjamin's project than Habermas's criticism suggests. For while the self-contained stasis of now-time may cut it off from politics, severing the kind of immanent relation to practice demanded by the Hegelian tradition, its very momentariness could be seen to redeem this failure, transforming it into the enabling condition for the re-establishment of a relation to practice (politics), enriched by the after-image of the 'now'. In this sense, it is not the temporality of Benjamin's metaphysics of historical experience that is the problem here, so much as the absence of an account of its subject (the dreaming collective) and, in particular, its conditions and modalities of action. For all its topographic thematization of space, its concern for cities and their architecture (Paris as the capital and the arcade as 'the most significant architecture' of the nineteenth century, for example),[141] there is no historico-philosophical consideration of the spatial side of the 'now', no geo-politics of the European 'here',[142] no sociological breakdown of the 'dreaming collective'. There is a failure to integrate the space/place of the 'now' into the concept of historical experience at anything like the same level of generality as that at which the issue of time is considered. Outside of the merely instrumental, Benjamin's concept of politics contracts into a politics of time.

We have already noted how, by the mid–1920s, the esotericism of Benjamin's early philosophy of language had come into conflict with his newly found political commitments. To begin with, this had less effect on his understanding of politics, as either instrumental or 'pure' means (either the violence of law-keeping or the violence of law-making),[143] than upon his understanding of culture. The idea of the 'supreme reality' of the 'isolated self-contained work' was replaced by an explicit identification with a politically defined cultural avant-garde.[144] But this was not because of a change in the philosophical status of politics, but rather because the avant-garde had become identified as the new cultural carrier of the idea of philosophical experience, suitably transformed. Gradually, however, as the immanently historical stance of his political orientation (Communism) began to erode the idea of a timeless truth, the idea of politics as 'means' was augmented, although never replaced, by a metaphysical conception of 'political experience' as a particular kind of historical experience: a redemptive but nonetheless 'revolutionary' action-generating orientation towards the past. This is the significance of the essay on Surrealism: the redefinition of the political as a mode of temporality or a specific *temporalization of history*. However, the articulation of this concept there remains faltering, and deeply problematic, because of the way it is associated with residual aesthetic impulses that are at once the object of the essay's critique and the means of expression for its apocalytic finale.

Indeed, one might go so far as to suggest that the 'aestheticization of politics' that appears so famously at the end of 'The Work of Art' essay as the sign of Fascism is already present, albeit in an ambivalent form, in Benjamin's account of Surrealism as the site of a suspended transition from 'art' to 'politics'. It was one of the things that attracted Benjamin to Surrealism. This is not to suggest that there are 'Fascist tendencies' in Surrealism, or in Benjamin's work. Rather if, as Buck-Morss has recently claimed, aestheticization is not something that Fascism 'creates', but something it 'manages',[145] then Surrealism may be understood as an attempt at its 'revolutionary' as opposed to its 'reactionary' appropriation. Yet if this is the case, then the conclusion to 'The Work of Art' essay ('Communism responds by politicizing art') is inadequate in at least two ways. On the one hand, on a restricted interpretation, even a politicized 'art' will be too narrow in its institutional form and social dynamics to combat an aestheticized politics. On the other hand, on a broader reading, the idea of a politicized art fails to distinguish Communism from Fascism in the first place. For Fascism is itself a 'politicization of art' in the sense of a particular political management of aesthetics, opposite in orientation, but nonetheless similar in form, to the project to put Surrealism 'in the Service of the Revolution'. Clearly, these parallels disturbed Benjamin, even though he never made them the explicit object of his thought.

If in 1929 he had identified the 'secret cargo' of *l'art pour l'art* as the 'profane illumination' of Surrealism, by 1935 he would come to see its 'consummation' in a Fascist conception of war as the provision of 'the artistic gratification of a sense perception that has been changed by technology', in which 'self-alienation has reached such a degree that . . . [humanity] can experience its own destruction as an aesthetic pleasure of the first order'.[146] Affirmation of Communism no longer seemed enough, as it did in 1931, to counter the danger that Benjamin's writings be 'placed at the disposal of the counter-revolution'. Now, the concepts themselves must be made 'completely useless for the purposes of Fascism'.[147] The beginnings of a positive account of an 'aestheticized', culturally and historically expanded, 'political experience' was stifled at birth in response to the emergence of Fascism, as Benjamin was quick to identify it as the ground of the opposition. His professed conception of the 'political' reverted to its earlier, instrumental form, but the one at stake in his intellectual practice continued to exceed it. It merely went underground.

In this respect, we may read the writings on both Kafka and Baudelaire as a working through of some of these problems at another level. As I have tried to show, what this material is primarily about is the way in which different temporalizations of history are articulated at the level of cultural form. In excavating these projections of history, Benjamin sought clues to the structure of an experience of history that would be 'revolutionary' in the strong (avant-garde) sense of not being dependent upon anything but the very latest cultural forms – a '*historical*-revolutionary' experience, not a 'conservative-revolutionary' one.[148] In each case, he identified a specific combination of 'conservative' and 'revolutionary' motifs. Thus, he came to see that Kafka's 'modernism' was actually the result of his revival of an archaic literary form (the fairy-tale), in the face of the elimination of the social form to which it corresponded (communicable tradition), while in Baudelaire he emphasized the way in which his modernism (his idea of the eternity of the transient) reproduced the classical idea of the self-contained work as independent of the social processes through which it survives. And in each case, there was a lesson. In Kafka, the lesson was a negative one, instructing us as to the futility of seeking a basis for historical understanding in anything but the very latest forms of social experience, however ostensibly they may lack historical self-consciousness, rather than hanging on to the form of tradition, however critically its perspective might appear to illuminate the present from a purely intellectual point of view. In Baudelaire, on the other hand, we snatch the first glimpses of a new modality of historical time ('modernity') amidst the classicism of his conception of poetic form. It was this mode of temporality that Benjamin had already picked up on in Surrealism, as the key to a new form of political experience (Baudelaire as the pre-history of Surrealism – Surrealism as the 'secret cargo' of aestheticism).

These readings enrich the texture of Benjamin's thought immeasurably; not just at the level of cultural-historical content, but more fundamentally, in its evolving philosophical structure. In Benjamin's work, cultural-historical interpretation and critique is inseparable from conceptual elaboration, all the way up to the most abstract philosophical ideas. (Failure to recognize this is one reason for the thinness of Habermas's methodological critique.) Yet the process of working through that these readings represent, along with the mass of material collected together in the *Passagen-Werk*, was hardly begun, let alone completed, by the time Benjamin came to produce his preliminary summary of results, 'On the Concept of History'. Most importantly, the political dimension of the concept of historical experience remained crucially under-determined. As the temporal structure of the new concept of experience – a sociologically based but Messianically expanded conception of the historical experience of cultural form – achieves increasing clarity, its political meaning recedes from view. The political, one might say, is the black hole at the centre of Benjamin's work. The linchpin of his project to fuse materialism with theology, the idea from which everything else derives its meaning, it is present, ultimately, only as a need.

There is an image in one of Benjamin's earliest letters, from before the First World War, that sums up his dilemma. Contrasting the logic of Jewish Messianism to the Tower of Babel, where the attempt to reach the heavens founders on the misunderstandings of the builders, Benjamin writes that the Jews 'handle ideas like quarry stones', but they 'build from above without reaching the ground'.[149] Benjamin, one might say, wanted to build simultaneously from above and below, but the two parts could meet only momentarily, for when they do, they shatter on impact, turning matter into energy. From the standpoint of redemption, 'small-scale victories' are all there is.

NOTES

I would like to thank Gregory Elliott and John Kraniauskas for their helpful comments on the draft version of this chapter.

1 *The Correspondence of Walter Benjamin and Gershom Scholem, 1932–1940*, edited by Gershom Scholem, translated by Gary Smith and Andre Lefevere (New York: Schocken Books, 1989), p. 14.

2 Walter Benjamin, 'On the Programme of the Coming Philosophy' (1917–18), translated by Mark Ritter, in Gary Smith (ed.) *Benjamin: Philosophy, Aesthetics, History* (Chicago, IL: University of Chicago Press, 1989), pp. 1–12 at p. 10. Cf. Benjamin's notorious conversational remark of 1918, recorded by Scholem, that 'a philosophy that does not include the possibility of soothsaying from *coffee grounds* and cannot explicate it cannot be a true philosophy'. Gershom Scholem, *Walter Benjamin: The Story of a Friendship* (London: Faber and Faber, 1982), p. 59.

3 Walter Benjamin, 'Ursprung des deutschen Trauerspiels', *Gesammelte Schriften* (hereafter abbreviated to *GS*), vol. I, edited by Rolf Tiedemann and Herman Schweppenhauser (Frankfurt am Main: Suhrkamp, 1980), pp. 211, 215, 210; translated by John Osborne as *The Origin of German Tragic Drama* (hereafter abbreviated to *OGTD*) (London: New Left Books, 1977), pp. 31, 36, 30. I have amended this translation throughout wherever a more literal rendering seemed philosophically preferable.

4 *GS* I, p. 214; *OGTD*, p. 34.

5 Anson Rabinbach, 'Between Enlightenment and Apocalypse: Benjamin, Bloch and Modern German Jewish Messianism', *New German Critique* 34 (Winter 1985), p. 107.

6 *GS* I, p. 217; *OGTD*, p. 36.

7 Benjamin, letter to Ernst Schoen, 19 September 1919, quoted by Rabinbach, 'Between Enlightenment and Apocalypse', p. 115.

8 Rabinbach, ibid., pp. 82, 97. The second reference is a quotation from Benjamin's letter to Ludwig Strauss, 21 November 1912. Cf. the opening sentences of the 'Theologico-Political Fragment' (1920–1): 'Only the Messiah himself consummates all history, in the sense that he alone redeems, completes, creates its relation to the Messianic. For this reason, nothing historical can relate itself on its own account to anything Messianic.' It is only nature that may be judged Messianic by reason of 'its eternal and total passing away'. The politics of this perspective is 'to strive after such passing'. Its method, Benjamin concludes, 'must be called nihilism'. Walter Benjamin, *One-Way Street and Other Writings* (hereafter abbreviated to *O-WS*), translated by Edmund Jephcott and Kingsley Short (London: New Left Books, 1979), pp. 155–6. Benjamin's 'programmatic anti-politics' is thus a nihilistic 'politics against politics' (Rabinbach) or, as Benjamin himself characterized it, a 'theocratic anarchism'. Rabinbach, 'Between Enlightenment and Apocalypse', p. 116.

9 *GS* I, pp. 215, 218, 228; *OGTD*, pp. 34, 38, 47–8. Emphasis added.

10 Benjamin, Notes for the *Trauerspiel* study, *GS* I, p. 918, quoted by Susan Buck-Morss, *Dialectics of Seeing: Walter Benjamin and the*

Arcades Project (Cambridge, MA: MIT Press, 1989), p. 21. Cf. Benjamin's much later description of Krauss's writing as 'a silence turned inside out', in 'Karl Krauss' (1931), *O-WS*, p. 262.

11 Benjamin to Adorno, in Walter Benjamin, *Briefe*, edited by G. Scholem and T. W. Adorno (Frankfurt am Main: Suhrkamp, 1966), p. 664. For some reflections on the metaphor of recasting, see Irving Wohlfarth, 'Re-fusing Theology: Some First Responses to Walter Benjamin's Arcades Project', *New German Critique* 39 (Fall 1986), pp. 3–24.

12 Walter Benjamin, *Passagen-Werk*, GS V, pp. 490–1 (K 1, 1–3); and 'Uber den Begriff der Geschichte', *GS* I, pp. 691–706, translated by Harry Zohn as 'Theses on the Philosophy of History', in Walter Benjamin, *Illuminations* (London: Fontana, 1973), pp. 255–66.

13 *GS* I, pp. 695, 701–3 (Theses VI, XIV, XVII), *Illuminations*, pp. 257, 263–5.

14 *GS* I, p. 47 *passim*. Cf. Irving Wohlfarth, 'On the Messianic Structure of Walter Benjamin's Last Reflections', *Glyph* 3 (1978), p. 212.

15 For a brief account of the differences between Judaic and Christian Messianism, and between nineteenth-century liberal Judaism and more orthodox interpretations of the relationship of history to redemption, see Gershom Scholem, 'Toward an Understanding of the Messianic Idea in Judaism' and 'The Messianic Idea in Kabbalism', in his *The Messianic Idea in Judaism and Other Essays on Jewish Spirituality* (New York: Schocken Books, 1971), pp. 1–36 and 37–48, respectively. Like Scholem, Benjamin always insisted on the catastrophic exteriority of redemption to history. Benjamin's review of Bloch's *Spirit of Utopia* was never published and is now lost. His relations with Bloch were personally friendly but intensely competitive intellectually. In particular, he feared that Bloch plagiarized his ideas, in a distorted form, while Bloch noted his own influence on Benjamin. In fact, the influences probably went both ways.

16 Sandor Randoti, 'Benjamin's Politics', *Telos* 37 (Fall 1978), p. 73.

17 Louis Aragon, *Treatise on Style*, translated by Alyson Waters (Lincoln, NE, and London: University of Nebraska Press, 1991), p. 90.

18 Benjamin, *Briefe*, pp. 496, 491, quoted in Richard Wolin, *Walter Benjamin: An Aesthetic of Redemption* (New York: Columbia University Press, 1982) and Bernd Witte, *Walter Benjamin: An Intellectual Biography*, translated by James Rolleston (Detroit, IL: Wayne State University Press, 1991), pp. 130 and 108, respectively.

19 Walter Benjamin, 'Surrealism: The Last Snapshot of the European Intelligensia' (1929), *O-WS*, pp. 225–39. One transition it does *not* stand for is the withering away of the 'intelligensia'. As Wolin points out (*Aesthetic of Redemption*, p. 292, n. 66), the translation of *Letzte* as 'last' here, as opposed to, for example, 'latest', is most misleading. The connotation is one of up-to-dateness, not finality – as in Moses Hess's *Die letzten Philosophen* (1845), rendered into English as 'The Recent Philosophers' in Lawrence S. Stepelevich (ed.) *The Young Hegelians: An Anthology* (Cambridge: Cambridge University Press, 1983). The essay is a classic example of Benjamin's appropriation of the genre of journalistic reportage as a medium for intellectual criti-

cism. Texts by Aragon and Breton discussed by Benjamin (*Treatise on Style* and *Nadja*) had only recently appeared in France, in 1928.

20 Scholem's claim (*Story of a Friendship*, p. 146) that the essay is 'still largely dominated by an absolutely pre-Marxist line' is unconvincing. As Witte puts it (*Walter Benjamin*, p. 106): 'when in his great essay of 1929 on surrealism, he traces the awakening of its political consciousness and its engagement on behalf of proletarian revolution, he is speaking primarily of the history of his own politicisation, which had received tangible expression in *One-Way Street*' – a work already decisively influenced by Surrealist writing, notably Aragon's *Paris Peasant* (1926).

21 *O-WS*, pp. 236–7.

22 'Benjamin's Einbahnstrasse' (1955), in Theodor W. Adorno, *Notes to Literature*, vol. 2, translated by Shierry Weber Nicholsen (New York: Columbia University Press, 1992), p. 323.

23 *GS* II, p. 300; *O-WS*, p. 229. Translation altered.

24 Already, by the end of 1927, a year before the composition of the Surrealism essay, Benjamin is describing his work on the Paris arcades as a 'philosophical Fortinbras, who will claim the legacy of surrealism'. Quoted in Witte, *Walter Benjamin*, p. 110.

25 Cf. Pierre Naville's identification of the basic antinomy of Surrealist thought as a contradiction between its metaphysical and its dialectical moments, in an essay much admired by Benjamin, *The Revolution and the Intellectuals (What can the surrealists do?)* (1927). For a discussion of Naville's relations to Surrealism and the impact of his critique upon it, see Maurice Nadeau, *The History of Surrealism* (1944), translated by Richard Howard (London: Plantin Publishers, 1987), pp. 127–72.

26 *O-WS*, p. 231.

27 *O-WS*, pp. 227, 226.

28 Peter Burger, *Theory of the Avant-Garde*, translated by Michael Shaw (Minneapolis, MN: University of Minnesota Press, 1984), ch. 2.

29 *O-WS*, p. 227.

30 'Paris – the Capital of the Nineteenth Century' (1935), in Walter Benjamin, *Charles Baudelaire: An Epic Poet in the Era of High Capitalism*, translated by Harry Zohn (London: New Left Books, 1973), p. 176.

31 *Correspondence*, p. 165.

32 *O-WS*, pp. 238–9. Contrast the way in which the aura will come to be described in 'The Work of Art' essay as 'the unique phenomenon of a distance, however close it may be'. *Illuminations*, p. 224.

33 *O-WS*, p. 239. Cf. Hegel's description of 'the true' as 'the Bacchanalian revel in which no member is not drunk' (*Hegel's Phenomenology of Spirit*, translated by A.V. Miller (Oxford: Oxford University Press, 1979), p. 27).

34 *GS* II, p. 310; *O-WS*, p. 239. Translation altered. Cf. the final section of 'One-Way Street', entitled 'To the Planetarium', *O-WS*, pp. 103–4.

35 *O-WS*, pp. 232–3, 236–8.

36 *O-WS*, p. 225.

37 *O-WS*, p. 230.

38 *GS* V, p. 491 (K 1, 2).

39 *Illuminations*, p. 263.

40 *GS* V, p. 595 (N 11, 3); Smith, *Benjamin*, p. 67.

41 *Correspondence*, p. 226.

42 See Howard Caygill's account of this double inscription, in this volume, pp. 3–12.

43 Benjamin, letter to Werner Kraft, 12 November 1934, quoted by Hans Mayer, 'Walter Benjamin and Franz Kafka: Report on a Constellation', translated by Gary Smith and Thomas S. Hansen, in Gary Smith (ed.) *On Walter Benjamin: Critical Essays and Reflections* (Cambridge, MA: MIT Press, 1988), p. 202. Cf. Benjamin's letter to Scholem, 15 September 1934, *Correspondence*, p. 139.

44 Benjamin, letter to Scholem, 12 June 1938, *Correspondence*, p. 225.

45 Wolin, *Aesthetic of Redemption*, p. 154. Wolin here follows the line of the polemics of the late 1960s and early 1970s which undialectically opposed the 'theological' to the 'materialist' aspects of Benjamin's thought.

46 Earlier, Benjamin had, as Randoti puts it, formulated his rapprochement with Marxism 'entirely in antinomies: Not as a theoretical problem, but as obligatory conduct' ('Benjamin's Politics', p. 73). This is particularly clear in his letter to Scholem of 26 May 1926 (quoted by Randoti, pp. 65–6): 'anyone in our generation who experiences and understands the current historical moment as struggle, and for whom this is not just a cliché, cannot hold back from studying and practicing that mechanism through which things and relations and masses affect each other'. It was the effect of such study on the pre-existing framework of Benjamin's thought that gradually transformed it. To begin with, he was concerned simply to avoid incompatibility: 'In my view, anarchist methods are unserviceable and Communist "goals" meaningless and non-existent. But the value of Communist action is not reduced one iota, since that action is the corrective for the goals and since meaningful *political* goals do not exist' (ibid., p. 66). By the mid–1930s, however, the pressure to confront the relations between these elements theoretically had become overwhelming.

47 Cf. Buck-Morss: 'for Benjamin, theology functions as an axis of philosophical experience'. *Dialectics of Seeing*, p. 248. The basic principle of historical materialism, Benjamin argues in the *Passagen-Werk*, 'is not progress, but actualisation'. *GS* V, p. 574 (N2, 2); translated in Smith, *Benjamin*, p. 47. For the difference between Benjamin's conceptions of Communism and Marxism in the early 1930s, see his letter to Scholem, 6 May 1934, where he protests that 'a credo is the last thing my communism resorts to', arguing that the practical affirmation of Communism in his writings (in the case at issue, a review essay on 'Problems in the Sociology of Language') 'leaves the theory (the credo, if you like) a much greater freedom than the Marxists suspect' (*Correspondence*, p. 110). He simultaneously identifies his work with 'Communism' and distances it from the 'Marxists' – those who offer the orthodox theoretical interpretation of the creed. That Benjamin was in no doubt as to the difficulty such a position raised for his relations to the Communist Party is clear from his earlier letter to Scholem of 17 April 1931, where he explicitly acknowledges that his writings look

'counterrevolutionary' (in inverted commas in the original) from the Party's point of view. Nonetheless, with characteristic intransigence, he insists that this makes it all the more important that he associate himself with Communism in order to counter the danger that they be 'placed at the disposal of the counterrevolution'. It was better that he 'make them definitely and reliably unusable for the counterrevolution at the risk that no one will be able to use them' than that he publicly clarify his differences with the Communist Party under the prevailing political conditions. (Scholem, *Story of a Friendship*, pp. 232–3.) Benjamin's intellectual objections to the narrowness of the Party 'creed' parallel those at stake in the tensions between the Surrealists and the French Communist Party. That his solidarity was more consistent than theirs was undoubtedly due to his more pragmatic stance towards politics as the domain of 'the lesser evil' (*Correspondence*, p. 110). The aspiration for his writing to be 'definitely and reliably unusable for the counterrevolution' recurs in 'The Work of Art' essay, the concepts in which, it is claimed, are 'completely useless for the purposes of Fascism' (*Illuminations*, p. 220). Whether this is possible at a general conceptual level, as opposed to at the more concrete level of *writing*, is doubtful. Indeed, the very declaration that it is, would seem to be part of a writing strategy based on just such a doubt. For a more extensive consideration of this issue from the standpoint of Benjamin's politics of language, see Chapter 2 by Alexander Düttmann in this volume.

48 *GS* I, p. 691 (Thesis I); *Illuminations*, p. 255.

49 See Benjamin, 'The Task of the Translator' (1923), in *Illuminations*, pp. 69–82. The translator, Benjamin argues, quoting Pannwitz, 'must expand and deepen his own language by means of the foreign language'. Only 'where a text is identical with truth or dogma', is it 'unconditionally translatable' (pp. 81–2). It is thus as mistaken to argue, as Scholem does ('Walter Benjamin and his Angel', in Smith, *On Walter Benjamin*, p. 82), that after this translation 'historical materialism is no longer anything but a puppet', and that 'frequently nothing remains of . . . [it] except the term', as it is to suggest that Benjamin's Marxism liquidates the theological dimension of his thought. As Kittsteiner puts it: 'Benjamin did not misunderstand Marxian theory. Nor did he want merely to interpret it differently; he wanted to change it.' H. D. Kittsteiner, 'Walter Benjamin's Historicism', *New German Critique* 39 (Fall 1986), p. 202. This was an attitude that was licensed by his reading of Korsch's *Karl Marx*. See *GS* V, pp. 606–8 (N 17, 17a); Smith, *Benjamin*, pp. 77–9. However, this is to not suggest, as Wohlfarth does, that theology and materialism, melancholy and revolution, are '*nowhere* . . . ultimately at odds with one another' in Benjamin's writings. Irving Wohlfarth, 'On Some Jewish Motifs in Benjamin', in Andrew Benjamin (ed.) *Problems of Modernity: Adorno and Benjamin* (London: Routledge, 1989), p. 202; emphasis added. This is hard to reconcile with Wohlfarth's own remark in the same essay (p. 194) that, as Benjamin presents them, 'the various idioms of Jewish Messianism do not seem capable of being reconciled even among themselves'. One might make a similar point about historical materialism. The stress generated by Wohlfarth's heroic attempt to

render Benjamin's *oeuvre* wholly consistent may be traced in the fault lines of his prose: 'nowhere . . . ultimately'.

50 The essay on Fuchs (1937) is located within a different frame of reference. Benjamin wrote it for the fee and often complained about the disruption to his other work caused by the obligation, putting it off until it could no longer be avoided. Nevertheless, perhaps because of these circumstances, it ended up containing a number of important formulations of methodological material culled directly from the *Passagen-Werk*.

51 *Illuminations*, pp. 127, 129. Benjamin's identification with the avant-garde was always a strong one. See in particular his letter to Scholem, 17 April 1931, where he refers to the 'small but extremely important avant-garde' in West Berlin of which he was a part and describes 'the most sophisticated civilization and the most "modern" culture' there as the 'very means' of his production. Scholem, *Story of a Friendship*, pp. 231–3. Not only is 'One-Way Street' one of the most important products of the German literary avant-garde of the 1920s, but Benjamin was tireless in his mediation of the French and German avant-gardes: presenting Surrealism and Proust to the German public (1929) and planning a series of lectures on 'The German Avant-Garde' (including one on Kafka, alongside others on Bloch, Brecht and Krauss) in French in Paris for March 1934. They were cancelled at the last moment. However, it is precisely the 'avant-garde' status of Kafka's work that is called into question as Benjamin's interpretation develops.

52 *Illuminations*, pp. 115, 114, 116, 117. Translation amended.

53 Ibid., pp. 120, 122, 128, 129.

54 Ibid., p. 130.

55 Gershom Scholem, 'Religious Authority and Mysticism', *On the Kabbalah and its Symbolism* (New York: Schocken Books, 1965), p. 12.

56 According to Benjamin's notes of a conversation on 6 June 1931, Brecht called Kafka 'the only truly Bolshevist writer' (Scholem, *Story of a Friendship*, p. 175), although, as we shall see, this was only one side of his analysis.

57 This structure is clear in the 'Idea for an Arcanum' that Benjamin sent to Scholem along with his letter from the end of November 1927, translated in Scholem, *Story of a Friendship*, pp. 144–5. See also Benjamin's remark in his letter to Scholem, 28 February 1933, quoting one of Scholem's definitions of revelation ('The absolutely concrete can never be fulfilled at all'): 'These words (putting aside the theological perspective) say more about Kafka . . . than that man Schoeps will ever be capable of understanding.' *Correspondence*, p. 28. (Schopes was a contemporary Kafka critic.) What it might mean to 'put aside' the theological perspective turned out to be the main issue in dispute.

58 *Story of a Friendship*, pp. 170–1.

59 *Illuminations*, pp. 122, 129.

60 *Story of a Friendship*, p. 170.

61 *Illuminations*, pp. 131, 136.

62 Ibid., p. 131.

63 See note 57, above.

64 Ibid., pp. 134, 117–18. 'Silence of the Sirens' is the particular story Benjamin cites.
65 Buck-Morss, *Dialectics of Seeing*, pp. 49, 271, 406 (n. 91). Benjamin rejected the title as 'impermissibly poetic' on returning to the project in 1934, immediately after writing the Kafka essay.
66 Benjamin, letter to Scholem 12 June 1938, *Correspondence*, p. 226. It seems likely to have been this affirmation of a combination of Jewish and German folk traditions in Kafka, in response to a distinctly modern set of problems, that provoked Brecht to charge Benjamin's essay with promoting 'Jewish fascism'. Walter Benjamin, *Conversations with Brecht* (London: New Left Books, 1973), p. 110. Mayer's thesis (Smith, *On Walter Benjamin*, pp. 189, 195), clearly influenced by Scholem, that what is apologetic about the essay is that, in explaining Kafka's failure, it served as a justification of Benjamin's own failure, is unconvincing, and in any case reductively biographical. Rather, as we shall see, Benjamin reacted to his deepening perception of Kafka's failure by intensifying the avant-garde element in his thought in his determination to avoid it.
67 *Illuminations*, p. 139.
68 *Conversations with Brecht*, pp. 107–11.
69 Each section is structured around a Kafkaesque quasi-parabolic tale.
70 *Hegel's Phenomenology of Spirit*, p. 6.
71 *Illuminations*, p. 223. Cf. the passage on p. 87, where we read that 'nothing would be more fatuous' than to want to see in the death of the art of storytelling 'merely a "symptom"' of decay, let alone a "modern" symptom'.
72 *Conversations with Brecht*, p. 111.
73 *Illuminations*, p. 233. If Benjamin takes his cue on the city from Brecht, and on industrial work from Marx, the recurring theme of the effect of modern warfare on the capacity for experience, although likely to have been influenced by Junger, receives a distinctive treatment of its own. See, for example, *Illuminations*, p. 84, and *O-WS*, pp. 103–4. It is combined with an acute foreboding about the tendencies towards war inherent in the existing system of production: 'Only war makes it possible to mobilize all of today's technical resources while maintaining the property system', *Illuminations*, p. 243. On the historical predominance of film as a medium, see *O-WS*, pp. 45, 61–2, and *GS* V, p. 498 (K 3, 3): 'all problems of contemporary art find their final formulation only in relation to the film'.
74 Indeed, his use of the fairy-tale represents a return to the origin of the story which illuminates its character as tradition. According to 'The Storyteller', *Illuminations*, p. 102, the fairy-tale is the first form of the story and 'secretly lives on' in it.
75 *Correspondence*, pp. 139, 224–6. First emphasis added.
76 Passages from Benjamin's record of his conversations with Brecht appear almost word for word in his letter to Scholem of 12 June 1938.
77 *Correspondence*, pp. 243, 224, 125, 128. Elsewhere, Benjamin extends this point about the comic character of the historically redundant to both Surrealism and the lyric. 'What is the meaning of the fact that music and lyric poetry become comic?' he asks Adorno. 'I can hardly

imagine that this is a completely negative phenomenon.' E. Bloch *et al.*, *Aesthetics and Politics* (London: New Left Books, 1977), p. 141. In the *Passagen-Werk*, Surrealism is described as 'the death of the last century via comedy'. *GS* V, p. 584 (N 5a, 2); Smith, *Benjamin*, p. 56. Such comedy is a product of the new form of historical time, and soon overtakes it in turn. As Adorno put it in the 1960s: even the label 'avant-garde' begins to conjure up 'comical associations', in this case of 'ageing youth'. Theodor W. Adorno, *Aesthetic Theory*, translated by C. Lenhardt (London: Routledge & Kegan Paul, 1984), p. 36.

78 *Illuminations*, pp. 97–8.

79 Ibid., pp. 88, 83, 90 (translation amended).

80 'Some Motifs in Baudelaire' (1939), in Benjamin, *Baudelaire*, pp. 112–17, 154, 132; 'The Work of Art', *Illuminations*, p. 239; 'A Small History of Photography', *O-WS*, p. 243. For an intriguing exploration of this 'neurological' side of Benjamin's understanding of modernity, see Susan Buck-Morss, 'Aesthetics and Anaesthetics: Walter Benjamin's Artwork Essay Reconsidered', *October* 62, pp. 3–41. In modernity, Buck-Morss argues, 'the cognitive system of synaesthetics has become, rather, one of anaesthetics' (p. 18). Such anaesthetics is 'the ground from which fascism can again push forth' (p. 41).

81 Georg Lukács, *Theory of the Novel* (1920), translated by Anna Bostock (London: Merlin Press, 1971).

82 Despite his focus on the 'periodicity of the triadic structure', Wohlfarth ('On the Messianic Structure') characterizes this standpoint only as the *Eingedenken* of *Eingedenken* – the 'remembrance of remembrance' (p. 198, n. 5), thereby sacrificing the complexity of the idea to the neatness of its formulation, slackening the tension between conception and expression that sustains the critical edge of Benjamin's thought. Nevertheless, this essay is a mine (a minefield, perhaps) of philological insights. As Wohlfarth points out (p. 155), it is in the exceptional figure of Proust alone that Benjamin finds a restoration of the story in his generation. The length of the work is taken by Benjamin as an index of the effort such a restoration required, and Proust's moment is in any case itself already past. Nonetheless, Proust's 'involuntary memory' does become a model for Benjamin, not merely through which to read Baudelaire's work (its function in 'Some Motifs'), but, more generally, for the fullness of the instant in which, in the conjunction of a specific present with a specific past, history as a whole becomes 'legible'. Like now-time, the time of involuntary memory is 'outside history': 'Each situation in which the chronicler is touched by the breath of lost time is thereby rendered incomparable and removed from the sequence of the days.' The problem with this parallel is, of course, that Proust's novelistic restoration of the story 'is part of the inventory of the individual who is isolated in many ways', whereas Benjamin aspires to reunite 'contents of the individual past' with 'material of the collective past', to recombine involuntary with voluntary memory. *Baudelaire*, pp. 143, 147, 113. Hence the turn to the Brechtian model of the film audience.

83 *GS* I, p. 577; *Baudelaire*, p. 74. Translation altered.

84 Critics have correctly noted that what goes under the heading of 'his-

toricism' in Benjamin's work is actually an amalgam of two quite discrete historiographic tendencies: an objectivism about knowledge of the past 'the way it really was' (Ranke) (*Illuminations*, p. 257), and an extension of the Enlightenment philosophy of history as progress. Outside of Benjamin's work, they are to be found in conflict with one another at least as often as they are to be found together. However, despite the terminological problem this introduces *vis-à-vis* other definitions of 'historicism' (of which there are many), I shall follow Benjamin's usage, taking care where necessary to specify which element is at issue, since what is ultimately at stake in his analysis is the concept they share of history as 'the subject of a structure whose site is homogeneous empty time' (*Illuminations*, p. 263). The affinity that Kittsteiner notes ('Walter Benjamin's Historicism', pp. 186–7) between the first of these tendencies and certain of the theological aspects of Benjamin's own critique of the philosophy of history is far less significant than Benjamin's opposition to their common temporal structure. Indeed, it can only be constructed by taking one side of Benjamin's concept of history (the theological) in abstraction from the other (the materialist or immanently historical). However, since the whole point of Benjamin's work is to try to hold these two sides together, such a procedure does too much violence to it to be acceptable as an interpretive strategy. This aspect of Kittsteiner's fascinating critique – its presentation of Benjamin as a 'materialist historicist' (p. 179) – may thus be reduced to a polemical exploitation of terminological differences.

85 Charles Baudelaire, 'The Painter of Modern Life' (1845), in *The Painter of Modern Life and Other Essays*, translated and edited by Jonathan Mayne (New York: de Capo Press, n.d.) (reprint of the 1964 Phaidon Press edition), p. 12. Emphasis added.

86 *GS* V, p. 610 (N 19, 3); Smith, *Benjamin*, p. 81; and 'Eduard Fuchs, Collector and Historian', *O-WS*, p. 360.

87 It is in reconnecting history to remembrance, against the 'bad' modernity of historicism, that the theological dimension of Benjamin's thought returns to the foreground: 'history is not just a science but also a form of remembrance [*Eingedenken*]. What science has "established", remembrance can modify. Remembrance can make the incomplete (happiness) into something complete, and the complete (suffering) into something incomplete. That is theology; but in remembrance we discover the experience that forbids us to conceive history as thoroughly a-theological, even though we barely dare not attempt to write it according to literally theological concepts.' *GS* V, p. 589 (N 8, 1); Smith, *Benjamin*, p. 61. Translation altered. 'Theology' stands here for that moment of transcendence of the given intrinsic to history and politics alike. It can no more be opposed to Marxism than Marxism can be reduced to positivism.

88 Benjamin, *Baudelaire*, p. 154.

89 For a more extended treatment of this approach to modernity, in the context of recent debates about historical periodization, see my 'Modernity is a Qualitative, Not a Chronological, Category', *New Left Review* 192 (March-April 1992), pp. 65–84.

90 See in particular 'Some Motifs', where the temporal correspondences

between the various different experiences are most explicit: 'The shock experience which the passer-by has in the crowd corresponds to what the worker "experiences" at his machine'; 'That which determines the rhythm of production on a conveyor belt is the basis of the rhythm of reception in film'; 'The jolt in the movement of a machine is like the so-called *coup* in a game of chance'. *Baudelaire*, pp. 133–4.

91 Benjamin to Scholem, 20 May 1935, *Correspondence*, p. 159.

92 Walter Benjamin, 'Central Park', translated by Lloyd Spencer, *New German Critique* 34 (Winter 1985), pp. 48, 36, 35, 49, 43, 46, 40. For a reading of the corresponding material in the *Passagen-Werk*, see Buck-Morss, *Dialectics of Seeing*, pp. 96–109. It was the reading of modernity as Hell, in what he referred to as the 'glorious first draft' of the *Passagen-Werk* of 1929, that Adorno was especially attracted to (Buck-Morss, *Dialectics of Seeing*, p. 57).

93 'Central Park', p. 43.

94 *Baudelaire*, p. 134. Benjamin takes this model of an 'exact' repetition, without difference, from the chapter on 'Machinery and Modern Industry' in Marx's *Capital*, vol. One.

95 *O-WS*, p. 156. See note 8, above.

96 'Central Park', p. 50.

97 *Baudelaire*, p. 117.

98 *GS* V, p. 495 (K 2, 3).

99 Ibid., p. 174. See also pp. 134–8. In the *Passagen-Werk*, Benjamin refers to historicism as 'the strongest narcotic of the century'. *GS* V, p. 578 (N, 3, 4); Smith, *Benjamin*, p. 51.

100 Ibid., p. 110. Emphasis added. Cf. his Freudian reading of Proust: 'only what has not been experienced explicitly and consciously, what has not happened to the subject as an experience, can become a component of the *mémoire involuntaire*' (p. 114).

101 Adorno, letters to Benjamin, 10 November 1938 and 18 March 1936, *Aesthetics and Politics*, pp. 128–9, 114; 'A Portrait of Walter Benjamin' (1950), in Theodor W. Adorno, *Prisms*, translated by Samuel and Shierry Weber (London: Neville Spearman, 1967), p. 237; 'Benjamin's Einbahnstrasse', *Notes to Literature* II, p. 324. See also in this context, Adorno's critique of Surrealism, 'Looking Back on Surrealism' (1956), in Theodor W. Adorno, *Notes to Literature*, vol. 1, translated by Shierry Weber Nicholson (New York: Columbia University Press, 1991), pp. 86–90. This is essentially an extended, sharpened up version of the earlier critique of Benjamin. The slightly misleading idea of Benjamin's thought as 'Surrealist philosophy' first crops up in Bloch's review of 'One-Way Street': Ernst Bloch, 'Philosophy as Cabaret' (1928), *New Left Review* 116 (July-August 1979), p. 96.

102 *Bertolt Brecht Poems, Part II 1929–1933*, edited by John Willet and Ralph Mannheim (London: Eyre Methuen, 1976), p. 193.

103 *GS* V, pp. 578, 608, 591–2, 495, 592, 576, 495, 578 (N 3, 1; N 18, 4; N 9, 7; K 2, 3; N 9a, 6; N 2a, 3; K 2, 3; N 3, 1); *GS* I, pp. 701–3 (Theses XVI, XVII, XIV). Translations: Smith, *Benjamin*, pp. 50, 80, 64, 65, 49, 50; *Illuminations*, pp. 263–5.

104 What follows is a condensed version of a discussion of the place of Benjamin's work in the history of the philosophy of time that will

appear as part of Chapter 3 of my *Modernity and Avant-Garde: The Politics of Historical Time*, forthcoming from Verso, London, 1994.

105 Aristotle, *Physics*, Book IV; Martin Heidegger, *The Basic Problems of Phenomenology*, translated by A. Hofstadter (Bloomington, IN: Indiana University Press, 1982), pp. 229–73, and *Being and Time*, translated by John Macquarrie and Edward Robinson (Oxford: Blackwell, 1962), pp. 472–9; Edmund Husserl, *Lectures on the Phenomenology of Internal Time-Consciousness* (1905), translated by James S. Churchill (Bloomington, IN: Indiana University Press, 1964). In the *Passagen-Werk*, Benjamin writes of the 'vulgar naturalism of historicism'; *GS* V, p. 575 (N 2, 6); Smith, *Benjamin*, p. 48. Heidegger thinks of the ordinary conception of time as a 'sequence of nows'.

106 *GS* I, p. 703 (Thesis XVIII); *Illuminations*, p. 265. Translation altered.

107 *GS* I, p. 704 (Theses, Appendix A); *Illuminations*, p. 265. Emphasis added. Habermas is thus quite wrong to refer to this experience as a leap into 'past *Jetztzeiten*' ('Walter Benjamin: Consciousness-Raising or Rescuing Critique', in Smith, *On Walter Benjamin*, p. 118). *Jetztzeit* is a mediation between different temporalities 'within' the present. 'Past *Jetztzeiten*' are not accessible as *Jetztzeiten*, but only as part of the past in the present *Jetztzeit*. As Augustine emphasized, the past is a part of the present.

108 For the critique of Hegelianism for its 'immobilization' of time, see Ludwig Feuerbach, 'Towards a Critique of Hegel's Philosophy' (1839), translated by Zawar Hanfi in *The Fiery Brook: Selected Writings of Ludwig Feuerbach* (Garden City, NY: Anchor Books, 1972), pp. 53–96. Benjamin's now-time is quite different from all three of the traditional philosophical concepts of eternity: perpetual duration, atemporality and the 'pure' present – for an exposition of which, see Michael Theunissen, 'Metaphysics' Forgetfulness of Time: On the Controversy over Parmenides, Frag. 8, 5', in Axel Honneth *et al.* (eds) *Philosophical Interventions in the Unfinished Project of Enlightenment* (Cambridge, MA: MIT Press, 1992), pp. 3–28.

109 *GS* V, pp. 576–7 (N 2a, 3); Smith, *Benjamin*, p. 49.

110 *GS* V, p. 600 (N 13a, 1); Smith, *Benjamin*, p. 71. Emphasis added. For an acute account of the relationship between the dialectical image, the allegorical image and the theological symbol, see Buck-Morss, *Dialectics of Seeing*, pp. 221–45.

111 See notes 8 and 17, above.

112 *GS* I, pp. 693–4 (Theses II, III); *Illuminations*, p. 256. Emphasis added.

113 *GS* V, p. 578 (N 3, 2); Smith, *Benjamin*, p. 51.

114 *GS* I, p. 216; *OGTD*, p. 36.

115 *GS* V, p. 578 (N 3, 2); Smith, *Benjamin*, p. 51.

116 *GS* I, p. 703 (Thesis XVIII); *Illuminations*, p. 265. Translation altered.

117 *Dialectics of Seeing*, pp. 240–52. See, in particular, the diagram on p. 242. This diagram errs, however, in giving Messianic time a direction. The Messianic axis should thus be read without the arrow. Similarly, it seems to me misleading to present the two dimensions of now-time as being internal to 'historical' time, as its 'Messianic' and 'empirical' dimensions respectively. Given the exteriority of the

Messianic to history, this opposition seems best represented as one between the Messianic and the historical. In now-time, historical time momentarily acquires a Messianic (that is, an extra-historical) dimension, but the Messianic does not thereby become historical. That would bring history to an end.

118 *GS* I, pp. 703, 704, 694 (Thesis XVIII, Appendix A; Theses II, III); *Illuminations*, pp. 265, 256.

119 *GS* V, p. 592 (N 9, 7); Smith, *Benjamin*, p. 64.

120 Ibid., p. 695 (Thesis V); p. 257.

121 Ibid., p. 700 (Thesis XII); p. 262.

122 *GS* V, p. 593 (N 9a, 7); Smith, *Benjamin*, p. 65.

123 The angel is a momentary, fleeting messenger from another world. (In Hebrew, the word for angel is the same as that for messenger: *malakh*.) As Benjamin puts it in his short text 'Agesilaus Santander': 'The *kabbalah* relates that in every instant God creates an immense number of new angels whose only purpose is, before they dissolve into naught, to sing His praise before His throne.' In Benjamin's case, however, the angel is delayed: 'Mine was interrupted in so doing.' The Messianic hovers over Benjamin's world, in the guise of the angel, at once ephemeral, yet delayed. Gershom Scholem, 'Walter Benjamin and his Angel' (1972), translated by Werner Dannhauser, in Smith, *On Walter Benjamin*, pp. 65, 57.

124 Quoted by Benjamin, *GS* V, p. 601 (N 14, 2); Smith, *Benjamin*, p. 72.

125 *Dialectics of Seeing*, p. 245.

126 See note 16, above.

127 Friedrich Schegel, 'Athenaeum Fragments' no. 80, in *Philosophical Fragments*, translated by Peter Firchow (Minneapolis, MN: Minnesota University Press, 1991), p. 27.

128 Smith, *On Walter Benjamin*, p. 117.

129 *GS* I, pp. 7–122. For a discussion of the abiding influence of Romanticism on Benjamin's thought, see Irving Wohlfarth, 'The Politics of Prose and the Art of Awakening: Walter Benjamin's Version of a German Romantic Motif', *Glyph* 7 (1980), pp. 131–48. The distinctiveness of Benjamin's understanding of Romanticism may be judged from his remark that 'the very centre of Romanticism' is its Messianism, *Briefe*, p. 208.

130 *GS* V, pp. 591–2 (N 9, 7); Smith, *Benjamin*, p. 64.

131 *GS* I, pp. 697–8 (Thesis IX); *Illuminations*, pp. 259–60.

132 'das Neue wiedererkennen', *GS* V, p. 493 (K 1a, 3). The translation follows Buck-Morss, *Dialectics of Seeing*, p. 274.

133 *GS* V, p. 608 (N 18, 4); Smith, *Benjamin*, p. 80.

134 *GS* V, pp. 491, 580 (K 1, 3; K 1, 2; K 1; N 4, 4); Smith, *Benjamin*, p. 53.

135 *GS* V, p. 490 (K 1, 1).

136 *GS* V, pp. 579, 571–2 (N 3a, 3; N 1, 9); Smith, *Benjamin*, pp. 52, 44–5.

137 Cf. Theodor W. Adorno, *Negative Dialektik* (1966) (Frankfurt am Main: Suhrkamp, 1982), p. 314 (translated by E. B. Ashton as *Negative Dialectics* (London: Routledge & Kegan Paul, 1973), p. 320; translation altered): 'Universal history is to be constructed and denied.' In Surreal-

ism, Benjamin had argued, 'the threshold between waking and sleeping was worn away'. *O-WS*, p. 226. For an interesting discussion of Benjamin's work as a 'science of thresholds', see Winfried Manninghaus, 'Walter Benjamin's Theory of Myth', in Smith, *On Walter Benjamin*, pp. 292–325.

138 Habermas, 'Consciousness-Raising or Rescuing Critique', Smith, *On Walter Benjamin*, p. 118.

139 Ibid., p. 310.

140 Ibid., p. 117. See note 107, above.

141 *GS* V, p. 1002; quoted by Manninghaus, in Smith, *On Walter Benjamin*, p. 304.

142 Except at the level of its unconscious – for which see John Kraniauskas's contribution to this volume, Chapter 5.

143 Benjamin, 'Critique of Violence' (1921), *O-WS*, pp. 132–54.

144 *GS* I, p. 235; *OGTD*, p. 55. See notes 46 and 51, above.

145 Buck-Morss, 'Aesthetics and Anaesthetics', p. 4.

146 *GS* I, p. 508; *Illuminations*, p. 244.

147 Benjamin to Scholem, 17 April 1931, *Story of a Friendship*, p. 233; *GS* I, p. 473; *Illuminations*, p. 220. See note 47, above.

148 For a critique of Habermas's identification of the redemptive with the conservative in his essay on Benjamin, see Peter Burger, 'Walter Benjamin's "Redemptive Critique"': Some Preliminary Reflections on the Project of a Critical Hermeneutics' (1979), translated by Nicholas Walker in Peter Burger, *The Decline of Modernism* (Cambridge: Polity Press, 1992), pp. 19–31.

149 Benjamin, letter to Ludwig Strauss, 7 January 1913, quoted by Rabinbach, 'Between Enlightenment and Apocalypse', p. 99.

4 Afformative, Strike
Benjamin's 'Critique of Violence'

Werner Hamacher
Translated by Dana Hollander

For Jean-Luc Nancy

Walter Benjamin's essay, 'On the Critique of Violence' ('Zur Kritik der Gewalt'), provides an outline for a politics of pure mediacy.[1] For Benjamin the means for such a politics may be termed 'pure' because they do not serve as means to ends situated outside the sphere of mediacy. Such ends could only be ambiguous – they would claim to be removed from or even superior to the sphere of means, but would in fact be merely historical positings whose mediacy is masked by isolation. Means which may be termed pure, on the other hand, are not on the order of posited norms – and certainly not on the order of legal norms or of models for binding interactions to be followed by the members of a society. Politics and violence can be termed pure only if they manifest a form of *justice* untainted by the interests of preserving or mandating certain ways of life, untainted by positive forms of law.[2] While all that is law must rest on a law-making, law-positing, law-imposing violence, and such law-imposing violence is represented in all law-preserving or administrative violence, the idea of justice cannot depend on the law's changing powers of imposition. Justice must therefore belong to a sphere equally distant from the law on the one hand, and from the violence of its imposition and enforcement on the other.

For all law – unlike justice – is dependent on a positing (*Setzung*), and no such positing manages without violence – without a violence that, with this positing, impedes, denies and compromises itself. The self-obstruction and corruption of positing and law-imposing violence become apparent every time such violence seeks to preserve itself. By turning from positing to preserving law, it must also turn against hostile forces of positing and thus indirectly against its own principle – the principle of positing itself. In order to remain what it is – violence of law imposition – law-imposing violence must become law-preserving, must turn against its original positing character, and, in this collision with itself, must disintegrate. This is why, as Benjamin writes, all positing and all imposition is 'ambiguous': in every positing, every stipulated positive legislation or law, the violence which has employed it must turn against itself – whether by ceasing to posit so as to preserve its position, or by opposing, for the same reason, other positing forces. In either case, the positing – and with it law and politics in so far as they are founded on positings – must weaken itself and leave itself to its own ruin. And in either case, the original positing violence – even if it was initially without purpose, not defined as an instrument for a particular purpose – must transform what it posits into its end and must thus itself wither into its means.

Every positing and every law is thus subject to a more powerful law that demands that it *expose* itself to another positing, and another law. This more powerful law is the law of historical change and internal structural transformation, dictated by the ambiguity of being both means and end. In connection with this ambiguity, Benjamin speaks of a 'dialectic' and its 'law of oscillation' (*Schwankungsgesetz*).[3] He leaves no room for doubt that the history of law and legislation, the political history of state authority and state institutions, develops according to a model that, in so far as it is under the prerogative of the dialectical ends-means relation, cannot bring about justice. As long as history remains constrained by the circular succession of imposing forces of law, it cannot be the medium of justice. Benjamin writes:

> A gaze directed only at what is closest at hand can at most perceive a dialectical rising and falling in the law-imposing and law-preserving formations of violence. The law governing their oscillation [*Schwankungsgesetz*] rests on the circumstance that all law-preserving violence, in its duration, indirectly weakens the law-imposing violence represented by it through the suppression of hostile counterviolence. . . . This lasts until either new forces or those earlier suppressed triumph over the hitherto law-imposing violence and thus found a new law, destined in its turn to decay.[4]

Thus, the law on which the dialectic of historical forms of violence is based is the law of an indirect suppression of violence, which nevertheless itself rests on the structure of positing – a suppression of violence that posits. Violence is suppressed not by another violence but by its own positing – by confining, obstructing and isolating itself, thus becoming an end external to itself. 'In its duration', writes Benjamin, law-preserving violence 'weakens' the positing violence it 'represents': for as long as it lasts, and *through* the duration that this preservation aims to secure, the demise of conservative violence brings with it that of positing violence. If the history of violence as the cyclical history of its own demise and restitution begins only with its claim to duration (and indeed historical duration is a category of positing and its decay), then one can say of a non-positing violence that it does not conform to any known temporal form, and never to temporality as a form of representation (*Vorstellung*), which is always also a form of positing; and one can say that this non-positing violence is contretemporal or anachronistic.[5] Just as pure violence is pre-positional, it is also pre-temporal and thus not representable. The representation of positing violence, however, brings on the demise of what is represented; positing violence weakens its preservation precisely by merely preserving it. The fact that no law-imposing violence manages without the support of a law-preserving violence in which it strays from itself shows that the violence of law imposition cannot by itself bring about a state of law, of legality or the legitimacy of actions: every violence must decay in its positing. According to the law of its historical dialectic, positing degrades the violence at work within it, transforming it from being pure means to being a means for stipulated ends. It makes violence into an instrument, places it in the service of something other than itself, and thus violates the principle of its unconditional mediacy. History is the realm of compromised, enslaved means, the realm of a violence which, by its consideration for self-preservation, security and duration renders itself impotent, and decays.

Benjamin leaves no doubt that even when the positing of law takes the form of a peacefully concluded legal contract, this positing rests on an instrumentalizing violence, because such a contract invests each of the contracting parties with the right to resort to violence in the case of breach of contract by the other party.[6] However, as Benjamin mentions in the cited passage, the presence of violence – which is at least latent in every judicial institution – complies with a dialectic that forces the disintegration not of the principle of violence itself and of the power it institutes, but only of its respective forms. Because at the moment when that which has been posited splits off from the positing and abandons itself to the preservation of its status, a legal form will have detached itself from what it 'represents': the positing decomposes in the law, which is consequently powerless and must succumb to *another* violence, *another* interest, previously separated, excluded, suppressed or ostracized from itself. Thus, every positing – according to its dialectical law – is dethroned by its internal reversal (*Umschlag*) into a positive institution, by its immediate self-alienation. This internal alteration may be represented by oppositional social or political forces, by interest groups, political parties, technical innovations or economic pressures. But all of these can only bring their power to bear because the alteration is already at work in the logic of the imposition of legal institutions. Whether imposition occurs as a process of seemingly non-violent, peaceful contractual agreements or by means of violent political interventions is irrelevant to the structure of this movement. As long as a legal institution does not rule out recourse to violence, its violence is one which *serves* that institution – if only to perpetuate it – and which, therefore, cannot be taken as a form of liberty, mediacy or justice. Indeed, it is doubtful whether liberty, mediacy and justice can be grasped in terms of the category of 'form' – that is, whether they can be objects of categorical knowledge. Historical change always proceeds from the inner structure of positing violence; it requires that this violence decay in its very positing. What is called history is nothing other than the decay of positing violence, the fall of positing.

Benjamin illustrates the logic of the decay of political and legal forms by citing an example from the early history of the Weimar Republic – the suppression of the mass Communist uprisings in the Ruhr region during the spring of 1920. ('Zur Kritik der Gewalt' was written in late 1920/early 1921.) Benjamin writes:

> When consciousness of the latent presence of violence in a legal institution disappears, the institution must fall into decay. In our time, parliaments provide an example of this. They offer this familiar, woeful spectacle because they have not remained conscious of the revolutionary forces to which they owe their existence. Accordingly, in Germany in particular, the last manifestation of such forces (*Gewalten*) bore no fruit for parliaments. They have no sense of the law-imposing violence represented within themselves.[7]

Benjamin's formulations do not entail a 'critique' of the institution of parliamentary democracy as such. Rather, they cite 'parliaments' of a certain historical period – that of the Weimar constitution – as an example for his observation that political institutions deteriorate from the moment they first seek to exclude the 'revolutionary forces', the 'forces' (*Gewalten*) to which they owe their existence, from their substantive decisions and their constitutional form. By way of this exclusion – in this case by the violent suppression of a mass strike – they deny not only the right of individuals and of groups to question the state's monopoly over violence, but also the very violence to which this monopoly historically owes its existence and thus 'the law-imposing violence represented within themselves'.[8] Thus, what is at issue in Benjamin's observations is not parliamentary democracy as such, but the specific historical form of restriction employed by a democratic system unable to do justice to the innovative impulses generated by the forces represented within it. This political system, like any other, must, as soon as its preservation and duration are at issue, behave in a restrictive manner toward its constitutive forces (*Gewalten seiner Einsetzung*). In principle, however, whether an existing institution or system is able to defend itself against attempts to overthrow it or whether it is in fact transformed by new social or economic forces remains irrelevant to the relation between violence and positing, between revolutionary forces and their representation. The alteration, corruption and decay of politico-judicial institutions, as an immanent and dialectical process, is not a transformation of the principle of judicial institutions positing itself. Rather, it is due to this very principle that legal institutions are transformed and replaced by ever other impositions, and that this series of transformations leaves unaffected the form of imposition and its origin in instrumental violence.

Now, Benjamin insists that legal contracts are not the norm for all forms of social and political interaction. Furthermore, he claims that the political realization of *other* forms of non-violent settlement could end the age of the 'dialectical' law of oscillation and inaugurate a 'new historical age'.[9] The logic of inaugurating this *other* history is not the logic of positing and intrinsic alteration, and accordingly not the logic of substituting one violence with another, or one privileged class with a hitherto oppressed one. Rather, it is the logic – assuming one can still speak here of logic – of 'deposing' (*Entsetzung*). Since antiquity the history of dialectically evolving legal conditions has proceeded in a circular fashion. 'Upon the breaking of this cycle maintained by mythical legal forms,' Benjamin now writes, 'upon the *deposing* [*Entsetzung*] of law with all the forces on which it depends as they depend on it, finally therefore upon the abolition of state forces, a new historical age is founded.'[10] And Benjamin continues with a remark that noticeably wavers between summary and hypothesis: 'But if the existence of violence beyond the law as pure immediate violence is assured, this is proof that revolutionary violence, the highest manifestation of pure violence by humanity, is possible, and by what means.'[11] It is not substitution (*Ersetzung*), then, but 'deposing' (*Entsetzung*), not the mythical metamorphosis, but the amorphization of positing violence – and finally of state violence – that inaugurates a new historical age. This 'deposing' is termed by Benjamin 'pure immediate' and 'revolutionary' violence, 'the highest manifestation of pure violence by humanity' – and, one might add, of ethical violence *par excellence*. If one now characterizes law imposition in the terminology of speech-act theory as a performative act – and specifically as an absolute, preconventional performative act, one which posits conventions and legal conditions in the first place – and if one further calls the dialectic of positing and decay a dialectic of performance, it seems reasonable to term the 'deposing' of acts of positing and their dialectic, at least provisionally, as an absolute *imperformative* or *afformative* political event, as *depositive*, as political *a-thesis*. Pure violence does not posit, it 'deposes'; it is not performative, but afformative. If the pure violence of de-posing exists even beyond the sphere of law, this pure, and thus non-violent, non-instrumental violence may at any time – if not universally at any time – break through the cycle of laws and their decay. In all acts, linguistic as well as political (that is, political in the narrow sense), in all acts of legislation as well as jurisprudence, at least an element of this afformative function – this deposing, pure violence – is in effect. Even the absolute performative of law-imposing – in fact, this performative first and foremost – not only must be exposed to its inherent historic disintegration, but must already previously, in its own effectuation, have been exposed to the absolute other of deposing, of afformance.[12]

The idea of deposing is by no means unproblematic. Linked to it, in fact, is a long series – perhaps an infinite series – of difficulties, none of which can be easily resolved. Thus, deposing for Benjamin is a historical event; yet it is one that puts an end to the cyclical history of legal institutions and that is not thoroughly determined by this history. Deposing is a political event, but one that shatters all the canonical determinations of the political – and all canonical determinations of the event. Deposing requires an agent, yet this agent can neither have the constitution of a collective or individual legal subject, nor be conceived of as an agent at all, that is, as a subject of positings. Deposing must be an event, but not an event whose content or object could be positively determined. It is directed against something, but also against anything that has the character of a positing, an institution, a representation, or a programme. Deposing is thus not encompassed by any negation, is not directed toward anything determinate – and therefore is not directed. Deposing could not be the means to an end, yet it would be nothing but means. It would be violence, and pure violence, but therefore entirely non-violent. As these aporias belong to the structure of deposing itself, they do not allow for resolution. However, the medium in which they occur – that is to say deposing itself as this medium – can be further specified.

Benjamin provides a few suggestions for such specification. Two of these will be considered here – the discussion of language, and the discussion of the proletarian general strike. Violence can be a means of justice only as *pure* means: as a means, as mediation, as transition, and as a transmittal that in a certain sense precedes the two extremes it links – a form of interpersonality which does not have as its initiator and its addressee already constituted subjects, but which from the outset constitutes them as mediated. Such means are thus essentially linguistically structured and are therefore defined by Benjamin as a technique of linguistic communication, or imparting (*Mitteilung*). The purity of these means lies in the fact that they cannot be derived from ends or reduced to impulses from beyond the sphere of their mediacy. Means are pure as long as nothing imparts itself in them but themselves, their own mediacy. It is only by virtue of this mediacy that they can turn – and indeed cannot avoid turning – into means towards ends and into instruments of imparting through which one can communicate something to an addressee. But just as mediacy is the condition of possibility of instrumental language, the language of pure mediacy and pure impartability is also its interruption. It is at once condition and caesura, and it can be both only because between the condition and the reality of instrumental language, between pure and instrumental language, there is no continuum – that is, because pure impartability is in itself heterogeneous and discontinuous. Language as pure means and pure violence is deposing – deposing not only all positings, but first of all deposing of itself. Language, pure violence, pure impartability (*Mitteilbarkeit*), imparts in that it divides (*teilt*) – and divides in the first place *itself*.[13]

After referring to the 'non-violent resolution of conflict' by way of 'the culture of the heart, . . . sympathy, peaceableness, trust'[14] – which can thus also be considered forms of pure violence – Benjamin emphasizes that pure means are never those of direct, but always those of mediated, solutions. They therefore never apply directly to the arbitration of interpersonal conflict, but do so only by way of things. The sphere of pure means unfolds in the most material human realm – conflicts relating to goods. For this reason technique [*Technik*] in the broadest sense of the word is its most proper domain. Its profoundest example is perhaps talk [*Unterredung*] as a technique of civil agreement. For in it not only is nonviolent agreement possible, but also the exclusion of violence in principle is quite explicitly demonstrated in connection with one significant relation: the immunity of lying from punishment. Probably no legislation on earth originally stipulated such punishment. This makes clear that there is a sphere of human agreement that is nonviolent to the extent that it is wholly inaccessible to violence: the proper sphere of 'mutual understanding,' language.[15]

Wherever something is said *about* something, wherever an action is performed *through* language – that is, wherever something is performatively posited – language must itself already be there as a form of mediacy and thus as sheer, pre-instrumental technique (*Technik*).[16] Thus, language is the means of mediacy – before it can and for as long as it might be the means to ends that could appear to lead us out of mediacy, allow us to transcend it, or claim to redeem us from it. Language is (to use a phrase that served as the title to an earlier political essay by Benjamin which is now probably lost) 'teleology without end' (*Teleologie ohne Endzweck*).[17] Since imparting occurs independently of legal forms or formal obligations (and therefore belongs to the realm of 'sympathy, peaceableness, trust' and 'the culture of the heart'),[18] and since it allows conflicts between speakers to be settled only by way of an objective third entity – by way of things which thereby themselves take on the linguistic status of pure means – imparting, as a technique prior to and in instrumentality, is never primarily or exclusively the means to projected ends or the imposition of such ends. Rather, imparting is a means which has no need of positings and which may undermine any established linguistic, political or legal institution at any time. Language in its mediality is pre-positional, preperformative – and, in this sense, afformative. Even before and even during its performative effects, language does not initially lay the foundation for anything outside itself, but rather offers itself as the form of mediacy between speakers, as their mediacy in a third entity, in a talk, an

Unterredung, an *inter* of their languages, without which they would not be language. While language originally imparts nothing but its own impartability, it does not lay claim to truth in all cases: Benjamin stresses that lying for a long time was not punishable and was exempted from any violent sanction. Language is not a medium that can be measured against an 'objective state of affairs' – a standard verifiable independently of this medium and already available outside itself. Rather, language is the articulation of a mediacy prior to any distinction between 'true' and 'false' and is therefore not subject to that distinction. Whoever speaks does not posit – that is, posits neither truth nor law – without exposing himself and his positings to the possibility of deposition in the mediacy of language, a deposition not determined by the distinction between truth and lying. Mediacy is the field of afformation. Whoever speaks is afformed and afforms.

This is true of everyone, and of everyone in a singular way. Singularity for Benjamin is a determination of justice – indeed, its determination *par excellence* – and thus a determination of pure mediacy. Laws require universality, but their claim to universal validity is founded on a logic of subsumption that views each individual situation only as a case under the law, disregarding its singularity. Like the logic of laws, the logic of performatives follows the principle of a subsumption, sacrificing the respective situation to statutory laws, conventions or codes, and can for this very reason never be appropriate to individual situations. Justice (*Gerechtigkeit*), however, consists essentially in being adjusted to suit situations (*Situationsgerechtigkeit*). Afformatives are singular. This is not to say, however, that they elude imparting. On the contrary, it means that afformatives alone are strictly impartable, while whatever is by the logic of positing subsumable under laws *cannot* be imparted. Thus, according to Benjamin, who may have had in mind the Kantian distinction between determining (*bestimmend*) and reflective (*reflektierend*) judgement, one must distinguish between universalizability (*Verallgemeinerungsfähigkeit*) and general validity (*Allgemeingültigkeit*). It is in this sense that Benjamin objects to

the stubborn habit of conceiving just ends as the ends of possible law, that is, not only as generally valid [*allgemeingültig*] (which follows analytically from the nature of justice), but also as universalizable [*verallgemeinerungsfähig*], which, as could be shown, contradicts the nature of justice. Because ends that for one situation are just, generally acceptable, and generally valid [*allgeme-*

ingültig], are so for no other situation, no matter how similar [the other situation] may be in other respects.[19]

From this, it follows for the theory of justice that pure means and just ends always apply to one singular situation alone, that only singular means and ends not subsumable under general laws may claim general validity, and that only singular laws may be regarded as just. Their singularity, then, is one which is not already cognized or ever cognizable according to rules, but one that demands universal recognition only in the absence of such rules. Since, however, the general validity of the singular can be demanded only in the medium of impartability and can in particular cases be recognized only in this medium – that is, where singularity and universality impart themselves to each other and are exposed to a *talk*, to a mediacy that permits neither the isolation of the individual nor the prerogative of a universal norm – the singularity of justice is always already given over to impartability, is always already an imparted and divided singularity, and always already one in which even the generality from which it demands recognition divides itself.[20] General validity, unlike universalizability, is the form in which the singular imparts itself to a generality and makes even it into a singular, and thus untransferable, and divided, partial generality, one which does not make further partitions and impartings superfluous, but which demands them just as does the particular situation from which it emerges. Justice – the singular, not prior to, but *in* its imparting – is the manifestation of a sociality free from the imposition of legal positings – the manifestation of freedom itself. Its structure is the structure of language.

On Benjamin's account, the technique of language as pure means (and thereby as pure violence), which enables peaceful agreements and 'mutual understanding' independently of any legal order, has its contemporary political 'analogue' in the strike, specifically in the proletarian general strike.[21] Benjamin's discussion of the strike may clearly be seen in the context of the strategic debates on the politics of striking which led in 1872 to the expulsion of the Anarcho-Syndicalists from the First International and whose last major political document was Rosa Luxemburg's 'Mass Strike, Party, and Unions', published in 1906.[22] However, Benjamin explicitly refers only to Georges Sorel's *Réflexions sur la violence*[23] and to Sorel's distinction between the political and the proletarian general strike. Sorel, writes Benjamin, was the first to distinguish these two essentially different kinds of strike. 'He contrasts them as the political and the proletarian general strike. They are also antithetical in their relation to violence.'[24] For whereas the political general strike is only concerned with inverting the relation of domination, and is still based on the preservation and strengthening of state violence, the proletarian general strike aims at nothing less than the abolition of the state apparatus and the legal order maintained by it. Citing Sorel, Benjamin characterizes the advocates of political general strike as follows:

> 'The strengthening of state violence is the basis of [their] conceptions; in their present organizations the politicians (i.e. the moderate socialists) are already preparing the ground for a strong centralized and disciplined violence that will be impervious to criticism from the opposition, capable of imposing silence, and of issuing their mendacious decrees. The political general strike . . . demonstrates how the state will lose none of its strength, how power is transferred from the privileged to the privileged, how the mass of producers will change their masters.' In contrast to this political general strike . . . the proletarian general strike sets [*setzt*] itself the sole task [*Aufgabe*] of annihilating state violence.[25]

The proletarian general strike is pure means, not means to an extortion that would effect modifications in the working conditions, in the distribution of power or the power structure and as such would be violent. Rather, it is a non-violent means of annihilation of legal as well as of state violence. The means of the proletarian general strike lies in the resolution – indeed it is itself the resolution – 'to take up only a wholly transformed work, one no longer enforced by the state'.[26]

The proletarian strike is pure political violence, pure means, and thus non-violent, as the strikers' aim is not one of new legislation or of modified work within the constraints of state violence – that is, not a positively determinable purpose beyond the strike but precisely the strike itself in its unmediated mediacy. This strike, directed toward the annihilation of state violence by way of suspension of all positing violence – in other words, directed toward *nothing* – can be described as being without intention. Following Sorel, Benjamin refers to a line from a letter written by Marx in 1869 to Edward Spencer Beesly, in which Marx reportedly wrote, 'whoever drafts programs for the future is a reactionary'.[27] For Benjamin, the strike is the social, economic, and political event in which nothing happens, no work is done, nothing is produced, and nothing is planned or projected. It is the manifestation of a sociality whose effectiveness neither conforms to a paradigm from the historical canon of politico-economic systems, nor aims at their simple recasting. This sociality is one which does not permit itself to become effective in any form other than as the bare minimum of its existence, the manifestation of the social *tout court*. The proletarian general strike, the eventual form of this sociality, is located outside any means-ends relation such as that which determines the political strike, in which political action defines itself as an instrument for the transformation of existing legal relations. This is why, unlike the political strike which takes place with a view toward an end, the proletarian strike can no longer be understood within a logic of positings and their decay, or within a dialectic of performatives or of production. It is, instead, imperformative, afformative. The strike is 'a non-action'; as an unconditional refusal to act it is tantamount to a 'severing of relations' – that is, of exploitative relations – and is thus 'an entirely non-violent, pure means'.[28] In this respect, the proletarian strike is 'analogous' to the 'proper sphere of understanding' – language.[29] Directed toward nothing, signifying nothing, not acting, the proletarian general strike, as the 'task' of political critique envisioned by Benjamin, is the 'annihilation' of all legal violence,[30] the 'annihilation of state violence [*Staatsgewalt*]',[31] and, like divine violence, is 'law-annihilating' – as opposed to mythical violence, which is 'law-imposing'. Thus, it is only in annihilation – not, certainly, the annihilation of mediacy, but the annihilation of the sphere of positing and its institutions by means of its *reduction to* mediacy – that the proletarian strike is 'the highest manifestation of pure violence by humanity'[32] and can be placed alongside the 'divine violence' of justice, twice called 'striking' (*schlagend*) by Benjamin.[33] The 'nothing' which takes place in the proletarian general strike is most readily distinguished from any *nihil negativum* or *nihil privativum*, from any logically or ontologically defined nothing, by the fact that in it the sheer mediacy of all social relations opens up, and all the formal and especially juridical restrictions of these relations are suspended.[34]

The proletarian general strike, whose method is the unconditional suspension of state power (*Staatsgewalt*) and whose form is justice, would be, in the political sphere, the violence of the political itself. It would thus be what language itself is in the sphere of language: afformative mediacy. Like language, the strike as pure means would be non-violent, neither coercion nor extortion, neither instrument nor the anticipation of transformed power relations, but, in its sheer mediacy, the overthrow itself: 'an overthrow that this kind of strike not so much causes as accomplishes'.[35] Not as a particular form of politics, but as a manifestation of the political as such, and of the only contemporary political force recognized by Benjamin, the proletariat; not as the application of one political means among others, but as an event of the mediacy of the political itself, the strike would suspend any politics oriented toward violently posited ends, and would thus itself be the sheer medium of the political: the only politics which does not serve as an instrument. With the proletarian strike, with the deposing of the rule of positive law, the imparting structure of language, the social itself would historically break through – and open up *another* history.

It may seem paradoxical, but is in fact only logical, that Benjamin makes the unconditional prerogative of mediacy into a criterion for rejecting as inadequate Kant's formulation of the categorical imperative. This is because Kant's formulation entails the license 'to use, or allow to be used, oneself or another in any respect also as a means'.[36] Why is absolute mediacy violated as soon as someone uses himself or another *also* as a means? Benjamin offers no answer, but from the context it is not difficult to propose one: the realm of ends (*Zwecke*) and purposiveness can only constitute itself by way of its relation to possible means, and thus cannot constitute itself otherwise than in the realm of unconditional mediacy. This is why persons or things could be means only with respect to this absolute mediacy, but not with respect to ends, which, as ideas, are foreign to them. If, however, one were to divide up the realm of mediacy into means and ends, one would risk introducing into the moral order a hierarchy of means, thus legitimating a process of infinite approximations, the unattainability of the 'idea of morality' and a politics of the prevention of just politics. The ambiguity of all means-ends relations in the realm of ethics becomes apparent in the fact that such relations cannot in principle eliminate unjust means and thus tend to support the continued dominance of injustice. Consequently, if the order of sheer mediacy would reserve a place for instrumental means, and if it also would tolerate the use of persons as instruments for ends, then, in short, this order itself would be abandoned. The programme of the categorical imperative in its minimal form – the injunction to 'act in such a way that at all times you use humanity both in your person, and in the person of all others, also as an end, and never merely as a means'[37] – demands too little, Benjamin suggests, because it continues to cling to an end beyond means, and because it does not also demand that one *never* make use either of oneself or another as a means to an end.

This consideration has consequences not only for the content, but also for the form of the imperative itself. For even if it demands only that one respect the humanity of each person as an end – and thus universalizes the sphere of ends as that of absolute mediacy – as a categorical imperative it nevertheless remains a law that subjects the realm of morality, and thereby the realm of the community as such, to a transcendental positing, an absolute performative, reducing everything that complies with it to a means of its fulfilment. But this unconditional law is itself dependent on at least one condition: it must articulate itself and is therefore dependent on a language which is neither posited by the law, nor a presupposition for the law – a language independent in principle from acts of positing. The non-thetic character of language is the condition for claiming the universality of *one* language as law, and the afformative, accordingly, is the condition for the possibility of a transcendental performative. The categorical imperative, this performative ground of all performatives, thus *does* nothing but *allow* the afformative of linguistic impartability to appear. It does not *posit* a universal rule or a law, but *exposes* to the unposited mediacy of its own language. Unlike all other, essentially performative imperatives, the categorical imperative, in Benjamin's radicalized version, is the deposition of anything that might cover over the mediacy of language through normative or regulative positings. Whatever manifests itself in it is at base (that is, where the premises of the philosophy of the positing and self-positing of subjectivity have been suspended) not an act of a transcendental subject, not an autoperformative of a transcendental language, but afformation: deposing of the law and exposing to that which, as sheer impartability, ineluctably precedes any positing. The moral law (*Gesetz*) that there shall be a community of speakers, that there shall be one language, is itself exposed to the unposited (*ungesetzten*) character of sheer impartability, of the possibility, and thus the pre-positionality, the pre-speaking (*Vorsprechen*) and the promise (*Versprechen*) of language.[38] Wherever this deposing *in* the categorical imperative of political action – this exposing *into* the afformative of the strike – is not experienced at all, one may assume that the realm of instrumental means and instrumentalized action has not, either analytically or practically, been left behind.

Benjamin terms the conception of the proletarian general strike, and thus the conception of pure violence which emerges within it, a 'moral' conception.[39] But his notion of pure violence as moral violence is nowhere as apparent as in his essay on Goethe's *Elective Affinities*, a text he worked on between 1919 and 1922 – the same period in which he wrote 'Zur Kritik der Gewalt'. The conceptual link between the two studies is most clearly in evidence in a passage from the 'Elective Affinities' essay devoted to the category of expressionlessness (*das Ausdruckslose*). Like the strike, expressionlessness is characterized as 'interruption', 'objection', 'fragmentation' of totality, and with it as the appearance of the 'sublime violence of truth'.[40] Like the strike, expressionlessness strikes (*schlägt*) and 'destroys' (*zerschlägt*); and expressionlessness in its striking (*schlagenden*) objection, its violence, is never positing, forming or transforming, but afformative. In this function it appears as 'the commanding word', as an imperative which brings the course of mere life to a halt, and preserves it in its rigidified state as the representation of a truth of which its moving appearance would not be capable.[41] Benjamin writes:

> Expressionlessness is that critical violence which, while it is unable to separate appearance from essence in art, does not allow them to blend. It possesses this violence as a moral dictum. In expressionlessness the sublime violence of truth appears as the one which determines the language of the real world according to the laws of the moral world. It destroys [*zerschlägt*] whatever survives in all its beautiful appearance as the legacy of chaos: false, erring totality – the absolute. Only this completes the work, by breaking it down, shattering [*zerschlägt*] it, making it into a fragment of the true world, a torso of a symbol.[42]

Just as aesthetic totality is ruined by the blow of expressionlessness that opens beautiful appearance to the dimension of the ethical, so the political totality of legal institutions and the illusion of reconciliation produced by their compromises must, according to the demand of 'Zur Kritik der Gewalt', be 'deposed' by the proletarian strike. The aesthetic of political statutes would have to be shattered (*zerschlagen*) by the strike as that event which no longer posits and which represents nothing – nothing but the unrepresentable, in which the superiority of the moral order over any political order of statutory law announces itself. Benjamin, clearly following Kant's conception of the sublime, speaks here of the 'sublime violence of truth' that appears in expressionlessness. Furthermore, in political history the strike would be analogous to the caesura in the realms of language and art. Citing Hölderlin's remarks on Oedipus, Benjamin, in the 'Elective Affinities' essay, defines this caesura as 'pure word, coun-

ter-rhythmical interruption', and observes that it becomes 'perceptible in the tragedy as the hero's falling-silent, and in the rhythm of
the hymn as objection [*Einspruch*]. Indeed, one could not characterize this rhythm more aptly than by asserting that something beyond
the poet interrupts the language of poetry [*der Dichtung ins Wort
fällt*].'[43] The 'pure word', also termed 'moral' by Benjamin, is thus
audible in the onset of muteness; objection (*Einspruch*) is not itself
a word, not a positing, but the interruption of propositional utter-
ance by something which neither speaks nor posits. So it is for
the strike: something beyond the order of positing interrupts law-
imposing and law-preserving actions and breaks the history of politi-
cal-legal forms, altering it into the fragment of another history. The
caesura opened up by the strike would be the critical, the moral,
the pure word: a wordless one belonging to no spoken language
because it would be its impartability, the very possibility of language
and social life themselves. The sphere in which this caesura intervenes would be that of aesthetic ideology in art and politics.

Benjamin's political theory is a theory of pure means that neither
present (*darstellen*) nor produce (*herstellen*) (for that would make
them into means for something other, serving the subjection and
exploitation of their mediacy), and that neither posit nor are the
act of positing itself (since positing is already bound to a temporal
form dictated by consideration for subsistence, and is thus a means
of its own preservation); Benjamin's political theory of pure means
which do not posit but depose, which do not produce but instead
interrupt production, is not only thematically about a revolution,
but itself effects a reversal of the perspective of classic political
theory: it no longer defines politics by reference to the production
of social life and its presentation in the 'moral organism' of the
state, but by reference to that which subverts the imperative of
production and self-production, which evades the institutions of its
implementation and suspends the paradigm of social self-production
– the law, the law-positing and law-preserving speech act. By defining the realm of the political from the point of view of the work
stoppage, and in terms not characterizable as linguistic *action*,
Benjamin's theory avoids the mistake of transcendental pragmatic
accounts of social and political life – the mistake of allowing the
production paradigm to be resurrected in the paradigm of performativity. The pure mediacy of language which Benjamin places at
the centre of his critique of the political does not depend on any
performative act or force of production, but only emerges in their
suspension: it is afformative. Unlike historical-transcendental

pragmatics, which are oriented toward historical forms of linguistic and social action, Benjamin's sketch of a politics of pure means is a theory not of positing, producing and presenting, not of forming and transforming action, but a theory of the *abstention* from action; it is, if you will, a theory of the transcendental strike which exposes the conditions of historical action, suspends its previous forms, and inaugurates another history no longer dominated by forms of positing and work, by forms of presentation and production, and no longer by forms. A strike, then, that even disrupts the form of the transcendental, the form of pure paradigmatic forms themselves, and thus the possibility of its cognition.

The decision reached by pure, critical violence cannot be made by cognitive means. The decision eludes judgement. Critique, as the advocate of historical justice, must present the possibility as well as the structural unavoidability of the strike and must take part in the strike in such a way that critique is itself 'striking' (*schlagend*).[44] For Benjamin, though, this does not mean that there can be any certainty about 'when pure violence was actual in a given case'.[45] This is to say that, for cognitive purposes, any strike must take place in the border region between political and anarchist general strikes, between negotiation or, rather, extortion and acts of positing new law on the one hand, and the pure violence of deposition on the other. For cognitive purposes, there can no more be a pure anarchism than there can be absolute afformatives. Afformatives can have unforeseen effects, precisely in so far as they 'strike' the cognition directed toward them with powerlessness. The more the event of afformation becomes possible and thus unpredictable in its effects for constative or thetic consciousness, the less the question of its actuality becomes cognitively decidable. Pure violence 'shows' itself precisely in the fact that it never appears *as such*. 'For only mythical violence, not divine [violence], will be recognizable as such with certainty, unless it be in incomparable effects. . . .'[46] The strike is not a matter of theory; it can be the object neither of prognoses nor of programmes; it belongs to the order of events that break through the continuum of history, as they do the commensurability of its cognition. Whoever speaks of the strike cannot be sure that he is not already affected by it, that he is not already participating in it. In his constatives, in his performatives, in his analysis of what has here tentatively been called the afformative, another already speaks – and acts – along with him, another, neither constative nor performative. An other, but not 'as such' – and thus at the very least also as constative and performative. *'Unless it be in incomparable effects. . . .'*

NOTES

The following reflections draw on W. Hamacher, 'Stonehand, This Sovereign, Strike' (lecture presented at the Hannah Arendt Memorial Colloquium, The New School for Social Research, New York City, 18 October 1989). For the paper at the 1 October 1990 Cardozo Law School conference 'On the Necessity of Violence for Any Possibility of Justice', these sections were partly expanded and partly condensed. Since then, the text has been reworked for publication. As it appears here, this essay is still a fragment in progress.

1 W. Benjamin, 'Zur Kritik der Gewalt', in *Gesammelte Schriften*, vol. II, ed. R. Tiedemann and H. Schweppenhäuser (Frankfurt am Main: Suhrkamp, 1977), p. 179. Translations of some passages from Benjamin's *Gesammelte Schriften* are based on W. Benjamin, *Reflections*, ed. P. Demetz, trans. E. Jephcott (New York: Fontana, 1986) (hereafter *Reflections*) and W. Benjamin, *Illuminations*, ed. H. Arendt, trans. H. Zohn (New York: Schocken Books, 1968).

2 Two sets of terms that appear frequently in my text are difficult to translate from German into English: (1) *setzend, rechtsetzend, Gesetz*; and (2) *Gewalt*. In general, *setzend, rechtsetzend* and *Gesetz* are rendered as *positing, law-positing* and *law-imposing*. *Gewalt* in German may have any of the meanings of the English words *force, power, might* and *violence*, depending on the context. It seems to me, however, that in the context of Benjamin's text there is no doubt that any translation other than *violence* runs the risk of euphemizing the problems in question here. Nevertheless, it should be kept in mind that where *Gewalt* appears in a standard expression such as *Staatsgewalt* (state power) or a formula such as 'Alle Gewalt geht vom Volke aus' (All power rests with the people), it can be translated only as *power*, or sometimes *force*. This is due to socio-historical, political and ideological differences between the English and German linguistic cultures that I cannot go into here. This cursory reference to certain linguistic – as well as non-linguistic – shadings lost in the transition from German to English says nothing about the particular logic Benjamin adheres to in his Kantian formulation 'pure violence'. However, it should be clear from the outset that what is at issue here is not 'brutality' and that the predicate *pure* does not represent a rhetorical hyperbole indicating an excess of such 'brutality'.

3 Benjamin, *Gesammelte Schriften*, vol. II, p. 202.

4 Ibid. See also *Reflections*, p. 300.

5 On the motif of contretemporality (*Unzeit*), see W. Hamacher, *Des Contrées des Temps*, in *Zeit-Zeichen*, ed. G. C. Tholen and M. O. Scholl, 1990.

6 Benjamin, *Gesammelte Schriften*, vol. II, p. 190.

7 Ibid. See also *Reflections*, p. 288.

8 Benjamin, *Gesammelte Schriften*, vol. II, p. 190.

9 Ibid., p. 202.

10 Ibid., emphasis added.

11 Ibid.

12 I have already indicated that the series *afformation, afformance* and *afformative* was formed in contrast to *performation, performance* and *performative*; similarly, the use of *afformative event* is to contrast with the use of *performative act* – implying that afformatives are not a subcategory of performatives. Rather, afformative, or pure, violence is a 'condition' for any instrumental, performative violence and, at the same time, a condition which suspends its fulfilment in principle. But while afformations do not belong to the class of acts – that is, to the class of positing or founding operations – they are, nevertheless, never simply outside the sphere of acts or without relation to that sphere. The fact that afformations allow something to happen without making it happen has a dual significance: first, that they let this thing enter into the realm of positings, from which they themselves are excluded; and, second, that they are not what shows up in the realm of positings, so that the field of phenomenality, as the field of positive manifestation, can only indicate the effects of the afformative as ellipses, pauses, interruptions, displacements etc., but can never contain or include them.

The afformative is the ellipsis which silently accompanies any act and which may silently interrupt any speech act.

What 'is' afformative can therefore never be represented in the form of a rule or a law. While every presentation depends on a positing and is essentially performative in character, the 'deposing' of which Benjamin speaks, the afformative, would not lend itself to presentation of any sort. Deposing is not posited. It is not the opposite of positing and cannot be defined as the negation – determinate or indeterminate – of a position as long as the logic of negation is governed by the premises of positional or propositional logic. Accordingly, Benjamin does not simply regard deposing as a historical consequence of unsuccessful political or legal impositions, but as the event of a 'pure immediate violence . . . beyond the law', that is as the manifestation of a violence independent in principle from positing (ibid., p. 202). Moreover, as 'pure immediate' violence, deposing is neither a historical nor even a causal consequence, but rather the absolute precondition of every historical positing violence. The afformative character of political deposing, therefore, does not stand opposed to particular legal positings; it lies beyond position and opposition and is – as athetical, immediate mediacy – the precondition for both, without, however, being expressible, representable or presentable in either of them.

Afformative is not *aformative*; afformance 'is' the event of forming, itself formless, to which all forms and all performative acts remain exposed. (The Latin prefix *ad-*, and accordingly *af-*, marks the opening of an act, and of an act of opening, as in the very appropriate example of *affor*, meaning 'addressing', for example when taking leave.) But of course, in *afformative* one must also read *aformative*, as determined by *afformative*.

Although deposing permits presentation, it is itself irreducible to any presentation. If one wished to speak of 'negative presentation', as Kant does in his analytics of the sublime (and indeed, it will have to be shown that the sublime is a mode of the afformative), then one would have to stipulate that this negativity is determined not in opposition to the positivity of an already instituted linguistic, social, political or anthropological substance. The 'negative presentation' of the afformative could not be oppositive, but at best only prepositive. And if, for Kant, being is defined as mere position, then one must say of the afformative that it 'is' not in the manner of being. It would rather be the pre-possibility which is 'realized' in no performative, let alone in a constative, and does not *strive* for 'realization'; it would be neither *essentia* nor *Wesen*, not even the essence of ontological difference – that is, it would be ultratranscendental and transontological.

If, however, it is necessary to say that the afformative stratum of language merely *lets*, but never *posits*, then it should also be said that all positings depend on this *letting*, preserve the memory of this letting, and are *indebted* to it: the letting, thus, does not simply let and does not leave itself out of the circle of mythical positings without a remainder, but, by way of indebtedness and what Benjamin calls 'fate', cleaves to the form of positing, of legal institutions, and thus to a violence which is not pure. As the sheer possibility of language as such, the afformative cannot help but preserve itself in the diversity of performatives. It cannot help becoming what it is not and will always have become what it never was: the atemporal relinquishes itself to the time of positing, of representation and of duration, exposing 'itself' to the dialectics of imposition and decay. (On the motif of indebtedness, see also note 46.)

13 These reflections are based as much on Benjamin's violence essay as they are on his study 'On Language as Such and on the Language of Man'. W. Benjamin, 'Über Sprache überhaupt und über die Sprache des Menschen', in *Gesammelte Schriften*, vol. II, p. 141. Although this Benjamin text dates from November 1916 and thus pre-dates 'Zur Kritik der Gewalt' by four years, one must assume that the two pieces are based on the same fundamental conception. In fact, each text can be read as the political complement of the other; those aspects of Benjamin's later text that concern his theory of language are hardly comprehensible unless they are read in conjunction with his earlier study. The relevant formulations on means and mediacy in 'Über Sprache überhaupt' read as follows: 'There is no such thing as a content of language. As imparting, language imparts a spiritual [*geistiges*] essence, that is, impartability pure and simple' (Benjamin, 'Über Sprache überhaupt', pp. 145–6). And further: 'all language imparts itself in itself; it is in the purest sense the "medium" of the imparting [*Mitteilung*]. The medial – the immediacy of all spiritual imparting – is the fundamental question of any theory of language' (ibid., p. 144). In opposition to what he terms 'the bourgeois conception of language' (ibid.), Benjamin insists on the immediacy of a mediality, which constitutes all isolated instances of the linguistic process and which is therefore not reducible to them. According to this bourgeois conception, 'the means of imparting is the word; its object, the thing; its addressee, a human being. The other [conception], in contrast, knows no means, no object, and no addressee

of imparting. It says: "In the name, the spiritual essence of man imparts itself to God" ' (ibid.). This statement leaves no doubt that God, for Benjamin, is not an addressee – that is, not an isolatable instance in the linguistic process, but the very mediacy of this process. God is the only immediacy of which one can possibly speak – that of mediacy pure and simple. If pure, unmediated violence is later termed *divine*, this predicate cannot refer to a God that is personally named and introduced as the agent of violence, but only to the unconditional nature of mediacy (*Mittelbarkeit*) and impartability (*Mitteilbarkeit*). God is nothing if not sheer mediacy. Just as language qua imparting imparts itself *in*, but not instrumentally *through*, itself, so the violence which is called divine is a means *in* which pure mediacy manifests itself, and not a means *by* which ends are pursued.

Thus, Benjamin does not deny that language is both sign and address, nor that any violence may serve as means to ends; but the instrumentality of language and of violence cannot even be thought, let alone critically analysed, unless irreducible mediality is thought as its absolute condition. Likewise, legal relations cannot be thought, criticized, or overturned, except in reference to a justice which is not derivable from such relations, either logically or practically, and which is not fully contained by any of them. Justice is one of the dimensions in which unconditional mediacy articulates itself. It is therefore without foundation and does not lend itself to any cognition in the form of positive objectivity – be it that of a fact or that of an intention. The same is true for any politics guided by the imperative not of positive legal forms and historical conventions but of justice alone.

The familiar attempts to localize observations of this kind historically by labelling them 'political theology' or 'Messianism' – which often enough means to discredit them – are based on an uncritical trust in the critical power of history. This trust was not shared by Benjamin. Indeed, such labels – as suggestive as they may be – remain empty as long as they are not developed in the course of a historical *and* formal analysis of the problems they indicate.

14 Benjamin, *Gesammelte Schriften*, vol. II, p. 191.

15 Ibid., pp. 191–2.

16 In this connection it should be noted again that the performatives discussed here are not those whose conditions of validity are already mapped out by conventions or institutions, but only those capable of instituting such conditions themselves. But if one assumes that language as such is not the executive organ of non-linguistically posited institutions, while at the same time insisting that it is essentially performative, then one must also assume that it posits itself in an act of absolute autothesis: that in order to be language, it must always presuppose itself. Thus, language understood as absolute autothetic and autotelic performance, rather than simply positing itself, would permanently – and this is the sign of its finitude – announce itself, speak before itself, speak itself as a language which is always arriving and always yet to come, one which, having never yet arrived, would never yet be language *itself*. This prestructure of language (*Sprache*) would make language as such into a promise (*Versprechen*) of itself. The absolute performative

of language would be the promise of language. Language does not speak; or rather, language speaks precisely in that it promises itself. Paul de Man and Jacques Derrida, following Heidegger, have particularly emphasized this prestructure of the performative trait of language. P. de Man, *Allegories of Reading* (1979), pp. 270–7; J. Derrida, *Mémoires pour Paul de Man* (1988), pp. 95–144. But if language in its absolute performativity always promises itself, then it does not, strictly speaking, promise itself, but promises its promise: the fact that it is infinitely yet-to-come coincides with its infinite non-arrival – so it always does not yet promise. It does not perform – and performs the not, and the always-not-yet, of its performation. The absolute performativity of language, its unconditional being-ahead-of-itself, accordingly implies – constitutively for language, deconstitutively for language as act – a dimension in which language itself does not correspond to itself *as act* and in which, instead of acting, language abstains from any action. This abstention from action is that dimension of language which is here – again tentatively – called affirmative. It is the dimension of the non-arrival of language (or of the contretemporality of language, for that which is ahead of itself and thus misses its own time is eminently contretemporal) which does not render itself present and cannot be oriented by any cognitive or temporal form of representation or, therefore, by any figure of subjectivity and its constitution. Thus, while any theory that thinks language as essentially autoperformative does so according to the model of the self-positing of the absolute subject that lays its own foundation, these reflections attempt to make clear that absolute performative self-foundation is exposed to an abyss of language, to its affirmative, which cannot be overcome by any speech act. (See further remarks on the motif of the 'promise' in note 38.)

Affirmation thus no longer means only dethronement, or deposition of what has been posited. Such deposition is possible only if there 'is' an area of the unposited. Accordingly, *afformation* means also *exposing* to the unposited, giving what cannot become a gift, an event of formation which is not exhaustible by any form.

17 See W. Benjamin, *Briefe*, ed. G. Scholem and T. Adorno (Frankfurt am Main: Suhrkamp, 1966), p. 247; Benjamin, *Gesammelte Schriften*, vol. II, pp. 943–5 (editorial annotations by R. Tiedemann and H. Schweppenhäuser).
18 Benjamin, *Gesammelte Schriften*, vol. II, p. 191.
19 Benjamin, *Gesammelte Schriften*, vol. II, p. 196.
20 Jean-Luc Nancy has developed furthest the notion of imparting, or *partage*, based on a commentary to Plato's *Ion*, and quite apart from Benjamin's reflections. J.L. Nancy, *Le Partage des Voix* (Paris: Galilée, 1982); J.L. Nancy, *La Communauté desoeuvrée* (Paris: Galilée, 1986). Corresponding suggestions are made in W. Hamacher, *The Second of Inversion*, in A. Fioretos (ed.) *Word-Traces* (essay on Paul Celan, originally published in 1984).
21 Benjamin, *Gesammelte Schriften*, vol. II, p. 193.
22 R. Luxemburg, 'The Mass Strike: The Political Party, and the Trade Unions', in R. Bland (ed.) *The Mass Strike: The Political Party, and the Trade Unions and The Junius Pamphlet 3* (1971).

23 Benjamin, *Gesammelte Schriften*, vol. II, p. 193 (citing G. Sorel, *Réflexions sur la Violence* (5th edn 1919)).

24 Ibid. (quoting *Réflexions sur la Violence*, at p. 250). See also *Reflections*, p. 291.

25 Benjamin, *Gesammelte Schriften*, vol. II, pp. 193–4.

26 Ibid., p. 194.

27 Ibid. This letter is not included in Karl Marx and Frederick Engels, *Werke*, vol. 32 (1965). There are references to a controversy surrounding Beesly's article, 'The Social Future of the Working Class', in a letter from Marx dated 20 March 1869 and in Engels's reply dated the following day. See Karl Marx and Frederick Engels, *Collected Works*, vol. 43 (1988), pp. 243–6. Benjamin refers to the account given by Sorel, who carefully adds: 'In this connection Bernstein says that [Lujo] Brentano may have been exaggerating somewhat, but that "the quotation is not too far from Marx's thinking". . . .' G. Sorel, *Über die Gewalt* (1981), p. 159. Benjamin's full sentence, which not only reports but in effect also endorses what it reports, reads: 'Taking up occasional statements by Marx, Sorel rejects any kind of program, of utopia, in short, any kind of law imposition, for the revolutionary movement.' Benjamin, *Gesammelte Schriften*, vol. II, p. 194. That Benjamin's position, in the sentence just quoted and in this whole text, is difficult to reconcile with the invocation of utopian visions in so much of the literature on him requires no further comment.

    With his reference to Marx, Benjamin rather cunningly manages to settle, by sleight of hand, the differences between Marxist politics and the politics of anarchism, in favour of anarchism. Following Sorel, he explicitly calls the proletarian general strike 'anarchist' (ibid.). And in his early notes in 'On the Problem of Physiognomy and Prediction', dating from 1918, Benjamin apodictically voices his conviction that ethics ought to be a doctrine of anarchy: 'Ethics, applied to history, is the doctrine of revolution[;] applied to the state, the doctrine of anarchy.' W. Benjamin, 'Zum Problem der Physiognomik und Vohersagung', in *Gesammelte Schriften*, vol. VI, ed. R. Tiedemann and H. Schweppenhäuser (Frankfurt am Main: Suhrkamp, 1985), p. 91 (hereafter Benjamin, 'Physiognomik und Vohersagung'). Another entry in Benjamin's notes, dating from the period between 1919 and 1920 – that is, from the time immediately preceding Benjamin's work on 'Zur Kritik der Gewalt' – reads: 'The significance of anarchy for the profane sphere must be determined from the historiophilosophical locus of freedom.' For Benjamin, this locus is characterized by 'the destruction and liberation of a (dramatic) presentation. Redemption of history from the actor [*Darstellenden*],' (ibid., pp. 98–9) – that is, liberation from the world as the scene of history, and from the actors, who, according to the master plan of redemption, are bound to play representative roles. This is why the 'doctrine of anarchy' in this fragment, as well as in the essay 'Zur Kritik der Gewalt', is a doctrine of revolutionary and divine violence, the violence of a language that does not represent, but manifests:

    The divine manifests itself in them [the contemporary manifestations of the social] only in revolutionary violence. Only in the community, nowhere in the 'social institutions', does the divine manifest itself non-violently and powerfully [*gewaltlos und gewaltig*]. . . . This sort of manifestation should be sought not in the sphere of the social, but in that of revelatory perception and finally and particularly in language – and first of all in holy language.

(ibid., p. 99)

This theology of a revolution that does not represent but that puts an end to all that represents in that it liberates in it the dimension of mediacy and thus liberates a presentation which does not manifest anything other than itself – this theology of the irrepresentable is, for Benjamin, at the same time an ethics that may be associated with the concept of anarchy. In notes from 1920, which discuss the problems of 'ethical anarchism', Benjamin writes:

To set forth this point of view is one of the tasks of my moral philosophy, a context in which the term anarchism may certainly be used for a theory which denies moral justice not to violence as such but only to any human institution, community, or individuality which awards itself a monopoly over violence . . . rather than revering it as a gift of divine power, as *perfection of power* in individual cases.

(ibid., pp. 106–7)

One's uneasiness at reading such formulations is not diminished if one recalls that they rigorously condemn any recourse to violence by people, institutions or communities as unjust and grant violence only to instances exempted from any human or social presentation: for how should something which in principle evades presentation and consequently also cognition be accessible to reverence without being compromised by it? And how could there be a 'gift of divine power' not claimed by someone, even collectively, and 'administrated' by its claimant? And could this violence, objectified in this way, still be revered without falling prey to mythologization? The thoughts in the last part of 'Zur Kritik der Gewalt' remain truer to the imperative of unrepresentability and demythologization than these formulations do. They state that only mythical violence – that is, positing violence – can be the object of cognition.

As little as the discussion of anarchism in Benjamin's early notes allows Benjamin's ideas to be traced historically to particular sources of anarchist theories (see, for example, B. Wille, *Philosophie der Befreiung durch das reine Mittel* (1894); R. Stammler, *Die Theorie des Anarchismus* (1894); G. Landauer, *Aufruf zum Sozialismus* (1911); and E. Unger, *Politik und Metaphysik* (1921) (studied by Benjamin while he worked on 'Zur Kritik der Gewalt')) it would be a mistake to take the references to Marx and the proletarian general strike simply as an avowal of Marxism, be it to the Marxism still known today as 'orthodox', or to a certain shade of Marxism, such as Sorel's. To Benjamin, working with uncompromising notions of language and politics, it was crucial to show that the only two political forces of uncompromising change in social relations were compatible. One of the questions, however, that one should ask in reading Benjamin's texts is what the link between pure violence and the proletarian general strike (which they – and, in the critical tradition, they alone – establish) might have to contribute to the determination of the proletariat. Clearly, for Benjamin proletariat is not a purely sociological concept, nor does it designate the representative of a violated universal legal norm. The proletariat is positively defined in these early Benjaminian texts only as that class which constitutes itself in and through the general strike and which, in this strike, deposes the state power and its apparatuses just as it ends the historical continuum of privilege and oppression. Since, according to Benjamin, one cannot say with certainty when pure revolutionary violence is actually present (Benjamin, *Gesammelte Schriften*, vol. II, p. 203), it follows that one cannot be certain who belongs to the proletariat. A resolution of this question would belong in the realm of prognoses and programmes and could thus only contribute to a crippling of revolutionary forces: it would reduce something to an object of cognition which is only possible as ethico-political experience.

28 Benjamin, *Gesammelte Schriften*, vol. II, p. 184.
29 Ibid., p. 192.
30 Ibid., p. 199.
31 Ibid., p. 194.
32 Ibid., p. 202.
33 Ibid., pp. 199, 202.
34 A detailed presentation of Benjamin's notions of annihilation and nothingness would have to take into account his familiarity with Hermann Cohen's methodologization of nothingness, H. Cohen, *Logik der reinen Erkenntnis* (1914) and his own treatment of these notions in conjunction with those of positing, position etc. in W. Benjamin, 'Der Begriff der Kunstkritik in der deutschen Romantik', in *Gesammelte Schriften*, vol. I, ed. R. Tiedmann and H. Schweppenhäuser (Frankfurt am Main: Suhrkamp, 1974), p. 7. Benjamin's later notions of *Destruktion* and the destructive character should also be read with reference to these discussions.

It should be self-evident that Benjamin's concepts of annihilation (*Vernichtung*) and destruction (*Destruktion*), aside from their names, have nothing to do with the corresponding propaganda terms of the so-called conservative revolution, or with the 'revolution of nihilism' (as the equation of radical democratic and totalitarian politics would have it, and as some critics by now do not hesitate to insinuate with explicit references to Benjamin). It should thus also be clear that the strike which Benjamin discusses in his piece has little in common with the 'state of emergency' (*Ausnahmezustand*) represented by the strike in the political theory of Carl Schmitt. For Benjamin, the strike is no state of emergency, is not the exception (*Ausnahme*) to a rule in need of protection, of the state's monopoly over violence, but the 'exception' of any system that can still operate with the political opposition of legal norm and state of emergency. Benjamin, consequently, had good reason, twenty years after 'Zur Kritik der Gewalt', in his thesis 'On the Concept of History' ('Über den Begriff der Geschichte'), to demand 'the bringing-about of a true state of emergency' – a remark clearly aimed at Schmitt. W. Benjamin, *Gesammelte Schriften*, vol. I, p. 697.

Herbert Marcuse, who was probably the first to point out the close link between the early study and the later theses, notes:

> The violence criticized by Benjamin is the violence of the status quo, which has preserved in that status quo itself the monopoly of legality, of truth, of law and in which the violent character of the law had disappeared so as to come to light with a vengeance in the so-called 'states of emergency' (which are, *de facto*, nothing of the sort). Such a state of emergency is, in regard to the oppressed, the rule; the task however is, according to the *Theses on the Philosophy of History*, to 'bring about a true state of emergency,' one capable of exploding the historical continuum of violence.

H. Marcuse, afterword to W. Benjamin, 'Zur Kritik der Gewalt und andere Aufsätze' (1965), pp. 99–101.

The passage Marcuse refers to reads: 'The tradition of the oppressed teaches us that the "state of emergency" in which we live is not the exception but the rule. We must attain a conception of history that is in keeping with this. Then we shall clearly realize that it is our task to bring about a real state of emergency. . . .' W. Benjamin, 'Über den Begriff der Geschichte', in *Gesammelte Schriften*, vol. I, p. 697.

35 Benjamin, *Gesammelte Schriften*, vol. II, p. 194.

36 Ibid., p. 187, n. 1.

37 Ibid., p. 187.

38 The problem of community which I have thus touched upon cannot, of course, be developed with adequate precision here. I simply wish to refer to Benjamin's observations in his treatise on language, according to which 'the material commonality of things [must be thought of] in its imparting [*Mitteilung*]', and according to which one must think of a 'communality' that 'encompasses the world in general as an undivided whole'. W. Benjamin, 'Über Sprache überhaupt', *Gesammelte Schriften*, vol. II, p. 156. Such speculations on the 'magical community' (W. Benjamin, *Gesammelte Schriften*, vol. VII, ed. R. Tiedemann and H. Schweppenhäuser (Frankfurt am Main: Suhrkamp, 1989), p. 796), which recall Böhme, Hamann and the Romantics no less than they recall Lévi-Brühl, always move in the proximity of a philosophy of totality, whose doctrinaire and obscurantist features Benjamin elsewhere exposed with all due disrespect. That Benjamin's political philosophy of language does not, however, have anything in common with the doctrines of mysticism should be clear – and should be made clear here – but this ought not to distract from the remaining ambiguities of his analyses.

The paradoxical formula 'teleology without end' most clearly suggests the central terminological difficulty in describing what Benjamin discusses here: pure mediacy shows itself in the critique of Kant's formulation of the categorical imperative as the end itself; and pure means are means toward nothing – that is, they are no longer any kind of means in a comprehensible sense. Pure violence, as a consequence, would be the cessation of any violence which could be employed for the implementation (*Durchsetzung*), or even for the positing (*Setzung*), of ends. Benjamin himself was quite aware of these difficulties in using the terms *means*, *ends* and *violence*. There is good reason to propose that the ambiguity of these terms, which is not entirely resolved by the predicate *pure*, marks the trace of the mythical in Benjamin's own language. The only passage in which Benjamin attempts to circumvent this ambiguity – and where he thus underscores it – turns out to be relatively vague: he speaks of 'a different kind of violence . . . that certainly could be neither the justified, nor the unjustified, means to those ends, that would not function as a means at all, but rather in some other way'. W. Benjamin, *Gesammelte Schriften*, vol. II, p. 196. In this sense, pure means are those which do not function as means, but in some indeterminable 'other' way. But despite this indeterminable otherness, even pure means remain *means* – thus marking the resistance of both the instrumental and of mediacy even in the alterity of the indeterminable.

I have discussed the motif of the promise and the prestructure of language – particularly in connection with the problem of positing and of the categorical imperative – in a different way than I do here in a 1983 essay: W. Hamacher, 'The Promise of Interpretation', in L. Rickels (ed.) *Looking after Nietzsche* (1990); see also Hamacher, 'LECTIO – de Man's Imperative', in *Reading de Man Reading*, vol. 59, ed. L. Waters and W. Godzich (Minnesota, 1989).

39 Benjamin, *Gesammelte Schriften*, vol. II, p. 194.
40 Benjamin, 'Goethes Wahlverwandtschaften', in *Gesammelte Schriften*, vol. I, p. 181.
41 Ibid.
42 Ibid.
43 Ibid., p. 182.
44 Benjamin on at least one occasion speaks explicitly of a 'striking critique' (*durchschlagende Kritik*). Benjamin, *Gesammelte Schriften*, vol. II, p. 187. In this connection, it should be kept in mind that the origin of the German word *Streik* in the English word *strike* would have been more widely remembered in the 1920s than it is today; in the nineteenth century it was still common in German texts to use the word *strike* in its English spelling. Engels's works are one of numerous examples. Benjamin would have been familiar with this spelling and with the meaning of the English word.
45 Benjamin, *Gesammelte Schriften*, vol. II, p. 203.
46 Ibid. The restriction of cognition to mythical or thetic violence is not a limitation which applies merely to a particular realm of cognitive objects, but a structural limitation on cognition itself: cognition is itself essentially thetic. The essay 'On Language as Such and on the Language of Man' (see note 13) is clearer on this point, and again can be read as a commentary on the study on violence. While that essay does say, 'Man is the cognizer [*der Erkennende*] in the same language in which God is creator', 'Über Sprache überhaupt', in *Gesammelte Schriften*, vol. II, p. 149, and also that 'the paradisiac language of man must have been one of perfect cognition' (ibid., p. 152), cognition in the language of names is 'abandoned' in the attempt to recognize good and evil – it 'steps outside itself in this cognition' and becomes a 'parody' of the immediate, creative cognition with which God said, on the seventh day of creation, that it was good (ibid., pp. 152–3). 'The Fall marks the

birth of the human word, in which the name no longer lives intact. . . . The word must impart something (other than itself). That is really the Fall of the linguistic spirit [*der Sündenfall des Sprachgeistes*]' (ibid., p. 153). Through this fall of the linguistic spirit – that is, through cognition of the known, an 'uncreative imitation of the creative word' – language thus becomes a means of imparting something outside itself, becomes a mere sign for something other than itself. This 'violation' of the organic link between creation and cognition, however, is rooted in the form of cognition (and also of creation) itself, in that each is directed toward something other than itself and bestows on this nameless thing a name. It is in this bestowal of a name, and in the possibility of 'overnaming' (*Überbenennung*) that it entails, that Benjamin sees the source of sorrow and of nature's falling silent, as well as the basis of guilt (ibid., p. 155). For anyone is guilty who receives from the sheer mediacy of language – the mediacy in which it imparts only itself – without being able to return what he has received in the same intact medium. Thus, any cognition is guilty which itself is not a creation, as is any imitation which is not immediately creative. This guilt is unavoidable; it is governed by law, without thereby exonerating the sinner. The 'judging word', which seals the expulsion from the paradise of the Adamitic language of immediate imparting, is, writes Benjamin, 'excited [*exzitiert*] in accordance with an eternal law, by which this judging word punishes – and expects – its own awakening as the only, the deepest guilt' (ibid., p. 153). According to this decisive statement in Benjamin's study, language as such disintegrates by way of 'excitation' – that is, by citation, exhortation and external agitation – out of a medium of pure impartability into one of instrumental designation, from speaking into what Benjamin, along with Kierkegaard, calls 'chatter' (*Geschwätz*), from a giving to 'the only, the deepest guilt' (ibid.). One might add that this 'excitation' not only transforms the language of perfect cognition into a parody of cognition, but also transforms that which is here called afformative into the performative as its parody. For the tree of knowledge stands in the paradise of language 'as an emblem of judgment over the questioner. This monstrous [*ungeheure*] irony marks the mythical origin of the law' (ibid., p. 154). The law which forces the empty question of good and evil at the same time disallows this question; it is not only an ambiguous law, but the law of ambiguity itself and thus the law (*Gesetz*) of the 'monstrous irony' of language as such, in that it allows for speaking only by giving it over to 'chatter' (*Geschwätz*), in that it permits no cognition that is not erroneous and in that it turns all positings into parodies of the unposited. But the tree of knowledge, this ambiguous sign of a colossal irony, though it is mentioned late in Genesis, stands as the possibility of parody in the paradise of language from the beginning, and there 'awaits' the fatal question which turns pure imparting into an imparting of something.

This law of irony – which is not the law of an ironic language as opposed to another language, but the law of the irony of language itself that allows for no decision as to whether it is language or sign, imparting or 'chatter', talk (*Unterredung*) or law – might also be called a law of bastardization. At the end of his study on violence, Benjamin writes:

5 Beware Mexican Ruins!
'One-Way Street' and the Colonial Unconscious

John Kraniauskas

We must rather picture this unconscious material
topographically . . .

Sigmund Freud[1]

I have long, indeed for years, played with the idea of setting out
the sphere of life – bios – graphically on a map.

Walter Benjamin[2]

AMERICA

Towards the end of his analysis of Walter Benjamin's city portraits,
Peter Szondi tells the following anecdote: 'At that time a story was
circulating in the emigrant community about a Jew who planned to
emigrate to Uruguay; when his friends in Paris seemed astonished
that he wanted to go so far away, he retorted, "Far from where?" '[3]
The time was 1933, and the Nazis had just seized power in Germany.
Towards the end of August seven years later, in 1940, escaping
from Nazi troops advancing on France, Benjamin began to make
his own way to the American continent. His journey would have
taken him across the Pyrenees and into Falangist Spain, and from
there on to join his exiled colleagues at the Institute of Social
Research in the United States.[4] Thanks to the help of Max Horkheimer he had been issued with a visa in the US Consulate in Marseilles. Some days later, however, he was detained by the Spanish
border authorities at Port Bou. Threatened with deportation back
to France, Benjamin committed suicide on 25 September 1940.
    America had beckoned before. Almost exactly five years earlier,
in a letter to Benjamin dated 23 September 1935, the literary historian Erich Auerbach mentions a previous attempt to provide him
with an opportunity to leave Europe for the 'far away' American
continent, this time to a teaching post in São Paulo, Brazil:

I thought of you once, at least a year ago, when they were looking for a professor to teach German literature at São Paulo. I found out your (then) Danish address through the *Frankfurter Zeitung* and communicated it to the relevant authorities . . .

But, continues Auerbach, 'nothing came of it . . .' (see Appendix). The full correspondence between Benjamin and Auerbach has not been published as yet, and so we do not know how he may have responded to such an idea, if at all. We do know, however, that his economic situation in 1935 was extremely precarious, and that he was finding it very difficult to survive on the stipend he received from the Institute of Social Research and to make a living as a writer. He may therefore have welcomed the opportunity to emigrate.[5] On the other hand, Benjamin's reluctance to leave Europe – and, for example, join Gershom Scholem in Palestine – is well known, as is his strong intellectual commitment to the Arcades Project, which by 1935 was quite well advanced. This reluctance, Benjamin insisted, had political content.[6]

First, there was the arena and traditions to which, as a Jewish intellectual, he believed his work was relevant. Bernd Witte is surely right, in this regard, to point out that Benjamin's reluctance to join Scholem in Palestine accords with his long held 'plea for an establishment for the spiritual values of Judaism in the context of European culture'.[7] Second, there was his commitment to deciphering the crisis-ridden present of that very tradition in the Paris of Baudelaire and the arcades. By September 1940, with the advance of Fascist forces on Paris, Benjamin finally decided to leave Europe. He would never reach America, however – be it the USA, Brazil . . . or even Uruguay. Nevertheless, America reached him – culturally – and not only in its most obvious US guise: cultural fordism (Hollywood).

Bernd Witte's recent intellectual biography of Walter Benjamin suggests that the latter's interest in language was 'awakened by studies with the Berlin teacher Ernst Lewy on Wilhelm von Humboldt and [most importantly for us here] furthered by his work with [Walter] Lehmann in Munich'. In October 1915, he goes on, Benjamin had moved to Munich where, until his departure in December 1916, he attended a number of seminars. According to his correspondence at the time, he was unhappy with his instruction there; except, that is, for a colloquium given by the Americanist Walter Lehmann 'on the language and culture of ancient Mexico'.[8] Witte's suggestion about Benjamin's interests in ancient Mexico confirms remarks already made by Scholem in his own earlier book *Walter Benjamin: The Story of a Friendship*:

> There [in Munich], under the Americanist Walter Lehmann, he [Benjamin] had already started his studies of Mexican culture and religion of the Mayas and Aztecs in the summer semester – studies closely connected with his mythological interests. In these lectures, which were attended by few people and by hardly any regular university students, Benjamin became acquainted with the memorable figure of Bernardo [sic] Sahagún, to whom we owe so much of the preservation of the Maya and Aztec traditions. . . . Some time later, in Berlin, I saw Molino's [sic] big Aztec-Spanish dictionary on Benjamin's desk; he had bought it in order to learn the Aztec language, but he never carried out his project.[9]

Witte concludes his own remarks on this subject as follows:

> The impetus to develop his thinking in written form was given by the intensive discussions with Scholem, who at the time was still studying mathematics but was already occupied with Jewish mysticism. Benjamin's pioneering essay, 'Concerning Language in General and the Language of Man', completed toward the end of 1916 in Munich, originated in his desire to continue his discussions with Scholem on the essence of language in a written forum.[10]

The narrative reconstructed here – from an 'awakening' to the 'development' of Benjamin's thinking on language – leaves little doubt as to the importance of his introduction to ancient Mexican culture for his subsequent intellectual development, and of the seriousness with which he originally pursued – albeit momentarily – his desire to speak 'Aztec'.[11] A critical appreciation of this interest may provide a new perspective on important aspects of Benjamin's work. America would not just be present in his work as the sign of the industrialization of culture (USA) but also, more problematically perhaps, as a site of its mythological critique (Mexico). The purpose of the following notes is to map out some of this ('underground') terrain with reference to Benjamin's 1928 avant-garde publication 'One-Way Street', and to ask after the significance of his subsequent reluctance to register Mexico or to address the questions of colonialism and imperialism in his work on cultural modernity.

GEOGRAPHIES: THE POINTS OF A COMPASS

Travel was, of course, fundamental to Benjamin's writing. Indeed, the point of Szondi's anecdote about the Jewish emigrant's intended voyage to Uruguay was to explain why Benjamin had stopped writing about his travels. The emigrant's retort, he believed, contained the germ of a possible explanation: 'With the loss of one's homeland' – in this case to Nazism – 'the notion of distance also disappears. If everything is foreign, then the tension between distance and nearness from which the city portraits draw their life cannot exist. The emigrant's travels are not the kind one looks back on; his map has no focal point around which foreign lands assume a fixed configuration.'[12] From 1933 onwards Benjamin's now exiled gaze remained fairly fixed on the arcades of his second home, Paris, as he gathered the materials necessary to produce their cultural history. So much so that, as we have seen, he left it until 1940 to attempt to leave Europe and join his colleagues in America.

The importance of the city portraits for Benjamin's Arcades Project has been underlined by Susan Buck-Morss in *The Dialectics of Seeing* in which she takes Benjamin at his word and sets out 'the sphere of [his] life . . . graphically on a map'. The cultural and political significance of the cities visited by Benjamin during the late 1920s and the 1930s is such that together they provide his life and work with a structure 'that locates the *Passagen-Werk* geographically, and lends it a spatial order'. Underlying Benjamin's work can be deciphered the traces of a political geography. Buck-Morss continues:

> To the West is Paris, the origins of bourgeois society in the political-revolutionary sense; to the East, Moscow in the same sense marks its end. To the South, Naples locates the Mediterranean origins, the myth-enshrouded childhood of Western civilization; to the North, Berlin locates the myth-enshrouded childhood of the author himself.[13]

It is the socio-cultural space constituted by the arcades – as at one and the same time 'commodity graveyards' and 'the unconscious of the dream collective' – that lies at the centre of the east-west/north-south axes, and gathers together – under one roof, so to speak – the revolutionary origins (past) and ends (future) of bourgeois culture. This particular map also contains, however, as Benjamin knew well, a fascism triumphant in the myth-enshrouded locations mapped out by Buck-Morss which, furthermore, eventually threatened to overtake Europe's past and future too. Benjamin's arcades thus become a complex spatio-temporal construct of modernity porous to unconscious desire and myth, dreams of the past and the future.[14]

There is something lacking, however, in a political geography of Benjamin's life and work – of arcades, cities and Europe – so dependent on Benjamin's own contextualization of his work, and it is the *internationality* of these spaces as structured by such concepts as *colonialism* and *imperialism*. 'I believe', says Theodor Adorno of Walter Benjamin's 'Paris – the Capital of the Nineteenth Century', 'that the commodity category could be greatly concretized by the specifically modern categories of *world trade* and *imperialism*. Related to this is the arcade as a bazaar, also antique shops as world-markets for the temporal.'[15] Adorno never took full note of this idea in his own work. Yet it is arguable that Benjamin did not follow up this criticism either, refusing to involve himself – and Baudelaire – in the international dimension of capitalism (imperialism/colonialism) signalled by the above critique. From Adorno's point of view the Paris of Benjamin's essay was not just a historical capital – the capital of a specific time (the nineteenth century) – but also a geographical capital – the capital of a specific internationalized *space* (imperialism).

Given Benjamin's interest in the phantasmagoria of World Exhibitions – the precursors of the culture industry[16] – and considering his interest in the materials and economy of the unconscious, this refusal appears unusual. For as Adorno suggests, in some places – bazaars and antique shops – the desires of purchasers and window-shoppers strangely acquired an international dimension, and the clue to such a geography of desire was precisely the historical specificity of the commodity form that so interested Benjamin – which, indeed, was at the theoretical centre of his enquiry. In this respect, both Adorno and Benjamin may have remembered the 'colonial goods' on sale in the shops of the recently unified – and Imperial – nation into which they were born.[17] The internationalized desire of colonialism, however, was subsequently denied and forgotten by both writers, as it has been by the criticism which has occupied itself with Benjamin's work.

The general context into which Walter Benjamin and his colleagues of the Frankfurt school were born was that of an Imperial – and recently unified – Germany in which nationhood and colonialism mutually re-enforced each other in the dominant ruling imaginary (and was to be suffered for years after the loss of colonies in 1918). If this denied international dimension is added to an appreciation of Benjamin's work – and both Witte and Scholem's references to his interest in ancient Mexican culture in the context of colonialism suggest that it should be – then its geographical contextualization must be modified so as to take it beyond Europe. Indeed, the name of the Americanist Walter Lehmann (1878–1939), whose seminar in Munich introduced Benjamin to the work of Bernardino de Sahagún (1499?–1590) and through him to the 'language and culture of ancient Mexico', can stand here as a sign for the comparatively early and rapid development of the discipline of ethnology in Germany (compared with France) during the second half of the nineteenth century. In this respect, note should also be made of the relationship between German colonialism, the discipline of ethnology and art: 'The acceleration of German colonial expansion after 1896', writes Jill Lloyd, 'coincided with developments in Western aesthetics and ethnology which encouraged *Jugendstil* artists to look towards non-European art for inspiration.'[18] Artists, like Kirchner, did not have to go far to find such inspiration. Colonial collections already existed, for example at the Ethnographic Museums of Dresden and Berlin, and were regularly visited. Benjamin himself may even have seen the accompanying side-shows – put on by impresarios and encouraged by governments as part of their colonial propaganda – which exhibited African villages, their inhabitants and dancers in the Zoological Gardens in which he remembered spending so much time as a child. From this interaction between art, colonialism and the institutionalization of ethnology there emerged a particularly strong primitivist mode of expressionism – a cultural form, like the *Jugendstil*, of particular interest to Benjamin.[19]

   In 'One-Way Street' Benjamin includes a fragment called 'Mexican Embassy' whose epigraph reads as follows: 'I never pass by a wooden fetish, a gilded Buddha, a Mexican idol without reflecting: perhaps it is the true God.' The text, interestingly, is by Charles Baudelaire, the literary object of the essay by Benjamin criticized by Adorno. The connection between Mexico and Baudelaire is not arbitrary, although it is not clear that for Benjamin it was ever more than literary. Indeed, Baudelaire's last years (1862–7) were the years of Napoleon Bonaparte's imperial designs on Mexico and the short-lived rule of Emperor Maximilian I – whose execution in 1867 was painted by his friend Manet, three times.[20] This is precisely the imperialism referred to by Adorno and which, according to Benjamin himself, Brecht even suggested was the background to Rimbaud's *Le Bateau Ivre*: 'what it describes is not an eccentric poet going for a walk but the flight, the escape of a man who cannot bear to live any longer inside the barriers of a class which – with the Crimean War, with the Mexican adventure – was then beginning to open up even the more exotic continents to its mercantile interests'.[21] As can be seen, Benjamin registers the imperial relation but seems unwilling to reflect upon it even after Adorno's suggestions. Could this be because he remains internal to an idea of European culture that in 1933 was threatened, and by 1940 destroyed?

UNDERGROUND WORKS

> I saw in a dream barren terrain. It was the market-place at Weimar. Excavations were in progress. I too scraped about in the sand. Then the tip of a church steeple came to light. Delighted, I thought to myself: a Mexican shrine from the time of pre-animism, from the Anaquivitzli. I awoke laughing. (Ana = ἀνά; vi = vie; witz [joke] = Mexican church [!].)[22]

'One-Way Street' is not a city portrait, although it self-consciously uses the city street as its organizing aesthetic principle. Given its status as an avant-garde literary work – it contains most of this movement's contradictory anti-institutional gestures – of all Benjamin's texts this one has received surprisingly little attention. This is because, paradoxically, it has not been *read* as an avant-garde text at all! 'One-Way Street' has rather been interpreted as marking an in-between stage in Benjamin's intellectual development where other works – the 'Work of Art' essay or the *Passagen-Werk* – are privileged. In 'One-Way Street' Benjamin, quite appropriately, is on his way elsewhere. From this point of view, it contains the seeds of another time, Benjamin's intellectual future, for example his reflections on the Paris arcades. Against the grain of narrative, however, 'One-Way Street' foregrounds, as in the above fragment, the symbolic organization of space: topography.

Rubbing his eyes, Benjamin 'takes on the task of dream interpretation'.[23] If the names of Berlin, Paris, Naples and Moscow take on symbolic values in Benjamin's eyes, what could this relationship between 'the market-place at Weimar' and 'a Mexican shrine' symbolize? Both are clearly places of fetishistic ritual (exchange and worship). But why Mexico? Could it be that, since attending Lehmann's seminar on the culture of ancient Mexico, it has come to stand for the colonial relation and, furthermore, a now Surrealist primitivism? Interestingly, the Mexican 'joke' is not located elsewhere, but *here*. And despite the temporality implicit in the '*pre*-animism', nor is it thought as merely a residue from the cultural past; it rather shadows the market *now*, underground. This is a crucial – spatial – dimension of colonialism that Benjamin registers without it becoming then, or later, an object of reflection. This is because the real joke for Benjamin is a Surrealist one.

In his dream, Benjamin unearths a Mexican church under a Weimar market-place: he awakes laughing at the joke. The problem with the Surrealists in his view was their 'undialectical conception of the nature of intoxication': they refused to wake up and see the joke. History for Benjamin, on the other hand, only 'begins with awakening'.[24] But in this dream-presentation history does not begin: the colonial is registered but not reflected. The joke that awakens Benjamin is the image of a Mexican church, which he presents – the function of the exclamation mark – as a puzzle for decoding. However, there is also the other joke: the shrine's contemporaneity and coexistence with the market. Benjamin registers this 'joke on the joke' only to scrape it away with the sand so as quickly to reveal the ridiculous Mexican church that awoke him. In other words, he moves back from the idea of a colonial presence 'fetishistically' underpinning and mirroring European markets to focus attention on that strange colonial object: a Mexican church! The joke contained in the, one supposes, invented Nahuatl ('Aztec') word *Anaquivitzli* is that despite colonization – the imposition of churches – the process of conversion in New Spain may have involved the spiritual overpowering of Christianity by the very religious system it was attempting to destroy. This possibility is implicit already in the Baudelaire epigraph used by Benjamin to frame his other Mexican fragment in 'One-Way Street' mentioned above.

MEXICAN EMBASSY

I dreamed I was a member of an exploring party in Mexico. After crossing a high, primeval jungle, we came upon a system of above-ground caves in the mountains where an order has survived from the time of the first missionaries till now, its monks continuing the work of conversion among the natives. In an immense central grotto with a Gothically pointed roof, Mass was celebrated according to the most ancient rites. We joined the ceremony and witnessed its climax: toward a wooden bust of God the Father fixed high on a wall of the cave, a priest raised a Mexican fetish. At this the divine head turned thrice in denial from right to left.[25]

Bernardino de Sahagún was one of the first Franciscan missionaries to arrive in New Spain soon after the conquest of the Mexica (Aztec) capital Tenochtitlan by Hernan Cortés. Would it be too much to suggest that it may be he that Benjamin has rejoined in a myth-enshrouded Mexico some years after having read and learned about him from Walter Lehmann in Munich? In this dream-presentation Benjamin does not include the moment of awakening. He rather confronts the reader with the message from Mexico to which he, with the surviving missionaries, is a witness and which God denies, three times. Is it the case, as suggested by Baudelaire, that the Mexican fetish 'is the true God'? Is the priest who raises the object entrapped by its magical powers and presenting it to the wooden image of God as his likeness, as an alternative, or even as his truth? This is why the idea of a Mexican church is a joke: it is a joke on the church.

There is a sense in which this fragment stages many of the tropes and figures of colonial narratives, particularly travel, confrontation, anxiety and even mimicry. As with those Surrealists who were to become intoxicated by Mexico – particularly André Breton and Antonin Artaud – whilst the direction of travel remains the same, the evaluative signs of colonialism are inverted. It re-stages a coloniality in which the embassy – mission and message – is from the traditional victims of colonization rather than its bearers. It is precisely the anxiety mapped out by such a context that provides the structural logic for the work of Bernardino de Sahagún in colonial Mexico (New Spain). Serge Gruzinski, for example, has recently told a similar story to the one contained in Benjamin's dream:

> since after 1525 the pre-Hispanic clergy that survived fled underground, the great liturgies and public sacrifices were no longer celebrated, the feasts of the calendar were only partially observed, and communication with the gods took place discreetly in a nocturnal half-light or in the secrecy of caves, hidden from the eyes of the friars or the indigenous neophytes.[26]

Although the 'old religious and political machinery' of the Mexica was 'irreparably cracked and flawed', continues Gruzinski, 'without means or men, without an adequate knowledge of the country, the Church did not yet offer a true alternative'. It was to provide this knowledge that, in large measure, the work of Sahagún was dedicated. He begins the prologue to his most important text – *Florentine Codex. General History of the Things of New Spain*

(1577–80 approximately) – foregrounding the purpose of such knowledge:

> The preachers and confessors are physicians of the souls for the curing of spiritual ailments. It is good that they have practical knowledge of the medicines and the spiritual ailments. . . . Nor is it fitting that the ministers become neglectful of this conversion by saying there are no sins among this people other than orgies, thievery, and lustfulness, because there are many other, much graver sins among them which are in great need of remedy. The sins of idolatry, idolatrous rituals, idolatrous superstitions, auguries, abuses, and idolatrous ceremonies are not yet completely lost. To preach against these matters, and even to know if they exist, it is needful to know how they practised them in the times of their idolatry, for, through [our] lack of knowledge of this, they perform many idolatrous things in our presence without our understanding it. And, making excuses for them, some say they are foolishness or childishness, not knowing the source from whence they spring (which is pure idolatry). And the confessors neither ask about them, nor think that such a thing exists, nor understand the language to inquire about it, nor would even understand them, even though they told them of it.[27]

The response to such colonial anxiety was to collect and document as much as possible of the history and culture of the society destroyed by conquest. The text thus authored by Sahagún and his informants was to be as complete as possible so as to enable missionaries to recognize correctly the idolatry practised right before their eyes. In other words, to assist in 'spiritual conquest'. In effect, Sahagún's is a paranoid and political book: a bilingual and visual collection designed to counter the mimetic abilities of the colonized, their perceived ability to *appear similar*, to appear to have been converted. The historical irony, however, is that given its very nature as a re-collection Sahagún's *Florentine Codex* has also been regarded as potentially subversive. This is because what it collected would enable the remembrance of the very same pre-conquest cultural practices that it was its avowed intention to destroy.[28]

PICTURES FOR THE UNCONSCIOUS

Benjamin was not particularly interested in colonial narratives as such but rather, as his imagistic writing suggests, in mythical topographies that organized space into symbolic above- and below-grounds. His attachment to the dream-worlds presented in both 'Mexican Embassy' and 'Underground Works' are nevertheless quite different from that contained in the following methodological fragment in 'Konvolut N' of the *Passagen-Werk*:

> To clear fields, where until now only delusion (*Wahnsenn*) ran rampant. Forge ahead with the whetted axe of reason, looking neither left nor right, in order not to fall victim to the horror beckoning from the depths of the primeval forest. At a certain point, reason must clear the entire ground and rid it of the underbrush of delusion and myth.[29]

As Walter Menninghaus has noted, the activity of clearing away in this passage seems remarkably close to the Enlightenment concepts of reason and truth of which Benjamin was famously a trenchant critic. Topographically, what in 'One-Way Street' constituted an occasion for a joke, here appears to be the scene of enlightened horror and recoil. The reversal is also accompanied by a geographical abstraction: from a jungle that is located, to another which is violently produced in opposition to an ideal of 'clarity'. The clue to an explanation for such a shift in view appears five entries later in 'Konvolut N', where he sets his work off from Louis Aragon's Surrealist *Paris Peasant* which had initially inspired both 'One-Way Street' and the later incomplete *Passagen-Werk*: 'whereas Aragon persistently remains in the realm of dreams, here it is a question of finding the constellation of awakening'. As we have seen, this is a critique that Benjamin had begun tentatively to elaborate in his 'Surrealism' essay. It is even rehearsed in the two fragments of 'One-Way Street' discussed above.

If 'Mexican Embassy' remains in the realm of slumber and thus, as in Aragon, blurs 'the threshold between waking and sleeping', in his enlightened riposte it is arguable that for the theory of historical experience that interested Benjamin – in which, according to Menninghaus, a truth aligned with reason in opposition to myth was insufficient – he was too awake.[30] The threshold of 'awakening' (designed to break down the enlightened opposition), however, is plotted into 'Underground Works' in the form of laughter. The point of 'awakening', says Benjamin, is 'the dissolution of "mythology" into the *space* of history'.[31] Does laughter do this work of taking myth into history in such a way as to remain partially attached to an experience of it and thereby redeem it?[32] As I have suggested above, it may be that it does not; that Benjamin, in a sense, remained at one and the same time too enthralled by both his aesthetic construction of myth (that is, too Surrealist) and his enlightened rejection of it (understandable in the context of the rise of a 'myth-enshrouded' Fascism).

Benjamin's images of Mexico in 'One-Way Street' were produced at the intersection of ethnology, aesthetics and psychoanalysis constitutive first of expressionism and then of Surrealism. With the invention of the unconscious by Freud a whole new realm of experience was made available to reflection. The unconscious itself, however, had to be narrativized and populated – colonized? – and provided with recognizable dramas that structured and explained it. Anthropology and literature, especially in their respective relationships to colonialism, provided many of the characters, dramas and scenarios – the primal hordes, Oedipuses and Electras, the undergrounds – for such experiences. The newly split European subject was thus provided with an unconscious that, in part at least, was explicable in terms of the anxieties of colonial history. Benjamin's images of overgrounds and undergrounds are arguably, from this point of view, colonial pictures both of and for the unconscious.[33]

Both the joke about the Mexican shrine from the time of pre-animism – that is, from before the subject-object split characteristic of the Enlightenment[34] – and the disturbing message to the missionaries register histories of colonialism. The geography and temporality of each, however, mean that church and shrine remain elsewhere and exist in another time, the past of myth. In this sense, these dream-images in 'One-Way Street' remain internal to a temporal structure of modernity that narrativizes history in terms of a master concept of 'progress' which on a global stage entails the idea of 'the non-contemporaneousness of geographically diverse but chronologically simultaneous times'.[35] Benjamin's colonial Mexico is located in another, non-contemporary time that, by definition, is not present.

This leaves the joke on the joke in 'Underground Works': the joke on the joke of the colonial Mexican church, which, as we have seen, in making the joke contemporaneous, becomes a joke on the market-place of Enlightened Europe – now, it is suggested, enslaved to fetishism (of the commodity) and myth (of the new) and whose roots, moreover, are to be found in '*primitive*' accumulation and *colonial* exploitation. This, however, is not the joke that wakes the dreamer. It is refused entry into 'the space of history' that would provide Benjamin's work – in response to Adorno's critique – with some insight into an international, that is, *imperial*, political geography that would explain the *place* of the Paris of Baudelaire (and Europe) within a colonial system. Encoded and disavowed according to the historically specific intertwining of the logics of aesthetics, psychoanalysis and ethnology, colonialism remains unconscious. Only after Benjamin's death will the crises of Fascism in Europe (particularly the Holocaust) and the subsequent anti-colonial struggles in Africa and Asia reveal – like photography with the optical unconscious – 'the secret . . . the existence of this [*colonial*] unconscious'.[36]

APPENDIX

23/9/35
Rome
Pensione Milton
Via di Porta Pinciana

Dear Mr Benjamin,

My wife has just discovered a contribution by you in last Saturday's *Neue Zuericher Zeitung*. What a joy – that you are still here, that you write, and that in your writings we hear the sounds of our far-off lost homeland. Please let us know immediately where you are and how you are doing. I thought of you once, at least a year ago, when they were looking for a professor to teach German Literature at São Paulo. I found out your (then) Danish address through the *Frankfurter Zeitung* and communicated it to the relevant authorities – but nothing came of the matter, and it would have been pointless to write to you from Germany. We shall probably be staying here until 4th Oct. and then, for a few days, with Dr Binswanger,[37] Castello-Firenze, Villa La Limonaia, Via di Quarto 9. I have had a very sad letter from Beverdell[38] in Prag; Bloch seems to be in Paris; his book,[39] which I have read recently, shows him, whether one likes it or not, in his whole and intact character.

We are well; I am still in office, but do not exercise it much. My *Privatdozent*, W. Krauss, teaches the main lecture course and the seminars and takes care of the examinations; he is proving to be of excellent calibre. Whether I shall still be teaching at all this coming winter seems very questionable; at least it is possible. It is impossible to give you an idea of the strangeness of my position. At any rate it has, for all its advantages, hardly a prospect to last, and is becoming more pointless by the day. I am therefore beginning to make contingency plans; but whether any of them are realizable is very uncertain.

Please write. Cordial regards and wishes from both of us.[40]

Yours

Erich Auerbach

NOTES

I would like to thank Carol Watts, Peter Osborne and Gordon Brotherston for their help in writing this chapter.

1 Sigmund Freud, *Introductory Lectures on Psychoanalysis* (Harmondsworth: Penguin Books, 1981), p. 488.

2 Walter Benjamin, 'A Berlin Chronicle' (1932), in *One-Way Street and Other Writings* (London: New Left Books, 1979), p. 295.

3 Peter Szondi, 'Walter Benjamin's City Portraits', in Gary Smith (ed.) *On Walter Benjamin* (Cambridge, MA and London: MIT Press, 1988), p. 31.

4 In a letter to Benjamin dated 13 April, Scholem compares the events of 1933 in Germany to the expulsion of the Jewish population from Spain in 1492 – the year, too, four hundred before the birth of Benjamin, of the expulsion of the Moors and the beginning of the conquest and colonization of America by Columbus. For many critics this date marks the beginning of the modern age. See Gershom Scholem (ed.) *The Correspondence of Walter Benjamin and Gershom Scholem 1932–40*, translated by Gary Smith and Andre Lefevere, Introduction by Anson Rabinbach (Cambridge, MA: Harvard University Press, 1992), pp. 38–9.

5 In a letter to Scholem sent in February 1939, however, he mentions the fact that the publisher Ernst Rowohlt was emigrating to Brazil without recalling Auerbach's suggestion. See ibid., p. 242.

6 'Every line we succeed in publishing today . . .', Benjamin wrote to Scholem in January 1940, 'is a victory wrenched from the powers of darkness' (ibid., p. 262).

7 Bernd Witte, *Walter Benjamin: An Intellectual Biography*, translated by James Rolleston (Detroit, IL: Wayne State University Press, 1991), p. 114.

8 Ibid., pp. 34–5. Witte bases his suggestion concerning the 'awakening' of Benjamin's interest in language on a statement made by Benjamin himself in a late curriculum vitae.

9 Gershom Scholem, *Walter Benjamin: The Story of a Friendship*, translated by Harry Zohn (New York: Schocken Books, 1987), p. 33. The dictionary Scholem is referring to is no doubt Alfonso de Molina's *Vocabulario de la lengua mexicana* (Leipzig: B. G. Teubner, 1880). Note the place of publication.

10 Witte, *Walter Benjamin*, p. 35.

11 On his own experience in this regard, Scholem writes: 'Remembering Benjamin's account of the atmosphere in the lectures, I was impelled to attend Lehmann's course when I went to Munich in 1919. Under his direction I read religious hymns, and I can still recite many of them in the original.' *Story of a Friendship*, p. 33.

12 Szondi, 'City Portraits', p. 31.

13 Susan Buck-Morss, *The Dialectics of Seeing: Walter Benjamin and the Arcades Project* (Cambridge, MA and London: MIT Press, 1989), p. 25.

14 The idea of 'porosity' comes, of course, from the city portrait written by Benjamin with Asja Lacis: 'Naples'. One of their images of such porosity seems, incredibly, to prefigure scenes from Gabriel García

Márquez's *baroque* fantasy *The Autumn of the Patriarch* (1975): 'Even the banal beasts of dry land become fantastic. In the fourth or fifth stories of these tenement blocks cows are kept. The animals never walk on the street, and their hoofs have become so long they can no longer stand.' *One-Way Street*, p. 175.

15 Theodor Adorno, 'Letters to Walter Benjamin', in Ernst Bloch *et al.*, *Aesthetics and Politics* (London: Verso, 1980), p. 118 (my emphasis).

16 Walter Benjamin, 'Paris – the Capital of the Nineteenth Century', in *Charles Baudelaire: A Lyric Poet in the Era of High Capitalism* (London: Verso, 1983), p. 165.

17 See E. J. Hobsbawm, *The Age of Empire 1875–1914* (London: Sphere Books, 1989).

18 Jill Lloyd, *German Expressionism: Primitivism and Modernity* (New Haven, CT, and London: Yale University Press, 1991), p. 4. I would like to thank my colleagues Annie Coombes and Lynn Nead for bringing this reference to my attention.

19 Ibid., pp. 21–49. Lloyd points out that one of the most important works of ethnography associated with aesthetic movements of regeneration and renewal was Theodor Koch-Grünberg's *Anfänge der Kunst im Urwald* (1907). The work of Koch-Grünberg on the Indians of the Amazon Forest also provided much of the material for Mário de Andrade's carnavalesque post-colonial primitivist novel *Macunaíma* (1928).

20 See Neil Larsen, 'Modernism, Manet and the *Maximilian*: Executing Negation', *Modernism and Hegemony. A Materialist Critique of Aesthetic Agencies* (Minneapolis, MN: University of Minnesota Press, 1990), pp. 32–48.

21 Walter Benjamin, 'Conversations with Brecht', in Bloch *et al.*, *Aesthetics and Politics*, p. 87.

22 Walter Benjamin, 'One-Way Street', in *One-Way Street*, p. 60.

23 Walter Benjamin, 'N [Re the Theory of Knowledge, Theory of Progress]', in Gary Smith (ed.) *Benjamin: Philosophy, Aesthetics, History* (Chicago, IL, and London: University of Chicago Press, 1989), p. 52.

24 Walter Benjamin, 'Surrealism: the Last Snapshot of the European Intelligentsia', in *One-Way Street*, p. 236; Smith, *Benjamin*, p. 52.

25 Benjamin, *One-Way Street*, p. 51.

26 Serge Gruzinski, *Man-Gods in the Mexican Highlands: Indian Power and Colonial Society, 1520–1800*, translated by Eileen Corrigan (Stanford, CA: Stanford University Press, 1989), p. 48.

27 Fray Bernardino de Sahagún, *Florentine Codex. General History of the Things of New Spain, Part 1: Introductions and Indices*, translated by Arthur J. O. Anderson and Charles Dibble (New Mexico: The School of American Research and The University of Utah, 1982), pp. 45–6. The *Florentine Codex* consists in its totality of a text in Spanish, a text in Nahuatl and a visual text (the above edition is an English-language translation of the Nahuatl version). Much of it was produced by Sahagún's native informants. For this reason it has been considered a prototypical work of ethnography. Much of Walter Lehmann's own work was based on the information provided in this text. He also translated sections of it.

It is interesting to note that Georges Bataille had also been a reader

of Bernardino de Sahagún, using the materials contained in the *Florentine Codex* on Aztec sacrifice to provide a historical chapter to his book
The Accursed Share. According to Pierre Klossowski, during the late
1930s Benjamin 'was an assiduous auditor at the Collège de Sociologie
. . . which crystallized around Bataille soon after his break with
Aragon'. However, as an exile from Fascist Germany he believed they
'risked playing the game of a pure and simple "pre-fascist aestheticism" '
(Pierre Klossowski, 'Between Marx and Fourier', in Smith, *On Walter
Benjamin*, p. 368). However distant Benjamin may or may not have
been from Bataille, he was close enough to leave two suitcases of
manuscripts that included much of the *Passagen-Werk* in his care. It is
this connection that has recently made Benjamin a figure of authority
in what has become known as 'postmodern ethnography'. See James
Clifford, 'On Ethnographic Surrealism' in his *The Predicament of Culture. Twentieth-Century Ethnography, Literature and Art* (Cambridge,
MA, and London: Harvard University Press, 1988); and Michael Taus-
sig, *Shamanism, Colonialism and the Wildman. A Study in Terror and
Healing* (Chicago, IL, and London: University of Chicago Press, 1987).

28 See the chapter on Sahagún in Howard F. Cline (ed.) *Handbook of
Middle American Indians*, vol. 13, *Guide to Ethnohistorical Sources,
Part Two* (Austin, TX: University of Texas Press, 1973), pp. 186–239.

29 Smith, *Benjamin*, p. 44. I have found Walter Menninghaus's article
'Walter Benjamin's Theory of Myth' in Smith, *On Walter Benjamin*,
pp. 292–325, very helpful here.

30 Ibid., pp. 297–8, 306. For the Benjamin quote, see 'Surrealism: the Last
Snapshot of the European Intelligentsia', in *One-Way Street*, p. 226.

31 Smith, *Benjamin*, p. 45 (my italics).

32 See Walter Benjamin, 'Theses on the Philosophy of History', in *Illuminations*, translated by Harry Zohn, edited and with an Introduction
by Hannah Arendt (London: Fontana, 1979), pp. 255–66, especially
Benjamin's second thesis.

33 Psychoanalysis, from this point of view, is not only a means of explaining
colonial histories. Colonial history, in its turn, provides an explanation
of psychoanalysis.

34 'We know of primitive peoples of the so-called pre-animistic stage who
identify themselves with sacred animals and plants and name themselves
after them . . .', writes Walter Benjamin in 'Program of the Coming
Philosophy' (1917–18), in Smith, *Benjamin*, p. 4.

35 Peter Osborne, 'Modernity is a Qualitative, Not a Chronological, Category', *New Left Review* 192 (March-April 1992), p. 75.

36 The history of racism would be crucial here (see note 4 above). The
quote is from Walter Benjamin, 'A Small History of Photography', in
One-Way Street, p. 243.

37 Ludwig Binswanger (1881–1966). A Swiss psychiatrist and neurologist,
who also wrote on art (*inter alia* 'Henrik Ibsen und das Problem der
Selbstrealisation in der Kunst', 1949).

38 It has not been possible to establish the identity of this person.

39 *Erbschaft dieser Zeit* (Zürich, 1935).

40 First published in *Zeitschrift für Germanistite*, vol. 6 (1988). Translation
by Peter Pollner.

6 No-man's-land
On Walter Benjamin's 'Destructive Character'

Irving Wohlfarth

THE CONSTELLATION

'Where is my place of work? In Berlin W[est]. . . . But do you really mean to forbid me . . . at my little writing-factory from hanging the red flag out of the window on the grounds that it's nothing but a scrap of rag? Given the "counter-revolutionary" nature of one's work – as you quite correctly characterize mine from a party standpoint – should one do the counter-revolution the further favor of explicitly placing oneself at its disposal? Shouldn't one rather methylate one's work, like spirits, to guarantee its unpalatability to the other side – at the risk of making it unpalatable to everyone?' (*Br* 531). Thus Walter Benjamin, a 'prisoner of [Berlin] West' (*GS* IV, 1, 287) – a middle-class neighbourhood – on his socio-literary situation in April 1931. The immediate occasion for this gesture of self-vindication had been the sharp response of his friend Scholem to his essay on Karl Kraus, which Benjamin had described as addressing the relation between the 'fundamentally metaphysical orientation' of his research and his 'application of the materialist approach' (*Br* 522–4). Scholem answered that the essay merely consolidated an 'illegitimate relationship', which he would merely need to join the Communist Party to discover to be an untenable and costly piece of self-deception. The 'tension' generated by 'playing with the ambiguities and interferences' of the materialist method, Scholem went on, could not but 'neutralize' the 'moral basis' of his insights (*Br* 526–7, 533). Benjamin for his part traced the 'ambiguity' of his work to the absence of a 'German Bolshevik revolution'. 'To respond in the right way – that is, with something "right" – to false circumstances', he pleaded, exceeded his powers. Right could in this situation only mean 'necessarily, symptomatically, productively false'. He did admit that the impossibility of 'unambiguously distinguishing oneself from the bourgeoisie' left him vulnerable to charges of ambiguity. 'Very well, I have reached a limit. Like one who keeps afloat on a shipwreck by climbing to the top of a mast that is already crumbling. But from there he has a chance to send out a rescue signal' (*Br* 530–2). The situation was indeed desperate. In July, Benjamin could still anticipate the imminent outbreak of civil war. But in October he recognized that with the massive rise in unemployment the National Socialists had replaced the Communists as the spokesmen of the masses. 'The German economy has as much stability as the high seas, and emergency decrees overlap like breakers' (pp. 536–7). Long-rang thinking was a thing of the past (pp. 539–40). The same month he mentioned to Scholem a newly written piece entitled 'The Destructive Character' (p. 542). Its model was a banker friend, Gustav Glück.

Seven years later the issue of materialism versus metaphysics revived around Benjamin's work on Baudelaire. Like the 'theologian' Scholem, Adorno, himself a 'materialist', feared that Benjamin was doing 'violence' to his innermost metaphysical powers. These, freed from Marxist 'self-censorship', would ultimately serve the materialist cause all the better (p. 787). Adorno was here practically citing the earlier Benjamin's against the later. This did not, in Benjamin's eyes, prevent the argument from being untrue to *present* priorities. There were truths and truths. Appeals to his 'most precious asset' (Scholem) or his 'very own substance' (Adorno) bore little relation to his own efforts to expropriate his 'little writing-factory' from within. This side of Russia no revolutionary 'melting-down process' of social and literary forms (*UB* 90) had materialized. His own thinking was, however, in the 'process of being totally overhauled' (*Br* 659), and this entailed the 'violence' (p. 793) about which Adorno was apprehensive. To evade a conflict that was incapable of non-violent resolution – *this*, as Benjamin saw it, was to 'neutralize' the strengths his well-wishers wanted to see preserved intact.

Brecht's *Versuche*, the first literary writings to which he could give his critical backing 'without (public) reservations', gave the most probing analysis, Benjamin maintained, of existing 'socio-political tensions' (p. 534). It was in their private exchanges that the mutual differences emerged. If Scholem and Adorno feared for his metaphysical powers, Brecht felt impelled to protect the interests of socialist praxis. 'Depth doesn't get you ahead,' he objected after reading Benjamin's essay on Kafka. Plumbing the depths, Benjamin replied, was his way of 'heading for the antipodes' (*UB* 110). From the destructive tension between materialism and metaphysics – neither a clear-cut choice (Brecht versus Scholem) nor their dialectical harmony (Adorno) – the latter was not, in short, the only one that stood to gain.

His various associates, despite their differences, were all agreed that such a tension of contraries was likely to result in their mutual neutralization. Benjamin for his part looked to their liberating intensification to spark energies which might explode the bastions of the common enemy. The danger he saw lay not in overextending oneself but in an absence of generative tension between potential allies. What distinguished his position from theirs was the effort to have the extremes interact, no less radically, with one another and *thereby* form a popular front (*l'énormité devenant norme*, as the author of earlier *Illuminations* had put it); to make himself a medium for antagonisms between which there could be neither choice nor mediation; and to do so without sitting on the fence. Already in 1927 he considered the political state of 'free-floating suspensions' (*GS* IV, 1, 486), with which Scholem was to reproach him, to be untenable both in fact and on principle. The historical 'disintegration of a "free" intelligentsia' (*GS* III, 174) constituted a definitive refutation of Karl Mannheim's still-born conception of a 'free-floating intelligentsia'. Choices had to be made on the vanishing ground between class lines. At the same time a stand had to be taken in the cross-fire between secretly interrelated positions in order that something might be salvaged of their ultimate unity. If this messianic goal was as neutral 'as white light to the colors of the spectrum' (*Ill* 95), its standard was red. Energies which could neutralize the powers that be were to be assembled in neutral, strategically organized territory, a (wandering Jew's) no-man's-land that kept lines open and space free for Elijah and Utopia.

All these motifs intersect in 'The Destructive Character' – unpalatable, objective ambiguity, the improvisation of a weak rescue signal, the right violence as the rallying-ground for the socio-literary vanguard of a dispersed opposition, the dismantling of hardening sectarian antagonisms, the breaking of new paths – not mediations – through seemingly impenetrable dilemmas, resolution at the crossroads, all in the impersonal person of an uncanny, providential nobody equipped to handle a runaway emergency and hold an untenable position between the lines. 'Where thinking suddenly stops dead in a configuration pregnant with tensions, it imparts to that constellation a shock by which it crystallizes into a monad' (*Ill* 262–3). As it moves between theology and historical materialism and establishes ('illegitimate', 'free-floating'?) relations between Moscow, Berlin West and Jerusalem, Benjamin's thinking suddenly stands still amidst a force-field – it was increasingly turning into a mine-field – of tensions and crystallizes around a figure (*Denkbild*) which leaves none of its points of reference intact.

THE DESTRUCTION OF CHARACTER, THE PURIFICATION OF DESTRUCTION, ALLEGORY

The destructive character is no 'character' in the psychological sense. Character is rather one of his targets. What emerges from its efface-ment is the faceless model of a positively conceived characterless-ness. Why, then, still call him a character? For Benjamin, like Wilhelm Reich, denounced the very idea of character as an 'armored concept' (*Br* 329). A short treatise written ten years earlier suggests an answer. 'Schicksal und Charakter' ('Fate and Character') sets about clearing away 'superficial' notions of character to 'make room' (*GS* II, 1, 175–7) for another, seemingly retrograde one based not on the psychological novel or 'modern physiognomy' but on the comedies of Molière and the old 'doctrine of the temperaments' (p. 179). The notion of character is progressively disentangled from its association with fate, divorced from 'moral evaluation', placed beyond 'psychological analysis' (p. 177), and thereby, a decade before the addition of the predicate 'destructive', made invulnerable to gossip.[1] 'While fate ravels the enormous complication of a per-son's guilt, the tangled skein of debt and liability, character consti-tutes an inspired solution to such mythical bondage. Complication turns into simplicity, fate into freedom' (p. 178).

What 'releasing the old words fate and character from their ter-minological shackles' (*Br* 239) ultimately intends is the liberation of the bourgeois subject from the tutelage of his pseudo-emancipation. The return to pre-bourgeois models opens up the possibility of a post-bourgeois character. A 'multiplicity of character traits', which is generally considered synonymous with the 'richness of a creative personality' (*UB* 97), figures in this context as a mythical 'net' (*GS* II, 1, 176–7). It is as a highly developed individual that one might not be clear of fateful complication. Conversely, reduction to a single, seemingly immutable character trait does not necessarily connote the unfreedom of a compulsive monomaniac but rather a capacity for single-minded action capable of cutting through the labyrinth of mythical 'ambiguity' (*GS* I, 1, 288). The ground is here already cleared for the destructiveness that everywhere clears ways. The destructive character too has no personal character traits. To be possessed of a single property is equivalent to ow(n)ing none. 'Anonymity' (*GS* II, 1, 178) of *character* liberates the individual *person* from a labyrinthine 'complex of law' (*Rechtszusammenhang*) and guilt (pp. 174, 176). Subject means subjection. 'The enormous complication of a person's debt' is liquidated by the discovery that the world is 'enormously . . . simplified when tested with a view to its destruction'. The 'Apollonian image of the destroyer' stands out against the darkening gloom of bourgeois inwardness as clearly as once did the comic hero, whom Benjamin characterizes as the 'sun of the individual in the colorless (anonymous) sky of man'. As a 'trigonometric sign' he illuminates the 'affinity' of freedom and logic (p. 178).

What the inverted commas around the 'destructive character' mark off is less a literal quotation – the phrase is not a standard one – than a summary translation of prattle into language calculated to reduce it to silence. The pseudo-quotation is a doubly false one inasmuch as no-one of that description appears in older characterologies either. This merely makes the quotation all the more destructive. An older notion of character is cited in order to clear away modern misconceptions. The *bourgeois* character had flourished between the eras of the old subject and the new predicate. Their conjunction marks its withering away. The destructive character expropriates 'possessive individualism' (C. B. MacPherson). Where once there was a variety of simple characters, the figure of the *terrible simplificateur* is now singled out as having the consistency with which to confront the present. Benjamin's *The Origin of German Tragic Drama* resurrects the actuality of a quite different character – the brooding melancholic, who embodies a buried allegorical interpretation of the world. The destructive character is his 'cheerful' counterpart. Instead of interpreting the world, he changes it. The one inhabits an inner labyrinth; all the other's 'paths' lead to 'success' (*GS* IV, 1, 349ff.). But the hostility he evokes in ideologists of creative individuality is of a piece with the bias against allegory on behalf of symbol.

'Fate and Character' destroys seemingly harmless ideas about character; Benjamin's later theses in 'The Work of Art in the Age of Mechanical Reproduction' 'brush aside a number of outmoded concepts, such as creativity, genius, eternal values and mystery' (*Ill* 218); and his concluding unscientific postscript 'Theses on the Philosophy of History' explodes the category of progress. 'The

Destructive Character' focuses on the loaded concept of destruction itself, summarily effecting *its* destruction.

That destruction is bad and creation good is a very old story. Where all was once darkness and void, the good Lord created light and the world: 'and, behold, it was very good'. A slot was thereby created for the evil (scape)goat. Goethe's Mephisto, to be sure, is a mere shadow of his former self – one indication, this, of his latter-day emasculation, the destruction of the destroyer. With Chaos and 'Mother Night' eclipsed by God the Father, Mephisto is relegated to impotent protest against the 'creative power' which 'inwardly unites the world' (*die Welt im Innersten zusammenhält*). The destructive 'bond' that, according to a slightly emended self-quotation from 'The Destructive Character', 'unites in harmony [*einträchtig zusammenhält*] all that exists' (*UB* 57) thus constitutes an inversion of the Goethean theodicy, where it is not the Destroyer but the Creator to whom the world offers 'a spectacle of the deepest harmony'. Not that destruction is now blasphemously rechristened, *à la* Sade, to function as a positive, natural principle mobilized against culture and religion. And far from helplessly trying to introduce diabolical discord into cosmic harmony, the destructive character has cheerfully made his peace with the world. Not fighting a losing battle against nature's god-given proliferation, he can, unlike Mephisto, be *cheered* by the knowledge that 'everything deserves to perish' (*Alles ist wert, dass es zugrunde geht*). It is destruction itself – and not its cunning Goethean or Hegelian recuperation – that is here divinely authorized. The unifying Goethean life-force (Ludwig Klages called it 'cosmogonic eros') is in this perspective indistinguishable from the universality of mythical guilt (*Schuldzusammenhang des Lebendigen*, in *GS* II, 1, 175). The *symbolic* cosmos, which relegates destruction to both impotence and damnation, is itself consigned to *allegorical* 'dismemberment' (*O* 186). 'The false appearance [*falsche Schein*] of totality evaporates. For the eidos is extinguished, analogy ceases to exist, the cosmos it contained shrivels up' (*O* 176). Goethe's *Verweile doch! du bist so schön!* now applies to the moment when beautiful appearances (*der schöne Schein*) are destroyed. Only then does 'Nature-History' (*Natur-Geschichte*), which appears to the melancholy allegorist as a 'death's head', 'Passion' and 'state of sin' (*O* 166) and to the angel of history as a mounting 'pile of debris' (*Ill* 260), assume a redeeming aspect. 'Where others shine forth as resplendently as on the first day' – *herrlich wie am ersten Tag* echoes the 'Prologue in Heaven' in

Goethe's *Faust* – 'the image of beauty' which baroque allegory 'holds fast' is that of 'the last' (*O* 235).

The same holds for the destructive character's 'Apollonian' appearance. Whereas Nietzsche's *Birth of Tragedy* had equated the Apollonian principle with *schöner Schein* and 'the deification of the individual', Benjamin's essay on Goethe's *Elective Affinities* defines the antidote to mythical nature in supra-individual terms as 'the expressionless'. 'For it smashes the surviving heritage of chaos beneath all beautiful appearances: the false, aberrant totality. What completes the work is its disintegration into a fragment of the true world, the torso of a symbol' (*GS* I, 1, 181). 'The Apollonian image of the destroyer' would thus constitute a paradox. Fair is foul, and foul is fair. 'Classical harmony of form' (*O* 166) has been implicitly transferred from the beautiful symbolic façade behind which the old chaos persists to the allegorical side of the opposition. As a result the destructive character's Apollonian features are as 'expression-less' as his cheerfulness is 'Chinese'. 'Whereas in the symbol destruction [*Untergang*] is transfigured and the radiant face of nature fleetingly revealed in the light of redemption, in allegory the observer is confronted with the *facies hippocratica* of history as a petrified, primordial landscape' (ibid.). In the figure of the destructive character the paralysed melancholiac has been transformed into a doer whose acts restore the light of judgement to an allegorically perceived world.

What binds the world together is an ancestral curse from which it is waiting to be released (*Ill* 254). This drastically revised version of 'the great chain of being' – a topos of the same great tradition which the allegorist's gaze unmasks as the ideology of the 'victor' (*Ill* 258) – results from a historical crisis which had shaken classical ontology to its foundations. Being no longer has an axiomatic *raison d'être*. Hegel's 'reason in history' has ceased to carry conviction. The world now has to show cause why it should *not* be destroyed. The destroyer's relation to the existing order is thereby inverted. *He* now calls *it* to account as if *he* represented the Last Judgement. No positive standard ('that life is worth living') is invoked, only a negative one ('destruction of what deserves destroying' (*GS* IV, 2, 1001) – but no *merely* negative one. Destruction neither takes the place of the destroyed as some new, positive value, nor does it remain subordinate to the status quo as its loyal opposition. The eternal objection that the destructive have no constructive ideas what to 'put in its place' is voided from the outset. The destructive character does, however, clear space as the lieu-tenant (*Mandatar*, in *GS* IV, 2, 999) of an absent power. Destruction is thus invested with a positive force unmatched even by the powers that be, let alone their powerless 'critic' – unless, that is, the latter is no longer conceived as a 'carper' (*GS* II, 1, 350) or 'Thersites' (*GS* IV, 2, 999) on the sidelines of world events, but rather, as in Benjamin's version of the critical annihilation practised by Karl Kraus, as a divine emissary 'on the threshold of the Last Judgment' (*GS* II, 1, 348). For the destructive character's sociability is poles apart from the 'unhappy consciousness' that is the lonely burden of the alienated social or cultural critic. Rather he embodies the solution to the unresolvable contradictions which threaten to reduce all resistance to spleen. His *faits accomplis* invalidate the unanswerable dialectical argument that unqualified destructiveness condemns one to 'abstract' or 'indeterminate' negation. Like Mephisto's, it would, on a Hegelian diagnosis, be at once dangerous and harmless, wreaking nothing but havoc yet also untenable and easily contained.[2] The destructive character is, rather, describable only in negative, tangential relation to existing models of destruction. He is no intangible *deus absconditus*, however, but rather the efficient executor of an eviction order.

THE AESTHETICS OF VIOLENCE

'The Destructive Character' identifies the prevailing prejudice against destructiveness as 'the most petty-bourgeois of all phenomena'. With the consolidation of bourgeois modes and relations of production all forms of destruction which do not in turn contribute to the turnover of capital are, with certain largely diversionary exceptions, generally tabooed, especially by small property-owners. What alarms them most is that those who need 'free space' do not shrink at 'suspending the rule of law' (*GS* II, 1, 202). These 'are called destructive'. During the last hundred years, the (anti) bourgeois avant-garde has regularly adopted as watchwords terms of abuse originally directed against it. The revaluation of the destructive is a case in point. So much so that the very gesture of modern literature has been plausibly seen in terms of a festive metaphorical destruction of the capitalist order.[3] The work ethic was to be recklessly abandoned, its accumulated fruits conspicuously consumed. In rehabilitating destruction, Benjamin does not, for his part, place a contrary taboo on the utilitarian. His strategy is no more identifiable with quasi-aristocratic forms of revolt than with bourgeois capitalism. Once again the oppositions have been realigned. For here it is the *destroyer* who husbands his resources. He does not squander his energies on uneconomical acts of protest but 'remains in control of his powers' (*Ill* 264). 'He reduces the existing to rubble, not for the sake of the rubble but of the path that extends through it.' This sentence itself breaks new ground through existing oppositions. Whereas Romantic nihilism, wanton destruction for its own sake, represents a mere mirror image of production for its own sake, and to that extent a harmless by-product of the status quo, the *effective* nihilist ' "enters" ', in (un)Hegelian fashion, ' "into his opponent's strength in order to destroy him from within" ' (*GS* II, 2, 481).

And yet the destructive character cheerfully lays himself open to the charge of aestheticism, without, however, flirting with it – for that would indeed constitute aestheticism. Though explicitly distinguished from nihilistic variants of 'art for art's sake', his portrait evokes undeniably literary associations. A first draft presents him (not as rising up from Dionysian depths but) as a 'contrasting image of positively Apollonian beauty' (*GS* IV, 2, 999). No phrase is more conducive to 'chatter' (*Gerede*, itself, since *Sein und Zeit*, another loaded term) than 'young and cheerful'. While still far removed from 'blond and blue-eyed', the phrase, taken in isolation, might seem indicative of Jewish self-denial or a dangerous proximity to superficially similar futurist motifs. The effort to distance himself unambiguously from the bourgeois 'neighborhood' of Berlin West would in that case have landed Benjamin in the enemy camp. He himself construed his strategy differently. He assumed that only advance positions had any prospect of success in the struggle against Fascism. Abandoning disputed territory for fear of operating in the vicinity of the enemy meant, on this view, withdrawing to defences that were bound to be overrun. Even barbarism was to be wrested away from the other side. As late as 1933 Benjamin was still siding with an avant-garde prepared, 'if need be', to survive culture with a Nietzschean 'laugh' that might 'at times sound barbaric' (*GS* II, 1, 219). Such a 'new, positive concept of barbarity' has, needless to say, nothing in common with 'the wrong kind' (pp. 215, 219). Benjamin's concept of destruction, while easily misunderstood, is no less unequivocal. That there were wrong ways of liquidating tradition and purging the world was not something of which in 1931 one needed to be reminded. But to abandon 'joyful wisdom' and the guilt-free beast of prey to the enemy – *this* was the short-circuit to be avoided. 'Young and cheerful' is a Nietzsche quotation that has been liquidated and 'hewn out' of (Fascist) context (p. 365), a 'tiger's leap into the past' (*Ill* 263) rather than the original predator.

'The Destructive Character' rests on the political assessment that liberal humanism is no match for a demonic perversion of the *Übermensch*. Only the new *Unmensch* (*GS* II, 1, 354, 367) who has no dealings with a 'noble, time-honored . . . image of man [*Mensch*]' but only, like Brecht, with 'people' (*Leute*; pp. 216–17) is equal to the situation.

Such realignments in no way efface the battle-lines. These are, on the contrary, sharply drawn where others blur them. 'The Destructive Character' alerts the reader to aestheticist misunderstanding; and the epilogue to 'The Work of Art in the Age of Mechanical Reproduction' (1936) unequivocally denounces both the Fascist ideology of futurism ('culmination of art for art's sake') and the actual Fascist 'aestheticization of politics' (*Ill* 243). Already one year before 'The Destructive Character' Benjamin had subjected the most recent version of political aestheticism to sustained critical annihilation. His review of *Krieg und Krieger*, a volume of essays edited by Ernst Jünger and devoted to the glory of modern warfare, was simply entitled 'Theories of German Fascism' (*GS* III, 238ff.).

BETWEEN LIBERALISM, MARXISM AND ANARCHISM

Benjamin saw in pacifism no alternative to the cult of war but only its mirror image. His own 'Critique of Violence' (1921) was a theory of the 'divine' counter-violence capable of arresting the continuity of 'mythical' violence (*GS* II, 1, 199). He rediscovered it in Georges Sorel's conception of a proletarian general strike which would aim not at political and economic blackmail but at the 'suspension of law' and the 'demolition of the state' (pp. 202, 194). As a 'pure means' such action, regardless of its possibly catastrophic consequences, would be 'non-violent'; the state, however, brands such action as violence pure and simple (ibid.). Awareness that the state and its laws were founded on revolutionary violence (*rechtsetzende Gewalt*) was, Benjamin argued, eroded by the latter's transformation into a law-and-order conservatism (*rechtserhaltende Gewalt*) which legitimized the suppression of subsequent revolutionary subversion merely by identifying it as violence. Modern parliaments thus exhibited a weakened 'sense of the constitutive violence vested in them' (pp. 190, 202). Unscientific though Benjamin's political analysis may have seemed, it was uncannily accurate. In the Weimar Republic liberal democracy and ideology were to prove no match for Fascist violence. 'While he spoke', Benjamin noted in 1938 after a political discussion with Brecht in Denmark, 'I felt the impact of powers equal to those of Fascism', powers that 'sprang from depths of history no less deep than Fascist power' (*UB* 120). The destructive character can take on the dark forces of latter-day, 'enlightened' myth only because his own force goes equally deep. It is a matching combination, at once modern surface and archaic depth, 'signal' and 'oracle'. Oracles do not, of course, abide by parliamentary procedures. To invoke such 'destructive state institutions' at the critical juncture when parliamentary democracy was trying to *preserve* itself from destruction was to invite political misunderstanding. Benjamin had invoked Sorel's rehabilitation of violence without feeling impelled to elaborate on its political ambiguity. Disregarding the rules of liberal scholarship, he had 'cited' it out of context. From a liberal standpoint this was tantamount to a leap into the wrong camp, a blurring of crucial distinctions.

But a middle-of-the-road verdict on the extremism of 'The Destructive Character' would itself have blurred decisive political dividing-lines. A comparison with Thomas Mann's *Doktor Faustus* indicates as much. So broadly are the interrelations between nihilism, aestheticism and political barbarism there construed that no positive notion of destruction can be visualized that is not a sinister portent of Fascist violence. From the old-world humanist standpoint of Mann's narrator Serenus Zeitblom no hard and fast distinction could ultimately be made between Benjamin's destructive character and Jünger's front-line hero. His portrayal of the so-called 'Kridwiss circle', a group of proto-fascist conservatives who champion Sorel in the name of a 'deliberate rebarbarization' (*Doktor Faustus* (Frankfurt am Main: Fischer, 1963), pp. 393, 397), is a case in point. 'Their world was at once old and new, revolutionary and regressive', no more or less reactionary than 'the path that leads back round a sphere' (pp. 393, 395). In the image of the sphere 'progress and regression', left and right, pre- and post-bourgeois impulses, both the reconciliation of myth and enlightenment and its diabolical parody, are interlinked as part of the same vicious circle. This no doubt accurate diagnosis of the dangerous games that certain intellectual cliques played simultaneously supplies the ideological scheme for an all-purpose defence mechanism. How 'The Destructive Character' would have been read on this basis can be deduced from Zeitblom's shocked reaction to the Kridwiss circle's claim that the First World War had definitively demolished bourgeois traditions. What most alarms him is that this should be announced in accents of joyful wisdom. That a cultural avant-garde should denounce the culture it feeds on – 'and cheerfully at that' (p. 392) – Zeitblom can only interpret as an act of 'self-denial' (p. 394). Anxious humanists might likewise be expected to confuse the destructive character with the common enemy. It is, however, a *different* 'relation of regression and destruction' (*GS* I, 3, 1244) that he embodies; and in shedding bourgeois selfhood, he rids himself in the process of its accompanying forms of self-denial.

If the destructive character lays himself open to the liberal confusion of left and right, orthodox Marxists could be counted on to charge him with anarchism. To protect him against them would indeed be 'senseless'. A strain of 'revolutionary nihilism' (*GS* II, 1, 299) is inseparable from Benjamin's writings. The old struggle between Marxism and anarchism was far from dead. But Benjamin felt no compelling need to decide between them. On the contrary, he regularly accentuated his anarchist sympathies whenever he made a move in the Communist direction, as if to test both in the border area between them. His essay on Surrealism wants anarchist 'revolt' inserted into the 'methodical and disciplined preparation of the revolution' (*GS* II, 1, 307); conversely, and synonymously, the political methods of the Communists are to focus on the anarchist goal of ending all political goals (*Br* 426). Marx, Bakunin (*GS* II, 1, 306) and Blanqui (*Ill* 262) variously figure in Benjamin's writings as comrades in arms. Such imaginary alliances, it could be objected, obscure actual historical conflicts. To this there is a concrete historical answer. Warring factions which no existing state socialism could reconcile were to be made to interact in the no-man's-land of an openly committed mind. Relations that had been prematurely broken off needed restoring. The destructive character posts himself at their intersection. He conjoins the contradictory forces of a divided yet common opposition. After all, not only anarchism but Marx too refuses to 'envision' the future, and thereby contaminate it with petty-bourgeois dreams; and, conversely, organization is Blanqui's watchword. More radical even than radicals, and better adjusted, too, the destructive character is an anarchist in the guise of a banker.

Praxis, according to one of Benjamin's letters, is only possible 'in religious or political terms': 'I do not grant any essential distinction between the two. Nor for that matter any mediation' (*Br* 425). 'The Destructive Character' in turn nullifies the standard alternative between political Romanticism and pragmatic realism. Oppositions which Benjamin disqualified, however, have reappeared in the secondary literature, most elaborately in the case of Rolf Tiedemann's appeal to a 'soberly' conceived 'historical materialism' against the nihilistic, apocalyptic aspects of a 'political Messianism' which, he claims, led Benjamin to aestheticize politics in ways he was elsewhere the first to condemn.[4] And whereas readings of Benjamin that came out of the German student movement tended to discount theology in favour of praxis, more recent philological work has rediscovered the theological dimension of Benjamin's thought only (in order?) to conclude that no political praxis can come of it. Where Scholem had warned against the *false* combination of politics and religion, the premise shared by Benjamin's younger readers is that the two cannot mix at all. He himself assumed the opposite: 'I speak here of an identity which emerges only from the paradoxical reversal [*Umschlagen*] (in whatever direction) of one into the other, the indispensable precondition being that action is contemplated unconditionally and radically enough. . . . Always radically, never consistently [*konsequent*] . . .' (*Br* 425).

'EFFACE THE TRACES' (BRECHT)

There is much evidence to suggest that Brecht was one of Benjamin's models for 'The Destructive Character', which was written during a period of intense discussion between them.[5] 'Differences arose over the criteria by which the critic measures what the truth is. Whereas Brecht . . . defines truth in terms of "what is socially practicable," progress towards it being achieved by the correction of "thought by reality," Benjamin . . . conceives it as the "radical demolition of the world of images." There are, he argues, two ways of achieving this goal: theology and materialist dialectics' (Bernd Witte, *Walter Benjamin – Der Intellektuelle als Kritiker* (Stuttgart: Metzler, 1976), p. 171). In 'The Destructive Character' Benjamin's strategy of alternately testing opposing positions against their most searching adversaries involves a further criss-crossing of opposites. In recording the corrective impact of the 'pragmatist' on the 'theologian', it also smuggles theology into the pragmatism. For truth is in this instance *both* 'what is socially practicable' ('ways') *and* the 'radical demolition of the world of images' ('envisions nothing', 'rubble'). The pragmatism borders on the miraculous, and the theology is identifiable only by the *depth* of its soberness and the *radicalism* of its profanation. The interplay between the poles is also interior to each. What seemed a one-way contact between impervious agent and passive observer turns out, at least retroactively, to exert a reciprocal impact. To that extent violence is also done to the destructive character's models. They are translated into a language in which polar opposites engage in a 'paradoxical reversal of one into the other' – a movement which Benjamin captures in such oxymorons as 'profane illumination' and 'holy-sober' (Hölderlin's *heilignuchtern*). 'The Destructive Character' invests a Brechtian figure with something of that 'aura' which, on a theory Benjamin was to elaborate four years later, is itself the chief target of revolutionary, Brechtian destruction. This is in turn subjected to (un)Brechtian reconstruction (*Umfunktionierung*; *UB* 93). Aura survives its demolition – without necessarily *outliving* itself and turning into an ideological smokescreen – as the aura of the auraless. Brecht was to return the compliment by translating Benjamin's paradoxes into the language of 'crude thinking' (*plumpes Denken*; *UB* 81). 'All so much mysticism', he later commented on the theory of aura, 'coupled with an anti-mystical stance' (*Arbeitsjournal* (Frankfurt am Main: Suhrkamp, 1973), vol. 1, p. 16).

'And if this soberness seems holy, it is, curiously, perhaps only in Goethe's eyes that it is not' (*GS* I, 1, 196–7). Two totally different versions of soberness underlie the exchanges between Benjamin and Brecht. The latter feels drawn to logical positivism, and considers Chopin and Dostoevski unwholesome (*UB* 114). Benjamin's notion of soberness goes back to German Romantic speculation, which conceived prose not as the sober antithesis of poetry but as its 'creative ground' (*GS* I, 1, 102), the colourless 'sober light' (p. 119) which comprises the whole spectrum within it. He rediscovers it in the 'dialectical optic' of the Surrealists, who recognize 'the everyday as impenetrable and the impenetrable as everyday' (*GS* II, 1, 307). In the figure of the destructive character one version of soberness is irradiated by the Messianic light of the other. While he 'envisions nothing' (*kein Bild*), his 'dialectical destruction' – the 'radical demolition of the world of images' (*Bildwelt*) – nevertheless opens up a Surrealist 'space of images' (*Bildraum*; p. 309), a Messianic world of 'liberated prose' (*GS* I, 3, 1235). The impenetrably everyday language of 'The Destructive Character' points towards that promised land. At once 'oracle' and 'signal', down-to-earth and *Luft von anderen Planeten*, it is generated by a tension between conflicting conceptions of language. The Brechtian component liquidates 'the barbarity of formulaic language' (*Br* 329). If faint traces of a dimension not wholly 'cleansed of all ceremony' (*GS* I, 3, 1235) can still be detected in the repetitive, almost ritual invocation of 'the destructive character', this is perhaps because, trapped in a 'necessarily false' situation, it subliminally enacts a litany which, like the theological ghost in the machine called historical materialism, 'has to keep out of sight' (*Ill* 253).

The Messiah, according to a 'great rabbi', will 'change the world not by violence but by the merest readjustments' (*GS* II, 2, 432). It is by similarly fractional realignments that Benjamin turns the violent impact of Brecht's 'crude thinking' to Messianic advantage. The Brechtian alienation-effect is itself slightly alienated by being conflated with Benjamin's 'dialectical optic' on history: '[Epic theatre] lets existence spurt up high from the bed of time and, for an instant [*Nu*], hover iridescent in empty space, the better to bed it afresh' (*UB* 13). Such penetration of the everyday is synonymous with 'profane illumination'. Seemingly incommensurable energies, the mystical *nunc stans* and the anarcho-syndicalist general strike, are to act in concert to bring history to a revolutionary standstill. The moment of alienating suspension – a politicized version of a classic, Schillerian definition of the role of art – is its aesthetic counterpart, an iridescence which contains the spectrum of possible futures. It is fleetingly lingered over. 'For a moment at least', life appears to have escaped the laws of inertia. The axioms according to which nature abhors a vacuum, makes no leaps etc. would, applied to society, constitute the mythical constants of its natural history. Benjamin conceives revolution as the leap that abruptly suspends it. To the stoppage of time, the 'Messianic cessation of happening' (*Ill* 263), corresponds the destructive expropriation of space; to the emptying of space, the instant that hovers in empty space. 'For deep down life does not', concludes the first version of 'The Destructive Character', 'go on . . . but from one extreme to the other' (*GS* IV, 2, 1001). At the surface no traces remain of these inner tensions. They are buried from view, like 'the traces of [the theatre's] sacral origins' since the 'filling-in of the orchestra pit' (*UB* 1). But it is only from the surface that they have disappeared. The pragmatic motto 'Efface the traces' will later be adapted to theological ends – another unBrechtian version, this, of Brechtian *Umfunktionierung*. The parable of a dwarf hidden inside a chess automaton whose hand it invisibly guides hints that theology too has to preserve its anonymity to be able to enter into secret partnership with its natural allies. Whether historical materialism knows that it should, or already does, incorporate theology, or whether the dwarf has to infiltrate it as a secret agent, the parable does not say. What does emerge is that the 'eristic dialectic, which . . . enters the opponent's strength' is complemented by the opposite strategy of bolstering one's allies from within. But it evidently belongs to the hide-and-seek – the cunning of Messianic reason – that the secret also be partly disclosed.

The destructive character is easily mistaken for a crypto-Fascist of the left or right. But his motto resembles nothing so much as the socio-economic imperative of bourgeois society itself. He taps its strength in order to turn it against itself. For it was bourgeois capitalism that was first motivated by the imperious 'need for free space', the better, of course, to 'occupy' it; that has effaced traces on a universal scale in order to create an imperialist 'world in its own image' (Marx); and that could finally proceed to remove some of the evidence of its own destruction. It represses the memory of its violent past so effectively as to be able to conceive it in evolutionary terms. Correlatively, the ' "scientific" character' of positivist historiography is achieved by the 'total eradication of everything that recalls its original vocation as remembrance' (*GS* I, 3, 1231). In the process no traces were more systematically erased than those of the destructive character himself. Revolutionary counter-violence was, in one exemplary case, silenced twice over – solitary confinement, the simple punitive answer to the need for free space, being further prolonged by subsequent oblivion: 'Within three decades [social democracy] managed virtually to erase the name of Blanqui, the rallying cry which had reverberated through the preceding century' (*Ill* 260). Such methodical destruction reduces the world to rubble *without* redeeming it. It would, unchecked, pave the way for a brave new world which, having removed the last vestiges of a past it considered obscene, would be left marking time. So-called 'progress', Benjamin argues, is predicated on the inert eternity of 'homogeneous, empty time' (*Ill* 262), the clock-time of Baudelairean spleen, which voids its history and effaces its destruction. Only a contrary evacuation, which produces 'the instant that hovers in empty space', can arrest its perpetual motion. Making empty space available for the new would thus constitute a mimetic redemption, an expropriation, of capitalist activity.[6] Each neutralizes the other's devastation. Capitalism is the most enlightened of mythical, the most mythical of enlightened forces. It both capitalizes on the mythical 'heritage of all who ever emerged victorious' (*Ill* 256) and brands counter-violence as atavistic. The destructive character's strength is that he does not belong among the 'primitive rebels' (E. J. Hobsbawm). He meets the double threat of a mythical enlightenment by welding disparate forms of resistance into a force which confronts the status quo with an apotropaic version of its own undeviating positivism.

The Brechtian motto puts a favourable construction on an unfavourable state of affairs. Benjamin's commentaries on the relevant poems accentuate its ambiguity. Thus the vagrants in the 'Handbook for City-Dwellers' have no individual traces to efface; those they do manage to leave behind, such as stains in a whore's bedclothes, are 'best unmentioned', and the 'precept . . . "Efface the traces" ' is 'supplemented by the adjunct: "rather that than have someone else efface them" ' (*UB* 64). There is, likewise, hardly any aspect of the destructive character that is not without its negative counterpart in some other text of Benjamin's. Brecht may be 'an expert in fresh starts' (*UB* 37), but 'starting all over again', 'the regulative idea of both gambling and wage-labor' is elsewhere equated with the unsalvageable emptiness of someone who has been 'reduced to reflex responses' and 'cheated of his experience, a modern' (*CB* 137). Such people 'live their lives as automatons and resemble Bergson's imaginary characters who have completely liquidated their memories' (p. 135).

There can be no *guarantee* that the individual, once rid of his inwardness, will, instead of becoming a hollow man, 'let go of himself' (*UB* 58) 'in the right way'; will, rather than succumb to collective inertia or the psychology of crowds, emerge 'new-born' from the 'matrix' of a critical mass (*Ill* 238). What, then, distinguishes right from wrong ways of liquidating the past, and mechanical alertness from true presence of mind? Benjamin banks on the 'exchange of a historical for a political perspective' (*GS* II, 1, 300), at the risk, no doubt, of *losing* perspective. But this is not necessarily the worst loss one can incur. A poor exchange can nevertheless constitute the right course of action, a liquidation of tradition which thereby restores whatever liquidity it still has: 'We have been reduced to poverty. We have surrendered one heirloom after another, often depositing them at the pawnshop for a hundredth of their value, in return for a few pennies in negotiable currency [*die kleine Münze des Aktuellen*]. Economic crisis looms ahead, and beyond it the shadow of impending war' (*GS* II, 1, 219). There can, under such conditions, be no biding one's time; the only right moment is the present. At least from the late 1920s on, Benjamin's writings constitute an 'uninterrupted series of tiny improvisations' (*CB* 70), strategies intended to quell despair, 'preventive measures and antidotes' (*Br* 556) calculated to cope with situations in which 'everything can go wrong'. Where everything is at stake, thought is driven to new levels of speculation. 'The Destructive Character', like 'The Work of Art in the Age of Mechanical Reproduction', is a historical gamble. The vindication of destruction in the one corresponds to the rehabilitation of 'disreputable' (*Ill* 239) categories in the other. As an attempt to wrest the solution from the very givens of the problem by giving a further twist to an already devious turn of phrase, Benjamin's version of 'Efface the traces' stakes its hope on a historical turn of events which failed to materialize. Only in foreshortened retrospect, however, did it never have a chance. To speak here of voluntarism would be to exchange back a political for a historical perspective. The destructive character, for his part, 'never thinks he "has a choice" ' (*GS* IV, 2, 1001).

The effacement of traces and, correlatively, the loss of aura are objectively ambiguous developments. Benjamin's response is two-fold. 'The Destructive Character' is counterbalanced by 'The Story-teller', which singles out the trace of the artisan's hand as the hallmark of a disappearing world of 'experience'. It is not, at least not primarily, these authentic traces that invite destruction but rather the secondary substitutes that cover up their actual historical effacement.[7] The scene of their monstrous accumulation is the bour-geois interior. Comfortably ensconced within it, celebrating their respective rituals, fussing over the velvet-lined 'traces of [their] earthly days' (Goethe) within the hermetic safety of their own four walls, dwell the *Etui-Mensch* and the 'creative individual' (*GS* IV, 2, 1000). Traces have come to belong to the artificial paradise of interior decoration. They are 'phantasmagorias of the interior' (*CB* 167) based on denial and substitute-gratification. To efface the sub-stitutes one merely need reapply the logic of the substructure to the ideological superstructure. All that the destructive character has to do is to introduce bourgeois matter-of-factness into places from which it has been elaborately screened.

Preserving *authentic* traces and destroying their *false* substitutes are complementary activities. But while they may share the same ultimate purpose, the two can in the short run prove irreconcilable. 'The Destructive Character' is predicated on the assumption that there are critical moments when it is only through 'destruction' that 'humanity . . . can prove its mettle' (*GS* II, 1, 367). 'Some hand things down by making them inviolable and conserving them; others pass on situations by making them handy and liquidating them.' The former ignore the *situations* from and into which seemingly self-sufficient traditions are handed down; a well-preserved façade of apparently inviolate *things* blocks the political view. Such tra-ditionalists include not merely ideologists who shuttle between the 'cultural treasures' and the respective historical 'victor' (*Ill* 256) but also those spokesmen for the oppressed who still subscribe to the reigning belief that ' "the truth won't run away from us" ' (*Ill* 255). 'The Destructive Character' implicitly defines itself against those conservatives in the socialist camp who, as Lukács will, invoke the past as a humanist 'heritage' (*GS* II, 2, 473) or a treasury of utopian traces (Bloch's *Spuren*).

CULTURAL BOLSHEVISM BETWEEN EAST AND WEST

'A fine phrase of Brecht's will help us out, a long way out: "Efface the traces" ' (*GS* II, 1, 217). For several years after visiting Moscow in 1927 Benjamin saw Soviet Russia as pointing the way out. 'The new perspective one gains on [Berlin]', he noted, 'is the most unquestionable advantage of a stay in Russia' (*GS* IV, 1, 316). The East-West comparison underlies a number of his subsequent writings; 'The Destructive Character' is also written in this margin. If it is in the 'wretchedness of the interior' (*GS* II, 1, 299) that the prisoner of Berlin West experiences the claustrophobia of bourgeois society, Russia figures, conversely, as the answer to the need for 'fresh air', the Archimedean point from which the old world might be moved.

In his own thinking Benjamin seeks to initiate an equivalent process to this 'world-historical experiment' in social transformation (*GS* IV, 1, 330), experimentally identifying it with the blank space in which solutions to the 'antinomies' (*UB* 89) of bourgeois society could be worked out. Where familiar notions 'have almost disappeared from the face of the earth' (*GS* II, 2, 743), the anonymous effacement of traces no longer connotes the social alienation that drives windowless bourgeois monads back into their shells. The abolition of private property has been implemented by 'sealing off everything private to an unimaginable extent' (*Br* 439), thereby clearing, for more than 'a moment', a *tabula rasa*, the 'empty space . . . where the thing stood, the victim lived'.[8] 'Every thought, every day and every life lie here as on a laboratory table. . . . On the shop-floor, in the houses and buildings, employees, offices and furniture are regrouped, transferred and shifted about' (*GS* IV, 1, 325). The furnishings inside Russian houses – which are 'merely used as camping-sites' – may only amount to a collection of 'petty-bourgeois odds and ends', but their weekly rearrangement constitutes a 'radical means of ridding the air of "snugness" [*Gemütlichkeit*] and its accompanying melancholy' (p. 328). In the West Sundays mark a weekly rendez-vous with the spleen that Baudelaire pictures as the hopeless, angry jangle of chafing church-bells (*CB* 144). Moscow, on the other hand, is 'practically liberated from the chimes which on Sundays spread such profound sadness over our large cities' (*GS* IV, 1, 344). The insides of overladen byzantine churches have 'not merely been cleared out but gutted like game' (p. 346).

Is, then, the destructive character the Bolshevik's Western counterpart and vice versa? 'What distinguishes the Bolshevik . . . from his Western comrades is his state of utter preparedness. He manages on so little that he is, year in year out, ready to give it up and start afresh. He would not otherwise be equal to the task' (p. 326). Inapplicable though it is said to be to the Bolshevik's Western comrades, this characterization also holds for the destructive character; conversely, the following sentence might have been formulated with the Bolshevik in mind: 'What matters to him are not private adventures but the permanent certainty of having a historical job to do' (*GS* IV, 2, 1000). The social arena as the essential dimension of existence, impersonal relations incompatible with a bourgeois or feudal order, authoritarian watchwords, the futility of suicide – these are among the motifs that recur in both contexts. But every common trait pinpoints the vast divergence between them. 'Being able to insert one's ideas into a pre-given field of force; a mandate, however implicit it may be; organized, guaranteed contact with one's comrades' (*GS* IV, 1, 327) – these advantages are not available to the destructive character, who first has to gather 'people' – not 'comrades' – around him and, significantly, receives *his* mandate from an *unnamed* authority. His borderline situation is also implicit in a comparison omitted from the final version: 'Contrast the builder: the conditions of his existence deteriorate daily; his sphere of action is increasingly narrow; and his equilibrium – closer, even at the best of times, to the unsteadiness of the creative temperament than the stability of the destructive character – is progressively imperilled' (*GS* IV, 2, 999). *Der Aufbauende* – itself an unconvincing neologism – falls unhappily between the 'creator' and the destroyer. He combines the former's nerves with the latter's commitment to praxis – a discrepancy which threatens to reduce his constructions to harmlessly 'creative' castles in Spain. The refined inmate of the bourgeois interior has from the outset sought shelter from the testing pressures with which builder and destroyer have to contend. That only the latter can cope with them is symptomatic of a specific 'historical' situation. He has 'a historical sense: a basic, invincible mistrust of the course of events'. That history is a permanent routine emergency has become a self-evident truth. It requires the individual to pawn things of sentimental value, above all himself, and 'exchange the play of his features for the dial of an alarm-clock' (*GS* II, 1, 310). Only the destructive character knows how late it is. Where the economy has 'as much stability as the high seas', the unsupported private initiative of the 'builder' lacks any foundations to build on. But where, as in Russia, the evacuation of the old coincides with the construction of the new, the alternative between building and destroying no longer obtains. If from within Berlin West Benjamin distinguishes the destructive character from the bourgeois nihilist, the two are from a Russian viewpoint practically indistinguishable. 'Everything is in the process of being built or rebuilt', writes Benjamin from Moscow, 'and almost every moment poses very critical questions' (*Br* 439). These, however, no longer place the whole society in question by exposing structural contradictions.

Some pass on 'situations by making them handy and liquidating them'. 'Nothing short of a German Bolshevik revolution' could decisively alter the destructive character's situation. Benjamin variously correlates the Russian experiment with the impulses of the disparate, necessarily superstructural avant-garde he identifies with Brecht, Loos, Klee, Le Corbusier and others. The Western counterpart to Bolshevik reconstruction is not the 'builder' but the 'constructor' who 'starts out from scratch' (*GS* II, 1, 215). In Russia culture is under standing orders to place itself in the service of an ongoing process of social renewal; in the West it is the gathering-place for frustrated social impulses violently at odds with the cultural ghetto within which they have been confined. 'The Destructive Character' practises a form of *cultural* bolshevism. Its constructor was aware that the Party would label him 'counter-revolutionary'. He did not contradict Scholem's contention that the Russians would have no use for his 'dynamite' except in the bourgeois camp (*Br* 527).

THE 'LIQUIDATION' OF THEOLOGY

Does the destructive character come to prepare the way for the Messiah, or is it his job to destroy theology too? Convincing evidence exists for either alternative. Scholem's reading of 'profane illumination' places most weight on the noun; others accentuate the predicate. Both are surely right only against the other. It was the difficult, compelling tension – not the well-trodden alternative – between the positions to which Benjamin responded.

It was, he conceded in a late jotting, beyond his powers to eradicate all traces of theology. 'My thinking relates to theology like blotting-paper to ink. It is totally soaked in it. But if the blotter had its way, none of the writing would remain' (*GS* I, 3, 1235). The blotter can only blot theology, it cannot blot it out. It is not content, however, to dry and thereby consolidate holy writ. Its ambition is to liquify and thereby liquidate it, to transform its canonic forms back into ink, leaving behind a *tabula rasa*. It can blot nothing, however, without thereby absorbing it; and its capacity for absorption has limits. Only a blotter more magical than Freud's 'mystic writing-pad', only an apparatus whose possibilities of self-evacuation matched its need for free space, could solve the dilemma. The blotter would have to be able to blot itself, to be constructed, in other words, like the destructive character. For to erase the tablets completely would require the capacity to efface both inner and outer traces of one's destruction. That is the destructive character's secret: he can continue to empty space because he himself never fills up. Only a blotter, a receptive 'witness to his efficacy', could, it is true, have registered his impact and formulated his impress. But by the same token a blotter can only *dream* of assimilating a mode of operation no longer based on the usual models of assimilation. Never immersing himself, the destructive character never gets bogged down. His work differs no less decisively from *Hegelian* immersion (*Versenkung*), with its 'patience of the concept' and its 'labor of the negative'. The 'indefatigable eater with the iron jaw' (*UB* 57) who has ' "eaten his way through" ' (*gefressen*) humanist culture and 'had more than his fill' (*GS* II, 1, 219) works reality over far differently from the *Weltgeist*. His relation to the past marks a clear departure from the Hegelian digestive system, an encyclopaedic, (anal-)retentive, self-interiorizing memory (*Er-Innerung*) which 'preserves-and-negates' (*aufheben*) the entirety of its prehistory. *Aufhebung* might be said, oversimply, to have split apart into its component meanings. Transposing the bourgeois 'phantasmagoria of the interior' to academic scholarship, historicism had reduced memory to the indiscriminate accumulation of bric-à-brac from a historical past which, Nietzsche insisted, it was wholly incapable of digesting and sometimes ought actively to forget. To such toothless eclecticism – historicism at one level, social democracy at another – Benjamin opposes 'destructive powers of mind' (*GS* II, 2, 481), which he equates with *his* version of dialectics (p. 478).

The blotter is not content to function as a secretarial *ancilla* to theology. For theology, the adversary of myth, is itself in need of redemption. Only where 'origins and destruction find one another' (*GS* II, 1, 367) will the reign of myth finally come to an end. Benjaminian demythologization differs markedly from standard versions of rationalization, secularization etc. Even his liquidation of theology is not without a hidden Messianic dimension. This does not, however, make it a 'negative theology'. And to view Benjaminian destruction, *à la* Scholem, in *exclusively* theological terms would be to reconstruct the traces instead of effacing them; to deny that the destructive 'process of transformation' on which Benjamin staked his development ever took serious effect; to be unwilling to concede *any* destructive powers, however '*weak*' (*Ill* 254), to the blotter. Nor, finally, is Benjamin's difficult, uneven relation to theology to be conflated with the steady filtered flow of metaphysical motifs into Adorno's 'negative dialectics'.

Were the blotter to succeed in erasing holy writ, it would have cleared the empty space that is the incognito of the new. Translation into the language of the profane would leave none of the original intact. But theology would not thereby have been simply superseded. Its liquidation would be its fulfilment, a void 'filled with the presence of the now [*Jetztzeit*]' (*Ill* 261). The destructive character 'envisions nothing'. But whenever Benjamin momentarily departs from the Jewish taboo on 'investigating the future' (*Ill* 264), the moveable feast that ensues is *openly* theological in character. With the unwriting of Scripture re-emerges the original Messianic language that preceded the written word, a language of 'ubiquitous and integral actuality' released from all prescription, 'integral prose that has burst the fetters of the written'. The multiplicity of fallen languages is translated into a single idiom that is no longer 'written but . . . festively enacted' (*GS* I, 2, 1238). It coincides with an uninterrupted *Messianic* effacement of traces, an *erotic* nihilism. For 'true actuality' is enacted by angels whose destiny it is, 'after singing their hymn before God, to cease and disappear into nothingness' (*GS* II, 1, 246); and the rhythm of this 'eternal and total transience' is the definition of 'happiness' (p. 204). For all this the destructive character, who cannot afford to divert any attention from the shifting *historical* moment, has no time. But its attainment remains 'the task of world politics, whose method will have to be called nihilism'.

'PESSIMISM OF THE INTELLECT, OPTIMISM OF THE WILL' (GRAMSCI)

'The Destructive Character' is the scene of a peculiar 'identification with the aggressor'.[9] Only in the intervening space it simultaneously creates could the text have come into being. The brief, self-reflexive preamble hints that one of the text's enabling conditions was the match made between a character who effaces traces and the writer who retains them. The destructive character, one of those moderns who have made it their business to 'free themselves from experiences' (*GS* II, 1, 218), is himself the object of an almost Proustian experience. 'Looking back upon one's life', one might, 'perhaps accidentally', be jolted into recognizing the pattern of one's 'deeper relations'. This could scarcely happen to anyone as shock-resistant as the destructive character. On the other hand, it is only by borrowing his technique that the 'blotter' can trace his portrait. In the interval between the shock and its articulation – the gap between the first paragraph and the rest of the text – the 'mimetic faculty' (*GS* II, 1, 210), which is itself destructive,[10] has been at work. Its object, the destroyer's strength, is itself mimetic – the protective mimicry it takes to negotiate the jungle of the cities. The way the text imposes itself corresponds to its subject's *faits accomplis*. It likens him to an oracle, and itself exercises an oracular authority all the more mysterious for having removed any overt traces of the occult. Instead of offering the reader a piece of well-developed characterization, it leaves empty gaps, eschews progress, makes fresh starts and prompts misunderstandings that it neither seeks nor avoids. It proceeds, in other words, like the destructive character himself. What began as a simple opposition turns out to be an elective affinity between secretly interrelated positions. To 'hand on' his version of the destructive character, the author has forged a destructive style; conversely, the destructive character 'stands in the vanguard of the traditionalists'. The lines are crossed: the no-man's-land is formed by the *x* of a chiasmus. Both the destructive character and 'The Destructive Character' are intersections of tensions. The *text* sets up an interaction between the *character*, himself a conjunction of forces, and his 'other'; and the destructive character is himself the product of that encounter. Was Benjamin himself a destructive character? A metaphysician, melancholiac and collector, he inhabited a far from empty space. He was by his own account no 'unwritten page' (*Br* 579) and hence could not bring himself to 'clear out' of Europe. But in Brecht, Baudelaire, Kraus, Loos,

Blanqui and others he was drawn to destructive characters that corresponded to and with his own.

Their *Denkbild* is both 'an image from involuntary memory . . . which suddenly appears at a moment of danger' (*GS* I, 3, 1243) and a construct 'designed on the drawing-board' (*GS* II, 1, 216). The authoritative, if not authoritarian, gesture of the text imparts self-actualizing power to a speculative construction. Like its subject, it forces, wills, open a passage. The closed formation of its assertions asserts them against the power of the facts. Its 'technique is that of the *putsch*' (*CB* 100); it too 'forestalls' normal expectations. Embracing a multiplicity of existing idioms, it 'prodigiously' simplifies them; a montage of heterogeneous materials, it is yet all of a piece. There is indeed scant trace of any breaks that would betray the hidden presence of inner tensions. They too have been effaced, no more and no less, to reinforce 'the unreality of despair'. Where the Baudelairean dandy represented a fictive *persona* who *redoubled* the individualism of the bourgeois monad in an effort to master the problematic situation of the 'lyric poet in the era of high capitalism', the destructive character has the task of rescuing a still bleaker situation by *dismantling* the subject. The *flâneur* 'makes a virtue out of necessity, and in this displays the structure which is in every way characteristic of Baudelaire's conception of the hero' (*CB* 70–1). The analogous brittleness of Benjamin's post-heroic hero is heroically denied by the contrary assertion of his unshakeable strength. But his robust doings remain a fragile fiction, his realism magical, and the leap beyond the merely literary perhaps still all too literary. In reality – a relevant criterion in his case, if also the touchstone of the 'victors' – the established order would have little trouble in containing or harnessing his subversion. What 'the drowning man clutches at' is a 'straw' (*GS* I, 3, 1243). How, then, decide whether the intended embodiment of total vigilance is any more than the mirage of a rescuing organizer, whether the 'organ of historical awakening' (*CB* 176) is not a last-minute dream that mistakes itself for its awakening, a phantasmagoria of the *exterior*, the trap of antiromantic Romanticism? Benjamin himself left the question open whether Blanqui's relative lack of interest in the theoretical underpinnings of socialism might not have been 'rooted in a deep-seated mistrust of the findings that wait for anyone who immerses himself too thoroughly in the structures that govern existence'.

This commentary has essayed a 'philological' reconstruction of the buried context in which 'The Destructive Character' intervened. Commentators and philologists are by profession preservers and readers of traces, 'collectors, conservative, conserving natures', who, rather than make 'situations . . . quotable' as destructive types do, seek to ensure that 'things' remain 'transmissible' (*GS* IV, 2, 1000). What nevertheless justifies the commentary in Benjamin's eyes is the urgent need to *preserve* texts *from* destruction. 'Tomorrow', he predicted, 'may bring disasters of such colossal dimensions that we can imagine ourselves separated from the texts . . . of yesterday as though by centuries' (*UB* 44). An 'exhaustive' archeology of *'The Destructive Character'* would, however, rebury it. What needs to resurface is its force. The only adequate response is to 'quote' it, thereby destroying it, but introducing 'prudence and circumspection into the destruction' (*Br* 709). For 'The Destructive Character' not merely describes its own destructive production, it also prescribes what its reception should be – an exchange at the going rate. 'Presence of mind is of the essence. . . . To interpret or to use [the signals], that is the question. . . . If we miss the chance, then, and only then, is it decipherable. We read it. But now it is too late' (*GS* IV, 1, 141). The present reading stops where intervention should, belatedly, begin.

NOTES

The original text is in *Gesammelte Schriften*, ed. R. Tiedemann and H. Schweppenhäuser (Frankfurt am Main: Suhrkamp, 1971–), IV, 1, pp. 396–8. Reference will also be made to the first draft (IV, 2, pp. 999–1001). Quotations are taken, where possible, from existing English translations; these are, where necessary, emended. For references in the text, abbreviations, followed immediately by the appropriate page numbers, will be used: *GS* for *Gesammelte Schriften*; *Br* for *Briefe* (Frankfurt am Main: Suhrkamp, 1966); *Ill* for *Illuminations*, ed. H. Arendt (New York: Harcourt, Brace & World, 1968); *UB* for *Understanding Brecht* (London: New Left Books, 1973); *CB* for *Charles Baudelaire. A Lyric Poet in the Era of High Capitalism* (London: New Left Books, 1973); *O* for *The Origin of German Tragic Drama* (London: New Left Books, 1977).

1 As a character in a pre-psychological sense, the destructive character is proof against the avenging reversals familiar to us from dialectics and psychoanalysis. His destruction does not take its toll on him. True, he does, in simplifying the world, also simplify himself; but his actions do not return to plague the inventor. On the contrary, they liquidate mythical guilt.

2 'This is the freedom of the void . . . the fanaticism of destruction . . . the elimination of individuals who are objects of suspicion to any social order, and the annihilation of any organization which tries to rise anew from the ruins. Only in destroying something does this negative will possess the feeling of itself as existent' (G. W. F. Hegel, *Philosophy of Right*, translated by T. M. Knox (London: Oxford University Press,

1942), p. 18). It is no accident that a philosophy of the state should choose the reign of terror as a paradigmatic example of 'abstract negation'. Undialectical destruction can then be condemned as a voluntarist threat to the social order. The destructive character, on the other hand, is likened to a 'destructive state institution'. If he momentarily savours a certain 'freedom of the void', then not for purposes of self-confirmation. Hegel too has a *psychological* theory of the destructive character. The destruction that Benjamin often equates with dialectics in fact *distinguishes* his thought from dialectical models. Jacques Derrida has shown how in Hegel's master-slave dialectic a contest between the masters is evaded in the interests of the slavish reproduction of the philosophical economy. Cf. 'De l'économie restreinte à l'économie générale', in *L'Ecriture et la Différence* (Paris: Seuil, 1967), pp. 369–407. The destruction that threatens to interrupt dialectical movement is suppressed by the destruction that is its motor. Likewise, Benjamin's 'dialectics at a standstill' (*CB* 171) is, 'for a moment at least', the standstill of the dialectic that makes the world go round. This poses the question of the relationship between Benjaminian destruction and Derridean deconstruction. . . .

3 In antithetical ways by Sartre in *Qu'est-ce que la littérature* (Paris: Gallimard, 1969) and George Bataille in 'La Notion de dépense', in his *La Part maudite* (Paris: Minuit, 1967) and *La littérature et le mal* (Paris: Gallimard, 1957).

4 Cf. his 'Afterword' to *Charles Baudelaire. Ein Lyriker im Zeitalter des Hochkapitalismus* (Frankfurt am Main: Suhrkamp, 1969), pp. 185ff., and his essay 'Historischer Materialismus oder politischer Messianismus?', in *Materialien zu Benjamins Thesen 'Über den Begriff der Geschichte'* (Frankfurt am Main: Suhrkamp, 1975), pp. 106ff.

5 Benjamin refers explicitly to Brecht's 'destructive character, which puts everything back in question almost before it has been achieved' (*UB* 119). Cf. also his commentary on the eighth stanza of *Of Poor B.B.*: 'Will survive of these cities what went through them: the wind! / The banqueter is glad to empty the mansion. / We realize that we are purely provisional / And after us will come – nothing worth mention' (p. 56). Reduced to his initials, B.B. is himself an interim stage: 'The best defender of a cause is one who has made a start by letting go of himself' (p. 58).

6 Effacing the traces – forgetting – is also as imperative a psycho-biological need as remembering. Cf. Freud's theory of consciousness – which grew out of research on war neuroses – as a transparent shield, the self-effacing outer layer of a 'mystic writing-pad' (Standard Edition (London: Hogarth Press, 1974), vols 18, pp. 24ff., and 19, pp. 227ff.). This is practically the only psychoanalytic account relevant to someone whose task is to be pure ('historical') consciousness. Self-adaptation in his case consists in dismantling the psyche. Like consciousness, and unlike the windowless monad, the destructive character – the product of a 'glass culture' (*GS* II, 1, 217) – is all wind-shield.

7 Cf. on a related problematic in Baudelaire my ' "Perte d'Auréole": The Emergence of the Dandy', *Modern Language Notes* 85 (3) (May 1970), pp. 529–71.

8 This phrase too is calculated to arouse political suspicions. But if the destructive character clears away, he does not purge. There are victims, but no sacrifice. Otherwise destruction would be still caught up in the toils of myth, which is 'mastered neither by purity nor by sacrifice' (*GS* II, 1, 367).

9 This concept of Anna Freud's recurs in Adorno's writings on Benjamin. Cf. *Br*, p. 16, and the following response to 'The Work of Art in the Age of Mechanical Reproduction': 'as if you were afraid . . . of the invading barbarity and had resorted to placing an inverse taboo on the feared object' (*Über Walter Benjamin* (Frankfurt am Main: Suhrkamp, 1970), p. 130). More generally, Benjamin's critics regularly reintroduce psychological categories precisely at those points where he himself was looking for ways out of bourgeois interiority. By contrast, Benjamin's 'One-Way Street' is dedicated to the woman who 'engineered it in the author' (*GS* IV, 1, 85). The destructive character evacuates 'object relations' and 'libidinal cathexes'; he no more 'invests' people than he 'occupies' space.

10 ' "In my [Karl Kraus's] case psychological insight is combined with the larger capacity to ignore psychological givens." This is the actor's inhuman, cannibalistic side' (*GS* II, 1, 358).

7 Objective Diversions

On Some Kantian Themes in Benjamin's 'The Work of Art in the Age of Mechanical Reproduction'

Rodolphe Gasché

Walter Benjamin's meditations on art and art criticism represent a continued debate with all the major positions punctuating the development of modern aesthetics. Yet although Benjamin's texts critically take up Enlightenment, *Sturm und Drang*, Kantian, Romantic and Idealist reflections on art, the aesthetic position – if it still is one – from which Benjamin levels his critique is difficult to ascertain. In view of this difficulty, the fact that only Kant emerges relatively unscathed from this debate becomes significant. By means of an analysis of 'The Work of Art in the Age of Mechanical Reproduction', I wish indeed to argue that Benjamin's understanding of art can best be approached by tracing its principal statements back to motifs in Kantian aesthetics.[1] First and foremost, Kant's detachment of the beautiful and the sublime from the object seems to have been Benjamin's model for the transformed perception of art, a perception free from the authority of the object, that he delineates throughout his 1935 essay. It is common knowledge that, in the *Critique of Judgement*, Kant develops a conception of the beautiful and the sublime in which beauty and sublimity are no longer attributes of objects, but rather refer back – in the reflective judgement constitutive of the judgement of taste – to the subject, more precisely, to the experience of pleasure or displeasure arising from the agreement of the faculties in a free play constitutive of the possibility of cognition in general, or their disagreement revelatory of the subject's supersensible destination. By thus detaching the beautiful and the sublime from the object, Kant occupies a most singular position in the history of aesthetics, at odds both with his Enlightenment predecessors for whom objects are beautiful if fashioned according to conventional rules of taste, and with the Idealists for whom art objects are beautiful and sublime because in them the idea has taken on sensible shape. Still, although Benjamin, in 'The Work of Art', continues this non-objective aesthetics, all the philosophemes that sustain Kant's foundation of aesthetics undergo significant transformations. Indeed, the Kantian notions of subject, object and reflective judgement emerge thoroughly altered in Benjamin's treatment. And yet, beyond all these modifications and transformations, the exposition of Benjamin's debt to Kantian objectives helps not only to situate the significance of Benjamin's provocative thesis that the loss of the aura in the age of mechanical reproduction allows the work of art to assume a political function, but, paradoxically, also serves to sketch out the limits, for Benjamin, of aesthetics – not simply its end, but also its restriction to a domain from which anything transcendental is ostensibly absent.

If in the Third Critique Kant can dispose of the object and concentrate on purposiveness with respect to form only, it is because the judgement of taste is only a pure judgement of taste if it is neither interested in, nor intrigued (as is the teleological judgement) by, the existence of the object. Free beauty is pleasurable because its perception assures the subject of its cognitive ability in general, and is achieved only where the judgement of taste has kept sensuous charm and moral connotations, both of which rest on the presence of the object, in check. Benjamin's separation of the effects of art in the age of mechanical reproducibility on its beholder from the work of art's phenomenal character coincides with his massive critique of the aura. By following Benjamin through the various facets of the process in which the aura is repudiated, both the similarities to and differences from Kant should become tangible.

From the start, let me emphasize that for Benjamin the loss of the aura in mechanically reproducible art is not something to be deplored as some of his Frankfurt School interpreters, in particular, have held. Nor is there a double response – positive in so far as it concerns the work of art, negative in the case of the human being – to be detected in 'The Work of Art', or anywhere else for that matter, as Susan Buck-Morss, for instance, sees it.[2] Undoubtedly, as long as the full implications of this decay of the aura in modern times remain unclear, it is pointless to discuss the beneficial or detrimental aspects of the loss in question. It must be admitted, however, that certain 'values' linked to the auratic make it difficult – especially when the elimination of the singular human being's aura is shown to be a function of his transformation into a mass being – to argue that Benjamin could indeed have endorsed its radical destruction. These 'values' happen indeed to be those of uniqueness, singularity and authenticity, and they explain to a large extent the ambivalence evident in Benjamin's treatment of the aura. Yet, in order to glimpse what the thesis of the loss of the aura is supposed to establish, it is necessary to interrogate what uniqueness, singularity and authenticity mean for Benjamin. This done, little doubt will remain that Benjamin must reject both the aura of art objects and the one attributed to the human being.[3]

Benjamin unambiguously endorses the radical reversal that comes with technical reproducibility of art, and which totally separates the new art forms from those that make up the uninterrupted continuum stretching from ritual art in mythic times to secular, autonomous art in bourgeois culture and society. He subscribes to this event without nostalgia. The 'comprehensive liquidation' of 'the traditional value of the cultural heritage', that goes hand in hand with the loss of the aura, is even viewed as a cathartic event (pp. 221; 478).[4] Indeed, 'for the first time in world history, mechanical reproduction emancipates the work of art from its parasitical dependence on ritual' (pp. 224; 481), Benjamin holds. With ritual and cult values radically severed from the artwork, a new era arises – 'a crisis and renewal of mankind' (pp. 221; 482) – in which art is 'based on another practice – politics' (pp. 224; 482). It is an entirely positive event for Benjamin – a liberating event, an event in which mankind becomes reborn – and Benjamin celebrates it without regret.[5]

He writes: 'We know that the earliest artworks originated in the service of a ritual – first magical, then the religious kind' (pp. 223; 480). Originally, artworks were 'instruments of magic', that were 'meant for the spirits' (pp. 225; 483), he holds. The link of the work of art to its function in cult is so fundamental that even where the cult value has become secularized, as in the cult of beauty, its ritualistic basis 'is still recognizable as secularized ritual' (pp. 224; 480). For Benjamin, 'it is significant [*von entscheidender Bedeutung*] that the existence of the work of art with reference to its aura is never entirely separated from its ritual function' (pp. 223–4; 480). *L'art pour l'art*, one of the last reactive movements in art against the advent of truly non-auratic, that is, ritual-free art, is a case in point. In mechanically reproducible art this essential link between art and cult is thoroughly cut. Art in the age of mechanical reproducibility is an art that no longer has even a secular ritualistic function. The crisis is radical: stripped of its cult value in a magical, religious and secularized sense, art has become entirely profane, free from all such dependences.

Yet, what constitutes the aura? It is highly significant that in order to explain what this concept implies for historical objects such as artworks, Benjamin has recourse to the aura of natural objects. Indeed, with this move, the aura is shown to be something which *fundamentally belongs to the order of nature*. I quote:

> The concept of aura which was proposed above with reference to historical objects may usefully be illustrated with reference to the aura of natural ones. We define the aura of the latter as the unique phenomenon of a distance, however close it may be. If, while resting on a summer afternoon, you follow with your eyes a mountain range on the horizon or a branch which casts its shadow over you, you experience the aura of those mountains, of that branch. This image makes it easy to comprehend the social bases of the contemporary decay of the aura.
>
> (pp. 222–3; 479)

Benjamin's distinction between historical and natural objects is not one between two different kinds of the auratic. Quite the contrary,

> the definition of the aura [of natural objects] as a 'unique phenomenon of a distance however close it may be' represents nothing but the formulation of the cult value of the work of art in categories of space and time perception. Distance is the opposite of closeness. The essentially distant object is the unapproachable one. Unapproachability is indeed a major quality of the cult value.
>
> (pp. 243; 479)

The aura is identical, a phenomenon of the order of nature in each case. If Benjamin continues to make a difference between the aura of natural and historical objects, it is for other reasons. Depreciation of the here and now through reproduction affects objects of nature as well as those of art, yet 'in the case of the art object, a most sensitive nucleus – namely, its authenticity – is interfered with whereas no natural object is vulnerable on that score' (pp. 221; 477). The difference between natural and historical objects concerns indeed this 'most sensitive nucleus', not a qualitative difference as regards their aura. As is obvious from the context, the nucleus in question, that is, the artwork's authenticity, corresponds to its authority to institute a tradition, that is, a *continuity* between its own unique existence and everything to which it becomes subject throughout the time of its existence (pp. 220; 475). The difference between objects of nature and artworks concerns the latter's power to inaugurate a cultural heritage, tradition and history.[6] Yet, although the nucleus characteristic of the artworks is termed most vulnerable to the destructive effects of reproducibility, here too Benjamin knows no regret. The history, tradition and cultural heritage to which artworks give rise, and through which the authority of the original holds sway, are flatly said to have their origin in cult. He writes: 'Originally the contextual integration of art in tradition found its expression in the cult' (pp. 223; 480). The difference between natural and historical objects is thus not one of their aura, but one of the power characteristic of historical objects such as artwork to extend the power of nature into the realm of the social and human. Tradition, heritage, history, with their value of continuity, are forms of natural, mythical interconnectedness.

But let us return to the definition of the aura, since it alone will explain the ease with which Benjamin is ready to relinquish it together with all the values attached to it. 'We define the aura [of natural objects] . . . as the unique phenomenon of a distance, however close it may be (*als die einmalige Erscheinung einer Ferne, so nah sie sein mag*).' Harry Zohn's translation is here in need of correction. Benjamin defines the aura as the unique *appearance* (*Erscheinung*), or appearing of a distance (*einer Ferne*), that is, not merely spatial remoteness or an open space, as the clause 'however close it may be' indicates, but *substantive*, if not substantial distance. What comes here into appearance is distance as 'something' distant, or unapproachable. First, then, auratic objects are appearances, that is, manifestations according to the forms (or categories, as Benjamin incorrectly writes) of space and time (the reference to the pure forms of intuition is obvious), of a distance, a remoteness, of 'something' that is beyond, that transcends the phenomenal. All appearing (of the suprasensible, or the noumenal, supposing that such a thing were possible) is necessarily a singularizing manifestation. Appearances in the Kantian sense are always singular (and merely give rise to a manifold). Auratic objects, for this reason, are *unique* singular appearances of the distance in question. That this distance must be read as 'something' distant is further supported by Benjamin's reference to the substratum of the artwork's uniqueness (*vom Substrat seiner Einmaligkeit*) (pp. 244; 481). The uniqueness of the appearance is rooted in a substratum, an existing support or ground, underpinning what of it comes into view as a singular object. Distance is such a substratum spreading or laying itself underneath its unique phenomenal existence in the auratic object. With this we are in a position to pinpoint Benjamin's understanding of uniqueness and singularity (*Einmaligkeit* and *Einzigkeit*) in so far as they represent qualifications of the auratic object whether natural or historical.

Uniqueness and singularity are a function of the phenomenal appearing, in space and time, in a here and now (*Hier und Jetzt*), of something non-phenomenal, something distant that transcends the phenomenal. The 'one element (*eines*)' that constitutes the auratic work of art is 'its presence in time and space [*das Hier und Jetzt des Kunstwerks*], its unique existence at the place where it happens to be' (pp. 220; 475). The uniqueness of the artwork, its quality of being *one*, is thus clearly a function of sensibility, in Kantian terms, of its being an object of nature, nature, however, having for Benjamin connotations of fallenness, entanglement and fate. I also note that the very appearing of a distant substratum explains why works of art are *authentic* (*echt*) and have *authority*. Benjamin writes: 'The presence [*das Hier und Jetzt*] of the original is the prerequisite of the concept of [its] authenticity.' But the original, singular object that is the work is also endowed with authority, and it has this authority *as* object, that is, as an appearance in space and time of a distant substratum (see pp. 220; 476 and 221; 477). But, in order to get a better grasp of why such a unique appearance of a distance is endowed with authority, we must return to the appearing substratum itself.

Benjamin claims that 'the uniqueness of the phenomena which holds sway in the cult image [*die Einmaligkeit der im Kultbilde waltenden Erscheinung*] is more and more displaced by the empirical uniqueness of the creator or of his creative achievement' (pp. 244; 481). In other words, the unique appearance of a distance in the cult object is that of an appearance that holds sway in it. In the auratic object, the unique appearance of a substratum is at work, and reigns in it. The cult object, but also the work of art as a cult object, is not only an instrument of magic meant for the spirits, it is inhabited by the appearance of a substratum that is actively at work in it. Such an object inhabited by a reigning substance is truly an *object*, or *Gegenstand*. It is set against the beholder, at a distance from him, unapproachable. Unapproachability is, indeed, the defining characteristic of the cult object whether belonging to ritual or art. (Yet, such unapproachability does not exclude, but rather implies attraction by it. Benjamin, putting forth the example of the mountain range on the horizon to illustrate his definition of aura as the unique phenomenon of a distance, might very well have had the following verse by Goethe in mind: '*und wenn mich am tag die ferne blauer berge sehnlich zieht*'; literally, 'and when during the day the distance of blue mountains longingly draws me'). With this, another aspect of Benjamin's definition of the auratic object as a unique appearance, as shaped according to the categories of space and time, by the here and now, comes into view. After having made the distinction between the cult and exhibition value of artworks, he notes that 'what mattered [for the works of art as cult objects] was their existence [*dass sie vorhanden sind*], not their being on view' (pp. 224–5; 483). The auratic is thus linked to the being present as object, or thing, of the distance. It is a function of this materialization of distance, its being effective in the shape of a present object. This objective quality is intimately linked up with the auratic. Objects as defined in this context are the unique material appearances of a distance that, like a power, holds sway in them. What the nature of these powers might be is not explicitly stated in 'The Work of Art'. Yet, in a footnote in which Benjamin credits German Idealism, Hegel in particular, for having anticipated, however confusingly, the distinction between the cult and exhibition value, as well as this link between object and the appearing in it of something noumenal, he gives us a hint when quoting the following passage from Hegel's *Lectures on Fine Art*: 'Worshipping . . . is concerned with the work as an object [*Ding*], for it is but a spiritless stupor of the soul [*ein geistloses Verdumpfen der Seele*]' (pp. 245; 482). What comes into appearance as a thing or object can therefore also only be of the order of the spiritless, dazzling, stupefying power, in short what Benjamin, elsewhere especially in the essay on Goethe's *Elective Affinities*, designates as the opposite pole to spirit (*Geist*), namely that which is of 'spectral [*geisterhaften*] origin'. Spiritless, the spectral – not only under the form of the deceased who bar the living's way, but especially as the superhuman daemonic forces, the dark powers of myth, the thirsty shadows – is associated in the Goethe essay with the cthonic element, the stagnant waters, the magnetism of the earth core.[7]

Yet the aura is not only the coming into presence of what Benjamin characterizes at one point – while describing in 'A Small History of Photography' a picture of Dauthendy, the photographer's wife – as 'an ominous [*unheilvolle*] distance' in which the gaze becomes absorbed (*saugend an eine unheilvolle Ferne geheftet*).[8] Its own structure has traits that betray its belonging to the order of nature and myth. The aura is the web itself, a tissue spun from the here and the now to produce the appearance of a distance. 'A Small History of Photography' asks: 'What is the aura, actually? A strange weave [*Gespinst*] of space and time: the unique appearance or semblance of a distance, no matter how close the object may be. While resting on a summer's noon, to trace a range of mountains on the horizon, or a branch that throws its shadow on the observer, until the moment or the hour become part of their appearance – that is what it means to breathe the aura of those mountains, that branch.'[9] The appositive, absent from the otherwise identical passage in 'The Work of Art', 'until the moment or the hour become part of their appearance', shows the aura to be constituted as a web in which space and time (*Augenblick, Stunde*) are interwoven so as to create the conditions for a mountain range or a branch to become the unique appearance of a distance. All by themselves insignificant, the weave of space and singular moment transforms these mountains and that branch into the singular coming into presence of a distance entirely different in kind from that of the far off mountains or the nearby branch.

To sum up, then, the auratic is the attribute of the thing, or object-like appearing, of something beyond appearances that thus becomes effective, actual, real. As such a materialization of a distance become power, the auratic object whether belonging to cult or to art is authentic, and has authority. It has authority in that in it powers hold sway. It is always unique and singular because in it a distance has taken on a concrete appearance. It is thus not surprising that Benjamin would reject along with the auratic work 'values' such as singularity, uniqueness, authenticity, since in essence they are nothing but the result of the appearing as thing or object of a spiritless substratum that thus acquires a power to hold sway. Benjamin writes: 'the unique value of the "authentic" work of art has its basis in ritual, the location of its original use value' (pp. 224; 480). Nor should it thus come as a surprise if Benjamin celebrates, together with the disappearance of the aura, the decay of the object in contemporary art as well.[10]

Yet before taking up that issue, the lack of any essential difference between the aura of objects and of human beings, and that, furthermore, Benjamin mourns the loss of neither, remains to be established. In Chapter VI of 'The Work of Art' – and it is mainly this chapter referenced by Susan Buck-Morss among others to claim a concomitant negative valorization by Benjamin of the decay of the aura – after having argued that although photography displaces cult value all along the line, it does not give way without resistance, Benjamin writes:

> It retires into an ultimate retrenchment [*ein letzte Verschantzung*], (that is, a temporally last form of retrenchment, before it will have been displaced for good): the human countenance [*Mensch-*

enantlitz]. . . . The cult of remembrance of loved ones, absent or dead, offers a last refuge for the cult value of the picture. For the last time the aura emanates from the early photographs in the fleeting expression of a human face [*Menschengesichts*].

(pp. 225–6; 485)

Undoubtedly, this passage in its melancholic beauty seems to display a sentimentality and nostalgia that one would deem appropriate under the circumstances. But is this not merely the honourable if not comfortable sentiment of a reader unaware of the fact that what Benjamin describes is a cult – the cult of remembering loved ones in pictures that have become the *objects* through which they look at us? First, it must be noted that the importance that Benjamin attributes in this chapter to Atget's photography clearly shows him to favour without regret an art that has entirely eliminated cult value for the benefit of exhibition value. 'A Small History of Photography' is even more explicit. 'He [Atget] initiates the emancipation of object from aura which is the most signal achievement of the latest school of photography,' Benjamin remarks.[11] His pictures, he adds, remove 'the makeup from reality', 'they pump the aura out of reality like water from a sinking ship'.[12] This achievement, prefiguring Surrealist photography's 'salutary estrangement between man and his surroundings', is largely the result of the emptiness and the absence of mood (*stimmungslos*) characteristic of his pictures.[13]

But more important is the fact that Benjamin does not valorize the human face or countenance, as have several of his interpreters. To make this point, it is useful to make recourse once again to 'A Small History of Photography', where Benjamin argues that the aura or 'atmospheric medium' that is about the people in early photographs, and that lends 'fullness and security to their gaze even as it penetrated that medium',[14] endows the human face (in the same way as the folds of the protagonists' frock coats into which the aura has seeped) with immortality. In these early portraits, 'the human countenance had a silence about it in which the gaze rested', because the portraiture of this period still shelters the reproduced from contact with actuality.[15] 'Everything about these early pictures was built to last,' Benjamin writes. They convey 'an air of permanence', and assure immortality to the portrayed not only as members of a rising bourgeois class, but as *living* human beings.[16] As the photography essay states, the aura of the human countenance in early photography is not only technically conditioned – it is indeed a function of 'the absolute continuum from the brightest light to darkest shadow', of the prevailing darkness and the penumbral tone of the early photographs[17] – it stems also from the ideological nature of these photographic objects – imperialist bourgeoisie – and in particular, and with this I return to 'The Work of Art', from them giving fullness, security, rest to the face in its mere natural singularity. If in the latter essay, Benjamin evokes the aura of the pictured human face, he primarily thinks of the faces of absent or dead beloved ones (*fern* or *abgestorben*). Singular living beings now absent or dead are portrayed in the early photographs, that is, beings in whose countenance *mere life* – natural, or biological life – has taken on phenomenal shape. The aura of the human being whether in pictures or in real living human beings is a function of the unique and singular appearance as thing of something for which Benjamin, continuing a tradition that originates in Aristotle, knows only contempt – *das blosse Leben*, mere natural life. Such life, he asserts in the essay on Goethe's *Elective Affinities*, is life that has become guilty (*verschuldetes Leben*).[18] As the singularizing shining forth of mere life, the human face is not essentially different from the unique and singular objects that are the coming into appearance of a distance.[19]

Benjamin's analysis of the difference between the actor on stage and the actor in front of the camera (*Apparatur*) in Chapter IX of 'The Work of Art' is a case in point. He writes:

> For the first time – and this is the effect of the film – man has to operate with his whole living person, yet forgoing the aura. For aura is tied to his presence [*Hier und Jetzt*]; there can be no replica of it. The aura which, on stage, emanates from Macbeth cannot be separated for the spectators from that of the actor. However, the singularity of the shot in the studio is that the camera is substituted for the public. Consequently, the aura that envelops the actor vanishes, and with it the aura of the figure he portrays.

(pp. 229; 489)

In front of the camera, unlike what happens in front of the eyes of stage viewers, nothing can appear or shine into singularizing presence. No distance can manifest itself here in the unique shape of a thing, human body or face. Indeed, Benjamin's whole discussion of what happens to the actor who represents himself to the camera presupposes that time and space, here and now, are no longer the forms that frame or shape what the camera 'eye' or film shot enregisters. The camera pictures are free pictures, detached from the outset from all space and time, and thus also reproducible from the start. The images are completely stripped of anything that could still make them appearances. The passage quoted above links the aura of the actor to the presence, here and now, on stage of 'his whole living person'. On stage, the whole *living* person comes into an appearance for the spectators. The aura that surrounds the actor is a function of this singularizing phenomenalization of the mere life that animates his whole person. Before the camera, by contrast, life loses its phenomenalizing power, it forgoes its ability to create appearances, and hence aura.

In conclusion to the preceding attempt to define 'aura', it must thus be remarked that if Benjamin, without hesitation or regret, rejects the singularity of both objects and human faces, it is because the human face too is an object in the sense discussed before – an objectified distance. Consequently, the singularity that he relinquishes is one that in his eyes is entirely mythical, and that deserves no salvaging or redemption. Rooted in what Benjamin elsewhere calls 'mythical boundary-setting [*mythische Grenzsetzung*]',[20] the singularity of the human face as it shows itself in the melancholic portraits of the early photographs is infinitely different from the human face as it is said (in the essay on photography) to figure in the best of the Russian films, or in the work of August Sanders. Yet, if Benjamin celebrates the human face in these films or photographs, it is precisely because it is no longer auratic. The human face that appears on film 'with new and immeasurable significance . . . [is] no longer a portrait', he writes. It is the 'anonymous physiognomy' of people 'who have no use [*keine Verwendung*] for their photographs'.[21] No longer representative portraits (*repräsentative Portraitaufnahme*), these pictures of human faces exhibit, on the contrary, the social provenance, role and function of the pictured, and train their beholder 'to read facial types', the ability for which, according to Benjamin, is 'of vital importance' given the 'sudden shifts of power such as are now overdue in our society'. Benjamin adds: 'Whether one is of the left or the right, one will have to get used to being looked at in terms of one's provenance. And one will have to look at others the same way.'[22] In the latter pictures of the human face, aesthetic distinctions have irrecoverably made room for social functions. Yet even more radically distinct from the representative portraits of individuals of the bourgeois class, or the auratic pictures of absent or dead beloved ones – radically different because without even a negative link – is the singular, lonely creature before God. As a reading of Benjamin's essay on Goethe's

Elective Affinities would demonstrate, the moral singularity of such an individual is the only one that counts for Benjamin.

From everything developed until now, it should be obvious that Benjamin's criticism of auratic art includes its status as an object – the authority of the artwork as a present thing. If Benjamin claims that art in the age of mechanical reproducibility assumes a political function, it is because it has succeeded in ridding itself of the spell that the phenomenal actualization of a distance casts on its beholder. Indeed, the traditional artwork is constituted, according to Benjamin, by 'an alluring appearance or persuasive structure [*lockender Augenschein oder ein überredendes Klanggebilde*]' (pp. 238; 502), that is (in more precise translation), by an enticing appearance or a sound formation that talks the beholder into doing something against his better sense. These unmistakably magical qualities of the auratic work get the viewer entangled in the work itself, rob him of his freedom, and bring him under the influence of the powers that dwell in the work as thing. By contrast, the non-auratic work of art is no longer a thing, and hence it allows the spectator a very definite autonomy. Indeed, as Benjamin's analyses demonstrate, the change in perception brought about by film permits the viewer to 'reflect' himself, as it were, into himself. Yet before further refining this point, let me first address Benjamin's contention that Dadaism is the art form that 'promoted a demand for film' (pp. 238; 502).

All art, Benjamin holds, produces the conditions for its own overcoming by creating a demand that can 'be fully satisfied only later. The history of every art form shows critical epochs in which a certain art form aspires to effects which could be fully obtained only with a changed technical standard, that is to say, in a new art form' (pp. 237; 500–1). In these critical epochs – not unlike the *dies critica* that designates the turning point in the course of an illness – a given art form points beyond itself, toward another art capable of superior techniques and that fulfils the demand and promise created by the first. Needless to say, this thesis is not to be measured against empirical facts. It is a historico-philosophical thesis which rests on the assumption that artworks are not in essence self-sufficient. Yet, works of art as cult objects, objects that are a singular manifestation here and now of a distance, repress the artworks' essential tendency to be overcome by another work, or form of art, and by ever more radical technical possibilities. Indeed, artworks critically call for their being transcended by technique, and above all by mechanical reproducibility. However, it is only in photography and film that this essential feature of all art is truly set free. According to this scheme, Dadaist art created a demand that only film came to fulfil. What is it then in Dadaism that helps us situate film? Dadaism, Benjamin holds, produced works that prohibit all contemplative approach to them. In Dadaist works, the aura of their creation is destroyed. But although the Dadaists branded their creations as reproductions, they did so 'with the very means of production' (pp. 238; 502). This limit is overcome by film. The fundamental reason why the Dadaist creations no longer allow for contemplation is their shock character. The Dadaist work of art is 'an instrument of ballistics. It hit the spectator like a bullet, it happened to him, thus acquiring tactile quality', Benjamin asserts. With this, he continues, 'it promoted a demand for film, the distracting [*ablenkendes*] element of which is also primarily tactile, being based on changes of place and focus which periodically assail the spectator' (pp. 238; 502). And he concludes: 'By means of its technical structure, the film has taken the physical shock effect out of its wrappers [*aus dieser Emballage befreit*] in which Dadaism had, as it were, kept it inside the moral shock effect' (pp. 238; 503).[23] In film, something held back by Dadaist art is fully liberated. But, as we still have to see, this is also a liberation from something, and for something.

Indeed, what precisely is it that happens in shock? In shock, the viewer becomes diverted from the object that causes the shock. With this, the possibility of contemplation (*Versenkung*), or collection (*Sammlung*) of, or in front of, the object comes to a stop. Instead, the beholder becomes bound up with reacting to the shock to which he has been subjected. Through the violent shake that the Dadaist work produces in the spectator, and with which he must come to grips in one way or another, the work itself deflects from itself, from the thing or object that it is. It distracts from its singular appearance, and diverts towards what at first would seem to be some sort of subjective reflection, or *Durcharbeitung*, by the subject of the violent disturbance that has occurred to him. With Dadaist art, and even more so with film since its distracting element rests on structural features such as cutting, montage etc., the object character of the artwork recedes entirely, and thus a radical diversion from what attracts – the singular object of the auratic work with its luring and enticing qualities – has effectively been achieved.[24] An aesthetics of shock is thus non-objective. In it the object has become diverted and deflected. It thus has all the allure of the Kantian aesthetics with its subjective bent. Yet, despite the striking similarities, is the subject who seeks to come to terms with his experience of shock the Kantian subject, and does he achieve his goal in a process of reflection or judgement?

Auratic works of art lure the spectator into a state of collection and contemplation, more precisely into immersing himself in the object. Benjamin writes: 'A man who concentrates before a work of art is absorbed by it [*versenkt sich darein*]. He enters into this work of art the way legend tells of the Chinese painter when he viewed his finished painting' (pp. 239; 504). Yet such absorption by the work presupposes that its viewer be an individual subject. The cult value of the work, Benjamin emphasizes, demands not only 'that the work remain hidden', but also that it can only 'be viewed by one person or by a few', 'the priests in the cella', or the private art collector (pp. 225; 483–4). Collection, contemplation, absorption presuppose a single spectator, or very few, who in front of the authentic, authoritative artwork lack the power to control themselves, or each other. The movie-goer, by contrast, is no longer the *one* single viewer. It is a mass public, a collective subject from the start. For the mass of individuals in the movie theatre, collection or contemplation of the artwork is out of the question. First, what they relate to is, as said before, no longer a thing that could lay claim to authority. Moreover, the content viewed by these movie-goers is not the representation of some spell-binding exotic reality (geographical or social) but, as Benjamin's emphasis on Russian movies demonstrates, *themselves* as actors, and workers at work.[25] Second, contemporary man, Benjamin insists, relates to what he views in a critical fashion. He writes that 'it is inherent in the technique of the film as well as that of sports that everybody who witnesses its accomplishments is somewhat of an expert' (pp. 231; 492). Film invites what Benjamin terms 'a progressive reaction'. It 'is characterized by the direct, intimate fusion of visual and emotional enjoyment with the orientation of the expert. . . . With regard to the screen, the critical and the receptive attitudes of the public coincide' (pp. 234; 497). This critical attitude, entirely at odds with the contemplative attitude demanded by auratic art, is the ownmost property of the mass individual, more precisely, of the mass audience. Indeed, as Benjamin claims, mass individuals check their reactions against one another. He contends that 'individual reactions are predetermined by the mass audience response they are about to produce, and this is nowhere more pronounced than in the film. The moment these responses become manifest they control each other' (pp. 234; 497). The subject who seeks to come to grips with the effects of shock experienced in film – Benjamin characterizes the movie theatre as a sort of exercise and training ground for acquiring the transformed mode of perception required by modern life – is thus, third, an autonomous subject of sorts. As a mass, the film audience is in self-control; it checks, collectively tests its reactions to shock – shock produced by a work that no longer exercises any authority over its beholder. Free from all domination, this collective subject, testing against one another the success of each individual in dealing with shock, reflects itself into a free, independent subject that gives itself the rule, as it were. This is the source of 'the great social significance' (pp. 234; 497) to which Benjamin attributes a non-auratic art form in which the object has been successfully repelled. If, with these new media, art assumes a new function, a political role to be precise, it is because art has become the training ground for the proletariat, or rather the masses, to constitute itself as a collective subject by developing all by itself the necessary skills to survive in contemporary society.

Yet what sort of autonomy is it that the movie-goers achieve in the dark depths of the movie house? Has this collective subject the substantial unity of the Cartesian, or the merely formal unity of the Kantian subject? Does the reflection upon self that comes with the repulsion of the object grant the subject an awareness of his cognitive and supersensible abilities? Can this process of coming to terms with the shock effect even be understood as a reflective coiling upon self? To answer these questions schematically, however, the effect brought about by the violent disturbance of shock needs to be addressed. As Benjamin puts it, referring to the effects of the film images, 'the spectator's process of association in view of these images is indeed interrupted by their constant, sudden change. This constitutes the shock effect of the film' (pp. 238; 503). Or, to refer to the photography essay, the camera's images 'paralyse the associative mechanisms in the beholder'.[26] In other words, the effect caused by shock is precisely to hamper a subject's constitution of itself, its ability to cohere with itself so as to form a centre. Benjamin quotes Georges Duhamel as a witness for this loss of all inner continuity with self. 'I can no longer think what I want to think. My thoughts have been replaced by moving images.' Whereas the spectator 'can abandon himself to his associations' before a painting, 'before the movie frame he cannot do so' (pp. 238; 502). It therefore comes as no surprise that Benjamin characterizes the new mode of participation of the mass audience in the movies as one of distraction (*Zerstreuung*). Not only does art in the age of mechanical reproduction deflect from the object, distract it, as it were, the collective subject of the critical reception of the new art forms is a distracted beholder. His associative mechanisms are interrupted by shock, and although he responds to the shocks that assail him through 'a heightened presence of the mind' (pp. 238; 503), he does so in a distracted manner. The collective subject, consequently, is neither a substantial nor a formal centre that would ground its autonomy. It is a distracted subject in all the senses of the word. Yet, compared with the individual who lets himself be immersed in the auratic work, or who in front of it weaves an equally mythical identity for himself while abandoning himself to his associations, this distracted collective subject and its behaviour towards art is according to Benjamin the answer to the questions that humanity faces today. The new kind of behaviour that issues from the mass's matrix (*neugebohren hervorgeht*) is, undoubtedly, a form that appears first in the 'disreputable form' of distraction as diversion, or entertainment, Benjamin admits (pp. 239; 503). Similarly, the new subject that collectively emerges with the loss of the aura coincides, at first, with what one contemptuously and condescendingly refers to as the masses. Yet this much is clear; both this distracted behaviour and centreless subject are credited by Benjamin with representing a solution to the problems of his time. The heightened presence of mind of this collective subject is not self-consciousness (individual or class consciousness). When Benjamin notes that, in contradistinction to the traditional viewer who becomes absorbed by art, 'the distracted mass absorbs (*versenkt in sich*) the work of art' (pp. 239; 504), it is not only to stress the scattering of the work of art as object in the mass, and its replacement by the shock effect, but to characterize the mass's state of mind as one which is so permeable that paradoxically it cushions against all attack.[27] But, perhaps more significantly, this remark forces us to conceive of the state of mind of the distracted mass, as set up by Benjamin, along lines akin to the classical divide between high and low culture. According to this opposition, the state of mind of the masses is characterized by absentmindedness, habitual modes of thinking, and unfocused, incidental relating to its surroundings. It is separated by a gulf from the self-consciousness of the (bourgeois) individual. Indeed, what Benjamin valorizes in the masses coping with shock are precisely these despised states of mind. Philosophically speaking, such a mental disposition is empirical consciousness.

In contradistinction from the transcendental unity of consciousness, or pure apperception, which secures the thoroughgoing identity of a manifold in intuition, 'empirical consciousness, which accompanies different representations, is in itself diverse [*zerstreut*] and without relation to the identity of the subject', Kant states in the First Critique.²⁸ This distracted consciousness is unable coherently to combine a manifold of intuitions into one consciousness, because it lacks the ability to represent in its synthetic efforts the identity of consciousness in the consciousness of the manifold intuitions themselves. Empirical consciousness is not only diverse and distracted in the different representations that it may accompany, it is distracted *in itself*, and thus in no situation authoritatively to secure self-coherence or self-identity. Its distracted nature prevents it from having any authority, any leverage, even regarding itself. In *Anthropology*, Kant defines distraction as follows: 'Distraction [*distractio*] is the state of diverting attention [*abstractio*] from certain ruling ideas by means of shifting to other dissimilar ideas. If the distraction is intentional, it is called dissipation; if it is called involuntary it is absentmindedness [*absentia*] [Abwesenheit *von sich selbst*].'²⁹ The distraction described by Benjamin is of the second kind. It is involuntary, and causes an absence from self. Although autonomous after having repelled the authority of the auratic object, the collective subject of the mass audience does not constitute itself as a unifying subject. Its rejection of authority in distraction goes so far as to deprive even itself of any authority. This rejection of self-authority is a constitutive feature of the masses, as analysed by Benjamin. Their distraction, he insists, is habitual.

In his discussion of distraction, Kant remarks that 'the reading of novels, in addition to causing many other mental discords, has also the consequence that it makes distraction habitual'.³⁰ This is not the place to discuss the relation between novel and film,³¹ but, as we have seen, the mode of perception fit for viewing the latter kind of art is a distraction entailed by the structural aspects of that art form. Moreover, the reading of fiction, according to Kant, not only makes distraction habitual, it 'makes for habitual absentmindedness [*Geistesabwesenheit*] (lack of attention to the present)'.³² It also bereaves the subject of self presence (Abwesenheit *von sich selbst*). Yet, while these characteristics of distraction are discredited by Kant, Benjamin approves of them wholeheartedly where they characterize the mass audience reaction to the shock effect of the film. Indeed, this critical achievement is accomplished not merely in a state of distraction, but by habit as well.

As Benjamin's discussion of architecture would seem to suggest, the kind of relation to art that becomes dominant with film is in truth a liberation of the modes of reception of buildings by the masses since time immemorial, modes repressed by auratic art. Since the beginning of civilization, the masses have appropriated buildings, not through 'attentive appropriation', but by habit. It 'occurs much less through rapt attention than by noticing the object in incidental fashion' (pp. 240; 505). Such habitual ways of appropriation determine both the tactile and optical reception of works of architecture. This mode of reception of art culminates in the masses' consumption of films, and has, according to Benjamin, 'canonical value. The tasks which face the human apparatus of perception at the turning points of history cannot be solved by optical means, that is, by contemplation, alone. They are mastered gradually by habit, under the guidance of tactile appropriation' (pp. 240; 505). Indeed, the thrust of Benjamin's argument is that the problems he refers to have only been successfully solved when they have been mastered 'in a state of distraction [since this] proves that their solution has become a matter of habit. Distraction as provided by art presents a covert control of the extent to which new tasks have become solulable [sic!] by apperception' (pp. 240; 505). Only a problem solving that occurs in incidental fashion but that has become habitual, and hence itself repetitive and reproducible, and not unique or singular, which consequently does not focus in or concentrate on what causes the problems, has a chance of succeeding in these times. Only the masses are up to these tasks, Benjamin claims. 'Individuals are tempted to avoid these tasks', presumably because of the fatal attraction that the causes, or objects, of these problems exercise. Against them the individual, acting alone, cannot protect himself. Only in conjunction with other individuals in a mass can he develop the repetitive habitual modes of reaction that prevent him from falling prey, through unique and singular modes of coping, to the spell of what obtains here and now. In the movie theatres, the mass audience exercises in distracted and habitual problem solving. 'The film makes the cult value recede into the background not only in putting the public in the position of the critic, but also by the fact that at the movies this position requires no attention. The public is an examiner, but an absent-minded one,' Benjamin concludes (pp. 240–1; 505). This distracted critic – who gives no direct attention to the film as an art object, who, in passing, cushions the shocks he receives by a heightened presence of the mind and habitual modes of handling them, modes that have been rehearsed and practised with other mass individuals in front of the movie screen – is a critic who has successfully cut himself free from the spell of the aura, and its object. They have lost all authority over him, who, as a collective subject, has also dismissed the authority of a self. This distracted critic is the first citizen of a world without magic.

Except for his denunciation in the 'Epilogue' of Fascism's attempt to pervert the revolutionary possibilities of film by pressing the apparatus 'into the production of ritual values' (pp. 241; 560), thus re-auratizing art, while at the same time abolishing the aura 'in a new way' – the Fascist way – through gas warfare, Benjamin ends his essay with the emphasis on a world resolutely become profane. In this world without aura, or magic, the power of myth and fate has been overcome in all its forms – ritualistic and secular. It is a stupendous transformation of the world that Benjamin describes, in which all forms of transcendence bastardized by myth have been evacuated from the realm of the present. It is a world so free that it has become empty. The aesthetic of shock expresses this loss of distance as the very texture of what exists, for the artworks. It is an aesthetics in which distance has made room for total proximity, and it remains, therefore, confined as well within the limits of what it depicts. Divorced from all transcendentalism, it has become empirical, at the limit of a discipline.

A strange silence hovers about this world emancipated from myth. No circumstantial reasons such as Benjamin's temporary affiliations with historical materialism, his friendship with Brecht, or his financial dependence on Adorno and Horkheimer, can explain the total silence about the Other of the profane. But silence 'speaks'. In its utter profanity, and blankness, the world void of myth points to what it cannot name, yet from which the very meaning of 'profane' remains suspended.

NOTES

1 Benjamin's borrowings from Kant do not exclude his rejection of major aspects of Kant's doctrine. Thus, in the essay 'Program of the Coming Philosophy' (translated by M. Ritter, in G. Smith (ed.) *Benjamin: Philosophy, Aesthetics, History* (Chicago, IL: University of Chicago Press, 1989), pp. 1–12), Kant, although positioned as the starting point for a new philosophy, is severely criticized for maintaining distinctions such as intuition/intellect, subject/object, epistemology/metaphysics etc. In the name of a higher concept of experience – higher than 'naked, primitive, and self-evident [empirical] experience', and in which experience is 'reduced to nadir, to a minimum of significance' – in which

'something absolute' is encountered, namely God, and which would characterize the coming philosophy as a theology, or a metaphysics, Benjamin, in order to overcome what he calls the remnants in Kant of the religious and historical blindness of the Enlightenment, relinquishes all the major distinctions constitutive of Kant's critical enterprise in the First Critique. But he disagrees with Kant's doctrine of aesthetic judgement as well and dismisses the phenomenology of experience on which it is based. As Claude Imbert has argued, Benjamin objects to Kant's aesthetics because of the reflective judgement's suspension of the phenomenology of the object, and on the basis, simply, that in this case there is no object to suspend. Yet, as I shall argue hereafter, Benjamin has recourse to Kant's aesthetics at the precise moment he needs to dispel the magic of the aura, and the auratic object as well. Imbert's contention that Benjamin objected to the unifying gesture of transcendental deduction, to what he called Kant's despotism, in other words, to his transcendentalism, is highly suggestive of what sort of Kant – a Kant folded back into the empirical, 'a criticist economy without transcendentalism' – is operative in Benjamin's own work. (See Claude Imbert, 'Le present et l'histoire', in H. Wismann (ed.) *Walter Benjamin et Paris* (Paris: Cerf, 1986), pp. 747, 769).

2 Susan Buck-Morss, *The Origin of Negative Dialectics* (New York: MIT Press, 1977), pp. 160–1.

3 In a superb essay entitled 'Zeit zur Darstellung. Walter Benjamin's Das Kunstwerk im Zeitalter seiner technischen Reproduzierbarkeit' (*Modern Language Notes, German Issue* 107 (3) (1992)), Eva Geulen, after having attempted to determine the epistemological point of view from which Benjamin writes the essay in question as that of a yet undecided future in whose perspective the present appears as past, accounts for the double nature of the loss of the aura which so many interpreters have pointed at on the basis of what she analyses as the simultaneity of method and object, that is, in terms of the performative dimension of Benjamin's criticism. She writes:

The theory of aura is the attempt to describe history not only in practical terms, but theoretically as well from a position for which no factual ground exists as yet. In other words, the concept of aura must mark out and localize itself in the essay itself. Aura belongs to the vocabulary of a possible, futural historiography. As anticipation of the future, the aura achieves intervention in history, stating, in this manner, what is now. That the specificity of traditional art consisted of its aura, can show itself only, when, and in so far as it has lost this character. The perception of aura arises from its loss.

(p. 598)

In passing I note that Geulen's interpretation of history in Benjamin as constructed, that is, represented, hence disfigured history, lays to rest objections such as those formulated by Peter Burger, *Theorie der Avantgarde* (Frankfurt am Main: Suhrkamp, 1974), according to which Benjamin's periodizations of art would be historically erroneous, and rooted in pseudomaterialist theorems (pp. 36–40).

4 The page references in the text are to Walter Benjamin, *Illuminations*,

translated by H. Zohn (New York: Schocken Books, 1969), and Walter Benjamin, *Gesammelte Schriften*, vol. I, 2 (Frankfurt am Main: Suhrkamp, 1974), respectively.

5 In a letter to Werner Kraft, of 28 October 1935, Benjamin describes the philosophical and historical viewpoint from which he approached the theory of art in the essay 'The Work of Art', a first programmatic version of which had been sketched out in September or October of that same year. He writes: 'As far as I am concerned, I try to direct my telescope through the bloody fog upon a mirage of the nineteenth century, which I seek to depict according to those features that it will show in a future state of the world liberated from magic' (Walter Benjamin, *Briefe*, vol. II (Frankfurt am Main: Suhrkamp, 1966), p. 698).

6 See in this context Chapter 2 by Alexander Düttmann for a detailed and extremely suggestive analysis of the notion of tradition.

7 Benjamin, *Gesammelte Schriften*, vol. I, 1, pp. 174, 179.

8 Walter Benjamin, *One-Way Street and Other Writings*, translated by E. Jephcott and K. Shorter (London: Harcourt Brace Jovanovich, 1978), p. 243.

9 Ibid., p. 250.

10 Since Benjamin also conceives in 'The Work of Art' of the destruction of the aura in terms of tearing or prying an object from its shell, that is, in terms that not only seem to be at odds with everything else said about the loss of the aura but that are used elsewhere, in the Goethe essay for instance, to warn against the philosophical barbarism of an art criticism that would seek to account for the beautiful by lifting its veil, it is necessary to interpret the simile in question in the context of what he establishes in the essay of 1935. Benjamin writes: 'To pry an object from its shell [*die Entschälung des Gegenstandes aus seiner Hülle*], to destroy its aura, is the mark [*Signatur*] of a perception whose "sense of the universal equality of things" has increased to such a degree that it extracts it even from a unique object by means of reproduction' (pp. 223; 479–80). According to this definition, the shell is what makes an object auratic. To pry it from its shell is to destroy the aura. Hence, the shell must correspond to the object's appearing in a phenomenal, that is, singular and unique, actualization. To tear the object from its shell, therefore, is to rob the object of its appearance with the result that it can no longer manifest itself as the unique appearance of a distance. An object deprived of its shell, of the phenomenal actualization that renders it distant, brings the object into the proximity of those objects that in everyday life are too close to us to warrant any particular attention. Only when sheltered behind its appearing can an object be distant and endowed with auratic magic, something like a 'thing-in-itself'!

11 Benjamin, *One-Way Street*, p. 250.

12 Ibid., pp. 249, 250.

13 Ibid., p. 251.

14 Ibid., p. 247.

15 Ibid., p. 244.

16 Ibid., p. 245.

17 Ibid., p. 247.

18 Benjamin, *Gesammelte Schriften*, vol. I, 1, p. 138.

19 The concept of the aura can only be a positive instrument of analysis if entirely recast. This is what Andrew Benjamin has set out to do in 'The Decline of Art: Benjamin's Aura', in Andrew Benjamin, *Art, Mimesis and the Avent-Garde* (London: Routledge, 1991), pp. 143–54.

20 Walter Benjamin, 'Critique of Violence', in *Reflections*, translated by E. Jephcott (New York: Harcourt Brace Jovanovich, 1978), p. 295.

21 Benjamin, *One-Way Street*, p. 251.

22 Ibid., p. 252.

23 Benjamin's analysis of Dadaism ought to be read in conjunction with parallel developments on the shock experience in the great nineteenth-century metropoles, in particular, in 'On Some Motifs in Baudelaire'.

24 Shock is thus not merely to be understood as the 'denial of sense', as Burger understands it in *Theorie der Avantgarde* (p. 108). With this, the meaning of shock is restricted to what Benjamin had called 'the moral shock effect'.

25 'Some of the players whom we meet in Russian films are not actors in our sense but people who portray *themselves* – and primarily in their own work process. In Western Europe the capitalistic exploitation of the film denies consideration to modern man's legitimate claim to being reproduced' (pp. 232; 494).

26 Benjamin, *One-Way Street*, p. 256.

27 A careful reading of Chapter III of Benjamin's 'On Some Motifs in Baudelaire' would be required here.

28 Immanuel Kant, *Critique of Pure Reason*, translated by N. Kemp Smith (New York: St Martin's Press, 1965), p. 153.

29 Immanuel Kant, *Anthropology from a Pragmatic Point of View*, translated by V. L. Dowdell (Carbondale, IL: Southern Illinois Press, 1978), p. 102.

30 Ibid., p. 104.

31 Everything, indeed, Benjamin advances about the genre of the novel in 'Der Begriff der Kunstkritik in der deutschen Romantik' – its prosaic, sober nature – suggests that the film is the novel's legitimate heir.

32 Kant, *Anthropology*, p. 77. For the important role of *absentmindedness* in the *flâneur*, see 'On Some Motifs in Baudelaire'.

8 Cosmos in Film

On the Concept of Space in Walter Benjamin's 'Work of Art' Essay

Gertrud Koch
Translated by Nancy Nenno

No essay by Walter Benjamin has led his readers and interpreters in as many different directions as 'The Work of Art in the Age of Mechanical Reproduction'. Not only is this the sole long and coherent text which the author wrote, and rather late at that (1935–6), on the subject of the new medium of the masses – film – but it develops a precarious and contradictory historical thesis. This thesis can be inserted in a stimulating way into the palimpsest of Benjamin's remarks on history and philosophy. That this essay, first written in Paris in 1935, bore an *intrinsic connection* with the Arcades Project beyond that of mere simultaneity is evidenced by several passages in his letters. Even if they were only to be interpreted as tactical evasive manoeuvres against the critique of the design of the Arcades Project, these passages still offer several interesting arguments for such a connection. Thus Benjamin wrote to Max Horkheimer on 16 October 1935:

> This time my project concerns itself with locating the exact site in the present which will be the vanishing point of my historical construction. If the book's subject is the fate of art in the nineteenth century, then this fate only has something to say to us because it is contained within the ticking of a clock, whose chiming has first penetrated *our* ears. By this I want to say that it is for us that the fateful hour of art has struck, and I have captured its signature in a series of preliminary reflections which is entitled 'The Work of Art in the Age of Mechanical Reproduction'. These reflections attempt to give the question of aesthetic theory a truly contemporary form, from the inside out, avoiding all *unmediated* connections to politics. These notes, which almost nowhere take historical material into account, are not extensive but are of a purely fundamental nature.[1]

Two more passages from letters written a short time after the one to Horkheimer betray how strongly Benjamin was preoccupied with work on his essay, or, more accurately, how much he was enamoured of his own idea, which he considered to be significant. On 23 October, he wrote to his close friend Gershom Scholem of his plans:

> This [essay] has recently furthered several fundamental discoveries of an art historical nature in a decisive way. Together with the historical schematism that I drew up about four months ago, I will build a kind of 'grid', a schematic plan, in which all the particulars will have to be inserted. These considerations anchor the history of nineteenth-century art in the recognition [*Erkenntnis*] of its contemporary situation as we experience it. I am keeping them very secret, since they are incomparably easier to steal than most of my ideas. Their preliminary title is 'The Work of Art in the Age of Mechanical Reproduction'.

> (*Briefe*, 695)

In a decidedly gloomy response to Werner Kraft on 28 October, Benjamin builds a bridge from his pessimistic speculations about the world situation, the cultures that perished in 'Blood and Horror', to his own project, which he describes with a lighter heart:

> For my part, I am seeking to focus my telescope through the bloody haze onto a mirage of the nineteenth century. This I attempt to sketch according to those contours that the telescope will show in a future world freed from magic. Of course, I had to build this telescope myself, and in the course of this attempt, I was the first to discover several fundamental principles of materialist aesthetic theory. At the moment, I am putting them down in a short programmatic essay.

> (*Briefe*, 698–9)

Perhaps the three cited passages are also interesting because of how different the addressees are. While he complains to his correspondents that the Eduard Fuchs study he was commissioned to write is a burden and an undesirable duty, he speaks at the same time about the 'Work of Art' essay to these three very different correspondents in a consistently enthusiastic manner. He recommends the study to Horkheimer on account of its immanent method ('and that is, from the inside out, avoiding all unmediated connection to politics') which corresponded to the Frankfurt School's programme of immanent critique. To Scholem he offers a secret bond born of the trust of their close friendship, at the same time referring to a 'schematism' in which he only needs to 'insert' his new findings, a claim which seems far better suited to the schema of the kabala and its exegetic traditions than to the model of historical materialism. Benjamin neutralizes a materialist critique in his note to Werner Kraft, whom he met through Brecht, by pointing to the utopian status of the matter 'in a future world freed from magic'. It would certainly be incorrect if one deduced from these observations that Benjamin related to his correspondents merely empathically. Rather, it is the *multiplicity of meanings* in his essays which finds expression in these passages. Scholem's biography contains reports of the discussion of the essay during the visit to Paris that show how Benjamin represented and defended all the elements which so many critics later wished to reduce to a single argument in favour of their own preferred position.[2]

All three explications of the plan for the essay are marked by a surprisingly vivid image which Benjamin connects with the idea of the essay, namely a representation of the history of nineteenth-century art from the standpoint of the twentieth century, that is, precisely with a view to its possibilities for mechanical reproduction. It is no accident that all three *images* are drawn from a sphere in which the technical apparatus simultaneously co-ordinates and constructs time and space: The 'clockwork' mechanism, whose ticking remained above suspicion in the nineteenth century, has intensified in the twentieth century into a fateful hour when it encounters '*our* ears', that is, when it pierces the space of the present. The grid provides spatial orientation – it structures the space of the earth's surface in terms of latitude and longitude – but it also contains datelines; the spatial model thus also determines temporal boundaries. Finally a 'telescope' that has been especially adapted for futuristic ages will reveal, through the 'bloody haze' of the present, the future of a 'world freed from magic' as a 'mirage' out of the nineteenth century, thus revealing a constructionistic undertaking whose method (technique) is an invention of the author, that secret weapon which he hesitates to reveal to Scholem. The image of time penetrating is constitutive of Benjamin's conception of the 'Theses on the Philosophy of History' which he develops in Thesis XIV in the following manner:

> History is the subject of a structure whose site is not homogeneous, empty time, but time filled by the presence of the now [*Jetztzeit*]. Thus, to Robespierre ancient Rome was a past charged

with the time of the now which he blasted out of the continuum of history.[3]

Benjamin ends his exposition of the 'Theses on the Philosophy of History' with a tiger's leap into the past of human history. The above passage telescopes the end of the text from 1940, making the 'Work of Art' essay, written five years earlier, more relevant for the contemporary debates within film theory.

'In relation to the history of organic life on earth,' writes a modern biologist, 'the paltry fifty millennia of homo sapiens constitute something like two seconds at the close of a twenty-four-hour day. On this scale, the history of civilized mankind would fill one-fifth of the last second of the last hour.' The present, which, as a model of Messianic time, comprises the entire history of mankind in an enormous abridgment, coincides exactly with the stature which the history of mankind has in the universe.

(p. 265)

One could call Benjamin's position a *negative anthropology*: here humanity is represented as a negligible dispersion within the cosmos of prehistory. Humanity is as dependent upon Messianic salvation – which certainly would be inconceivable without it – as Hannah Arendt's human being who is born into dependency, relying upon the care of others. It is this broken anthropology that occupied Benjamin early on and from which a connecting thread may be drawn to the emphatic construct of the technological mastery of the spheres of time and history that he attributes to film in the 'Work of Art' essay.

Central to Benjamin's aesthetics are concepts such as perception, experience, expression and mimesis, which either refer to what Adorno terms the 'Prehistory of Subjectivity' or to phenomenological anthropologies of philosophy. The description of man as deficient appears in an early notation, which is clearly influenced by the debates about the epistemological problem of perception, a problem Benjamin remarked on in his notes on the philosophy of language. In this version of the notorious problem that runs through the work of writers from Ernst Mach to Jacques Lacan, Benjamin postulates the inability of human beings to grasp themselves entirely:

On account of our physicality, in the end most immediately through our own bodies, we are put into the world of perceptions and thus into one of the highest linguistic realms. We are, however, blind, mostly unable to distinguish between the natural body, between the appearance and the being [*Sein*] of the messianic form. It is very important that our own body is inaccessible to us in so many ways: we cannot see our face, our back, not even our whole head, that is, the most noble part of our body.[4]

In search of a better representation of the problem, Benjamin then turns to the 'case study' of the child 'who without prehensile organs and immobile would develop its visual world: a different hierarchy of distances' (p. 647). Precisely this 'case study of the child' has developed into the paradigmatic description of the position of the spectator in one branch of recent film theory. The masochistically tinged passivity of the spectator position, the experience of powerlessness, the inability to enter into the screened action which is a dead ringer for reality takes centre stage. Film, as a technical apparatus which permits one to forget anthropological lack, was related, above all through Jacques Lacan's notion of the mirror stage, to the old Machian problem of man having only an incomplete image of himself because he cannot view himself as a whole body.[5]

At this point Benjamin takes a distinct step away from the anthropological question by drawing a connection between perception and myth: 'There is a history of perception which, finally, is the history of myth.'[6]

The anthropology of natural history, which Benjamin later dissected in 'Schemas of the psycho-physical question', admittedly appears to have borrowed this Gnostic dualism wholly from theology and cosmology. In this anthropology, myth no longer chronicles changing perceptions of the body in natural history (itself subject to change), but rather body (*Leib*) and corpus (*Körper*) are completely separated from each other: 'With body and corpus, man is bound to universal connections. But differently in each case: in body, he is related to humanity, in corpus, to God' (p. 80).

In one passage of the fragment, Benjamin also draws the same conclusions for the corpus as he did earlier for the body, but jottings permit such uncertainties which perhaps need not always be meaningful. Nevertheless, this passage makes it clear that Benjamin thought of negative anthropology as the other side of the theological coin: he clearly assigns both 'dissolution' (of the body) and 'resurrection' (of the corpus) to 'natural history' in which humanity most certainly also has its share. This theory of perception and experience remains anthropologically tinged precisely because it conceives of man and myth as engaged in a natural-historical conflict with body/corpus. My thesis for a new reading of the 'Work of Art' essay is derived from these commentaries on anthropology which stem from the 1910s and 1920s. Although they are, for the time being, unresearched fragments, they nevertheless appear to be meaningful as threads which later interweave the concept of history in the 'Work of Art' essay as it delegates revolutionary Messianism to the technology of film.

As I hope to show in this essay, Benjamin constructs the recording apparatus of film as a kind of demiurgical eye that is capable of approaching the bodily quality of the physical world in a manner that remains inaccessible to the embodied human eye. This provides the basis for the Messianic-prophetic power of the camera, its function of disclosure and revelation. The camera does not establish a realm apart from the physical world, but instead explodes the prevailing world into rubble, piercing the veil of dissimulation. This is consistent with Jewish theological tradition, according to which Messianic redemption is not ascribed to another world but takes place on earth.

In his book on Benjamin, Gershom Scholem describes how, from 1916 to 1920, Benjamin's thought revolved around a complex amplification of a concept of myth taken from Jewish religion, history and philosophy (and ethnology). These early attempts by Benjamin differ from the later project of the 'Dialectic of Enlightenment', less in the original intention (to include different fields of knowledge and modes of thought) than in their conception of analogy (which is more strongly committed to simultaneity, which cannot be resolved dialectically, but rather corresponds more readily to a dualistic cosmological structure).[7]

The argument on film theory in the 'Work of Art' essay can be reconstructed as an early variation of the apparatus theory which considers technical equipment, as well as the camera and projection apparatus, as the material basis of film aesthetics. Benjamin arrives at this thesis by amalgamating a Brechtian conception of the audience with a precise analysis of the technical conditions of filmic production. He develops his conception of the apparatus *à propos* the filming of an actor:

> The artistic performance of a stage actor is definitely presented to the public by the actor in person; that of the screen actor, however, is presented by a camera, with a twofold consequence. The camera that presents the performance of the film actor to the public need not respect the performance as an integral whole.
>
> ('Work of Art', 228)

From here Benjamin argues that the audience assumes the role of a tester *vis-à-vis* the film, since it and the apparatus might be said to subject film's performances to optical tests. Thus, Benjamin later concludes, the aura of the actor's persona disappears. The second consequence is that the screen actor is no longer in direct contact with the audience, and thus the latter takes up 'the position of a critic, without experiencing any personal contact with the actor' (p. 228). Above all, this thesis appears dubious because it excludes the possibility that the apparatus itself might be perceived to be a naturalized fetish with which the audience identifies – less on the level of an instrument with which to test the actor than on the narcissistic level of an enormous extension of the perceptual apparatus. If one discounts the Brechtian conclusions of Benjamin's analysis, one beholds a remarkable and bold vista through which Benjamin outlines the construction of a specifically filmic space.

In Benjamin's conception, the physically real space in which an actor (or some other object) communicates here and now with a physically present audience dissipates. The apparatus appears in its place, representing the audience in its mirroring function. Benjamin overlooks that in this way not only is the actor in the here and now deprived of his human aura, but the audience, which steps into the position of the apparatus, remains imaginary. Only when the (edited) film is screened by the projection apparatus, without possibility of intervention, does the audience appear as real. The audience identifies with the apparatus instead of with the actor. In a later passage, Benjamin writes: 'The singularity of the shot in the studio is that the camera is substituted for the public' (p. 229).

This collapse of the audience and the apparatus into one, which for Benjamin should create distantiation, in the sense of the Brechtian aesthetics of theatre, establishes the opposite effect: it prevents precisely this distancing because it literally cannot envision or permit any space for this. This appeal to the theory of the actor, which Benjamin borrowed from Pirandello,[8] does indeed aid in explaining the loss of aura through the dispersion of the physical time-space continuum into the fictional realm of arbitrary pictorial details and montages. However, it also underestimates the explosive potential of the observation when the whole argument in inverse form still remains fixated on the actor. At best, Benjamin requires this argument systematically in order to be able to connect his thesis concerning reproduction to a history of the decline of aura. However, what is revolutionary about the filmic apparatus lies elsewhere, and this is precisely what Benjamin saw in those passages where he puts the favourite child (the eschatological philosophy of history) to bed in the baby carriage of historical materialism.

In Section XI Benjamin finally arrives at the decisive analysis of that which makes film new and different from earlier, aura-laden art forms:

> The shooting of a film, especially of a sound film, affords a spectacle unimaginable anywhere at any time before this. It presents a process in which it is impossible to assign to a spectator a viewpoint which would exclude from the actual scene such extraneous accessories as camera equipment, lighting machinery, staff assistants, etc. – unless his eye were on a line parallel with the lens.
>
> ('Work of Art', 232–3)

Regardless of the production's technical apparatus which destroys illusions, the film produces an extreme illusionistic effect, which is precisely what makes film interesting:

> Its illusionary nature is that of the second degree, the result of cutting. That is to say, *in the studio the apparatus has penetrated so deeply into reality that its pure aspect freed from the foreign substance of the apparatus is the result of a special procedure, namely, the shooting by the specially adjusted photographic apparatus and the mounting of the shot together with other similar ones.* The apparatus-free aspect of reality here has become the height of artifice; the sight of immediate reality has become an orchid [*Blaue Blume*] in the land of technology.
>
> (p. 233, translation modified, emphasis added)

In contrast to more recent apparatus theory which locates the ideological function of film squarely in the naturalization of the technically produced impression of reality, Benjamin discovers amid the collapse of artifice and immediacy precisely the *kairotic* constellation: the proverbial 'orchid in the land of technology'. In this construction of a constellation, a notorious Benjaminian concept flashes brightly, that of 'prehistory', of the 'primeval moment', which he attempts to capture in historical phenomena as a 'mirage' which spreads its roots into the present of the new medium. Benjamin's remarks on the projectionist[9] clarify the way in which the noteworthy, romantic passage in the 'Work of Art' essay locates its site of meaning in the construction of history as a kinetically activated space in which the camera moves through different levels:

We take recourse to an analogy which is based upon the concept of the *Operateur* that comes to us from surgery. The surgeon represents one extreme, while the magician represents the polar opposite. . . . The surgeon does exactly the reverse; he greatly diminishes the distance between himself and the patient by penetrating into the patient's body, and increases it but little by the caution with which his hand moves among the organs. In short, in contrast to the magician – who is still hidden within the medical practitioner – the surgeon at the decisive moment abstrains from facing the patient man to man; rather, it is through the operation that he penetrates into him. Magician and surgeon relate to one another like painter and cameraman. . . . There is a tremendous difference between the pictures they obtain. That of the painter is a total one, that of the cameraman consists of multiple fragments which are assembled under a new law.

('Work of Art', 233–4, translation modified)

The 'web of circumstances' into which the camera penetrates (p. 233) salvages phenomenological immediacy as the telos of artifice. Revolutionary pathos and eschatological motive walk hand in hand during Benjamin's trip through the pile of rubble which the cinematic technologies have blown open. In this way he remains faithful to his announced position that only the immobilization of time in the *spatial image* counts as the moment of salvation. The fact that cinematic technology does not actually present (*Darstellen*) movement but rather represents (*Vorstellen*) it illusionistically through a series of photographically fixed moments, turns it, in the wake of photography, into a medium in which time is immobilized in space. Only in this immobilization does the *corpus* emerge out of the anthropologically untenably constructed *body*, explosively liberated into the image of the 'heavenly' from the space of the 'optical-unconscious'. Benjamin's citation on slow motion comes from Rudolf Arnheim:

So, too, slow motion not only presents familiar qualities of movement but reveals in them entirely unknown ones 'which, far from looking like retarded rapid movements, give the effect of singularly gliding, floating, supernatural motions'. . . . Even if one has a general knowledge of the way people walk, one knows nothing of a person's posture during the fractional second of a stride. The act of reaching for a lighter or a spoon is a familiar routine, yet we hardly know what really goes on between hand and metal, not to mention how this fluctuates with our moods.

Here the camera intervenes with the resources of its lowering
and lifting, its interruptions and isolations, its extensions and
accelerations, its enlargements and reductions. The camera introduces us to unconscious optics as does psychoanalysis to unconscious impulses.

(pp. 236–7)

In the moment of liberation, the camera itself becomes the subject, the demiurge which builds a new world out of the rubble of
the old one, a new world that had always been there but had never
been unveiled: the camera becomes the telescope of prehistory
through which 'entirely new structural formations of the subject
appear' (p. 236). His own ideas tend towards an aesthetics of unveiling. Instead of tests, the discussion now focuses upon the 'exploration of commonplace milieus under the ingenious guidance of the
camera' (p. 236, translation modified) – something that film should
accomplish and with which Benjamin comes much closer to filmic
aesthetics of apparatus production. In the end, the somatic effects
of the shock, the altered apperception, 'under the ingenious guidance of the camera' are the benchmarks of the cinematic revolution:

Our taverns and our metropolitan streets, our offices and furnished rooms, our railroad stations and our factories appeared
to have us locked up hopelessly. Then came film and burst this
prison-world asunder by the dynamite of the tenth of a second,
so that now, in the midst of its far-flung ruins and debris, we
calmly and venturously go traveling.

(p. 236)

NOTES

1 Walter Benjamin, *Briefe*, vol. 1, ed. Gershom Scholem and Theodor W.
  Adorno (Frankfurt am Main: Suhrkamp, 1966), pp. 690f. Unless otherwise indicated, all notes are by the author and all translations by the
  translator.
2 Gershom Scholem, *Walter Benjamin – Die Geschichte einer Freundschaft*
  (Frankfurt am Main: Suhrkamp, 1975), p. 257. English version: *Walter
  Benjamin. The Story of a Friendship*, translated by Harry Zohn (Philadel-
  phia, PA: Jewish Publication Society of America, 1981).
3 Walter Benjamin, 'Theses on the Philosophy of History', in *Illuminations*,
  translated by Harry Zohn (London: Fontana, 1973), p. 263.
4 Walter Benjamin, *Gesammelte Schriften*, vol. VI, ed. Rolf Tiedemann
  and Hermann Schweppenhäuser (Frankfurt am Main: Suhrkamp, 1987),
  p. 647.
5 Walter Benjamin, 'The Work of Art in the Age of Mechanical Repro-

duction', in *Illuminations*, translated by Harry Zohn (New York: Schocken Books, 1968) pp. 230–1.

The feeling of strangeness that overcomes the actor before the camera, as Pirandello describes it, is basically of the same kind as the estrangement felt before one's own image in the mirror. But now the reflected image has become separable, transportable. And where it is transported? Before the public.

6 *Gesammelte Schriften*, vol. VI, p. 67.
7 On 18 March 1936, Adorno wrote Benjamin a long letter which emphasizes differences and similarities in this matter. This famous response to Benjamin may be intensified into a critical reproach against Benjamin for allowing one-sided dialectical mediation to befall the concept of the work of art, while completely ignoring the dialectics of reproduction and the masses. In this way he is able to arrive at a hasty adoption of the autonomous character of works of art, and at the apologia for film, both of which are mediated dialectically through each other. *Gesammelte Schriften*, vol. I.3, pp. 1000–6. That Benjamin arrests dialectical mediation too early is at the centre of Adorno's critique of Benjamin's concept of the commodity as a 'dialectical image', as he formulated it for the Arcades Project.
8 *Gesammelte Schriften*, vol. VI, p. 67.
9 The German word *Operateur*, from the French, has three meanings that are relevant here: surgeon, cameraman, and the projectionist in the cinema.

9 Time and Task

Benjamin and Heidegger Showing the Present

Andrew Benjamin

OPENING THE PRESENT

Writing takes place in time. There is, in addition, the time of writing. This twofold positioning of time – an ineliminable doubling of time, the recognition of which becomes the affirmation of anoriginal difference, the truth of ontology – is here from the start, in this particular presentation, mediated by another presence.[1] In this instance the mediation is given by the effective presence of an announced task. The task's enactment, an enactment which must maintain a link to its founding articulation within intentionality, reiterates the twofold temporality already located in the connection between writing and time. What emerges from this given relation is the interplay of writing, time and task. What is involved in this relation is the possibility of thinking the relation between politics and time. This possibility arises because such a thinking must occur in a 'now' that in eschewing its reduction to the *nunc stans* while nonetheless maintaining a relation to it, a relation that marks a presence that takes place at the same time, demands to be thought at the present as the present. In opening this 'now' what is opened up is the ontology of the present. What is proposed therefore, with Benjamin, is the possibility for a philosophical thinking of the present.

In broad terms what is involved here is a specific opening of the present. This is a task made all the more difficult by the demand that it also involve an already existent consideration, at the present, as the present, of the possibility of thinking philosophically philosophy's history. (The problem of the relationship between history and philosophy's history is raised thereby.) As the present is thought within the work of Benjamin and Heidegger, to engage with their thinking is itself to take up the present and therefore to move towards a consideration of the ontology of the present by maintaining it as the site in which such movements are sustained. The identification of the present determines the nature of the philosophical task. Reciprocally, of course, the nature of the philosophical task will have a determining effect of the construal of the present. One cannot be thought without the other.

As yet, however, the need for taking up this particular emergent connection between time, task and writing is yet to be announced. It is not as though need is yet to be given a specific determination within philosophy. Amongst other possibilities need can be taken as opening both the Cartesian and the Hegelian philosophical projects.[2] (Its presence in Heidegger and Benjamin will be just as insistent.) In both instances need is present as what advances a necessity that orients the project and which in its projections continually comes to be addressed by them. As such it is maintained within, while maintaining, an ineliminable reciprocity. Need in both instances is a demand given by the present – the present being the construal of the contemporary at (and as) the time of writing, again need's time – as such the response to need is itself contemporary.[3] With need, with its instantiation, its having a time at a given instant, a relation to the given is established. In other words if need is a response to what is given – the gift of tradition creating the specificity of the moment – then the response occurs at a particular instant. The instant while bearing a date is not the present as such. The reason is that thinking the present will necessitate taking the construal of the given and its (the given as construed) enjoined response. Articulated as need the response can be formulated as a specific stand in relation to a particular repetition. Repetition here is the reiteration of the already given. Need exists in relation to the gift and yet the gift, what is taken to have been given, is itself determined by need; again the presence of a founding and original reciprocity. Accepting the generality of this description cannot obviate the necessity of giving it specificity and thereby opening up the multiplicity inherent in the stance. Indeed what must be maintained is the position that it is in terms of its actual specificity – the effective interplay of dating, present and need – that any philosophical thinking of the political will come to be acted out since it is the differences given at the level of this interplay that mark the primordiality of conflict. Regarding their actual projects the point of connection and divide between Benjamin and Heidegger can be located at this point. Multiplicity therefore becomes the site of conflict. Once given a precise designation it becomes a site that resists the possibility of any automatic synthesis.

In sum, and if only to provide a name with which to work, the present as giving rise to a specific task – where of course that specificity is itself moulded and determined by the construal of the present – will be termed the *epochal present*. Such a present gives itself. It is given within its own self-conception. It is not the giving of that which is distanced because of its being either originating or primordial and which, were it to be present, its presence (and hence its being present) would then become the epochality of the founding and maintaining origin. In working with the abeyance of such a conception of epochality, and moreover in allowing for the determining interplay of the epochal present and the *nunc stans* (the latter being the time of dating, the temporality of the instant), this will serve to maintain the ineliminable presence of a different politics in so far as this other possibility (a politics thought within a different philosophical frame) can be reworked as the primordial conflict over the present. Such a reworking sustains the present as that site while at the same time it provides a different instantiation of the primordial. What is proposed is a conflict that cannot be resolved by a simple deferral to the instant. The conflict between Benjamin and Heidegger is political for precisely this reason. The inability of the instant – the specific referent – to resolve conflict opens up the necessity, not just to rethink its presence, but to take its presence as determining and thus as real. However, the reality in question is not coextensive with the instant (the latter as marking both the ontological as well as the temporal location proper to the time and place of dating). The epochal present as a name names another, yet related, reality.

The ineliminable reciprocity between the ontology of the present and action, the latter being a constitutive part of an inherent actative dimension forming an integral part of the present, is of an order such that it will sanction the possibility that this engendered construal may become the present within philosophy's history. The actative is simply the constitutive part of the present that will demand action and thus be what gives rise to a task while at the same time sanctioning its reality. The epochal present will as a consequence always attempt to legitimize actions done in its own name. An additional point must be made, namely that it will always be possible for the epochal present to be declared to be, in all senses, commensurate with the time marked by 'calendars' and 'historical occurrences'. However, such a conception becomes no more than the intended unmediated positing of objectivity which, in the attempt to rid the present of its construction and thus its proper reality, in the end only maintains that relation and with it therefore the distance between the present and the instant by representing it in the guise of objectivity (reality here marking out the space of conflict). The doubling of objectivity resists obviation and it is thus that the positing of objectivity will always occupy the space of construction. Objectivity in other words becomes a part of an interpretive structure given by construction.

What is central within this opening, in its having opened an approach to the present as it figures in Benjamin and Heidegger, is that it entails working through the site of the task's founding formulation; in other words the task and its interpretation demand working through the foreword.[4] With the foreword and even in allowing for a certain plurality, namely an oscillation between the formal (an actual foreword) and projection (an intended project), there is always an attendant risk. The risk is simply that the foreword may always be viewed as being either provisional or redundant and thereby as no more than an addition that can be either subtracted or added; it could even become a gratuitous afterword. Nonetheless, it is by beginning with a foreword that Benjamin will set the scene for his writings on *Trauerspiel*, Baudelaire, Paris and the nineteenth century. As he indicates in a letter to Scholem which links the foreword to the *Passagen-Werk* to the much earlier foreword to *The Origin of German Tragic Drama*, writing these forewords was a necessary task.[5] Both works brought with them – as an integral part of their work – their own 'theories of knowledge'.

In Benjamin's case what would seem to jeopardize the works, real or envisaged, that take place after these forewords (a similar problem will also be present in Heidegger, in the case of *Time and Being*) is that the form that the works will have to take is marked by the difficulty of enacting, if not the potential impossibility of realizing, the project set out in and thus demanded by the foreword. In general terms within his work, the complex relationship between allegory and symbol, the use of the monad as a mode of presentation checking the power of representation, the privileging of showing and image over expression, narrative and stories have at least one straightforward consequence: the question whether the text could ever contain, in the way envisaged, that which the foreword sets up as the project. The problem, as has already been indicated, is reducible neither to style nor genre but pertains to the construal of a task and thus of its present and then how that task comes to be enacted.

It should not be thought that the question of presentation has to be added to the work of either Heidegger or Benjamin. Benjamin's study of the German *Trauerspiel*, for example, begins by locating the necessity for philosophy of 'representation' (*Darstellung*).

> It is characteristic of philosophical writing that it must continually confront the question of representation [*der Frage der Darstellung*].[6]

In writing to Scholem, Benjamin expresses a doubt that can be seen as touching on precisely this point – the task's possibility, its own effective realization – in relation to what is there identified as the 'Arcades'. Of the *Passagen-Werk* he states

> I can foresee neither whether it will find a form of representation of its own [*eine selbständige Darstellung*], nor to what extent I may succeed in such a representation.[7]

While this letter was written in 1935, four years before the final drafting of the *Passagen-Werk*, it remains the case that the question of success, let alone its criteria, remains as open after the drafting as it did before.

The foreword's own reiteration of a projected impossibility of completion – of a textual enactment in narrative – will demand a response, a response to the text, a response, perhaps, to the text's own interpretations, that has the intention of distancing both the interpretive and the hermeneutical and their subsequent replacement by experience. It is the presentation of the problematic status of interpretation and the centrality of experience that brings Heidegger and Benjamin into a specific philosophical relation. Despite the problems that will emerge in pursuing it, it is this relation – the relation given within experience – that will be of central importance. Approaching it, an approach that will of course already be a part of it, can begin with an opening citation.

In *A Berlin Chronicle* the limits of narrative and a certain construal of the politics of memory are advanced. The analogy of archaeological investigation is central to the text's effect since such investigations will demand that the politics of display – incorporating display's time – be taken up.

> Fruitless searching is as much part of [excavating] as succeeding, and consequently remembrance [*die Erinnerung*] must not proceed in the manner of a narrative [*erzählend*] or still less that of a report, but must, in the strictest epic and rhapsodic manner,

assay its spade in ever new places, and in the old ones delve to ever-deeper layers.[8]

There are two difficulties with this passage. The first is understanding the claims being made. The second is tracing their consequences. The presentation of Benjamin and the related consideration of the present – the interrelationship between politics and time as constitutive in any attempt to take up the ontology of the present – will continually have to return to these difficulties; returning, perhaps, by readdressing them.

Returning to the present means working with the recognition that, as has been suggested, the presentation of a task, and in consequence its writing, take place in time, a time that is from the start complex. Complexity arises because it is a time which, while it may occasion a date, at times even enjoining one, is nonetheless to be distinguished from that which is dated. Within the passage of time the self-conception of the task to be enacted is instantiated. It is this self-conception that will be of concern here, for with it what arises is the time of the task; in other words the conception of the present in which the task is to be enacted at the present, and with it therefore of the present as that which sustains and maintains the task and its self-enactment. The reciprocity here is essential. Presenting these interdependent elements in this way will allow for the possibility of thinking through the nature of the relation between the present and 'now-time' (*Jetztzeit*). The 'present' (*die Gegenwart*) within the frame of 'Konvolut N' while cited in a number of entries is, for the most part, a term that is still to be clarified and yet of course this lack of clarity should not obviate the necessity of recognizing the weight that it – the present – has to carry,[9] a weight indicated in the following examples. 'The present' (*die Gegenwart*) is included within the historical task. 'The present' is that which is placed in a 'critical condition' by 'the materialist presentation of history' (N 7a, 5). Moreover it is 'the present' that 'polarizes the event into fore and after history' (N 7a, 8). The question that endures concerns what this 'present' is taken to be. In addition, it will have to include a consideration of the link between 'the present' as a temporal moment, the moment within the temporality of the instant and thus a moment which also brings its own ontological considerations with it, and that which is presented, where the latter involves a presentation of and thus also within the present; present instant-iation.

The 'present' – in part Benjamin's construal of the epochal present

– and presencing are inevitably linked in his work to the presence of critique. Part of the critique of Jung that takes place in 'Konvolut N', and elsewhere, concerns how presencing occurs, and with its occurrence what is thought to have been carried over into the present; 'translated into the language of the present' is Jung's own expression, a line quoted by Benjamin (N 8, 2) in order to establish a critical distance from Jung. With Jung, for Benjamin, the error lies not in the preoccupation with incursions into the present but in the way both the process and the content of presencing are thought. An intrinsic part of the critique of Jung is the effective presence of a construal of the present in which, perhaps for which, Jung's project is not simply vulnerable philosophically but reiterates a politics – the politics of a particular expressionism – that is once again the subject of critique. It is a stance that forms a part of Benjamin's general critique of expressionism. And yet with Jung – with a more generalized preoccupation with Jung in the *Passagen-Werk* – what is involved is more complex. A way of formulating this problem would be to suggest that Jung allows for a present in which what is received from outside of it – the outside as an archaic past, presencing in Jung's words as 'an unconscious animation of the archetype' (N 8, 2) – becomes, despite the appearance of difference, a repetition of the Same.

In less specific terms it will emerge that in taking up repetition, the present, and hence the differing conceptions of the epochal present, work within the complex of repetition. In other words repetition will contain the very differences that serve to work the present as a site of conflict. With repetition, even in its complexity, experience is introduced, since experience delimits the stance in relation to repetition and this despite the stance's textual and thus written formulation. Furthermore, forming a fundamental part of what is involved in any consideration of the present is the reciprocal conception of experience that such a present demands. A way into this present will stem from the recognition that, with Benjamin and Heidegger, it is the place and thus the time of 'showing'. With this showing, what remains open is how the experience of showing is to be understood. What is it therefore to experience the shown as such?[10]

HEIDEGGER'S PRESENT

While they may lack any predetermined and therefore pre-given presentation, aspects of this initial taking up of Benjamin's work are intended in the first place to connect, reconnect, albeit on a general level, the projects of Heidegger and Benjamin. Connecting and reconnecting occur in so far as a constitutive part of each project is the relationship between showing and experience. Nonetheless it goes without saying that the specific formulations of that relationship serve to open up an important difference between their projects, thus forcing a consideration of how that difference is itself to be thought. As difference eschews simple positing its location is paramount (perhaps as a more generalized art of setting 'sails'). Here of course it turns on the present. More concretely this particular point of departure is also intended, in the second place, to take up, again as an example, Heidegger's *Nietzsche*, in particular the final part of the section entitled 'European Nihilism',[11] a text in which 'metaphysics', the history of metaphysics, bears on by bearing the present.

Before presenting Heidegger it should be noted that this presentation is itself intended to take up significant aspects within Benjamin's own philosophical forewords, though more emphatically the relationship between the forewords and that which the forewords intend to have follow them. Since it can be taken to harbour the project itself the foreword inevitably becomes more than a given site – even a preliminary site – within a textual topology. It is the latter component, the inherent complexity of the foreword, which as has already been indicated must form a fundamental part of any real philosophical engagement with it. Here the work of Benjamin and Heidegger is such that one tracks and tacks on the other. Neither their opposition nor their similarity can be taken as given. Sails will always have to be trimmed. The problem will always pertain to the nature of the calculation.

Heidegger's final considerations of Nietzsche's metaphysics could be said to incorporate 'today''s location.

> 'Today' [*Heute*] reckoned neither by the calendar, nor in terms of world-historical occurrences, is determined by the period in the history of metaphysics that is most our own: it is the metaphysical determination of historical mankind in the age of Nietzsche's metaphysics.
>
> (pp. 195, 254)

The actual quality of this 'today', its uniqueness, is clarified in the lines that follow.

> Our epoch reveals a particularly casual matter-of-factness with respect to the truth of being as a whole.
>
> (pp. 195, 254)

And yet within the frame of the same formulation this casual attitude is mediated by the presence of another and greater 'passion'. Again it attests to the age by giving it a specific particularity.

> Such an indifference [*Gleichgültigkeit*] to Being in the midst of the greatest passion for beings testifies to the thoroughly metaphysical character of the age.
>
> (pp. 195, 254)

The particular force of this description, one to which it will be necessary to return, is that for Heidegger it is a characterization that comes from Being, which is sent by it. The present for Heidegger is therefore always already given by the history of Being. As such it is, in part, constitutive of that history. It is the precise nature of the given coupled to the mode of access to it that is presented at the end of the text.

> The age of the fulfilment of metaphysics – which we descry when we think the basic features of Nietzsche's metaphysics – prompts us to consider to what extent we find ourselves in the history of Being. It also prompts us to consider – prior to finding ourselves – the extent to which we must experience [*erfahren müssen*] history as the release of Being into machination, a release that Being itself sends, so as to allow its truth to become essential for man out of man's belonging to it.
>
> (pp. 196, 256)

For Heidegger the quality of the present resides in what could be described as a givenness that is always more than the simple instantiation of the given. Again its quality discloses itself in its forming the present and yet forms it in such a way that its 'originality' can always be shown as present. The predicament of human being – a predicament that is the being of human being (identified earlier by Heidegger, in *Being and Time* for example, with the term Dasein) – is given by Being; it is part of Being's destiny, in that human being belongs to Being. In Heidegger's terms grasping that this is the case will necessitate that 'experience' in which what is proper and original to human being is taken over in its propriety as establishing, though in a sense also re-establishing, the 'original' belonging together of Being and human being. The reluctance to separate establishing and re-establishing in any systematic way indicates the extent to which propriety is in some sense already there. The belonging together of Being and human being – the latter as the being of being human – has already been worked through in *Being and Time* in terms of questioning. There Heidegger presents Dasein as that for which the question of being, and with it its being, is always, that is, originally, a question. Ontology takes the place of any simple humanism.

The expressions 'indifference', 'casual matter-of-factness' and 'passion for beings' as employed by Heidegger attest to the present epochality of Being and yet they can also be taken as descriptive of the present, the time of writing. Remembering the functional reciprocity between description and task, it becomes a description that demands a particular task. The demand is located in expressions of the form 'we must experience'. The 'must' in marking the intended elimination of 'indifference' brings to the fore the inherently actative dimension within the present. It is this dimension that gives rise to a specific task, a task formulated by the present and thus forming a fundamental part of its constitution. As such this reciprocity takes the present beyond Heidegger's own description. Heidegger's present is no longer either the 'Today', or the 'age', or the current epochality of Being. Rather, they are all interrelated with the task they demand (to give one side of the reciprocity) and thus form the epochal present for Heidegger. The constitutive elements must be retained and examined within their given reciprocity.

The 'passion' Heidegger identifies is for the other side of the divide within ontological difference. Consequently while this 'passion' may define the age it is because of its place within that divide that at the same time it gives rise to a task. Present and task are interarticulated. One works within the other. Here what this entails is, first, overcoming the given 'indifference' and stemming contemporary 'passion', and second, thinking Being in its differentiation from beings and thus as differentiated from them. The force of the description that presents 'today' as the 'release of Being' allows for the recognition of the current epochality of Being, that which Being forms and informs 'today', while indicating that it is within the very structure of this presencing, because of what it is, that it becomes possible to consider the conditions of possibility for the thinking of Being itself. (The epochal present will always have recourse to a form of the transcendental, since what such a conception of the present will give are conditions of possibility – conditions in which the present is also given.) The latter possibility arises out of 'today's' situation, the present, and is moreover predicated upon experience, more significantly an experience that 'we' must have. (Again a separate though important line of inquiry would concern the identity and thus ontology of this 'we'. Not the question of who we are, but of who is the intended subject of this experience.) The difficulty that resides in experience, in what the term stakes out, pertains to how it is to be understood. It goes without saying that this is a difficulty that arises with the acceptance, as a point of departure, that experience cannot be posited. Perhaps more significantly, however, there is the related problem of how it is that experience's intended effect is to be realized. What is the registration and thus what is it that is registered in the experience that 'must' be had? The recognition of the actuality of such experience, leaving the question of its specificity to one side, is what locates the present as the present. Recognition works to intensify it. And yet the temporality of this intensity is far from straightforward. As will be indicated, it is an intensity that is for Heidegger released in an openness and thus within the calm of having experienced. Calmness and the open in their link to the future are given as originally determined by propriety. Present intensity for Benjamin will be significantly different.

Allowing for the present as given by the 'release of Being' locates the present as historical. The quality of the present – and thus of Heidegger's formulation of what has already been described as the epochal present – is determined in advance. However, what it is that is determined must be experienced as such, as that determination. It follows that once that experience has taken place and only within the actual terms given by what it is that will have been experienced, it then becomes possible to think, for Heidegger, the condition of the present itself. Perhaps more accurately it is then possible to think at the present that which gives to it – the present – its present determination. Such a thinking is essentially futural in the precise sense that it breaks up the present by taking the present's propriety – that is, that which is proper to the present, namely Being – as its own exclusive object of thought. It will be a thinking of the present that takes place at a particular point in time, a date, that will serve to differentiate the present from itself. In the thinking of Being the future is possible. While this is to employ terms such as present and future beyond the purview of Heidegger's own specific use, it nonetheless accords with the implicit construal of the future – future possibility – that is at work, for example, in a text such as *Time and Being*, a text which is of fundamental significance for any serious attempt to understand what it is that a foreword may be and thus of being able to plot the relationship between time and task. It can be added here that the project and thus the strategy of *Time and Being*, along with, for example, the programmatic claim in the opening section of *On the Way to Language* in which the project is advanced as an 'experience' with language and thus in the distancing of the said remaining open to the saying, work to reorient the task away from interpretation and the textual and towards experience and action. The precise nature of this experience endures, with any encounter of Heidegger's text, as the dominant interpretive problem.[12] With it the question of the status of the hermeneutic is reopened.

The importance of *Time and Being*[13] is that it is a foreword to a text that in some sense has yet to be written – there is even the very real possibility that it cannot be written – and to that extent the possibilities that it holds open, open the future, while at the same time indicating the nature of the task set. What is meant by doubting the possibility of its being written pertains to Heidegger's understanding of the 'propositional statements' (*Aussagesätzen*) that characterize philosophical writing. The text reiterates the impossibility of such 'statements' doing justice to the task at hand. The difficulty is stated in the text's opening and is announced again at its end. 'Statements' are in Heidegger's terms one of a number of 'hindrances' to the task that is given. The task is thinking Being 'without relation to metaphysics' (*ohne rücksicht auf die Metaphysic*) (pp. 24, 25). It is the 'without' – thinking 'without' – here that is of singular importance. Before taking it up it is essential to examine what the distancing – establishing the limits – of philosophical writing is going to entail. These entailments work to construct an important link to Benjamin's foreword; moreover they seem to forge a bridge in regard to presentational method. In both instances they will be connections which distance.

Time and Being was initially a lecture. Responding to it therefore was intended to be a different exercise than that demanded by reading. Indeed reading, because the very practice means that within it there is the necessity of being forced to respond to the movement of statements and propositions, is as a consequence inherently problematic (again the difficulty of any immediate reconciliation of interpretation and experience). Heidegger takes up the difficulty of what he is about to present, to say, in the following way:

> Let me give a little hint on how to listen. The point is not to listen to a series of propositions, but rather to follow the movement of showing [*dem Gang des Zeigens*].

(pp. 2, 2)

It is this formulation of Heidegger's that recalls the frequently cited though nonetheless still difficult passage from 'Konvolut N' in which Benjamin describes his own work's method. The possible paradox inevitably generated by Benjamin's juxtaposition of method and montage needs to be noted from the start. What is noted therefore is the possibility of holding method and montage together. Were they to fall apart then the way demanded by the foreword would be a way the following of which would always be proved impossible.

> Method of the project: literary montage. I need say nothing only showing [*nur zeigen*]. . . .
>
> (N la, 81)

Benjamin's showing is of course significantly different. What then of Heidegger's showing? What does the showing itself display? Asking what is shown is to recognize – though here this recognition is neither Benjamin's nor Heidegger's – the presence of an ineliminable doubling within showing itself. It should be remembered that the central issue here is the present, the task's time and thus the epochal present (in Heidegger's own formulation). The doubling is the complexity engendered by what the showing shows. It is thus equally, at the same time, generated by it, a reciprocity demanding another take on complexity.

HEIDEGGER'S 'AGE'

Heidegger's concerns at the end of 'European Nihilism' can be read as yielding a construal of the present in which the present has the quality of having been given by Being even though the 'age' remains 'indifferent' to the question of Being. The nature of the present as that which is constituted by Being forces through the present the task of thinking Being, thus causing the present to become – and the becoming brings with it a complex future – reconciled with itself. The reconciliation is, of course, premised upon the forced actualization of what was described above as thinking 'without'. The task as formulated in *Time and Being* turns around within the 'without'. Heidegger formulates it thus:

> To think Being without [*ohne*] beings means to think Being without regard to Metaphysics.
>
> (pp. 24, 25)

The 'without' can be taken, at least provisionally, as the overcoming of 'indifference', the stemming of 'passion' etc. It will in the end

involve a similar movement to the one occurring (perhaps envisaged) in what Heidegger describes, in the same text, as 'leaving
metaphysics to itself'. And yet this 'metaphysics' is not just an
option for thinking, a way of doing philosophy – though clearly it
is that as well – 'metaphysics' here is a description of the 'age' and
consequently it involves the present. It circumscribes the epochal
present. 'Leaving metaphysics to itself' or doing 'without' it is an
act in the present which opens the future, but it opens it towards a
possibility that is there in the present even though by definition it
could not occur either 'in' the present or 'as' it. The future becomes
the space for the realized possibility of a reconciliation between
that which gives the present – the epochal present – its present
determination but to which the present is 'indifferent'. In the end
what must occur is a reconciliation with that which is proper to
human being; that is, the taking over of the question of Being itself.
Being reconciled with what had already been there. Nothing will
have been rescued, the work of return will have been precluded,
the present will have been sacrificed, given away.[14]

The intensity of the present is generated by its being the site of
misidentifications (Being as 'idea', 'energia', 'will' etc.), and thus
the perpetual repetition of irreconcilability; a state whose existence
must be experienced, acknowledged and then perhaps even resolutely affirmed. In taking over the present, in taking a stand within
it, the present projects a future. The present will never be worked
back onto itself. Heidegger is scrupulous in *Time and Being* in
recognizing the possible incursion of the retroactive – what will
reappear beyond his immediate concerns as the movement of *Nachträglichkeit* (iterative afterwork) – and then in attempting to rid
those concerns of precisely that possibility. Hence the importance
of 'originality', of the already there. The privileging of original
propriety over the effective of iteration – iteration's work – is signalled by Heidegger in *Time and Being* that what is proper to Being
and time in the sense of 'what determines time and being in their
unique propriety [*in ihe Eignes*]' (pp. 19, 20) is not what he then
describes as a 'relation retroactively [*nachträglich*] superimposed
upon being and time' (pp. 19, 20).[15]

The present must – and the 'must' is the sign of the task as well
as the necessity for resoluteness – abandon itself, leave itself behind,
do without itself for the future. In so doing it emerges as the future.
Time and Being precedes that which it cannot state and moreover
that which cannot be stated. It follows therefore that the text is
almost, in a literal sense, a foreword indicating what is to be done

while at the same time not doing it. As a text it identifies what will hinder the effectuation of the task, and in the act of identifying it indicates what might be involved in order that its restrictive and blocking powers be diminished. The present must be differentiated from itself. The problem is what sustains the differentiation. In sum, the 'without', in order to be maintained, enjoins either forgetting – a forgetting of that which will have been done 'without' – or sacrifice, a task involving metaphysics having been given away; from '*Aufgabe*' to '*aufgibt*'. Tracing the necessity of either sacrifice or forgetting enables the development of a critical stance in relation to Heidegger's construal of the epochal present. Their necessity becomes an important limit.

Sacrifice and the doing 'without' are necessarily connected. They are tasks demanded by the specific construal of the epochal present. Here, for Heidegger, they enjoin the future. It is this link to the future, a future opened up by the necessity of what is presented, that must be seen as arising out of the project engendered by that which is present as the text's foreword. The projected impossibility lies in the relation to what it is that must be experienced and the impossible eventuality of its being given within the language of philosophy and thus within metaphysics. It is with Benjamin that the linkage between experience, future and reconciliation will be sundered. It will be broken up by the necessity of destruction and thus of the caesura. To deploy the phraseology of the final part of the *On the Concept of History*, the future is forbidden precisely because it cannot be thought outside of the twofold possibility of progress and ultimate reconciliation.[16] It is precisely this state of affairs that is captured in the presentation of 'dialectical experience'.

> It is the unique property of dialectical experience to dissipate the appearance of things always being the same. Real political experience is absolutely free from this appearance.
>
> (N 9, 5)

BENJAMIN, MONAD, REPETITION

In order both to maintain the difference between Heidegger and Benjamin and to give it philosophical force, what must be taken up is the present within Benjamin's own presentation of the term; opening up, at the same time, the epochal present in Benjamin's writings (in this instance Konvolut N of the *Passagen-Werk*, its 'foreword'). Here the presentation of the term 'present' is announced as part of a particular task which is itself located in what amounts to a foreword. In other words in retaining the importance of the actative what this involves is taking up the interplay of ontology and action announced within the recitation of 'the present'; that is, the positioning of another epochal present positioned as projecting a task to be completed in writing. At a later stage in the drafting of the notes that comprise 'Konvolut N' – the period 1937–40 – 'the present' is drawn into the consideration of history in ways that serve to highlight 'the present' as a site, while at the same time attempting to distance continuity construed as either sequence or repetition.

> For the materialist historian, every epoch with which he occupies himself is only a fore-history of the one that really concerns him. And that is precisely why the appearance of *repetition* [*Wiederholung*] doesn't exist for him in history, because given their index as 'fore-history' those moments in the course of history that matter most to him become moments of the present according to whether this present is defined as catastrophe or as triumph.
>
> (N 9a, 8, my emphasis)

A beginning can be made with this 'present'. Here something becomes a 'moment' of the present; it becomes it because of its introduction into 'the present'. The question that emerges is the extent to which this introduction is constitutive of the present and is thus to be taken, in this aspect of Benjamin's work, as forming an integral part of the construction of the epochal present. Any attempt to take this question up will necessitate considering the status of 'fore-history', in its differentiation from 'after-history', and therefore in its being formulated as that which in some sense precludes repetition. It is essential that 'repetition' (*Wiederholung*) be given the specificity that is demanded by the passage, rather than its being assumed to mark out repetition in general (as if there were repetition in general). It will be necessary therefore to return to this 'repetition', a return signalling the abeyance of essential thinking.

The distinction between 'fore-history' and 'after-history' figures in a number of places in 'Konvolut N'. Almost invariably it is linked to either 'the present' or the attempt to formulate historical time. For example, at N 7a, 8,

> It is the present [*die Gegenwart*] which polarises the event into fore- and after-history.

and again, at N 11, 5,

> The present [*die Gegenwart*] defines where the fore-history and
> the after-history of the object of the past diverge in order to
> circumscribe its nucleus.

At a slightly earlier stage the 'foundation of history' is linked to
what is called the 'afterlife' of the object of historical understanding.

> Historical understanding is to be viewed primarily as an afterlife
> [*nachleben*] of that which has been understood; and so what
> came to be recognised about works through the analysis of their
> 'afterlife', their 'fame', should be considered the foundation of
> history itself.

> (N 2, 3)

The 'foundation of history' is then that which is to be located not
beyond the original – as though there could ever have been an
original founding moment to which a return could be made let alone
a moment of original propriety – but in a present incursion. The
continual repositioning, the privileging of the 'afterlife' in the place
of 'life', is not intended to be taken as an anti-realist gesture that
in some way denies reality by countering the material with the ideal;
rather reality comes to be invested with a different power, one
which will complicate the nature of that reality. The power is of
course Messianic. As Benjamin states, the method proper to a
'commentary on reality' (*der Kommentar zu einer Wirklichkeit*) is
theology. Theology as opposed to philology concentrates on the
'*nach*'. With this concentration, however, there arises the inevitable
question of limits. Does a *nachleben* always survive? Is there a limit
therefore to this '*nach*' and thus to any *nach*? Can the life of the
'afterlife' (*nachleben*), the 'afterhistory' (*nachgeschichte*), come to
an end? These are questions for Benjamin's own formulation of
time. The problem to which they allude concerns the twofold possibility of fulfilment and reconciliation.

In their varying forms these questions turn around the Messianic,
turning in the end towards *the* Messianic question. And yet what is
at stake here is not theology as such – understood as either the
language of/for God, or God reasoning – nor the Messiah as the
redeemer of a fallen humanity. Here the intersection of time and
politics is thought, provisionally, within the frame of the theological
in which the Messiah may be present but only as a figure; figuring,
perhaps, in the same way as the '*Flâneur*' or '*Lumpensammaler*'.
What is intended by this frame is that the Messianic is descriptive

of the power that enables the 'event' to have an afterlife; its capacity to live on is explicable in terms of Messianic power. That power is not theological. It is not the consequence of God's word or deed. Indeed it can be added that a limit to Benjamin's own adventure lay in his having to have recourse to the figure of theology to explain this occurrence rather than to the ontology of the 'event' – the limit therefore which becomes the limiting of the philosophical within his work.

A significant number of the theological motifs he employs turn on time. In a sense this is not surprising given the contention that theology is the site in which the thinking of time is sustained in his writings. However, the presence of such motifs brings with them a number of attendant problems, not the least of which is the nature of the relationship between motif and motive. This emerges quite clearly with the term 'apocatastasis'. Despite its decontextualization – perhaps a move envoking another afterlife? – it remains the case that the word is essentially Christian. One unproblematic occurrence of it in the Christian Bible is Acts 3:21:

ἄχρι χρόνων ἀποκαταστάσεως πάντων (until the time for restoring everything).

What is evoked is both a fall and a restoration located within totality. (Here πάντων is the Absolute, its having become actual, the giving of the totality gathered in time, given as the place of complete reconciliation.) What is designated in this instance in the Christian biblical context is the restoration of a totality that had come apart. The intended reality of absolute reconciliation is projected. (It will be vital, in this regard, to try and differentiate between the Christian concept of 'apocatastasis' and the Judaic, or more properly the Kabbalistic, concept of '*tikkun*'. While the distinction may not be immediately self-evident, maintaining the difference, it could be argued, is of considerable importance.) Within the Christian frame, the absolute nature of the term is essential, as indeed is the fall from completion. What is restored is that original completion and reconciliation of Man and God. What is restored is that which was originally always already there in Man though retained after the fall, in part in terms of the 'image of God', and in part in terms of that image involving a transcendence which in turn denied to the material present the possibility of its own redemptive, and therefore Messianic, possibility. Partiality is excluded as is a possible infinity. In the restoration of the 'all' the necessity for the continuity of any 'afterlife' would have ended.

The transformative and continually destructive power of 'now-time' (*Jetztzeit*) – a destruction already indicative of a denial of any impartiality and therefore, in addition, also of a resisted universality – would have become otiose.

What then of Benjamin's use of the term? With this question the problem of the '*nach*' ('after') is compounded for the question of the nature – the ontology – of what it is that is unending will come to insist. As it does not instantiate the theological, thought as the sacred – the sacred in its disassociation from the mundane – it must follow that in the end the enforced actuality of the Messianic will simply not do. Maintaining theology as the language and reasoning concerning God, were that to be a possible option, would involve thinking its relation to politics rather than taking it as that which provided politics with its temporality. These considerations, ones which will take Benjamin's concern beyond the limits he has provided for them, come to the fore with the use of a term such as 'apocatastasis'.

In 'Konvolut N' the word 'apocatastasis' occurs as part of what is described there as a 'minor methodological recommendation', concerning the contrasting and then the recontrasting of the putative positive and negative parts of an epoch. The point of this movement was to indicate that one only has value against the backdrop of the other. Retaining the negative – the 'backward' and 'extinct' parts – will involve contrasting them with different 'positive' elements in order that they be positioned anew. Original oppositions are thereby broken up. This breaking is at the same time the critique of historicism – be it Ranke or Hegel – and indicative of the radical nature of Benjaminian destruction. Benjamin concludes this recommendation in the following way:

> And so on *ad infinitum* [*Und so weiter in infinitum*] until all of the past has been brought into the present [*die Gegenwart*] in a historic apocatastasis.
>
> (N 1a, 3)

The value of this recommendation, which repeats the structuring force of the archaeological analogy from *A Berlin Chronicle* by the past being brought to the present as though to the surface, is that it allows for the effective distancing of oppositions such as major/minor, good/bad etc. when they are put forward as no more than the constitutive parts of an either/or; especially the given either/or of tradition.[17] Contrasts are to be dialectical and not straightforward oppositional juxtapositions (positing and counter positing). These contrasts may be, he suggests, as elementary as 'nuances'. What these contrasts allow for, however, is a continual renewal. As he puts it, 'it is from them that life always springs anew [*das Leben immer neu*]' (N 1a, 41). It is precisely this type of formulation that raises difficulties, since what it demands is a confrontation with the question of how the finality and totality of 'apocatastasis' is to be squared with the continual renewal of life – the continuity of the '*nach*', the 'always new' (*immer neu*) – especially as it is buttressed by the effective presence, in the passage under consideration, of the '*ad infinitum*'. The difficulty of answering this question indicates in part why residues of historicism are thought by some commentators to have been retained by the process marked out and thus enacted by the term 'apocatastasis'.[19]

What arises is in the first place the impossibility of 'all the past' ever being brought into the 'present'. It is not just that the reference to infinity renders it impossible; it is more exactly that the methodological procedure being suggested is precluded first by this type of finality and second by the 'monadological structure' of the 'historical object' (*des historischens Gegenstandes*) (N 10, 3). (It will be essential to return to the question of the monad for with the monad the force of the disruptive nature of Benjamin's construal of time will emerge.) What is wanted by Benjamin is a continual restoration that does not intend to restore the original paradisiac site nor aim at completion – a completion invoked by the 'all' – but rather a continual restoration in which each restorative moment is new, in the precise sense of a renewal of life as the afterlife. This particular theological term, therefore, while gesturing toward a state of affairs that is demanded methodologically, nonetheless belies the force of what is wanted. Benjamin used theology to think the relationship between politics and time. As a consequence he presents the challenge of thinking time and action beyond the conceptual purview of theology, thereby freeing theology for God.

In the passage under consideration (N 9a, 8) the relationship between 'fore-history' and 'after-history' is given in terms of the present as either catastrophe or triumph. What is located outside of their possible interconnection is 'the appearance of repetition' (*den Schein der Wiederholung*). But what here is repetition? It is that which is obviated in the first place – as a category – by the existence either of a dialectical image (the singular insistence and synonymy of Now and Then) and in the second place by the possible continuity of the always the Same. The use of 'fore-history' intends to rid history of repetition, and yet even with this twofold exclusion of repetition the question that still endures is: How is the 'after-history' or 'after-life' to be thought?

The question strikes at the heart of this attempted extrusion of repetition since it would seem to be the case that the 'after', the whole strategy of the present constructed by another giving, is itself unthinkable except as a form of repetition. Given this possibility what will then have to be argued is that what is involved in the distinction is a reworked concept of repetition. What this will entail is a repetition that has been subjected to the process marked out by the distinction between 'fore-history' and 'after-history'. It is only the interpolation of such a construal of repetition that will allow further insight into Benjamin's response to Horkheimer's insistence of a dialectical formulation of incompleteness and completeness and why Benjamin's introduction of 'a form of memoration' (*eine Form des Eingedenkens*) checks the dialectical presentation of history via the introduction of memory, but in so doing maintains the dialectical image as the ground of the historical itself. It is as though Engels were in debate with God; the God, that is, of Benjamin's theology.

The problem of repetition can be taken a step further by taking up the reference to the already cited insistence, by Benjamin, on the 'monadological structure' of the 'historical object'. Leaving to one side Benjamin's examples, as well as the question of the continuity of references to monads throughout his work, the passage in question positions the object, 'the historical object', in relation to its 'fore-history' and 'after-history' in the following terms:

> If the historical object is blasted out of the historical process, it is because the monadological structure of the object demands it. This structure only becomes evident once the object has been blasted free. And it becomes evident precisely in the form of the historical argument which makes up the inside (and, as it were, the bowels) of the historical object, and into which all the forces and interests of history enter on a reduced scale. The historical object, by virtue of its monadological structure, discovers within itself [*findet er in seinem Inner*] its own fore-history and after-history.

(N 10, 3)

Present here is an ontological formulation of the 'historical object'. The 'demand' that it makes is not a contingent possibility. On the contrary, it is a demand that stems directly from the mode of being proper to the 'historical object' in its being a historical object. What must be questioned therefore is the nature of this monad. What, in the above, is the monad in question? It is the enormity as well as the centrality of this question that suggests an approach which, while maintaining history and acknowledging the importance of memory, is concerned, nonetheless, with nature of the 'object' and thus with ontology and time.

References to the monad inevitably raise the possibility of a relation to Leibniz's own formulation of the monad in the *Mona-dology*.[19] What must be sought here is that which in Leibniz's own philosophical writings offers a type of illumination. (The possibility of a historical continuity, or the attempt to establish the same, even the continuity of influence, must be recognized for what it is.) As what is involved is the internality of the 'historical object' the obvious point of entry is Leibniz's own construal of the internality of the monad. In section 11 of the *Monadology* Leibniz argues that

> the natural changes of the monads come from an internal prin-ciple, since an external cause could not influence their inner being.

Slightly later at *Monadology* 15 this 'internal principle' is described as 'appetition' and then further clarified as what 'causes the change or passage from one perception to another'. What is significant about these descriptions is that the monad's change or development comes from within the monad itself. Change, and change here if it is translated into a different idiom, is going to involve the monad's 'after-life'. It will be an 'after-life' that is already part of its life in the strict sense that it is a possibility that is already within the monad. Furthermore, when Leibniz argues that the monad reflects the totality and thus in some sense contains all of its possibilities within it, it looks as if Leibniz as well as Benjamin construe monads in a similar way. However, there is a fundamental difference. In this instance, it is a difference involving time; not the temporality of the monad as such but the temporality of that in which the monad plays a constitutive part. Constitution here means that time brings ontological considerations with it.

The time in question pertains to what Leibniz identifies within his writings as 'pre-established harmony'; in other words time here pertains to the time of this harmony. It will be a time that precludes a straightforward singularity. In *Monadology* 59 the 'universal har-mony' is presented as that according to which

every substance exactly expresses all others through the relations
it has with them.

This mutuality of infinite relations expressed in the monad opens
up for Leibniz the need to distinguish each monad from God since,
if this infinite – the infinite of both 'division' and 'subdivision',
Monadology 65 – were clear to each monad and in addition the
necessary presence of distance did not introduce a type of confusion,
it would then follow, as Leibniz himself suggests at Monadology 60,
that 'each monad would be a deity'. (This is an identity established
and secured by Leibniz's own law of the identity of indiscernibles.)
The relation of monads to the infinite is more complex and is
explicable in terms of 'appetition'; in terms, that is, of the monad's
internality, and thus of the ontology of the monad. The interpretive
difficulty within this explication stems from having to recognize the
abeyance of stasis and with it the centrality of the ontology of
becoming.

> In a confused way they all go after/towards [*vont à*] the infinite,
> the whole; but they are limited and differentiated through the
> degrees of their distinct perceptions.

> (*Monadology* 60)

The movement is harmonious. Moreover, it follows from Leibniz
arguing in *Monadology* 7 that because the source of all change is
internal to the monad all changes have to be reflected in the whole,
such that the totality accords with itself. Again, this is possible only
for ontological reasons. In sum it is because the monad, as Leibniz
defines it in the opening line of *Principles of Nature and of Grace*,
is 'a being [*un être*] capable of action'.[20] Action is not a contingent
predicate of substance. The actative is in part constitutive of the
monad itself. The internal and complete accord – an accord *in toto*
– is 'pre-established harmony'. The difficulty here is God. It is,
however, a precise difficulty. If the totality is present in God, then
in some sense the infinite to which all substance moves – a move,
the consequence of desire, which is itself explicable in terms of the
monad's inscribed desire for completion and thus, in a sense, to be
God – is already present for God. In being present for God, and
even if appetition provides the continuity of completion, it remains
the case that for God the completing harmony is in some sense
already complete. (While there may be an ambivalence in Benjamin's work with regard to how reconciliation is to be understood,

Leibnizian teleology would be nonetheless a simply untenable proposition.)

While the ontologico-temporal considerations proper to God raise important problems for any sustained interpretation of Leibniz, it is nonetheless also directly relevant for understanding the time of 'pre-established harmony'. (It is the time proper to this harmony that will establish, and maintain, the significant divide between Benjamin's and Leibniz's conception of the monad.) The harmony is continued and continuous self-completion – completion, as it were, to infinity – is always already enacting the completing that is proper to it (establishing thereby a necessary link for Leibniz between ontology and the actative). While this does not preclude free will what it nonetheless renders impossible is the existence of that act in which the time of completion and thus with it both the ontology and the temporality of harmony – an always already pre-existent harmony – could be subverted, destroyed, let alone blasted apart. It is of course precisely this possibility that, Benjamin argues, can occur precisely because of the monadological structure of the 'historical object'.

It is possible to argue that for Leibniz what could be described as the temporality proper to freedom – the time in which, for example, evil and good acts are committed – is historical or chronological time, the time of dates, while the temporality of 'pre-established harmony' is the time of the universe held in infinite time with God and as such is not a time in which actions with determining results can occur. The reason for this impossibility is almost definitional in so far as the implicit Leibnizian conception of the universe and the temporality proper to it are such that they incorporate the totality of substance and therefore the totality of actions. With Benjamin the temporal structure is going to be importantly different. If there is any connection to 'pre-established harmony' within a philosophy of history then it would lie in the move that would turn the past into a given historical continuity that remains impervious to intervention or disruption. It would be as though the historical past created an accord that determined the historical task as the necessity to reproduce that founding and already existent accord, such that the reproduction itself accorded with the past. The historical object, the object of/in history, would therefore only reveal itself – reveal itself as it is, a revelation demanding the effective presence, *contra* Leibniz, of the ontology of stasis – in that founding accord.[21]

BENJAMIN'S REPETITION AGAIN

Even though there is an important difference between them that arises here, it should be noted that it is at this point that the complexity of Benjamin's debt to Leibniz emerges. It is precisely the status (the ontology) of what for Benjamin is the 'historical object' that allowing for that founding accord – the putative natural-izing of historicism – at the same time occasions the object being 'blasted out' of that pre-given continuity in order then to reveal itself – and to reveal thereby that which is reflected in it – in another setting. The revelation in another setting, a revelation constructed by that setting, is the explosive 'now-time', the instantiation of the present by montage; by the movement of montage (a montage effect whose determinations are yet to be fixed). It will be a montage that involves temporality as well as objects and images. Consequently it is not just that this present remains complex; there is a more insist-ent problem, namely, whether montage could ever be provided in a sustained and intentional way such that it avoided being simply arbitrary, and as such no more than a weak imagistic flutter (a flutter present as the figure, amongst others, of irony). In other words could there be a 'method of montage' that worked to preclude any response other than 'dialectical experience'?[22]

It is with these questions that the problem of the foreword, as the site where the task is announced such that what proceeds from it is the task's enacting, returns. Again, this is not a state of affairs simply added on to Benjamin's concerns; indeed the frame in which a return can be made is provided by Benjamin (N 1, 9) in his bringing 'project' (*Arbeit*), 'theory' and 'montage' together in order to provide a formulation of the undertaking, as a foreword.

> This project must raise the art of quoting without quotation marks to the very highest level. Its theory is intimately linked to that of montage.

If the approach indicated in this passage is taken up what remains problematic is the relationship between 'quotation' and the monad. A way of addressing this is provided by thinking through the differ-ence between quotation and 'quoting without quotation marks'. What may need to be argued is that montage while allowing for its being descriptive of images and pictures is in the end not merely descriptive of images or pictures. Montage in moving from images and pictures while at the same time incorporating them will have become a description of time. In other words, independently of

actual montage, montage will be a way of constituting the present
(the epochal present rather than the instant, the dated present). It
will awaken a possibility in which the present as temporal montage
will reorient itself in relation to the given and thus to that which is
given to it. It is this eventuality that can be identified as present at
the beginning of 'Konvolut N'.

> Comparison of others' attempts to setting off on a sea voyage in
> which ships are drawn off course by the magnetic north pole.
> Discover that North Pole. What for others are deviations, for me
> are data by which to set my course. I base my reckoning on the
> *differentia of time* [*den differentialen der Zeit*] that disturb the
> 'main lines' of the investigation for others.
>
> (N 1, 2, my emphasis)

The possibility gestured at here is that the 'differentia of time' could
be temporal montage, the co-presence of different times. (If this
state of affairs can be maintained then there will be no necessary
link between temporal montage and imagistic montage; the specific
art form.) The linkage between montage and time – temporal montage – will have to be taken up at the same time as returning to the
foreword, and attempting to plot the effect of the presence and
absence of 'quotation marks'.

These three elements combine in an important way. The 'quotation marks' raise the problem of repetition. The 'differentia' gesture towards a complex time at/as the present. While the foreword
instantiates the methodological and thus projective problems that
are sustained by one take on 'quotation marks' and 'differentia',
these problems are overcome by another take. With this other take
it will emerge that the problems are distanced by the repetition of
what is marked by 'quotation marks' and 'differentia'. 'Repetition',
the term that is to be restricted if not dismissed as long as it remains
in quotation marks, will turn out to play a redemptive role within
the project, projected and projecting beyond its given confines,
though only once the quotation marks are removed. Moving from
'repetition' (N 9a, 8) to repetition crystallizes the general problem
of understanding the loss of 'quotation marks'. To juxtapose images,
it may be that the crystal works as a *mise-en-abyme*. The radical
consequence of this opening up of repetition, presented within the
play of quotation marks, the continuity of their own oscillation, is
that again, though now for slightly different reasons, merely rehears-
ing Benjamin's own undertakings should not be assumed, in any
real sense at all, to be continuing the project of the *Passagen-Werk*.

Moreover, if they are repeated then their viability will not be able to be assessed in straightforwardly Benjaminian terms. Once more, it is not that Benjaminian montage amounts to the sustained juxta-position of chronologically separate images, it is rather that montage is a term that pertains to time. The importance of montage lies not in the chronologically disparate nature of the images but in the presence of the chronologically disparate being present.

The possibility of 'quoting without quotation marks' is another formulation of Benjaminian destruction. A movement that as has already been noted involves blasting 'the historical object . . . out of the historical process' (N 10, 3). Destruction here in opposition to either Cartesian destruction, which is the attempt to differentiate the present from itself in an absolute and all encompassing manner, or Heideggerian sacrifice, in which the present ('metaphysics') is given away for a specific end (the thinking of Being), will necessitate the centrality of relation and with it of repetition. (Heidegger's 'without' (*ohne*) will not dominate.) Destruction for Benjamin, Benjaminian blasting, it can be argued, is maintained by relation. Both the dialectical image and 'now-time' are relations. And yet they are more than simple relations. Part of the departure from simplicity pertains to time and part to repetition. It goes without saying that these two parts are related. Opting for the distinction within quotation – the absence and presence of marks as always signifying more than that which is given by the either/or of absence/presence – will capture these two interrelated parts. What has to be taken up, therefore, is quotation, to be understood as a form of repetition.

In its most general sense to quote means to restate what has already been stated. Any citation therefore must also re-site. And yet with citation there is a convention: the presence of tradition. The use of quotation marks, apart from introducing the continuity of convention, works, conventionally, to mark the act of recitation and hence of what could be described as a re-sitation. What the convention brings with it, in addition to itself, is a form of con-tinuity. The quotation marks indicate that what is cited (and re-sited) is not new but is the reiteration of what has already been; an intended repetition of the Same in which the singularity of the past's content is itself maintained. (As will be indicated it is Benjamin's description of the "historical object" having a monadological struc-ture that will render this singularity impossible. To which it should be added that it is an impossibility derived from ontological con-siderations.) The absence and presence of quotation marks within a given narrative indicates the presence of different moments of historical time – chronological time – which are made present as continuous and thus as part of a more general continuity within narrative. Benjamin can be taken as addressing precisely this possibility – the effective presence of enforced continuity – at N 19, 1:

> It could be that the continuity of tradition is only an appearance. But if this is the case, then it is precisely the persistence of this appearance of permanence that establishes continuity.

The force of this description is that it gives to tradition the structure of narrative, namely a structure in which tradition is present as a continuous and therefore unfolding sequential temporality. It is in this sense that tradition incorporates progress; its own progress however. The intricacy of the link between tradition and progress is that their reciprocity provides further constitutive elements of Benjamin's construal of the epochal present. Here both progress and tradition are themselves part of the necessary interarticulation of time and task.

The use of quotation marks sustains the continuity of tradition – its 'permanence' – while allowing, as has been indicated, the intrusion of the discontinuous. It is, however, a discontinuity that is absorbed and as such becomes part of the 'permanence'. Another type of discontinuity – itself discontinuous with the type cited above – is present in 'quoting without quotation marks'. In this instance the discontinuity is intended to endure. (It is thus that narrative and monadological structure are in a fundamental and effective opposition. Each will demand a different time and, with time, ontology, such that their difference is really only explicable in ontologico-temporal terms.) The absent marks signal the disruption of context. And yet the interplay of absence and disruption on its own is far from sufficient as a description. The mark's absence is not the only determination. Despite this absence there is still a quotation and thus a form of presence. All that is missing is that which maintains it, the quotation, as a quotation, namely the marks. Absence and presence, in this context, are not mutually exclusive. What this means here is that the contrast – the absent and present quotation marks, coupled to the continuity of quotation – is between two fundamentally different forms of repetition. What is emerging therefore is that far from providing either a false path or the simply peripheral, repetition, though more significantly the anoriginally present divisions within repetition, can be taken as central to any understanding of Benjamin's construal of the task at the present; a construal demanding the recognition of the ineliminable presence of reciprocity. The centrality of repetition plus repetition's constitutive divisions will allow the larger problems raised by Benjamin's use of such terms as 'apocatastasis' to be redressed with greater precision. The problems are inevitably linked to the unstated and therefore unacknowledged presence of repetition. What remains, however, is to set up the differing types of repetition and their enacted inter-relation with time and the announced task (the site of the foreword). Enactment here is intended to mark out the ineliminable presence of the actative. Action will always be part of the present's weave.

Repetition once thought beyond the purview of the Same opens up the possibility that what is given, repeated, is presented such that its occurrence may be the result of a working through, or a reworking, that is itself no longer contained by the Same. What is given is given again. The re-giving is neither simple iteration nor a repetition of the Same. Work is the divide. The re-giving therefore needs to be thought as an iterative reworking. The process of reworking re-presents the given in such a way that other possibilities that are in some way already inscribed within, and thus which are brought with it, are able as a consequence of that work – and thus also as constitutive of the work – to be revealed. It is this possibility that is based on the 'monadological structure' of the 'historical object'. The affinity here is, of course, with Freud's conception of 'working-through' (*Durcharbeiten*) and the way in which the tem-poral structure of *Nachträglichkeit* is incorporated as the temporality of 'working through'.[23] Perhaps the most important way of examin-ing the prospects held open by iterative reworking (the other rep-etition) and the monad is by reintroducing the concept of the fore-word and with it the relationship between foreword and repetition.

With Heidegger, the foreword presented that which could not be followed. This has to do with the language of metaphysics and the way in which experience in opposition, and thus in contradistinction to writing and language, functioned in his formulation and presen-tation of philosophical work. For Benjamin the problem of the foreword, while different, still raises problems touching on the possi-bility of the realization of the task demanded by the foreword. In Benjamin's case this will be linked to the nature of montage and with it to the possibility of methodological montage. Again, experi-ence will play a pivotal role in any understanding of this complex set-up. In both instances, Heidegger and Benjamin, the present is to be differentiated from itself. In Heidegger's case this is necessary because the present is taken to be metaphysics – the 'age' – and therefore the task involves 'leaving metaphysics to itself' and thus to think 'without' it. Here there is a differentiation that necessarily eschews relation. With Benjamin the differentiation occurs by an act of repetition, a repetition that can be thought and thus presented in a number of different ways; for example as 'memoration', as 'quotation', as 'awakening'. In each instance there is a juxtaposition or constellation that breaks the effect of continuity.

If what has been identified as temporal montage, taken in conjunction with 'quoting without quotation marks', and formulations of a similar nature are themselves all linked – a linkage that, in the end, will come undone for reasons both ontological and temporal – to the 'dialectical image', then that constellation can be pursued in order that constitutive elements be taken both together and in their sundering. Of central importance here are the methodological components provided in the formulation of the image. The significance of this particular adventure is that it highlights the problem of the interplay of method and experience.

> The dialectical image is a lightning flash. The Then must be held fast as it flashes its lightning image in the Now of recognizability. The rescue [*Die Rettung*] that is thus – and only thus – effected, can only take place for that which in the next moment is irretrievably lost.
>
> (N 9, 7)

The epochal present for Benjamin therefore comprises the unfolding of a continuity that can be blown apart at any moment. The flash of lightning coupled to loss, the irretrievable loss, harbour that residue of apocalyptic thinking that also inhabits the use of the term 'apocatastasis'. The question is whether Benjamin is only an apocalyptic thinker. Answering this question necessitates attending to a divide within the work. To the extent that this conception of the 'dialectical image' is retained then there can be no text, no enacted writing, that follows from this 'image' presented and thus serving as a foreword and thus not presented as itself. The apocalypse is not methodological. Not even the presentation of forced and enforced juxtapositions can rehearse the potential of 'lightning'. Irony is too strong to allow this rehearsal – the forced enforcement – to function unproblematically. On the other half of the divide however – a divide in which the elements present in each half will always inhere in the other – there is the potential inherent in the 'historical object'. Potential pertains to the ontology of the object. It goes without saying that the 'historical object' and the 'dialectical image' are not the same. The latter pertains emphatically to experience, while the first brings different ontological and temporal considerations to bear. It is the 'monadological structure' that can be taken as allowing for the 'dialectical image' and yet, and this will be the point of greatest significance, it does not have to have that result. The 'monadological structure' will allow, equally, for another repetition; repetition as iterative reworking. (Here repetition has come to be subjected to the process that it names.) This time it will be a repetition in which, to redeploy the same language, continuity has been 'blasted' apart because of the presence of a quotation which, while referring to its context and thus while bringing its context with it – a bringing to be thought as a reflection to be released – comes to be released at the present. Its release is therefore, at the same time, an integral part of the present. This other repetition arises because of the ontology of the monad; Benjamin's monad.

While there can be no foreword and thus no afterword to the apocalyptic, there can be nonetheless a foreword that incorporates and acts out the rescue and thus the redemption of repetition. With repetition the present will always be characterized by the 'differentia of time'. It will be repetition that while eschewing prediction will give the present as the site that is given in being worked through. Benjamin's construal of the epochal present therefore can be taken as bearing on the present, bearing it.

In sum, therefore, and in returning to Benjamin's initial formulations, it is the 'present' as that which 'polarizes the event into fore- and after-history' that becomes a site sanctioning its own constitution, though always as a further and furthering reconstitution, taking place and thus having a place through repetition. It is thus that the future is forbidden. This constitution, the act of constitution, not only introduces the primordiality of conflict, the flight from the homogeneous into the present, it allows at the same time the present – the present's potential – to stand apart from the homogeneous passage of time. There are two levels of destruction. Both are necessary if conflict is to be maintained and simultaneity sundered. Both enact the departure from the pre-established. It is the twofold nature of destruction that is announced in N 9a, 6. It is a destruction that is the province of historical materialism, the other name, for Benjamin, for the co-presence of politics and time.

Historical materialism has to abandon the epic element in history. It blasts the epoch out of the reified 'continuity of history'. But it also blasts open the homogeneity of the epoch. It saturates it with ecrasite, i.e., the present [*Gegenwart*].

Even recognizing the intrinsic difficulties of its formulation the present – the epochal present – is the site of an action connected to experience.

What then of showing? Remembering, if only as a contrast, that Heidegger's showing pertained to the presence of that which had already happened; showing was linked to the already there. The refusal of the retroactive was intended to maintain that 'originality'. Its refusal can be understood, if only initially, as the attempt to rid the historical and experiential of that form of repetition identified by the term *Nachträglichkeit*. Having cited part of the section concerning showing (N 1a, 8), its complex mediation needs to be introduced. The extract is completed in the following way.

> Only the trivia, the trash – which I do not want to inventory, but simply allow to come into its own the only way possible; by putting it to use.

The reference to the marginal brings back not simply the allusion to archaeology and the need to investigate the castings but the whole – if the use of such a term is not here oxymoronic – of allegory (the whole being both the ontology as well as the temporality of allegory). At this stage, this is not the central point. Rather, it is the contrast between something obeying its own law 'coming into its own' and being 'put to work to use'. The contrast here is stylistic. The opposition vanishes with the recognition that one is the other. The propriety of what is, is its being used. Showing is use. The doubling of showing, in showing, to which allusion was made above is now affirmed. Showing cannot eliminate reworking and can never obviate the process of a retroactive and thus iterative reworking. The recognition of this ineliminable possibility will occasion another reworking of experience. The present is partial and intense because it is the site of repetition, the place continually structured by repetition as a working through, iterative reworking, and thus as the potential site of its disruptive continuity. This is Benjamin's potential. The 'without' – the philosophy working with without – founders, yielding its place to the inevitability and ineliminability of the other repetition, as that which works the present.

NOTES

1 This chapter takes up and continues a discussion of ontology outlined in A. Benjamin, *Art, Mimesis and the Avant-Garde* (London: Routledge, 1991), and presented in a more systematic manner in A. Benjamin, *The Plural Event* (London: Routledge, 1993).

2 This particular construal of the Hegelian and Cartesian philosophical undertakings is presented in much greater detail in *The Plural Event*. Fundamental to each is the way in which their philosophical concerns are construed as contemporary.

3 The importance attributed here to writing is not intended to rehearse the issues involved in authorship. Nor moreover is it envisaged as raising generic problems, for example the relationship between philosophy and literature. Writing here attests to the necessarily textual nature of philosophy's presentation. Writing is therefore the site where the task – the philosophical task – is announced.

4 'Konvolut N' of Benjamin's *Das Passagen-Werk* and Heidegger's *Time and Being* are, for reasons to be advanced at a later stage, attributed the status of forewords. All page references are given in the text, the English pagination preceding the German. (This will be the case for all subsequent references.) The references are W. Benjamin, 'N [Re the Theory of Knowledge, Theory of Progress]', translated by L. Hafrey and R. Sieburth, in G. Smith (ed.) *Benjamin: Philosophy, Aesthetics, History* (Berkeley, CA: University of California Press, 1983); W. Benjamin, *Gesammelte Schriften*, vol. V.1 (Frankfurt am Main: Suhrkamp, 1991); M. Heidegger, *On Time and Being*, translated by J. Stambaugh (New York: Harper & Row, 1972); M. Heidegger, *Zur Sache des Denkens* (Tübingen: Neimeyer, 1938).

5 G. Scholem (ed.) *The Correspondence of Walter Benjamin and Gershom Scholem 1932–1940*, translated by G. Smith and A. Lefevre (New York: Schocken Books, 1989), p. 159.

6 W. Benjamin, *The Origin of German Tragic Drama*, translated by J. Osborne (London: New Left Books, 1977), p. 27. Benjamin, *Gesammelte Schriften*, vol. I, 1, p. 207.

7 Scholem, *Correspondence*, p. 159.

8 W. Benjamin, *One-Way Street*, translated by E. Jephcott and K. Shorter (London: Verso, 1985), p. 314. Benjamin, *Gesammelte Schriften*, vol. V.1, p. 486.

9 Part of this weight is the recognition that the present, even 'the present', within these passages from 'Konvolut N', while not made specific, mark out and therefore incorporate the site of the task's enactment. The present, given that the project here involves thinking through the ontology of the present, has in virtue of that project a double burden.

10 What experience will demand, in the end, is to be rethought in terms of the problem of agency. What this involves is a rethinking that arises out of the impossibility of the singularity, even a complex singularity, of agency. While it is a problem of considerable intricacy it is still possible to argue in general terms that another limit within the work of Benjamin and Heidegger concerns agency. With Heidegger it is the retention of the necessary singularity of the agent, while for Benjamin

it will emerge as the inability to account, in his terms, for the agent of 'dialectical experience'.

11 M. Heidegger, *Nietzsche*, vol. 4, translated by F. Capuzzi (San Francisco, CA: Harper & Row, 1982); M. Heidegger, *Nietzsche*, Zweiter band (Pfullingen: Neske, 1961). All page references are given in the text.

12 While it cannot be pursued here it is nonetheless worth noting that the emphasis on experience is presented most systematically in the opening of 'The Nature of Language', in *On the Way to Language*, translated by P. Hertz (San Francisco, CA: Harper & Row, 1982).

13 Fundamental to the comments made here about *Time and Being* is the 'without' (*ohne*). What must be addressed is the possibility of this 'without'. Not just what it means but what is involved in maintaining a thinking that is predicated upon a founding doing 'without'. Central to such an undertaking will be sacrifice.

14 While the projects are different it should still be noted that the discussion of reconciliation presented here has been greatly influenced by Rebecca Comay's remarkable paper 'Redeeming Revenge: Nietzsche, Benjamin, Heidegger and the Politics of Memory', in C. Koelb (ed.) *Nietzsche as Postmodernist* (New York: State University of New York Press, 1990). While memory has not been addressed within the confines of this chapter, it has been taken up in *Art, Mimesis and the Avant-Garde*, ch. 4, and in 'Kiefer's Approaches', in A. Benjamin and P. Osborne (eds) *Thinking Art: Beyond Traditional Aesthetics* (London: Institute of Contemporary Arts, 1991).

15 For a more sustained treatment of *Nachträglichkeit* within psychoanalysis see the recent collection of papers by and about Jean Laplanche: J. Fletcher and M. Stanton (eds) *Jean Laplanche: Seduction, Translation, Drives* (London: Institute of Contemporary Arts, 1992).

16 The reference here is to W. Benjamin, *Illuminations*, translated by H. Zohn (London: Fontana, 1973), p. 226. While the passage warrants a detailed analysis it is nonetheless essential to note the way within it that the question of time – to be understood as the question of the present of historical time – is reposed away from a simple gesturing towards the future.

The soothsayers who found out from time what it had in store did not experience time as either homogeneous or empty. Anyone who keeps this in mind will perhaps get an idea of how past times were experienced in remembrance – namely in just the same way. We know that the Jews were prohibited from investigating the future. The Torah and the prayers instruct them in remembrance, however. This stripped the future of its magic, to which all those succumb who turn to soothsayers for enlightenment. This does not imply, however, that for the Jews the future turned into homogeneous, empty time. For every second of time was the strait gate through which the Messiah might enter.

17 Tradition may seem to admit of a plurality, it may seem that there are many traditions. And yet any such description misses the role of power within tradition. There is a dominant tradition. Its unfolding is construed as the site of continuity; the continuity, in addition, of certain power

relations. Blasting it apart therefore is more than the simple critique of a posited singularity.

18 See in particular H. D. Kittsteiner, 'Walter Benjamin's Historicism', *New German Critique* 39 (Fall 1986).

19 References to Leibniz are to the *Oeuvres Philosophiques de Leibniz*, vol. II, ed. P. Janet (Paris, 1866). For the 'Monadology' the English edition, edited and translated by Latta, has been used: E. Latta, *Leibniz's Monadology* (Oxford: Oxford University Press, 1972).

20 Leibniz, *Oeuvres*, p. 608.

21 The position under attack is brought out in Benjamin's quotation of Grillparzer;

> To contrast the theory of history with Grillparzer's comment, translated by Edmond Jaloux in 'Journaux intimes' (*Le Temps*, 23 mai 1937): 'To read into the future is difficult, but to see *purely* into the past is even more so; I say *purely* which is to say without mixing that retrospective gaze with everything that has happened in the meantime.' The 'purity' of the gaze is not so much difficult as impossible to attain.
>
> (N 7, 5)

> The impossibility in question is not explicable in terms of the historian's failure. In other words the point being made does not concern the ability or inability of the historian to complete a specific task. Furthermore various historians and philosophers will always claim to have achieved the 'gaze' that Benjamin is describing here as impossible. The reason for the impossibility has to do in part with the ontology of the 'historical object' and in part with the way memory works both to inform and construct the present.

22 The substantive methodological point here is that presentation of works – even if they were accompanied by written text – which oriented themselves around the juxtaposition of images, drawings and photos in the belief that this illuminated Benjamin's project, would have taken the references to montage far too literally. As such they would have missed what is essential to montage, namely time.

23 For a detailed treatment of the philosophical implications of the Freudian concept of 'working through' see the final section of *The Plural Event*.

10 Benjamin's Endgame

Rebecca Comay

July 12, 1934. Yesterday, after a game of chess, Brecht said: 'If Korsch comes we shall have to work out a new game with him. A game in which the positions do not always remain the same; where the function of the pieces changes if they have stood for a while on the same square: then they become either more effective or weaker. Like this, the game does not develop; it stays the same too long.'

(Benjamin, 'Conversations with Brecht')

There is a well-known story [*Bekanntlich soll es gegeben haben*] of an automaton constructed in such a way that it could play a winning game of chess, answering each move of an opponent with a countermove [*Gegenzug*]. A puppet in Turkish attire and with a hookah in its mouth sat before a chessboard placed on a large table. A system of mirrors created the illusion that this table was transparent from all sides. Actually a hunchback dwarf who was a master chessplayer sat inside, and guided the puppet's hand by means of strings. One can imagine a philosophical counterpart [*Gegenstück*] to this apparatus [*Apparatur*]. The puppet called 'historical materialism' is supposed to win all the time. It can easily be a match for anyone if it enlists the services of theology, which today, as is well-known [*bekanntlich*], is small and ugly and has to keep out of sight.

('Theses on the Philosophy of History',[1] First Thesis)

The first thing to be noted about Benjamin's first thesis on history is its radical uninterpretability. I am referring to the frequently remarked tension if not contradiction between the actual 'apparatus' or image (the hunchback chess 'master' (*Meister*) covertly *pulling the strings* of a passive puppet) and its purported 'philosophical counterpart', interpretation or meaning (historical materialism actively *enlisting the services* of a servile and hunched theology). Who is the master and who the servant? Not only does the giant puppet, in enlisting the dwarf's services, become the puppeteer of his own puppeteer, jerking the line that will jerk him. So too the dwarf, deformed by the double handicap which marks, in fact, his real advantage, is himself burdened by the reification he would control: stunted, doll-like, puppet to the puppet who sits astride him.

Despite this chiasmic formulation and the apparent reciprocity of the bondage, this is not a dialectical or symmetrical exchange of power resolvable along Hegelian lines. For if the master-slave dialectic in Hegel (or, for that matter, Marx) was to issue in the increment in meaning which marks the self-escalation of a self-consciousness, neither the puppet nor his puppeteer here will profit from this backstage contest. The very labour of recognition – recognition as the reciprocity of desire which will determine history for Hegel as, indeed, the history of labour – such a labour will have been from the outset blocked or circumvented in this furtive tug-of-war game in which neither party achieves the productive freedom of an 'I'. What for Hegel was the essential theatre of recognition – 'life' as the ultimate presupposition of every struggle, and most specifically of that struggle to the death which inaugurates the dialectic of self-consciousness – this scene will have no pertinence in this secret puppet-show in which both players are already, in a real sense, dead. If Hegelian desire is that ordeal which puts life itself in jeopardy (but thereby naturally capitalizes on its own venture), the combatants here would risk both everything and nothing in so far as the stakes – 'life' – are from the outset lost. The specularity of intersubjective recognition (that is, the rational commensurability of a common risk or venture) will have already been subverted by the 'system of mirrors' that manufactures transparency (and thus the assumed transparency of face-to-face encounter) as one more conceit.

What is the precise nature of this entanglement? If the oscillation of master and servant suggests perhaps less a Hegelian dialectic than a carnivalesque derangement, the specific logic of this saturnalia – both its intoxicating and its Saturnine dimensions – still needs unravelling.

I

Chess, tshes, n.s. A nice and abstruse game, in which two sets of
puppets are moved in opposition to each other.

(Samuel Johnson)

The mirrors not only misrepresent a crowded box as a transparent
table. They also suggest a *mise-en-abyme* or series of self-reflecting
(but also, as in an eye or camera, self-inverting) images in which
the scene recapitulates its own effect. Are not the chess-pieces
themselves like little dolls on stage? Miniature 'men' animated with
the life their master both conceals and lacks? Puppets of a puppet
to the third degree? Does not the giant puppet therefore turn into a
kind of Bunraku puppet-master, inconspicuous in his very visibility,
exposed in the non-illusionistic (perhaps even Brechtian) theatre in
which all the moves are on the surface – 'without a thread', as
Barthes succinctly puts it[2] – and therefore gestic, bodily, outside?
If the large puppet's overt manipulation of the chess-pieces would
seem to repeat or reflect (in inverting) the dwarf's covert manipulation of the puppet, it is perhaps less a question of exposing,
theatricalizing or expressing the latter's secret than of subverting
our habitual assumptions regarding exposure or theatricality as such.
For despite the apparent symmetry of the antithesis – giant/dwarf,
manifest/hidden, outside/inside, high/low, inanimate/animate and so
on – it is ultimately unclear just how this opposition is to function.
The giant's ostentatiously visible manoeuvres would in fact undermine the very idea of exposure as the externalization of an interiority on which every theatre of expression (that is, Western theatre
as such) relies. Does not the relation between hidden and manifest,
inner and outer, here need to be rethought?

For if the allegory would seem to invoke a familar enough series
of antitheses – puppet and dwarf as outer and inner, body and soul,
expression and meaning, the Cartesian machine and its operator –
it will resist any *mechanical* or *automatic* (so to speak) interpretation
along such lines. Tempting as it may be to explicate the image in
terms of a co-ordination or synthesis, closer reading complicates the
matter. In insisting on the co-implication of 'historical materialism'
and 'theology', Benjamin is neither *proposing* nor *exposing* their
final unity.

This is not, on the one hand, a conventional plea for co-operation
(the engineers of the human soul need to find a soul, intuition
without concept is blind, concept without intuition is empty, and so
on). Nor is it really, on the other hand, a question of demystification

or unmasking, whether banal (Marxism is just another 'creed', the Enlightenment harbours false gods) or sophisticated (as in Hegel's analysis in the *Phenomenology* of the reciprocity of faith and insight; or, more pointedly, as in Nietzsche's excoriation of socialism as a slave morality, and hence a prolongation of the ascetic ideal it would surmount; or, yet again, to cite an example taken up by Benjamin himself, as in Karl Löwith's depiction of Marxism as a secularization of providential eschatology).

If the puppet, dressed in 'Turkish', recalls the 'Turkish fatalism' denounced by Nietzsche,[3] and if his hookah suggests that the materialist drug squad shares the addictions of organized religion, that the opiate of the people is imbibed even, or especially, by its most vigilant detractors (see, for example, Nietzsche on the bad alcoholic odour of the positivist[4]), it would be too quick to assume that it is here an issue of another false consciousness to be unduped or undoped. For since any such hermeneutics of suspicion would be captured in advance by the logic it would expose, the very success of the unmasking would *a priori* constitute its failure. (See *Zarathustra* on the ascetics of the spirit.[5]) In his 'Surrealism' essay, Benjamin had insisted on the need 'to win the energies of intoxication for the revolution' (II.1, 308; *R* 189f.). Benjamin, himself an earnest (if somewhat studious) hashish smoker, will insist on a 'dialectical conception of intoxication' which would displace the very terms of the opposition between sobriety and inebriation – Hölderlin's *heilignüchtern*[6] – thereby forcing us to consider whether our wearisome habit of trying to kick the habit might not itself stand in need of defamiliarization.

In other words, the exposure of the dwarf in the machine would not be a demystification or secularization in the Enlightenment sense. 'Truth is not an unveiling which destroys the mystery, but a revelation which does it justice' (I.1, 211; *OGT* 31). It is not a question, therefore, of achieving the rationalization announced by Hegel as the supersession of religion by philosophy, that is, the revelation that even revealed religion essentially obfuscates what it would unveil. If to some extent Benjamin (with Nietzsche) shares Hegel's critique of organized religion – specifically, of the compensatory, never-never land temporality of its redemptive claims[7] (a temporality which structures the once-upon-a-time narratives of all historicism) – there can be no question of a similar passage to conceptuality or thought.

'Truth', according to Hegel, is that 'Bacchanalian revel in which no limb or member is not drunk [*kein Glied nicht trunken ist*]'.[8] From the standpoint of Absolute Knowing, such a delirium will have been a provisional disorder within the system, enjoyed in order to be overcome (indeed nowhere more markedly, as Derrida has argued, than in the binges of religion itself as it proceeds from fruit to wine, from wine to blood, from the oblations of natural religion to the sacramental wine transforming itself into the blood of a God resurrected in worship and comprehended in thought).[9] The torn body of Dionysus, of a Dionysus turned Christ turned Spirit, the body of a thought beside itself in the ecstasy of absolute *Zerissenheit*, this shattered body will be reassembled. In the sober 'court' of memory, every 'member', as a member – that is, in its very partiality or dismemberment – will have been judged inadequate and thus sublated.

> Because each member collapses as soon as it drops out [detaches itself: *sich absondert*], the revel is just as much transparent and simple repose. Judged in the court of this movement, . . . in the *whole* of this movement . . . what distinguishes itself therein, and gives itself particular existence is something that *recollects* itself [*sich erinnert*], whose existence is self-knowledge and whose knowledge is just as immediately existence.
>
> (ibid.)

Hegelian *Erinnerung* is just this *re*-membering. Recollection would be precisely the resurrection of the idealized, transfigured body, a body restored to its organic unity and spiritual integrity as a whole.[10]

Benjamin, in contrast, re-*members*. That is, for Benjamin as for Proust – for Benjamin above all as a reader of Proust – memory is in the first place a *mémoire des membres* (double genitive) (I.2, 613n; *CB* 115n): the incoherent, multiply situated reawakenings of shattered body parts re-encountering themselves in time and space. For Proust, such an encounter had the power to arrest the homogeneous flux of time: *faire reculer le soleil*.[11] In the 'Berliner Chronik' Benjamin describes the work of memory as the ceaseless, 'rhapsodic' excavation of vestiges: 'ruins or torsos in a collector's gallery', fragments broken off from the chain of prior connections so as to stand unassimilated in the 'sober chambers' of retrospection. Like the *disjecta membra* strewn across the baroque theatre stage, allegorical 'rebuses' resisting the symbolic harmonies of a 'transfigured nature' (I.1, 352–5; *OGT* 176–9), the shards of memory frustrate the conciliations of organic closure, announcing the endlessness of a mourning which keeps on exhuming or unearthing what has been buried. Memory, *Erinnern*, retrieves the hidden interiority of the earth, *Erdinnern*, as the broken outwardness or exteriority which breaks away from (*ausbrechen*) every inwardness.

> He who seeks to approach his own buried past must conduct himself like a man digging. This determines the tone, the posture of genuine reminiscences [*Erinnern*]. They must not be afraid of returning again and again to the same matter, to scatter it as one scatters earth, to turn it over as one turns over soil. The matter itself is only a deposit, a stratum which yields only to the most meticulous examination what constitutes the real treasure hidden within the earth [*Erdinnern*]: the images, severed from all earlier associations [*aus aller früheren Zusammenhängen ausgebrochen*], that stand – like precious ruins or torsos in a collector's gallery – in the sober chambers of our later insight.
>
> (VI, 486; *R* 26, slightly modified)

Far from resolving the fragmentation of experience into the spiritual interiority of consciousness, sobriety, for Benjamin, dissolves or disintegrates (but thereby reconfigures) what is already in a state of disintegration: the dismembered, inorganic body, reminder of incurable mutilation.

In his 'Surrealism' essay, Benjamin rewrites Hegel's formula. According to his thinly veiled quotation of the *Phenomenology*, 'no limb remains unrent' (*kein Glied unzerissen bleibt*) in the transformed, Dionysian body of a collective stimulated to revolutionary pitch (II.1, 309; *R* 192). This is Benjamin's own materialist version of 'dialectical justice' (*Gerechtigkeit*) as a 'dialectical annihilation' (*Vernichtung*) (pp. 310; 192) or catharsis in which a radically fragmented body discharges its innervations in an 'ecstasy' doubling as the 'humiliating sobriety' (pp. 299; 181) of a revolution calculating its war-moves to the most banal degree. Such 'dialectical' intoxication ('profane illumination') would be a 'true, creative overcoming of religious illumination' (pp. 297; 179) – whether the 'humid backroom' of Surrealist 'spiritualism' (pp. 298; 180) or Hugo's dabblings with the occult (I.2, 565f.; *CB* 63) – an 'overcoming' which although (or perhaps because) 'dialectical' would refrain from mediating or conceptualizing what it takes up.

Whereas for Hegel revealed religion betrayed its own mandate by its final adherence to the graven images of *Vorstellung* (therefore requiring the cleansing prose of thought), Benjamin insists that in any act of elucidation 'there remain a residue': *Es bleibt ein Rest* (II.1, 310; *R* 192). Despite ('indeed, precisely after') the 'dialectical

annihilation' which announces 'the overcoming of religious illumination', there persists a 'sphere of images and, more concretely, of
bodies' (ibid.). The 'dialectical image' would be the concatenation
or constellation (for Hegel, oxymoronic) of image and concept,
figure and thought, marking Enlightenment itself as, in effect, a
chronically 'unfinished project' (Habermas).

Nor is it a question of prying loose the shell of the apparatus so
as to *recover* theology as a repressed or hidden content. That gesture
of recovery – interpretation as the reprise or elucidation of a lost
or buried original – would be no more pertinent than the hermeneutics of suspicion or unmasking which in fact, as Ricoeur has
argued, it so closely resembles.[12] For since 'theology' stands in here
not for any determinate content to be remembered but indeed for
the very power of remembrance – in his notes Benjamin describes
remembrance as the 'quintessence' of a Jewish theological representation of history (I.3, 1252) – it is unclear just how such a quintessence could ever essentialize itself so as to emerge intact. For if it is
memory itself and not a *determinate memory* which remains hidden
or occluded, it remains by this very token inaccessible to any hermeneutic retrieve. The hunchback, 'as we know, is small and ugly
and has to stay out of sight'. What has been occluded or forgotten
is in fact the only power against forgetfulness: memory as such has
become distorted or displaced.

Irving Wohlfarth points out that for Benjamin (as no doubt for
Freud, or for that matter, Hegel or Heidegger), deformity or 'distortion' (*Entstellung*) – literally, 'misplacement' or 'displacement' – is
the essential hallmark of oblivion:[13] one's own body becomes 'the
most forgotten alien land' (II.2, 431; *Ill* 132). Thus Benjamin enu-
merates the stigmata of Kafka's blighted creatures, the 'hybrids'
(pp. 414; 116), 'abortions' (pp. 430; 131) and 'bastards' (pp. 431;
132) of a swampy 'intermediate world' (pp. 430; 131). Dogs, bugs,
monkeys, mice, moles, butterflies, monstrous kitten-lambs yearning
for the butcher's knife of redemption: the human body has become
undecipherable to itself, a site of exile, 'a village whose language
[one] does not know' (pp. 424; 126). The spool-shaped Odradek,
'standing upright' only by means of elaborate prostheses, is relegated to the attic, staircase, corridor and hall (pp. 431; 133).
Displaced, without a place in (but equally without escape from) the
household economy of the 'family circle' (pp. 414; 116), such a
creature embodies oblivion as the guilty deferral which marks our
time (as a time, that is, of merely marking time). Benjamin remarks
that with their low ceilings, attics, like lawcourts, are 'places of

discarded, forgotten objects' (pp. 431; 133), sites of the neglect distorting both space and time. One puts off opening the dusty trunks in the attic as assiduously as Joseph K. would postpone (until 'retirement') concluding his day in court (pp. 431; 133).

'The prototype of distortion' is 'the hunchback' (II.2, 431; *Ill* 133). Wohlfarth has articulated the issue with great rigour. 'Among the images in Kafka's stories, none is more frequent than that of the man who bows his head far down on his chest' (pp. 431; 133). Fatigued officers, doorkeepers, 'descendants of Atlas' (pp. 410; 112) bearing the burden of the universe in every object: 'it is the back on which this is incumbent' (pp. 432; 133). Thus too the 'archaic apparatus' multiplying the inscriptions on the condemned prisoner's back in the 'Penal Colony' (pp. 432; 133): 'an immense apparatus of officialdom [*Beamtenapparatur*]' directed by authorities whose crippling power is indeterminate (*ungenau*) even to their 'executive organs' (*Br* 760). In an early diary entry quoted by Benjamin, Kafka describes falling asleep with arms crossed like soldiers carrying a heavy backpack: forgetfulness is the guilty somnolence of our days and nights (II.2, 432; *Ill* 134).

The hunchback, while the Messianic agent or augur of remembrance, is at the same time thus the supremely guilty instance of forgetfulness – a secret agent, then, in every sense. Deformed because forgotten, his deformity requires that he, in turn, be forgotten: his hump is simultaneously both the symptom and the occasion of his withdrawal. His double distortion – 'small and ugly', dwarf and hunchback – marks the doubleness or duplicity of all distortion: 'displacement' as such is never quite in its place. His exclusion or seclusion thus has the reflexive circularity of all forgetting: a repression that needs in turn to be repressed. 'The main feature of forgetting', writes Benjamin, 'is that it forgets itself.'[14] (We are close here to Freud's sense of 'primal repression' as the (repressed) presupposition of all repression. But perhaps equally to the redoubled concealment – *die Verborgenheit der Verborgenheit* – which inaugurates Heidegger's history of Being.)

In his essay on Karl Kraus, Benjamin describes the 'falling sickness' evoked in the products of Viennese Expressionism, the 'stepped, steeped' terraces of human shoulders, necks and backs (II.1, 351; *R* 256f.). Like the 'mysterious' figures depicted in medieval miniatures, 'leaning' or 'inclining' together with 'wide-open eyes', the Expressionist figures display a radical 'curvature' or 'concavity', typically most visible when viewed from behind. Clenched or huddled in 'steep steps' which despite appearances 'lead less toward heaven than downward', the human body becomes a stepping stone for higher powers, 'climbed like heaped up rocks or hewn stones' (pp. 351; 257). 'The nameless power toward which the backs of people are bent', writes Benjamin, is 'guilt' (ibid.). By 1912 Kraus had already denounced the 'pitiable' subservience of the 'obedient masses', led astray 'not by an unknown will but by an unknown guilt'. 'Whatever powers may have fought out their spiritual battles on these shoulders', comments Benjamin, '. . . we are able to call one of them by its name' (ibid.).

The name of the game, of course, is capital. In nineteenth-century Paris, the sandwichman or 'poster-man' (*l'homme-affiche*) was observed carrying on his shoulders the burden of consumer capitalism, an edible offering to the system he was to advertise.[15] In twentieth-century Marseilles, the hunchbacks, remarks Benjamin, like beggarwomen, wear lurid pink – 'colour of shame, of poverty' – gleaming like stinking carcasses thrown to a system recycling its refuse to the last degree (IV.1, 359; *R* 131).

Under such conditions, it would be idealism of the worst sort to celebrate, à la Bloch, the orthopaedia of the upright posture. In his Kraus essay, Benjamin comments that 'developing man' – the child, the 'monster' (*Unmensch*), the demonic messenger of a 'more real' humanism (II.1, 366; *R* 272) – is 'recognized by the posture which the fight with exploitation and poverty stamp upon him' (II.1, 365; *R* 270). Whereas the tradition of bourgeois idealism (from Schiller to Stifter) would celebrate the 'classical ideal of humanity' (pp. 355; 261) – whether as the individual bearer of abstract 'rights' (ibid.), as 'Romantic creature of nature' (pp. 364; 270) or even, suggests Benjamin, as the Nietzschean 'overman' (pp. 361; 266) – a 'real' (that is, anti-essentialist, anti-idealist and ultimately even anti-humanist) humanism would contest this 'idol' (pp. 364; 270) of a 'harmoniously and perfectly formed' humanity (pp. 348; 253): that is, the 'phantom of the unpolitical or "natural" man' (pp. 364; 270).

Benjamin comments that 'distortion will overcome (or sublate) itself [*sich aufheben*] in the passage to redemption' (II.3, 1201). Forgetfulness, already once forgotten, is in being remembered to be, precisely, re-forgotten: to remove the hump is to engage in a kind of 'active forgetfulness', in Nietzsche's sense. In Grimm's story, the dwarfish Rumpelstiltskin disappears forever upon being named or recognized by the princess (cf. II.1, 345; *R* 250). The little hunchback in the German folksong 'will disappear with the coming of the Messiah' (II.2, 432; *Ill* 134). The dwarf, already marked by the stigmata of his twofold occlusion, is, inconspicuously, to write himself out. In the meantime, his deformity stands as a secret indictment of social existence: pure *Lumpengesindel* (IV.1, 303), a 'stumbling-block' (II.2, 565; *UB* 67) in society's way. Like the child in Brecht who 'didn't want to wash', he disrupts every 'orderly household' (ibid.), ruins the Kaiser's visit, smashes dishes, leaves a pile of debris (IV.1, 303).

II

But how does this pair of sideshow freaks become a winning number? The puppet team, according to Benjamin, is 'supposed to win each time'. The claim is striking not only because it is one of Benjamin's more flagrant misreadings or interpolations into the Poe subtext he is reworking here – Poe, in fact, specifically emphasizes the *fallibility* of the automaton as the telltale sign of its hidden operator[16] – and not only because it is unclear how this uneasy partnership, divided against itself and without internal coherence, could possibly form a united front. Would not the machine's ability to perform a successful 'countermove' (*Gegenzug*) be thwarted under the impact of the 'philosophical counterpart' (*Gegenstück*) which in effect jams the gears mid-circuit? The claim is also striking because in fact it makes no sense. For the figure (as so frequently in Benjamin) is being made to function in an argument which will in effect undermine its explicit meaning. What could it mean to invoke the notion of automatic victory to introduce a text the essential point of which will be, after all, to problematize the very notion of victory, automatic or otherwise, as being the ideology of those on top?

Historical materialism (henceforth without scare quotes) will above all expose the ultimate illegitimacy of every victory, reminding us that victory as such implies victimization, a 'triumphal march' trampling over its casualties like so many pawns swept 'prostrate' (*am Boden liegen*) underfoot (§7). It will have been, of course, the fatal error of the Social Democrats to believe that the automatic victory of the proletariat – an automatism dressed up precisely as an organicism, that is, an evolutionism and specifically a neo-Darwinism[17] – it will have been Social Democracy's credulity to think that such a victory would irresistibly propel Europe through its darkest hour (§13). Benjamin argues that such a faith will have only accommodated barbarism in the name of progress, maiming or 'cutting' the workers' 'sinews' in the misguided celebration of a future which could only – in its very zeal for compensation – cheat (§12). A similar 'faith in progress' will have led Stalin to his devil's pact with Hitler, reducing fascism's opponents to 'prostrate' under-lings (*am Boden liegen*), puppets entangled in the 'snares' (*Netzen*) of an 'apparatus' (*Apparat*) 'uncontrollable' in its own success (§10).

In 'One-Way Street' – the 'one-way' sign simultaneously both marking a certain historical irreversibility and warning against any naively progressivist or linear rendering of this irreversibility – Benjamin had already spelled it out. In a fragment entitled, appro-priately, 'Fire Alarm', he dismisses any determination of the class struggle which would 'romanticize' by obscuring what is essentially a tactical (or 'technical') intervention as a 'chivalric' ordeal or 'trial of strength' (*Kraftprobe*). If according to the laws of historical materialism the bourgeoisie is condemned in advance, that is, auto-matically, to extinction, the crucial question remains just how, or more precisely, when, this inevitability is to transpire – a question, for the proletariat, of *timing*.

> The notion of the class war can be misleading. It does not refer to a trial of strength to decide the question 'Who shall win, who shall be defeated?', or to a struggle the outcome of which is good for the victor and bad for the vanquished. To think this way is to romanticize and obscure the facts. For whether the bourgeoisie wins or loses the fight, it remains doomed by the inner contradic-tions that in the course of development will become deadly. *The only question is whether its downfall will come about through itself or through the proletariat*. The continuance or the end of three thousand years of cultural development will be decided by the answer. . . .
>
> (IV.1, 122; *OWS* 80, my emphasis)

In other words, there are victories and then there are victories. Toughing it out ('chivalrously') in the certainty of a preordained triumph would be inevitably to embroil oneself in the series of reformist adjustments that simply keeps the gears well-oiled. In the *Passagen-Werk*, Benjamin describes the insight (actually, a decision) that 'capitalism will die no natural death' as 'the experience of [his] generation' (V, 819). The kind of 'natural' demise which concludes an evolutionary sequence – for the proletariat, a victory chronically deferred by reason of its inevitability – becomes mythical, Pyrrhic, too late in the day.

The true politician reckons only in dates. And if the abolition of

the bourgeoisie is not completed by an almost calculable moment
in economic and technical development (a moment signalled
by inflation and poison-gas warfare), all is lost. Before the
spark reaches the dynamite, the lighted fuse must be cut. The
interventions, dangers, and tempi of politicians are technical –
not chivalrous.

(ibid.)

The 'stupidity and cowardice' which rosily assumes that 'things can't
go on like this' (IV.1, 94; *OWS* 54) – together with its 'unphilosophi-
cal' counterpart, the complacent 'amazement' that 'the things we
are experiencing are "still" possible' (§8) – is blind precisely to the
truth that the fact 'that "things keep going on like this" *is* the
catastrophe' (V, 592; N 9a, 1). The continuum – continuation as
such – is the catastrophe. 'For the suffering of individuals as of
communities there is only one limit beyond which things cannot go:
annihilation' (IV.1, 95; *OWS* 55). What is already falling, as Nietzsche observed, needs to be kicked. 'Before the spark reaches the
dynamite, the lighted fuse must be cut' (IV.1, 122; *OWS* 80).

Hegel had described the triumphal march of history as a 'slaughterbench'.[18] Benjamin, observing a 'humanity' that had come to
'prove itself by destruction' (II.1, 367; *R* 273) – a humanity that in
the age of 'total war' had indeed come to construe production *as*
destruction (I.2, 632n; *CB* 133n), thereby aestheticizing its own
destruction as its most essential act of self-production (cf. I.2, 506–8;
Ill 241f.) – Benjamin speaks of the need to counter (self-)destruction
with destruction. What presents itself according to conventional
piety as a progressive 'chain' of events (§9) – a 'smooth thread' (I.3,
1233) or a consoling 'rosary' (§A) – is to be grasped as a burning
wick. Beneath the pre-established harmony of a clockwork universe
– a 'cosmic clock' (II.2, 489; *OWS* 370) humming inanely to the
'ticktock of a small happiness' (Nietzsche)[19] – beneath this cheerful
machine lurks a time bomb. 'Before the spark reaches the dynamite,
the lighted fuse must be cut.'

In other words, the clock must be stopped. For what strikes the
beat of the victory parade is, of course, the 'homogeneous, empty
time' (§B) assumed by every ideology of progress from the Enlightenment to this day. Nietzsche had already spelled out the vested
interests that such a metaphysics both presupposes and sustains.
According to such a metaphysics, time would be determined as
the empty succession of identical now-points – inertly observed,
indifferently exchanged – the site of the will's own impotence and

'gnashing of teeth' before the past. Petrified as 'ground' or 'cause' or 'thing in itself' (a 'heavy stone', says Zarathustra, a 'prison'), the past becomes the site of unredeemed possibilities for a generation of 'angry spectators'. The future becomes the compensatory 'fable' of a time of final judgement, 'progress' the vengeful payoff for a prior impotence before the past. He who pays the piper is of course the one who calls the tune: the chant of progress ultimately vindicates the present as the final measure of all times. What is celebrated in every victory march is 'the tyranny of the actual';[20] beneath the parade regalia lies a 'naked admiration for success'.[21] Its participants become 'Chinese mechanical doll[s]', says Nietzsche, nodding to whatever power pulls the strings.[22]

It is, for Benjamin, a question of jamming the gears in this happy clockwork universe. Or, more precisely: a question of rigging the clock in such a way that as it stalls it sounds the alarm. In an age where talk of progress can only mask the real 'retrogression of society' (§11), continuity is itself the catastrophe threatening humanity as a whole. An ideologue such as Carl Schmitt mystifies the continuum as an 'exception', normalizes catastrophe, therefore, as an accident or aberration (a 'state of emergency') thereby legitimating authoritarian intervention. 'It is our task', writes Benjamin, 'to bring about a real state of emergency' (§8).

Zarathustra had threatened to 'wind and wound' (*aufziehen*) the 'cheap clocks' of the virtuous, to overwind these mechanical dolls with his mockery until they whirred no more.[23] Writing in 'One-Way Street', not long after the debacle of the *Trauerspielbuch* and his own expulsion from the academy, Benjamin recounts a dream about strolling as a fledgling Privatdozent through the mausoleum of culture. Peering into a glass museum display-case, he 'blushes' to see hanging in the mouth of a golden statue's head the jewels of a dismembered watch (IV.1, 118; *OWS* 77). The Surrealists, staring in the face of the humanism that peddles barbarism in the name of culture – or, more precisely, staring this gift horse in the mouth and finding there, like Benjamin, the vagina dentata of a precision clockwork – overwind this clock and set it ringing. 'They exchange . . . the play of human features for the face of an alarm clock that in each minute rings for sixty seconds' (II.1, 310; *R* 192).

Among the scattered notes to the 'Surrealism' essay gathered under the laconic rubric 'clock motif', Benjamin cites the case of 'the American who hangs his clock on the wall and shoots it'. Breton, also quoted, writes of the 'crackling of the wood of a clock which I throw into the . . . fire in such a way that it dies ringing the hour' (II.3, 1031). In the fifteenth thesis, Benjamin cites an unnamed 'eye-witness' of the July revolution who on the first evening of fighting claims to have observed the clocktowers being fired at 'independently and simultaneously' from several places in Paris. The 'eyewitness' is actually a pair of self-proclaimed *'poètes-citoyens'* from Marseilles who write (and Benjamin quotes) as follows:

> Qui le croirait! on dit qu'irrités contre l'heure
> De nouveaux Josués, au pied de chaque tour,
> Tiraient sur les cadrans pour arrêter le jour.[24]

I cannot explore now the slightly circular if not paradoxical logic informing this spontaneous revolutionary calculus, so very punctual in its anarchy, this calculus to end all calculi, announcing the very advent of the incalculable: how did the militants know what time, exactly, to start shooting at all the clocks? Nor do I want to dwell on the peculiar irony at work in Benjamin's rather chilling invocation, in 1940, of the Israelites' triumphant vendetta against their enemies, the Amorites, at Gibeon, the day the sun stood still (cf. Joshua 10:13). And I shall not linger on the oddity of this apparently historicist appeal to the 'eyewitness'. At the very least, the authority of such a gesture would have undermined itself with the erasure of the authors' names, and with the vaguely sardonic suggestion that the witness 'may have owed his insight' (actually 'divination', or, more ambiguously, in the French version,[25] 'clairvoyance') to 'the rhyme', that is, to the – somewhat automatic – exigencies (or contingencies[26]) of rhetoric rather than to the objectivity of fact. But I would like to set aside these peculiarities for the moment so as to focus on the peculiar nature of the temporal caesura at work.

Why shoot the clocks? Baudelaire's 'deepest wish' – 'the wish of Joshua' – is 'to interrupt the course of the world'.[27]

> Not so much the prophetic; for he did not think much of change. From this wish sprang his violence, his impatience and his anger. From it too sprang the ever renewed attempts to strike at the heart of the world or to sing it to sleep. Out of this wish came the encouragement with which he accompanied Death in his works.
>
> (I.2, 667; *CP* §15)

What for Baudelaire exemplifies itself in the arrested present of the hashish trance[28] – compare Zarathustra's 'strange drunkenness' at noontime[29] – 'can also', remarks Benjamin, 'be applied to the definition of revolutionary historical consciousness' (V, 602; N 15, 1).

If intoxication (at least in its 'dialectical' form) resembles revolution in its congealed temporality, such a moment is 'not so much prophetic' as turned backward, 'accompanying Death' by marking the irretrievable pastness structuring every time. 'Revolutionary historical consciousness' (V, 602; N 15, 1) freezes or 'crystallizes' time by administering the posthumous 'shock' (§17) by which the 'historical' as such is founded (§A), thus exposing history to the traumatic structure of *Nachträglichkeit*, in the Freudian sense.[30] The past becomes 'historical' retroactively through its citation (§14) 'at a moment of danger' (§6), suspending or 'blasting open' (§14) the continuum of events unfolding along historicism's 'causal chain' (§A).

As when mourners stop the clock so as to mark the moment of dying, the revolutionary caesura 'accompanies death' by registering its untimely rigor as the 'Golgotha' (I.1, 405; *OGT* 232) ruining every time. Such untimeliness disrupts the self-identity of the living present, exposes this present as the 'transfixed restlessness' (*erstärrte Unruhe*) (V, 410) or explosive stasis which resists integration into a linear exchange. If the singularity of death marks the very limits of exchangeability (including the temporal exchangeability of indifferent now-points), its recognition involves the awareness of a future radically unthinkable because unassimilable to what is on hand. Mourning thus involves the inherently 'revolutionary' sense of a future 'absolute' (Levinas) in its heterogeneity: to perceive history as corpselike is already, strictly speaking, to negotiate an opening to a future radically new. Thus 'the standstill is utopia' (V, 55; *CB* 171). If, for the angel, history appears as a rubble heap (§9) – a 'death's head' or 'petrified landscape' (I.1, 343; *OGT* 166) – such rigidity signifies neither the embalming nor the sanctification of what has past, but on the contrary points to the limits of organic assimilation and hence to the 'utopian' non-identity of what may arrive. Reification is turned against itself. To perceive history (allegorically) as the 'natural history' of a frozen 'landscape' (I.1, 343; *OGT* 166) – a 'puppet-play' (pp. 303f.; 124f.) or 'tableau vivant' (pp. 369; 193) – is to refute the idealism which would see 'eternal life' (pp. 353; 178) in what comes to pass. 'How can one speak – of progress, to a world sunk into rigor mortis [*Totenstarre*]?' (V, 420). To an idealism which would mask or spiritualize death as the organicity of 'becoming', allegory opposes the spectacle of a 'life' rendered inorganic or immobilized in the cadaverous fixity of the ruin. In at least this respect, Baudelaire, Gryphius and the 'July revolutionaries' are in accord. '*Je hais le mouvement . . .*' (cf. V, 388). To register such ruinousness – blasting the continuum, shooting the clocktowers – is to beat the 'irregular rhythm of the constant pause', a rhythm which announces 'the sudden change of direction' (I.1, 373; *OGT* 197) of a future radically new.

Memory, *Eingedenken* – the 'Ein– ' prefix signifying here in fact precisely the *opposite* of the unifying inwardness of a thought affirming its self-actualization as a culture returning to itself in the recollection of its own formation or *Bildung* (the opposite, in a word, of the Hegelian *Erinnerung* which it lexically recalls) – Benjamin's *Eingedenken* is no longer strictly one or inward (*Ein-*) and no longer strictly thought (*-Denken*). It announces, rather, a mindfulness or vigilance which refuses to take in (or be taken in by) a tradition authorizing itself as the continuity of an essential legacy, task or mission to be transmitted, developed or enacted. The site of an intensity turning against itself – 'turned intensively towards the exterior' (V, 570; N 1, 3) – *Eingedenken* marks the impasse or 'standstill' of thought as such: the 'flow' of inference is interrupted (§17). In 'blasting open' the continuum, *Eingedenken* inaugurates repetition as the return of that which strictly speaking never happened: it announces the redemption of a failed revolutionary opportunity at the moment of most pressing danger. 'Hope in the past' (§6). Such repetition arrests the apparent continuity of inherited power relations by remembering precisely what official historiography had to repress.

Eingedenken thus announces the return of lost possibilities as the return of the repressed. It signals the entry into history of those forgotten or trampled in the victory march of the conquerors. It is not here a question of recuperating those previously excluded by means of a more capacious or inclusive memory – bringing the margins into the centre, essentializing the inessential, thus turning losers into winners according to the endlessly familiar dialectic (for Nietzsche, ultimately, a slave logic) of the *qui perd gagne*. For in challenging 'every victory, past and present, of the rulers' (§4) – this in the face of an enemy which 'has not ceased to be victorious' (§6) – historical materialism in fact overturns the very logic of victory *and its obverse* by thinking the unthinkable (because contradictory) double imperative or double bind of a past which is at once both irretrievable and yet – for this very reason – incomplete. Such an imperative expresses the twofold impossibility either of reanimating or of neutralizing the past, whether as the site of empathic fusion or as the inert object of contemplation (that is, whether to be relived or safely buried). A present emerges which neither recuperates nor cuts its losses, whether by spiritualizing or by letting bygones be bygones, but rather exposes the double pressure of a memory which strictly speaking exceeds the alternatives of memory and forgetting, thus opening history to the endlessness of a mourning which neither resuscitates nor lays to rest the past.

Such mourning displaces the antithesis between idealization and foreclosure – the double aestheticization of loss whether as indirect gain or as simple absence – thereby upsetting the economy of every victory narrative as such. What is ultimately subverted or exceeded is the very opposition (but therefore also the essential reconciliation) of life and death as the final horizon of every narrative. Death neither terminates nor is redeemed by the life which it not only ends or 'finishes' but in fact marks as radically 'finite' and, as such, unfinished. Neither resurrection nor proper burial, neither a spiritualization of death nor its securing as life's antithesis, can now be thought.

If, for the victims, remembrance always comes too late to make good the losses, they are not for this reason immune or exempt from further risk. If the storm of progress prevents the angel from 'lingering, awakening the dead, making whole what has been smashed' (§9) – Benjamin similarly disqualifies the historicist attempt to resuscitate the vanquished Carthage – it is equally true that 'not even the dead will be safe from the enemy if he wins' (§6). Benjamin adds that the enemy 'has not ceased to be victorious' (§6). Neither securely dead, then, nor spiritually recuperable, the dead exert their uncanny pressure on their survivors who are in turn reduced to living dead.

III

. . . the blank is folded

(Derrida, *Dissemination*)

At the moment of *Stillstand*, clock time gives way to the time of calendars. Like a 'historical time-lapse camera' which condenses temporally remote images into the synchronicity of a moment, the calendar inaugurates repetition in the form of holidays – in memorializing the past it anticipates the future as a future memory – thus marking time as a 'perpetual recurrence' (*Wiederkehr*), perhaps in Nietzsche's sense (§15). 'Thus the calendars do not measure time as clocks do' (ibid.). Elsewhere Benjamin remarks that 'to write history means giving dates their physiognomy' (V, 595; N 11, 2);

'the true politician reckons only in dates' (IV.1, 122; *OWS* 80). At once both singular (or unrepeatable) and, in this very singularity, repeatable, the date is the very possibility (but by this very token, the impossibility) of commemoration as such. Like every idiom, proper name or signature, the date is both utterly unique and profoundly iterable; Derrida will remark on the 'madness' (*Wahnsinn*) of the 'when' (*Wann*).[31] The date serves as witness to an event after every possible witness (and every witness of every witness) will have vanished, constituting (but for this very reason also obliterating) the event it is to commemorate, thus rendering the 'once' as a 'yet again'. The date both confirms and effaces the cryptic singularity of what is dated, rendering its idiomatic exclusivity both accessible and unreadable to those coming later. Like every signature, it binds with the force simultaneously of obligation and of promise.

As a form of promise or alliance, the date reveals itself as essentially Messianic in its logic, exemplified in the holiday or *Feiertag*. In his Baudelaire essay, Benjamin writes of holidays as 'heterogeneous, conspicuous fragments' punctuating the chronological regularity of the continuum (I, 642; *Ill* 184): 'slivers of Messianic time' (§A). While marking time in the worst sense, the calendar also re-marks the past thereby effecting a radical unmarking or erasure: to institute remembrance is to initiate a future irreducible to the official inscriptions of any regime. In its very repeatability, the holiday announces the recurrence of what cannot in fact return, thus opening up the space of the unforeseen. The calendar commemorates in negotiating a certain blank or emptiness: repetition marks just the possibility of the radically new. *Eingedenken* is thus the opposite of an imprinting or preservation of self-identical, enduring traces. Closer to Nietzsche's active forgetfulness than to Platonic anamnesis, it leaves blank precisely what will have been commemorated. This is in fact the force of memory's promise. If not exactly a blank cheque or *tabula rasa*, it reminds the reader that for now at least a page of history remains unwritten.

> To have combined recognition of a quality with the measurement of a quantity was the work of the calendars in which the places of recollection are left blank [*die Stellen des Eingedenkens gleichsam aussparen*], as it were, in the form of holidays.
>
> (I, 642; *Ill* 184)

Hegel, observing the 'slaughterbench' of Spirit's progress,[32] comments that, in the chronicle of history, periods of happiness are like 'blank pages' (*leere Blätter*),[33] blank in the sense of an utter absence of determination: the vacuous harmony or slackness arising when 'the antithesis' (between individual and universal) is 'in abeyance' (*Perioden des fehlenden Gegensatz*).[34] Benjamin, taking the measure of the sacrifice and refusing the consolations of philosophy – Hegel's 'retreat into the selfishness' which knows 'that what has happened could not be otherwise'[35] – tries to read these blanks.

Or, more precisely: he tries to think what is strictly speaking illegible within the terms of literacy set forth by the victors, thus marking a new 'coming to legibility' (*zur Lesbarkeit*) (V, 577; N 3, 1) – historicity – of the past. He calls these blanks holidays. That is: he thinks the very interval or spacing of the blank, the condition of the possibility of the blank, the gap or fissure – *Sprung* – which ruptures the catastrophic continuity of tradition (V, 591; N 9, 4), exposing this as the merely factual continuity of hereditary power lines, thus revealing a jagged foothold for a new beginning (cf. V, 592; N 9a, 5). Like a blank page inserted into the weighty annals of the conquerors, the holiday marks simultaneously the condition and the limits of legibility, commemorating what by definition cannot be recalled. Like blotting paper saturated with the infinite inkstain of theology (to cite another Benjaminian image (V, 588; N 7a, 7)), indeterminate through indeed an excess of marking or determinacy, the blank page is both unreadable and for this very reason demands to be reread.

The blank page is thus the condition of the possibility (but that means also the necessity) of rereading, marking the structural impossibility, therefore, of any first reading: a memorial which testifies precisely to the irrecuperability or unreadability of what is recalled. In 'One-Way Street' Benjamin writes: 'like a clock of life on which the seconds race, the page-number hangs over the characters in a novel. Which reader has not once lifted to it a fleeting, fearful glance?' (IV.1, 118; *OWS* 76). The novel – unitary in its thematic focus (II.2, 454; *Ill* 98), inexorable in its destination – resembles historicism in its temporal commitments: the bourgeois genre par excellence (cf. III, 310). Benjamin remarks that the novel's ending excludes all supplementation or revision, a 'Finis' immobilizing and thereby sanctioning what has transpired (II.2, 455; *Ill* 100). Historical materialism, like storytelling, would explode the 'cosmic clock' (II.2, 489; *OWS* 370) of progressive history, dispersing by endlessly rewriting what can be told (II.2, 454; *Ill* 98). The blank page interrupts the continuous pagination of the book of history – whether the 'ticking of the seconds' of *spleen* (I.2, 642; *CB* 143) or the rosary beads enumerating the roll-call of tradition

(§A) – unnumbered, a testament to the innumerable dead. Of course this makes us only more aware than ever (if 'fleetingly') of the 'fearful' power of the suspended sequence: it both exposes and undermines this sequence as the violent arbitrariness it is. The blank contests the inevitability of every ending as fulfilment or completion, tangling the story-line just where classical narrative would provide the satisfaction of a closure or denouement.

Writing of Kafka, Benjamin compares remembrance to the ('old people's') practice of 'reading backward'. At Svendborg, the summer of 1934, Brecht had read Kafka's little parable 'The Next Village' as a variation on Zeno's paradox of motion: to decompose a journey into its smallest elements means to renounce ever reaching any goal, even the most modest, reformist target of 'the next village'. Upon which the pragmatist Brecht had snapped that life's just 'too short' for such ruminations (R 209). According to Benjamin's reading of Kafka's story, however, the rider in the story never reaches the next village because he keeps on endlessly reverting back to and rewriting the beginning, a revision which shatters both the self-identity of the subject ('a different person from the one who started the ride arrives at the village') and the 'unity of life' (R 209).

> Retrospectively, [remembrance] traverses life with the speed of lightning. As quickly as one turns back a few pages, it has gone back from the next village to the point where the rider decided to set off. He whose life has turned into writing, like old people's, likes to read this writing only backward. Only so does he meet himself, and only so – in flight from the present – can his life be understood.
>
> (R 210)

Elsewhere Benjamin will describe the past as a palimpsest (1.1.125), as a photographic plate waiting to be irradiated by a posthumous flash of recognition (R 56) or to be developed by chemicals of the future (V, 603; N 15a, 1), a text thus constituted by the very process of rewriting. In short: the past poses the demand, in Hofmannsthal's words, 'to read what never was written' (I.3, 1238). Like a seed of grain embalmed within the pyramid of collective memory, a story releases its germinating power only belatedly, 'preserving and concentrating its strength . . . and unfolding it even after a long time' (II.2, 446; Ill 90). In 'One-Way Street' Benjamin describes the retroactive force of memory as a fluorescent light (re)activating a buried phosphorescence – what will be labelled in the *Theses* as a 'secret heliotropism' (§4) – exposing the past as but the mournful prophesy of the present, the present as the guilty belatedness of the survivor.

> When you are taken unawares by an outbreak of fire or the news of a death, there is in the first mute shock a feeling of guilt, the indistinct reproach: did you really not know of this? Did not the dead person's name, the last time you uttered it, sound differently in your mouth? Do you not see in the flames a sign from yester-day evening, in a language you only now understand? And if an object dear to you has been lost, was there not, hours, days before, an aura of mockery or mourning about it that gave the secret away? Like ultraviolet rays memory shows to each man in the book of life a script that invisibly and prophetically glosses the text.
>
> (IV.1, 142; *OWS* 99)

Legible/illegible, the blank space marks the opening of historicity. It marks both our guilt and the possibility of redemption, the reminder both of lost possibilities and of our 'secret agreement' (§2), rendez-vous, contract or alliance with the dead. 'The historical materialist is aware that this claim cannot be settled cheaply' (§2). The blank is thus not the pristine innocence of a new beginning, not a new immediacy or neutrality susceptible to whatever comes. Benjamin will have elsewhere identified such innocence with the amnesiac 'starting all over again' which is in fact 'the regulative idea' of both gambling and wage-labour (I.2, 636; *CB* 137): the 'narcotic' addiction to a game in which a Satanic 'second-hand', in Baudelaire's words, 'wins always, without cheating – it's the law!'[36] Such a game reduces the players to drugged out puppets jerked forward by the numbing promise of the 'next' move (I.2, 635; *CB* 136), strung out and strung along by the 'empty' (§B) march of time. 'They live their lives as automata', remarks Benjamin of these 'modern men' who in their Cartesian zeal for fresh beginnings have 'completely liquidated their memories' (I.2, 634, 636; *CB* 135, 137).

It is thus not a question of a carte blanche or blank cheque indifferently redeemable to any buyer. The blank marks rather the site of a highly determinate indetermination – the guilty whiteness or inky dissolution or absolution – of a responsibility and a redemption both infinite and infinitely finite. 'Like every generation that went before us,' writes Benjamin, 'we have been endowed [*mitgege-ben*] with a *weak*' – emphasis Benjamin's – 'Messianic power' (§2). The blank is therefore not the sign of voluntarism – not a 'new tablet' awaiting the will's diamantine inscriptions (cf. Zarathustra's 'become hard!')[37] – but rather the cipher of that which exceeds the limits of figurality as such. In marking the radical unreadability of the past it also signals a future unforeseeable – unwritable – from the perspective of what is either given or even conceivable within the categories available to the present day.

Brecht's epic interruptions break the stream of life, making it 'for an instant, hover iridescent in empty space [*im Leeren*]' (II.2, 531; *UB* 13). The destructive character who 'clears away' without a constructive 'vision' of the future leaves 'for a moment, at least, empty space [*leere Raum*]' (IV.1, 397; *R* 301) in which 'ways' or 'crossroads' might open up (IV.1, 398; *R* 303).[38] 'No image', similarly, inspires the revolutionary: neither 'the ideal of liberated grandchildren' (§12) nor the utopia 'painted in the heads' of the Social Democrats (§13). The angel of history catches not even a glimpse of the future to which his back is turned (§9). The moment of 'writing history' (§16) rather signals the radical unwritability or unrepresentability of history as a 'sequence of events' (§A) to be recounted (or, by this token, predicted), thus announcing the advent of what arrives.

The *Stillstand* – an arrest both of the flow of events (§11) and of the 'flow of thoughts' (§17) – exposes 'a present which is not a transition' (§16): a 'Messianic cessation of happening' (§17). This present is 'not a transition' because logically there can be no bridge or transition to what is unforeseen. The angel 'has the idea it is *about* to move' (§9); the revolutionary classes are 'aware that they are *about* to make the continuum of history explode' (§15); at the 'moment of danger' the oppressed class senses that 'a conformism is *about* to overpower it' (§6, my emphasis). The *Jetztzeit* announces the *imminence* of that which, impending, resists the *immanence* of what is given or presentable: an 'absolute future' in, perhaps, Levinas's sense.

The *Jetztzeit* is thus nothing like a present, but rather that which undermines the very presentability of that which comes. The 'Messianic cessation of happening [*Geschehens*]' is not an 'occurrence' or event *in* time, but rather the opening of history (*Geschichte*) itself as the infinite responsibility of the pure event. The *Jetztzeit* is thus anything but 'the mystical *nunc stans*', as Zohn would have it (*Ill* 261, translator's note). In coming to a 'standstill', time itself '*einsteht*' (§16): not exactly 'stands still' (Zohn) but stands in for, answers for, pledges responsibility for a past which permits no substitutes, nor therefore any retroactive warrants or guarantees.

Kafka, even while practising his livelihood selling insurance policies, preaches with 'unrestricted pessimism' the ultimate untenability of all guarantees (*R* 209). Baudelaire similarly renounces every attempt to find in organic nature (hence equally in the organicized history of historicism) any security or 'warrantee' (*Unterpfande*) (I.2, 680; *CP* §32). The 'Messianic cessation of happening' is thus the response to and responsibility for that which strictly exceeds all contracts or securities: 'put differently, a revolutionary chance in the fight for the oppressed past' (§17).

A chance: that is, 'we have been endowed with a *weak* Messianic power' (§2). For a generation swept along in the 'stream of tradition' (I.3, 1160; *CB* 103) or lulled into 'moving with the current' (§11), *Eingedenken* offers only 'the smallest guarantee, the straw at which the drowning man grasps' (I.3, 1243). In the face of an 'enemy [who] has not ceased to be victorious' (§6), the hunchback's infallible 'countermove' becomes in fact the belated response to what is, as such, unanswerable: a pure promise without authority or will.

Stalled or shortcircuited in the suspended moment of its standstill, history comes to a head as a Medusa head:[39] a 'death's head' (cf. I.1, 343; *OGT* 166) arrested and arresting the spectator with the double prospect of a past unviewable except with horror (§9) and a future undeterminable from the perspective of the present day. Such a twofold opacity marks the disastrous constellation of the present as Messianic in the sense of containing both a promise and an imperative all the more pressing for being undefined.

In this caesura opens up the 'space of history' (*Geschichtsraum*) (V, 571; N 1, 9). The forgotten prophesies of the past, legible only posthumously, speak only of the radical prematurity of all prediction and hence of the ultimate undeterminability of every end. In his notes to the *Theses*, Benjamin compares the historical materialist to the physicist, discerning 'Messianic power' just as the latter identifies in the spectrum the presence of ultraviolet rays. Such 'power' – not only 'weak' (§2) but in fact as intangible as the 'pure, colourless light' of written history[40] – refuses to determine itself empirically as a self-legitimating force (as in, for example, the 'infinite power' of Hegelian Reason[41]). 'Whoever wants to know how a "redeemed humanity" would be constituted, under which conditions it would be constituted, and when one can count on it, poses questions to which there is no answer. He might as well ask about the colour of ultraviolet rays' (I, 1232). Jean Paul: 'Unlike Orpheus, we win our Eurydice by looking back and lose her by looking forward.' If memory functions photographically as a 'flash' (*R* 56) or 'developer' (V, 603; N 15a, 1) or 'darkroom' (II.3, 1064), advance exposure would simply ruin the film.

What is exposed, in the 'Messianic cessation of happening', is that which simultaneously conditions and resists all disclosure: time itself as the 'precious but tasteless seed' (§17). Such a 'seed' – elsewhere: 'temporal kernel' (*Zeitkern*) (*PW* 578; N 3, 2) (one should return to the 'seminal logic' underpinning this whole discussion) – manifests itself in withdrawing from the ontic, phenomenal order of perception, thus offering a 'nourishment' exceeding the culinary order as such. (We are not far here, despite Benjamin's aversions, from a Heideggerean problematic.[42])

This is not an idealistic or ascetic renunciation of the body. The turn away from the consumerist sampling or 'tasting' of visible or determinate options is precisely a commitment to the 'struggle for crude and material things' (§4). (We are explicitly allied here with a Marxist problematic.) Hegel's somewhat ironic injunction to 'seek nourishment and clothing first'[43] – Brecht's truculent 'Erst kommt das Fressen . . .' – announces, in Benjamin, a materiality exceeding (while conditioning) the fungible order of representation as such. (Here we can begin to trace a merging of the Marxist and the Heideggerean problematics.) Such a turn constitutes the 'most inconspicuous of all transformations' (§4) – inconspicuous according to a 'secret heliotropism' (§4), 'secret contract' or 'secret index' (§2) – pointing us to a future all the more binding for being undisclosed. (And here, finally, we can begin to see the Heideggerean-Marxist ban on representing the future join forces with the Biblical *Bilderverbot*.)

The empty space turns every page into a potential blank page, but blank with a peculiar determinacy – '(ful)filled' or 'laden' (§14) or 'saturated' (§17) with the pressure of the *Jetztzeit* – which is 'anything but homogeneous, empty time' (§B). In an age when, as Caillois argued, the holiday has degenerated into the vacation[44] – rationalized as entertainment, 'days off' functioning only to keep the workers in their place[45] – no day, but by this very token, potentially every day, can be a holiday. The possibility of sober intoxication presents itself at every turn. Visiting Moscow (a city whose churches 'all preserve their incognito' (IV.1, 344; *R* 126) Benjamin enthuses that the Russians, 'if we believe them', intend to eliminate Sundays in favour of 'moveable holidays' – a 'sign of the transparency' of both space and time (IV.1, 197). (Benjamin had earlier observed a similar 'porosity' in modern Naples; 'a grain of Sunday is hidden in each weekday, and how much weekday in this Sunday!' (IV.1, 311; *R* 168).) Such transparency would overcome the organizing 'rosary' (§A) of official clock time (institutionalized in the bound rhythms of liturgical performance): thus Benjamin writes of a 'feast' freed of the 'shackles' of all 'festive songs'.[46] The holiday, secularized, becomes the site of a generalized awakening, engaging the possibility of redemption at every step. For 'the Jews', prohibited from 'investigating the future', 'every second of time was the strait gate through which the Messiah might enter' (§B).

But alternatively: if 'every second' becomes potentially the Messianic *Jetztzeit*, the Messiah's very 'presence', as Blanchot will argue, 'is no guarantee'.[47] Messianic arrival cannot complete or close off the history it interrupts, in the sense of a final judgement to secure salvation or eternal peace. In this endgame to end all endgames, the Messiah's coming signals only the belatedness of what cannot arrive on time – 'not on the last day but on the day after', as Kafka put it – introducing the endlessness of a vigil without hope of resolution and the hopelessness of a belated hope. Kafka:

> The Messiah will come only when he is no longer necessary; he will come only on the day after his arrival; he will come, not on the last day, but on the day after.[48]

Blanchot glosses:

> His being there, then, is not the coming. With the Messiah, who is there, the call must always resound: 'Come, Come.' His presence is no guarantee. Both future and past (it is said at least once that the Messiah has already come), his coming does not correspond to any presence at all. . . . And if it happens that to the question 'When will you come?' the Messiah answers, 'Today,' the answer is certainly impressive: so, it is today! It is now and always now. There is no need to wait, although to wait is an obligation. And when is it now? . . .[49]

IV

Pascal's *il ne faut pas dormir* must be secularized . . .

(Adorno, 'Commitment')

A clock ringing 'sixty seconds out of every minute', though in one sense of course not a very good alarm clock, is in another sense the perfect one. Like Tinguely's self-destructing machine (or like Heidegger's broken hammer), it has in its hyper-functional dysfunctionality the inert conspicuousness of every out-of-work tool. Both sleep and wakefulness become, strictly speaking, quite impossible, leaving only an uneasy vigilance or alertness no less imperative for being uncontrolled.

Thus the parade of the great insomniacs: Breton, Proust, Kafka, Kraus. The Surrealist 'dream wave' of images wears away 'the threshold between sleep and waking' (II.1, 296; *R* 178). Proust, 'obeying the laws of night and honey', stays up writing in his cork-lined study day and night (II.1, 312; *Ill* 202f.). Kafka's 'indefatigable assistants' – like children, fools or students – never go to bed (indeed, remarks Benjamin, that's no doubt the best part about studying, however useless, at least it keeps you up all night) (II.2, 435; *Ill* 136). Kraus, ' "in these loud times" ' (II.1, 338; *R* 243), works the 'nightwatch' (pp. 354; 260): in his own words, simply, ' "I work day and night" ' (pp. 354; 259). Thus, too, the travelogue of the great nocturnal cities: the gas-lit streets of Paris becoming the scene of a generalized *noctambulisme* (I.2, 553; *CB* 50), the little children of Naples staying out all hours of the night (IV.1, 314; *R* 172).

'Waking', writes Benjamin, 'is the paradigm of remembrance' (V, 491). If the essential task here is that of 'waking from the nineteenth century' (V, 580; N 4, 3) – from the 'dream sleep' (V, 494) (Marx's 'nightmare'[50]) by which capitalism keeps us in its thrall – such an awakening presupposes no ultimate opposition between sleeping and waking consciousness and therefore implies no final lucidity or self-control. If Benjamin's own 'Copernican revolution' (V, 490), like Kant's, involves a certain awakening from our dogmatic slumbers – in this case, from the historicist addiction to the 'narcotic' objectivism of the 'once upon a time' (V, 578; N 3, 4) – the 'heliotropic' turn to the present 'sun rising in the sky of history' (§4) subverts every heliocentrism (and hence the heliopolitics of any community founded in the enlightened contemplation of a self-certain truth[51]). For the sun is here in eclipse, permitting only fleeting 'images' or snapshots of the past.

> It isn't that the past casts its light on the present or the present casts its light on the past: rather, an image is that in which the past and the now-time flash into a constellation.
>
> (V, 576; N 2a, 3)

The 'leap in (or under) the open sky of history' (§14) thus implies neither a Platonic emergence from the nocturnal cave or puppet-theatre of oblivion nor Marx's emancipation from ideology as from the *camera obscura* of our benighted dreams.[52] In an age where artificial lighting and glass architecture will have obliterated the distinction between inside and outside as between daytime and night-time – thus Benjamin cites a description of Baudelaire going out in his bedroom slippers, using the quay and sidewalk as his writing table (V.316), at home equally (which is to say not at all) on the streets as within his own four walls (I.2, 573; *CB* 70) – in an age in which the very difference between inside and outside will have been erased or rendered futile, the notion of emancipation as the emergence to solar clarity becomes quite inoperative. Nor is the Cartesian discrimination tenable here between sleep and waking – ultimately a banishing of the spectre of the automatism threatening the clarity and distinctness of our conscious life.

If the present announces itself as 'the midday of history' (V, 603; N 15, 2), such a solar moment is darkened by a putrefaction threatening the pellucid clarity of any retrieve. By 1940, this diurnal blindness will have a special determinacy of its own; the summer solstice also marks the date of Pétain's armistice, the final blow to Hitler's French opposition (and hence, for Benjamin as for so many others, the beginning of the end).

'One of the implicit presuppositions of psychoanalysis', remarks Benjamin, 'is that the opposition between being asleep and being awake has no validity for empirical forms of consciousness' (V, 492). As a form of vigilance towards the past which grasps danger as precisely the imminence of what has already happened, waking (*Erwachtsein*) is the 'dialectical breaking point' (V, 579; N 3a, 3) which precedes the distinction between sleeping and awakened consciousness, announcing a responsibility exceeding the 'interest' of every subjective (or intersubjective) being. (We are clearly approaching Levinasian insomnia,[53] the 'nocturnal intensity' of which Blanchot writes.[54]) Thus a 'presence of mind' (*Geistesgegenwart*) is initiated in which both 'presence' and 'mind' are divested of their identity and authority, thereby moving – to quote Benjamin quoting Engels – ' "beyond the field of thought" ' (V, 595; N 10a, 2).

'That things "just go on" ', writes Benjamin, '*is* the catastrophe. It is not that which always lies ahead but that which is always given. Thus, Strindberg . . . : Hell is not something that awaits us, but our own life, here and now' (V, 592; N 9a, 1). If the catastrophe is not impending in some abstract future but inscribed as always already past, the broken alarm clock calls us to a vigilance and a responsibility all the more urgent for being invoked too late.

V

Sometimes the awakening call, that chance event which gives
'permission' to act, comes but too late – when the best part of youth
and the strength to act has already been used up in sitting still;
and how many a man has discovered to his horror when he 'rose'
up that his limbs had gone to sleep and his spirit was already too
heavy. 'It is too late' – he has said to himself, having lost faith
in himself and henceforth for ever useless.

(Nietzsche, *Beyond Good and Evil*)

In 'One-Way Street', Benjamin describes the child's experience of being 'enclosed in the world of matter'. Hiding behind the curtain he turns gauzy, becomes a statue crouched beneath the dining table, 'is himself door' behind the door. At the striking of the clock, he turns puppet-like, his grimace congeals into a death mask, flesh turns to stone.

> In such a manner does a man who is being hanged become aware of the reality of rope and wood. Standing behind the doorway curtain, the child becomes himself something floating and white, a ghost. The dining table under which he is crouching turns him into the wooden idol in a temple whose four pillars are the carved legs. And behind the door he is himself door, wears it as his heavy mask and as a shaman will bewitch all those who unsuspectingly enter. At no cost must he be found. When he pulls faces, he is told, the clock need only strike and he will remain so. The element of truth in this he finds out in his hiding place. Anyone who discovers him can petrify him as an idol under the table, weave him forever as a ghost into the curtain, banish him for life into the heavy door.
>
> (IV.1, 116; *OWS* 74)

But if 'life' is itself the lateness of an unfinished dying, every hour sounds the death knell: every face turns into a death mask, every child a wooden doll. The baroque 'theatre of cruelty' (I.1, 392; *OGT* 218) presents this clearly, the human body already fragmented or decomposing (pp. 391ff.; 216ff.), interludes pantomimed as 'expressive statuary' (pp. 368; 192f.), actors playing stiff-limbed puppets or playing-card kings (pp. 304; 125).[55] An 'Italian trick' displays the living body as acephalic, the actor's head emerging disembodied through a covered tabletop, the concealed body hunched dwarf-like underneath (pp. 393; 219): man plays at being a machine. The body's own excrescences stage the chiasmus of a living dying. What for Plotinus exemplified the most extreme corruptibility of matter – hair and fingernails 'growing' in the grave[56] – signals for Benjamin the ultimate undecidability of life and death as such: what is 'cut away as dead matter from the living body' proliferates on the corpse as if still alive (pp. 392; 218). Thus 'a *memento mori* is aroused in the physis': death no longer appears simply as or at 'the end of life' (ibid.) but as the very condition of (im)possibility of life as such.

Thus Beckett's Clov: 'there's no more nature'.[57] Adorno, reading *Endgame* as the story of 'complete reification', writes of Spirit's reduction to 'dead inventory'.[58] If for Benjamin the Marxist rubric of reification[59] cannot entirely capture what he describes as the thoroughgoing 'destruction of the organic' (II.1, 670; *CP* §19), the age of capitalism nonetheless gives ample evidence of its demise. It would be more or less mechanical to multiply the examples. The dismembered body of the baroque *Trauerspiel* becomes the automaton of modern times. Thus Poe's pedestrians adapt themselves to machines and, like gamblers, drunks or factory-workers, 'express themselves only automatically': ' "if jostled, they bowed profusely to the jostlers" ' (I.2, 632; *Ill* 176). Flaubert's St Anthony fetishistically visualizes the 'reduction of the living to dead matter' (V, 448): ' – Désormais tu n'es plus, ô matière vivante!/Qu'un granit entouré d'une vague épouvante . . .'[60] For Baudelaire – whose own 'jerky gait', 'eccentric grimaces' (I.2, 616; *Ill* 163) and 'sadistic' passion for animated toys and clockwork (V, 447f.) betray a certain 'empathy with the inorganic' (I.2, 558; *CB* 55) – man becomes 'a kaleidoscope equipped with consciousness' (I.2, 650; *Ill* 175).[61] Woman becomes a 'jet-eyed statue' (V, 416).[62] By 'lowering the barriers between the organic and the inorganic' (V, 118), fashion 'prostitutes the living body to the organic' (V, 51; *CB* 166). 'The rights of the corpse' are represented (ibid.). The bourgeois *intérieur* of the Second Empire becomes a doll's house for its occupants, who are 'encased' or 'embedded' in plush like 'dead fauna' fossilized in granite (I.2, 549; *CB* 46). Photography introduces the 'inhuman, one might even say deadly' (I.2, 646; *Ill* 188) experience of being posthumized in one's own lifetime. In the age of technical reproducibility, the human body becomes fragmented, unrecognizable to itself – 'experiments have proved that a man does not recognize his own walk on the screen or his own voice on the phonograph' (II.2, 436; *Ill* 137) – decorporealized and 'deprived of reality, life [and] voice' (I.2, 489; *Ill* 229).

Thus 'the unfreedom, imperfection, and collapse of . . . beautiful nature' (I.1, 352; *OGT* 176). Nature's mortification as 'ruin', 'decay' or 'eternal transience' (pp. 355; 179) punctures every fantasy of 'eternal life' (pp. 353; 178). The baroque vision of 'the total disappearance of eschatology' (pp. 259; 81) shatters equally every *Heilsgeschichte* or 'universal history' (§17) consummated in eternal rest.

The dwarf is already puppet: nothing remains to animate the automaton or machine. Every attempt to find the 'little man' within the machine's interior[63] yields only the infinite exteriority of a Deleuzian 'assemblage' strung together by a rhizomatic network of puppet strings, 'nerve fibres' without a puppeteer.[64] The demystification of the 'wooded interior' (I.1, 342; *OGT* 165) of the Romantic symbol spells simultaneously both the 'rending' (II.1, 309; *R* 192) of Cartesian inwardness and the impossibility of any final 'transfiguration' (*Verklärung*) (I.1, 343; *OGT* 166) of a deadened life. 'There is not the faintest glimmer of any spiritualization of the physical' (pp. 363; 187). No *deus ex machina* intervenes to repair the wreckage left in the tempest's wake (§9). What idealism puts forth as 'mind' or 'soul' or 'consciousness' is exposed as already spectral and 'figural' (I.1, 363; *OGT* 187): a ghost in the machine. Gryphius provides this 'marvellous translation': ' "If anyone should find it odd that we do not bring forward a god from the machine [*einen gott aus dem gerüste*], like the ancients, but rather a spirit from the grave [*einen geist aus dem grabe*], let him consider what has occasionally been written about ghosts" ' (pp. 313; 134).

What has been more than occasionally observed about ghosts, of course, is that they represent the impossibility of either dying or living: what has been improperly or unsafely buried (cf. §6) comes back to haunt the living in the eternity of a recurrence without resurrection or the consolation of an eternal life (cf. §9). The ghost thus expresses the recurrence of what cannot, as such, return or make good the losses. Every afterlife becomes the 'overlife' (*Überleben*) (IV.1, 10f.; *Ill* 71) of an 'over-ripeness [*Überreife*] and decay' (I.1, 355; *OGT* 179).

In the age of Fascism, 'the face of nature' has congealed into the 'Hippocratic features' of a death mask, frozen as the 'Sphinxlike countenance' of a nation propping itself on the mysteries of blood and soil (III.1, 247f.; *TGF* 126f.). In this context, any appeal to 'life' can only serve to blur 'the fact that there is life no longer'. *Das Leben lebt nicht.* Adorno writes:

To speak immediately of the immediate is to behave much as

those novelists who drape their marionettes in imitated bygone passions like cheap jewelry, and make people who are no more than component parts of machinery act as if something depended on their actions. Our perspective of life has passed into an ideology which conceals the fact that there is life no longer.[65]

'Life' has become the ideology of a class society which needs to mask its own exclusions under the homogeneity of raw 'experience'. *Erlebnis* is the 'euphemism' (I.2, 681; *CP* §32a) concealing the mortified mediacy of a life 'none of us has time to live' (II.1, 320f.; *Ill* 211). German Fascism celebrates as *Urerlebnis* the bloody experience of the battlefield, naturalizing what it castigates as the ' "senselessly mechanical machine war" ' it seeks to vitalize and, as such, prolongs (III, 247; *TGF* 127). Technology is either demonized as 'boring' (ibid.) or mystified vitalistically as 'storm of steel' (Jünger).[66] The dream of fusion only occludes the imminent reality of 'millions of human bodies . . . chopped to pieces and chewed up by iron and gas' (III, 249; *TGF* 128). 'Life' and 'machinality' here simultaneously reinforce and occlude each other as presocial, abstract forces. What Heidegger announces as the complicity or *Zugehörigkeit* of *Machenschaft* and *Erlebnis*,[67] Benjamin exposes as the joint mystification of technology and nature in the modern age (III, 247; *TGF* 126f.).

Understood in its 'entirely non-metaphorical objectivity [*Sachlichkeit*],' writes Benjamin, 'life' in fact exceeds the domains of 'organic corporeality', 'animality' and 'soul'.[68] 'In the final analysis, the range of life must be determined by history rather than by nature' (ibid.). History is, then, life's own excess to itself as a sur-vival (*Über-leben*) of an outlived or obsolescent 'nature': the 'over-ripeness' which marks the limits of every teleology of development or growth. 'Nature was not seen by [the baroque writers] in bud and bloom, but in the over-ripeness and decay of her creations. In nature they saw eternal transience, and here alone did the saturnine vision of this generation recognize history' (I.1, 355; *OGT* 179). If 'life' is marked by purposiveness or *Zweckmässigkeit*, its 'end' disturbs the rational entelechy of every organism; 'the relationship between life and purposiveness [is] . . . almost beyond the grasp of the intellect [*Erkenntnis*]' (IV.1, 11; *Ill* 72). The 'completely different teleology' of the baroque contests the anthropocentric optimism of the Enlightenment, holding out not for 'human happiness' but for 'instruction' (I.1, 347; *OGT* 170).

This 'completely different teleology'[69] disturbs the aesthetic plenitude of all idealism. The organic harmonies of Kant and Schiller are suspended. The baroque determination of 'life' as a 'game' or 'puppet-play' (I.1, 261; *OGT* 82) contests the autotelic sufficiency of Kantian purposiveness, together with its correlate, the self-sufficient self. Such a game therefore implies neither the consoling aestheticism of a Tieck (II.2, 538; *UB* 21) nor the bourgeois phantasmagoria of the interior ('his drawing-room became a box in the world theatre' (V, 52; *CB* 168)). 'Historical materialism is not diverted' by the pretty 'spectacle' of the 'stream of tradition' (I.3, 1160; *CB* 103). The aesthetic ideology of *schöne Schein* is interrupted (cf. I.2, 491; *Ill* 230). 'The false appearance [*falsche Schein*] of totality is extinguished' (I.1, 352; *OGT* 176). *Schein* is no longer the illusionistic 'sheen' or 'radiance' (cf. pp. 356; 180) which forgives or consecrates the given by harmonizing it, but a 'shade' or 'shadow' haunting the plenitude of life.[70] The *lebende Gestalt* of Weimar classicism is disrupted. The conciliations of every *Spieltrieb* are turned back. History, construed as 'scene' or 'setting', becomes in fact *ein andere Schauplatz* of dismembered body-parts and animated stage props (I.1, 311; *OGT* 132), 'merging into the setting' as ruin (pp. 353; 178) or 'scattered like seeds over the ground' (pp. 271; 92).

Brecht's actors 'play at acting' – paradoxically pretend to act, dramatize their own theatricality – in a performativity which short-circuits the reflexive plenitude of Romantic irony and thus self-consciousness (II.2, 538; *UB* 23). For Kafka, 'man is on the stage from the beginning': the Nature Theatre of Oklahoma accepts 'everyone' on the condition that they 'play themselves' (II.2, 422; *Ill* 124) – compare the opportunity provided to the Russian workers to 'play themselves' on the movie screen[71] – according to a paradoxical logic of (self)-mimesis. Such a mimetology subverts the *adaequatio* assumed by every classicism – in fact exposes this as strictly contradictory – by positing the originary self-dissimulation of the imitated 'self'. 'Play' becomes an endless effect of 'framing and miniaturization' (I.1, 262; *OGT* 83), 'spaced' or 'quoted' according to a 'dialectic' which preserves an essential distance between what 'shows' and what is 'shown' (II.2, 592; *UB* 12). Cathartic reconciliation is thus pre-empted. The play's own non-identity to itself 'paralyses' (*lähmet*) the audience's 'druglike' tendency to empathy or identification (II.2, 537f; *UB* 21) and thus prohibits every identification with the aggressor (cf. §7). History thus refuses the rosy optimism of Hegel's panoramatic 'picture gallery',[72] with its theatrical conciliation of viewing subject (*für uns*) and object viewed (*für es*). Its puppet-play becomes a 'lugubrious game'[73] or 'mourning play' – a chess-game staged against an unseen enemy and before an unnamed audience[74] – an endless *Fort-Da* commemorating an infinite loss.

VI

CLOV: 'Fit to wake the dead! Did you hear it?'
HAMM: 'Vaguely.'

(Beckett, *Endgame*)

'Sometimes inadequate, even childish measures may serve to rescue one.'[75] Another fragment of 'One-Way Street' portrays a fairground shooting range. The customer proves his marksmanship by hitting the bull's eye, which activates a series of miniature puppet theatres representing automated scenes of torture or degradation: Joan of Arc in prison, death by guillotine, 'a penurious interior', a dancing bear, the damned in hell, penal servitude and so on. Benjamin suddenly remarks that one 'could also imagine' an alternative sequence of events being triggered.

> One must think of the fairy-story [*das Märchen*] of the brave little tailor, and could also imagine Sleeping Beauty awakened with a shot, Snow White freed of the apple by a shot or Little Red Riding Hood released by a shot. The shot breaks in magically [*märchenhaft*] upon the existences of the puppets with that healing power that hews the heads off monsters and reveals them to be princesses.
>
> (IV.1, 127; *OWS* 85)

By such 'magical' intervention the mythical automatism of history is interrupted. The shot would thus disrupt the very violence which it automatically and otherwise perpetuates – a *pharmakon*, simultaneously within and outside the system – a 'healing' partaking of the destructive logic it would subvert. Benjamin's rewriting here of Grimm is decisive. Elsewhere it is said to be the noisy tumult of the class struggle which is to wake up the Sleeping Beauty (*Br* 418). If the 'shock' that crystallizes or arrests the continuum (§17) also reiterates and thus prolongs the 'shock experience' of a debased *Erlebnis* (cf. I.2, 629–32; *Ill* 174–6), nothing unambiguously distinguishes Messianic 'saving' from mythical 'danger'. *Wo aber das Rettende ist, wächst Gefahr auch* . . . (to rewrite Hölderlin). 'The merest summons can distract me from anything', writes Aragon, 'save from my own distraction'.[76] Adorno, who at one point chastises Benjamin for his 'undialectical' adherence to the (capitalist) logic of distractibility,[77] elsewhere accuses him of invoking the revolution as a '*deus ex machina*'.[78] A more precise formulation would read: *machina ex machina*. If 'ambiguity' is the essential feature of Benjamin's 'dialectics at a standstill' (V.1, 5; *CB* 171), the dream sleep is inevitably prolonged by what disturbs it. As anyone knows who has simultaneously failed both to sleep through and to wake up to an alarm clock, the moment of awakening is perhaps also the most intense moment of the dream. 'The dialectical image is therefore a dream image' (ibid.).

Benjamin remarks that 'with cunning, not without it, we extricate ourselves from the realm of dream' (V, 234). Elsewhere he writes that 'reason and cunning [*Vernunft und List*] have inserted tricks into myth', such that 'their forces cease to be invincible' (II.2, 415; *Ill* 117). Waking is said to stand within the dream's interior as a 'Trojan horse' (V, 495) or immanent exterior: a wooden puppet concealing living men. (According to Baroque mythography, Palamedes, who conceived the horse, also invented chess while killing time – in more than one sense – at Troy.[79]) Waking is thus the automatism that interrupts the automatism of the dreamwork, apotropaically repeating what it would resist.

There is thus a 'teleological moment' whereby the dream 'secretly awaits its own awakening': the dreamer 'awaits the second at which he wrests himself with cunning from [death's] grip' (V, 492). This is clearly not the providential teleology of the Enlightenment – from Kant to Schelling to Hegel – according to which a universal Reason actualizes itself through the exploitation of unconscious individual passions. If Hegel's 'cunning of Reason' (*List der Vernunft*) achieves its end by the 'sacrifice' and 'abandonment' of particular existence,[80] the 'cunning' described by Benjamin in fact outwits Hegelian cunning by exposing the latter's collaboration in the mythical reproduction of the Same. 'As long as there is a single beggar, there is still myth' (V, 505). 'Waking is the dialectical, Copernican revolution' (V, 491) which disorients the solar trajectory of Hegel's 'great day's work of Spirit'[81] by recalling what every 'theodicy'[82] of reconciliation forgets. 'Courage, humour, cunning, and fortitude' manifest themselves in the class struggle, writes Benjamin, by 'constantly calling into question every victory, past and present, of the rulers' (§4). Hegelian Reason proves its cunning by its ability to remain immune from or uncontaminated by what it inflicts on its unwitting puppets, thus overcoming the death it dishes out. The cunning of historical materialism is to expose that teleology to be, in fact, the spurious instrumentality whereby present powers legitimate their rule. The 'teleological moment' of awakening is therefore, in Benjamin, a 'completely different teleology' (I.1, 347; *OGT* 170) from Hegel's. Death is neither absorbed nor absolved by the consciousness which would commemorate it: one 'extricates oneself' (V, 492) from death without surmounting it.

According to 'Russian folk belief,' writes Benjamin, resurrection is less a 'transfiguration' (*Verklärung*) than a 'disenchantment' (*Entzauberung*) (II.2, 459; *Ill* 103): a kind of 'magical escape' (*märchenhaft Entrinnen*) (ibid.) from the 'nightmare' placed by myth upon man's chest (pp. 458; 102). A demythologized magic thus turns against the mythical rationality of the Enlightenment. The fairytale's (*Märchens*) 'happily ever after' (pp. 457; 102) contests the narcotic (V, 578; N 3, 4) 'once upon a time' of historicism's 'bordello' (§16). Such 'magic' defies every idealism. The gunshot that 'magically breaks in upon the existence of the puppets' (IV.1, 127; *OWS* 85) neither spiritualizes their wooden materiality nor redeems their fate.

The little child petrified among the furniture 'does not tire of the struggle with the demon'. Dwarfish, puppet-like beneath the table, he pierces the silence of the idols with his sudden shout. A disenchanted magic finds in the Golgotha of the *intérieur* the cipher of resurrected flesh.

> At the seeker's touch he drives out with a loud cry the demon who has so transformed him – indeed, without waiting for the moment of discovery, he grabs the hunter with a shout of self-deliverance. That is why he does not tire of the struggle with the demon. In this struggle the apartment is the arsenal of his masks. Yet once a year, in mysterious places, in their empty eye-sockets, their fixed mouths, presents lie. Magic discovery becomes science. As its engineer the child disenchants [*entzaubert*] the gloomy parental apartment and looks for Easter eggs.
>
> (IV.1, 116; *OWS* 74)

VII

Towards the end of the *Meno*, after putting the slave boy through his motions, Socrates explains to Meno the need to convert *doxa* into knowledge (97e–98b). If left untethered by the logos, opinion has the wantonness attributed to writing in the *Phaedrus*. Like the moving statues of Daedalus which run away if no one ties them – or, adds Socrates, like a slave who keeps on giving you the slip – unbound opinions 'run away from a man's mind'. Opinion is the automatism which disrupts while simulating the paternal logos: 'a fine thing so long as [it] stay[s] in [its] place'. Socrates adds: 'but [it] won't stay long'. Memory, the self-recollection of the logos, is here the master pulling the strings of the automaton: a 'magnificent creation', remarks Socrates, of the latter, if tethered; if set loose, a renegade slave.

Benjamin's hunchback pulls the strings but, although a *Meister*, is no master. And the string is both tangled and frayed. If the 'Penelope work of *Eingedenken*' (II.1, 311; *Ill* 202) resembles, in its involuntariness, the forgetfulness of an automatism, something invariably escapes. Plato's tether becomes, in Benjamin, a weave, that is, a textile, a *textum*: or, as he writes at the end of his Proust essay, a net 'cast into the sea of the *temps perdu*' (pp. 323; 214). He observes of the mess of Proust's galleys that 'no one's text is more tightly woven' (pp. 311; 202). But if memory is that infinite rewriting of the past we call 'experience', the web's tightness is no guarantee of a final catch. For what tightens the mesh is precisely what loosens it: the possibility of endless revision puts the object (if in fact there is one) forever in abeyance. To 'seize hold [*bemächtigen*] of a memory' (§6), to 'capture [*festhalten*] the past as an image' (§5) is precisely to relinquish all mastery and control. What escapes is, of course, the image that 'flashes up' never to be seen again (§5): 'a fragile reality', Benjamin remarks (II.1, 314; *Ill* 205).

Historicism (like Plato's Socrates) thinks the 'truth won't run away from us' (§5), inertly available, self-identical, like a 'whore' (§16). Benjamin alerts us to the secret interests at work in such an assumption, exposes the hidden power plays for what they are. A memory that unravels as it weaves breaks the smooth thread of progress (I.3, 1233) – the causal 'rosary' of historicism (§A), the 'chain' of tradition (§9), ultimately the 'snare' of the 'apparatus' (§10) – and, perhaps, thereby (but too late, of course) sets the slave free.

NOTES

1 'Über den Begriff der Geschichte', in *Gesammelte Schriften*, 7 vols, vol. I.2 (Frankfurt am Main: Suhrkamp, 1980–9), p. 693; 'Theses on the Philosophy of History', in *Illuminations*, translated by Harry Zohn (New

York: Schocken Books, 1969), p. 253. All quotations from the 'Theses' will henceforth be indicated in the text by thesis number or letter. All German references to the *Gesammelte Schriften* will be indicated simply by volume (Roman numeral), part (Arabic) and page number. All other quotations from Benjamin will be indicated according to the following abbreviations: *Br, Briefe*, ed. Gershom Scholem and Theodor W. Adorno (Frankfurt am Main: Suhrkamp, 1978), 2 vols; *CB, Charles Baudelaire: A Lyric Poet in the Era of High Capitalism*, translated by Harry Zohn (London: Verso, 1976); *CP*, 'Central Park', translated by Lloyd Spencer, in *New German Critique* 34 (1985), pp. 32–58; N, 'N [Re the Theory of Knowledge, Theory of Progress]', translated by Leigh Hafrey and Richard Sieburth, in Gary Smith (ed.) *Walter Benjamin: Philosophy, Aesthetics, History* (Chicago, IL: University of Chicago Press, 1989), pp. 43–83; *OGT, The Origin of German Tragic Drama*, translated by John Osborne (London: Verso, 1977); *OWS, One-Way Street and Other Writings*, translated by Edmund Jephcott and Kingsley Shorter (London: Verso, 1979); *R, Reflections*, translated by Edmund Jephcott (New York: Harcourt, Brace, Jovanovich, 1978); *TGF*, 'Theories of German Fascism: On the Collection of Essays *War and Warrior*, edited by Ernst Jünger', translated by Jerolf Wikoff, in *New German Critique* 17 (1979), pp. 120–8; *UB, Understanding Brecht*, translated by Anna Bostock (London: Verso, 1983). Unless otherwise indicated, I will cite the existing translations, with modifications where appropriate.

2 Roland Barthes, 'A Lesson in Writing', in *Image-Music-Text*, translated by Stephen Heath (New York: Hill & Wang, 1972), p. 174.

3 Nietzsche, 'The Wanderer and His Shadow', §61, *Human, All Too Human*, translated by R. J. Hollingdale (Cambridge: Cambridge University Press, 1982), p. 325.

4 Nietzsche, *On the Genealogy of Morals*, III. §26, translated by Walter Kaufmann (New York: Vintage, 1969), p. 159.

5 Nietzsche, 'The Magician', in *Thus Spoke Zarathustra*, Fourth Part, translated by Walter Kaufmann in *The Portable Nietzsche* (New York: Viking, 1968), pp. 363–70.

6 See, for example, I.1, 104; II.1, 125; IV.1, 171.

7 For Hegel's critique of the traditional Christian depiction of Jesus as a historically remote event of incarnation presaging a reconciliation distant in an otherworldly future, see *Phänomenologie des Geistes*, ed. Eva Moldenhauer and Karl Markus Michel (Frankfurt am Main: Suhrkamp, 1970), p. 574; translated by A. V. Miller as *Phenomenology of Spirit* (Oxford: Oxford University Press, 1970), p. 478. Henceforth abbreviated as *PhG; PS*.

8 *PhG* 46; *PS* 27f.

9 Jacques Derrida, *Glas* (Paris: Galilée, 1974).

10 Compare a similar trope in Novalis, cited by Benjamin in I.1, 101, together with Irving Wohlfarth's comments in 'Messianic Prose and the Art of Awakening', *Glyph* 7 (1980), pp. 131–48 at p. 137.

11 Proust, *A la recherche du temps perdu*, I, *Du côté de chez Swann*, 1 (Paris: Gallimard, 1954), p. 15.

12 Paul Ricoeur, *Freud and Philosophy: An Essay on Interpretation*, translated by Denis Savage (New Haven, CT: Yale University Press, 1970).

13 In the following remarks I am greatly indebted to Irving Wohlfarth, 'Märchen für Dialektiker: Walter Benjamin und sein bücklicht Männlein', in K. Doderer (ed.) *Walter Benjamin und die Kinderliteratur* (Weinheim: Juventa Verlag, 1988), pp. 121–76. See also his 'On the Messianic Structure of Walter Benjamin's Last Reflections', in *Glyph* 3 (1978), esp. pp. 159–62.

14 Quoting Willy Haas on Kafka's *Trial*. See II.2, 429; *Ill* 131.

15 See V, 242; V, 562. Cf. Susan Buck-Morss, 'The Flâneur, the Sandwichman and the Whore: The Politics of Loitering', *New German Critique* 39 (1986), pp. 99–141.

16 See E. A. Poe, 'Maelzel's Chess-Player', in *The Complete Tales and Poems of Edgar Allan Poe* (New York: Modern Library, 1938), p. 433.

17 II.2, 487f.; *OWS* 369f., and V, 596; N 11a 1.

18 Hegel, *Vorlesungen über die Philosophie der Geschichte* (Frankfurt am Main: Suhrkamp, 1970), p. 35; translated by J. Sibree as *Philosophy of History* (New York: Dover, 1956), p. 21. Henceforth abbreviated as *VPG*; *PhH*.

19 'On Virtue that Makes Small', *Thus Spoke Zarathustra*, Book III, *Portable Nietzsche*, p. 281.

20 Friedrich Nietzsche, 'On the Uses and Disadvantages of History for Life', in *Untimely Meditations*, translated by R. J. Hollingdale (Cambridge: Cambridge University Press, 1983), p. 106.

21 Ibid., p. 105.

22 Ibid., p. 105. Cf. my 'Redeeming Revenge: Nietzsche, Benjamin, Heidegger and the Politics of Memory', in Clayton Koelb (ed.) *Nietzsche as Postmodernist* (Albany, NY: State University of New York Press, 1989).

23 'On the virtuous', *Thus Spoke Zarathustra*, Book II, *Portable Nietzsche*, p. 207 (Kaufmann's translation).

24 Barthélemy and Méry, *L'Insurrection. Poème dédié aux Parisiens* (Brussels: Louis Haumann, 1830), p. 17.

25 I.2, 1265 (Benjamin's own translation).

26 In the French version: 'Un témoin dont la clairvoyance pourrait être dûe au hasard des rimes, écrivit . . .' (ibid.)

27 Compare also the lines of Kraus quoted by Benjamin at II.1, 365; *R* 271. 'Let time stand still! Sun, be consummate!/. . ./. . . Had I but Joshua's power,/ I tell you, Gibeon would be again!'

28 'However long it appeared to me . . . it nevertheless seemed that it had only lasted several seconds . . .' (from *Les paradis artificiels*, quoted in V, 603; N 15, 1).

29 'And he got up from his resting place at the tree as from a strange drunkenness; and behold, the sun still stood straight over his head. But from this one might justly conclude that Zarathustra had not slept long.' 'At Noon', *Thus Spoke Zarathustra*, Book IV, *Portable Nietzsche*, p. 390.

30 My thanks to Andrea Sauder for this insight.

31 Jacques Derrida, 'Shibboleth', in Geoffrey Hartman and Sanford Budick (eds) *Midrash and Literature* (New Haven, CT: Yale University Press, 1986), p. 336.

32 *VPG* 35; *PhH* 21.

33 *VPG* 42; *PhH* 26.

34 Ibid. Elsewhere Hegel mocks the void as a kind of 'holy of holies' (*PhG* 117f.; *PS* 88f.).

35 *VPG* 35; *PhH* 21.

36 'L'Horloge', cited at I.2, 636; *CB* 137.

37 Cf. 'Of Old and New Tablets', *Thus Spoke Zarathustra*, Book III, *Portable Nietzsche*, p. 326.

38 Cf. Irving Wohlfarth, 'No-Man's Land: On Walter Benjamin's "Destructive Character" ', Chapter 6 in this volume.

39 I owe this formulation to Eduardo Cadava. See his 'Theses on the Photography of History', forthcoming in *diacritics*, special issue on Walter Benjamin.

40 II.2, 451; *Ill* 95. Cf. Irving Wohlfarth, 'The Politics of Prose and the Art of Awakening' (see note 10 above).

41 *VPG* 21; *PhH* 9.

42 Cf. my 'Framing Redemption: Aura, Origin, Technology in Heidegger and Benjamin', in Arleen Dallery and Charles Scott (eds) *Ethics and Danger* (Albany, NY: State University of New York Press, 1992).

43 Quoted in §4. On Hegel's rewriting of the Biblical verse and its reworking in Benjamin, see Ian Balfour, 'Reversal, Quotation (Benjamin's History)', *Modern Language Notes* 106 (1991), pp. 622–47.

44 Roger Caillois, 'Théorie de la Fête', in *Nouvelle revue française* (Jan 1940), pp. 58f., cited by Theodor W. Adorno and Max Horkheimer in *Dialectic of Enlightenment*, translated by John Cumming (New York: Continuum, 1972), pp. 105f.

45 Adorno and Horkheimer, ibid.

46 I.3, 1235. 'Festive songs' are curiously enough identified here with 'writing', or at least with Scripture (*Schrift*). See generally Irving Wohlfarth, 'The Politics of Prose and the Art of Awakening' (note 10).

47 Maurice Blanchot, *The Writing of the Disaster*, translated by Ann Smock (Lincoln, NE, and London: University of Nebraska Press, 1986), p. 142.

48 Franz Kafka, 'The Coming of the Messiah', in *Parables and Paradoxes*, bilingual edition, ed. Nahum Glatzer (New York: Schocken Books, 1946), pp. 80f.

49 Blanchot, *Writing of the Disaster*.

50 Marx, 'The Eighteenth Brumaire of Louis Bonaparte', in Karl Marx and Frederick Engels, *Selected Works* (Moscow: Progress Publishers, 1970), p. 96.

51 Cf. Jacques Derrida, 'Violence and Metaphysics', in *Writing and Difference*, translated by Alan Bass (Chicago, IL: University of Chicago Press, 1978), pp. 90f.

52 See Irving Wohlfarth, 'History, Literature and the Text: The Case of Walter Benjamin', *Modern Language Notes* 96 (1981), p. 1012.

53 Cf. Emmanuel Levinas, 'Dieu et la philosophie', in *De Dieu qui vient à l'idée* (Paris: J. Vrin, 1986), pp. 93–127, at pp. 98f.

54 Blanchot, *Writing of the Disaster*, p. 49.

55 See Rainer Nägele's suggestive reading of the *Trauerspielbuch* and Rilke, 'Puppet Play and *Trauerspiel*', in *Theater, Theory, Speculation: Walter Benjamin and the Scenes of Modernity* (Baltimore, MD: Johns Hopkins University Press, 1991), pp. 1–27.

56 Plotinus, *Enneads* IV.4, 29.

57 Samuel Beckett, *Endgame* (New York: Grove Press, 1958), p. 11.

58 Theodor Adorno, 'Trying to Understand *Endgame*', in *Notes to Literature*, translated by Shierry Weber Nicholson (New York: Columbia University Press, 1991), vol. 1, pp. 245, 243.

59 For Benjamin's reservations, see for example his letter to Adorno of 7 May 1940, in *Br* 849; also in I.3, 1134.

60 Baudelaire, second 'Spleen' poem in *Les Fleurs du mal*, quoted *inter alia* at V, 448.

61 See generally Christine Buci-Glucksmann, *La raison baroque: de Baudelaire à Benjamin* (Paris: Galilée, 1974).

62 On the theme of fetishism and the female body in Benjamin, see Buck-Morss, 'The Flâneur, the Sandwichman and the Whore' (see note 15, above); also Angelika Rauch, 'The *Trauerspiel* of the Prostituted Body, or Woman as Allegory of Modernity', *Cultural Critique* (1988), pp. 77–88, as well as Buci-Glucksmann, *La raison baroque*.

63 Cf. Maurice Merleau-Ponty, *The Visible and the Invisible*, translated by Alphonso Lingis (Evanston, IL: Northwestern University Press, 1968), p. 210.

64 Cf. Gilles Deleuze and Felix Guattari, *A Thousand Plateaus*, translated by Brian Massumi (Minneapolis, MN: University of Minnesota Press, 1987), p. 8.

65 Theodor Adorno, *Minima Moralia: Reflections From Damaged Life*, translated by E. F. N. Jephcott (London: New Left Books, 1974), p. 15.

66 Cf. Jeffrey Herf, *Reactionary Modernism: Technology, Culture, and Politics in Weimar and the Third Reich* (Cambridge: Cambridge University Press, 1984).

67 Martin Heidegger, *Beiträge zur Philosophie (Vom Ereignis)*, *Gesamtausgabe*, vol. 65 (Frankfurt am Main: Klostermann, 1989), pp. 127–9.

68 'The idea of life and afterlife in works of art should be regarded with an entirely unmetaphorical objectivity. Even in times of narrowly prejudiced thought there was an inkling that life was not limited to organic corporeality. But it cannot be a matter of extending its dominion under the feeble sceptre of the soul, as Fechner tried to do, or, conversely, of basing its definition on the even less conclusive factors of animality, such as sensation, which characterize life only occasionally' (IV.1, 11; *Ill* 71).

69 In an early letter to Scholem, Benjamin writes of a 'teleology without a goal' (1 December 1920, *Br* 247).

70 Etymologically, *Schein* derives from the same root as English 'shine' and 'shimmer', as well as the Greek *skia* (shadow).

71 Writing of the way in which film technology allows 'everyone' the 'opportunity to rise from passerby to movie extra', Benjamin appeals to the Soviet experience of 'polytechnic' authorship. 'Some of the people whom we meet in Russian films are not actors in our sense but people who portray *themselves* – and primarily in their own work activity' (I.2, 493, 494; *Ill* 231, 232).

72 *PhG* 590; *PS* 492.

73 Cf. Georges Bataille, 'The "Lugubrious Game" ', in *Visions of Excess*, edited by Allan Stoekl (Minneapolis, MN: University of Minnesota Press, 1985), pp. 24–30.

74 *The Anatomy of Melancholy* warns against chess as being 'a testy cholerick game'. Montaigne remarks that this 'absurd pastime' is 'over serious'. Michel de Montaigne, 'On Democritus and Heraclitus', in *Essays*, translated by J. M. Cohen (Harmondsworth: Penguin, 1958), p. 132. The Renaissance assimilates chess to the *Totentanz* or *danse macabre*, a contest in which Death will have always already won. Baroque still-life paintings connect the vanity of life to the vacuity of chess-games: chessboard, flowers, skull and moneybag are repeatedly shown lying heaped together as images of transience, emblems of a life already dead. See Marion Faber, *Das Schachspiel in der europäischen Malerei und Graphik (1550–1700)* (Wiesbaden: Otto Harrassowitz, 1988). The paralysis or 'mating' of the king thus only dramatizes a prior mortification: both players and chessmen will have been marked as spectres in the game of life. Every victory as such becomes less than a final victory: sacrificial, Pyrrhic, without real gain.

75 Franz Kafka, 'The Silence of the Sirens', in *Parables and Paradoxes* (cited above, note 48), p. 89. Quoted by Benjamin at II.2, 415; *Ill* 117f.

76 Louis Aragon, *Le paysan de Paris* (Paris: Gallimard, 1926).

77 Letter from Adorno to Benjamin, 18 March 1936 (I.3, 1003f.); *Aesthetics and Politics: Debates between Bloch, Lukàcs, Brecht, Benjamin, Adorno*, translated and edited by Ronald Taylor (London: New Left Books, 1977), p. 123.

78 Letter from Adorno to Benjamin, 2 August 1935 (*Br* 680); *Aesthetics and Politics*, p. 117.

79 Faber, *Das Schachspiel in der europäischen Malerei und Graphik (1550–1700)*, pp. 120ff. Numerous seventeenth-century engravings show the Greeks (sometimes dressed in Turkish clothing) playing chess outside the walls of Troy.

80 *VPG* 49; *PhH* 32f.

81 *VPG* 134; *PhH* 103.

82 *VPG* 538; *PhH* 457.

Index